AF183264

Investment Aftercare Explained

This book is the first to systematically map the last step of the foreign investor's journey, usually referred to as post-investment, aftercare or business retention and expansion. It provides a wide range of approaches and strategies for host economies to better retain foreign investors, encourage follow-on expansions and achieve greater local economic embeddedness through a multi-stakeholder dialogue, leading to improvement of the overall business climate.

Global foreign direct investments reached US$1.5 trillion in 2019, but this figure reduced by over 42% in 2020, due to the pandemic. Against this backdrop, retaining established investors became even more important. Numerous organisations all over the world are dedicated to attracting foreign companies to invest in their markets. Facilitating this effort is a dynamic and competitive industry that involves international organisations supporting capacity building, think tanks, academia and consultants. However, once foreign companies decide to invest, a critical question arises: how can host economies *grow and retain* these foreign investments? Many host governments could do much better, as there is very little post-investment support for these foreign companies to help them grow their businesses throughout different stages of investment, business and economic cycles. This is where aftercare comes in. In this book, the authors include diverse examples from around the world to demonstrate aftercare best practices in action.

This book is an essential read for all public administration staff related to FDI attraction and promotion, practitioners in the private sector and FDI consultants. It will also be of great interest to multilateral organisations seeking to organise seminars and training courses for capacity building. The book will also benefit researchers, academics and postgraduate students of international relations, foreign trade and internationalisation.

For further information, see www.aftercareexplained.com.

Carolina Arriagada Peters is one of the very first international consultants specialised in Aftercare and Post-Investment. She advises governments on how to maximise long-term foreign direct investment. A former practitioner from her tenure at London & Partners, the international promotional agency from the British capital, she is the Managing Director of Cities & Collaboration and Founder of fdiCampus, providing tailored strategy consultancy, training and mentoring to FDI executives globally. She holds a bachelor's degree in Communications, an MBA from Universidad Adolfo Ibáñez, Chile, and an MA in Communications from Westminster University, UK.

David Coble is a Senior Economist at the Central Bank of Chile. His main research interests are International Economics and Applied Macroeconomics. He was previously the Chief Economist and Head of Research at InvestChile – the Chilean Government's Foreign Investment Promotion Agency – where he worked developing the first Investment and Business Climate Survey and a system for evaluating the impact of InvestChile's services to foreign companies. He holds bachelor's and master's degrees in Economics from the University of Chile, and a PhD in Economics from the University of Chicago, USA.

Toby X. Li is Assistant Professor of Strategy at Texas A&M's Mays Business School, USA. His main research focus is corporate strategy and international business, covering topics that include alliances, contracting, stakeholder management and organisational learning. Prior to academia, he worked in the energy sector, where he was involved in helping formulate foreign investment and diversification strategies. He holds a PhD in Strategy from Rice University's Jones Graduate School of Business, USA, an MPhil in Business Economics from the University of Cambridge, UK, and a BA in Economics from Brown University, USA.

Brendan Lewis is the President of RealSAM Inc in the United States, an artificial intelligence business with operations in the US, the UK, Australia and Italy. His past experience includes being a foreign investor into Vietnam, Indonesia and Romania, as well as representing Greater London in Australia for investment attraction, for 6 years. He holds qualifications in Information Systems from Curtin University, Australia, and Accounting from Monash University, Australia.

"Aftercare is arguably more important than the initial landing of FDI. This book demonstrates that with on-going business aftercare, the greater the client's chances are of expansion and economic prosperity."

Craig O'Kane MBE, *Former Director of FDI and Capital – The UK Department for International Trade (Australia and New Zealand)*

"Read the book and get out to visit your foreign investors; you will discover the difference you can make to your host economy when looking after them."

Anne Have Kjærholm, *Head of Tech – Expert in Business Retention & Expansion – Copenhagen Capacity, Denmark*

"As an Economic Development Practitioner, I could not put this book down. This is exactly what practitioners need as a guide in doing effective Aftercare. This book provides an easy-to-understand roadmap with examples that every economic development professional should reference as they work in FDI."

Erik Collins, *Director of Economic Development in Montgomery County, Dayton, Ohio, USA*

Investment Aftercare Explained

A Guide for FDI Practitioners and Policymakers on How to Grow and Retain Investors

Carolina Arriagada Peters, David Coble, Toby X. Li and Brendan Lewis

Routledge
Taylor & Francis Group
LONDON AND NEW YORK

Cover image: © Getty Images

First published 2022
by Routledge
4 Park Square, Milton Park, Abingdon, Oxon OX14 4RN

and by Routledge
605 Third Avenue, New York, NY 10158

Routledge is an imprint of the Taylor & Francis Group, an informa business

British Library Cataloguing-in-Publication Data
A catalogue record for this book is available from the British Library

Library of Congress Cataloging-in-Publication Data
Names: Arriagada Peters, Carolina, author. | Coble F., David, author. |
Li, Toby X., author. | Lewis, Brendan, author.
Title: Investment aftercare explained: a guide for FDI practitioners and
policymakers on how to grow and retain investors/Carolina Arriagada
Peters, David Coble, Toby X. Li and Brendan Lewis.
Description: Abingdon, Oxon; New York, NY: Routledge, 2022. |
Includes bibliographical references and index.
Identifiers: LCCN 2021021875 (print) | LCCN 2021021876 (ebook) |
ISBN 9781032006277 (hardback) | ISBN 9781032006246 (paperback) |
ISBN 9781003174950 (ebook)
Subjects: LCSH: Investments, Foreign–Government policy. |
International business enterprises–Government policy. | International economic relations.
Classification: LCC HG4538 .A663 2022 (print) |
LCC HG4538 (ebook) | DDC 332.67/3–dc23
LC record available at https://lccn.loc.gov/2021021875
LC ebook record available at https://lccn.loc.gov/2021021876

ISBN: 978-1-032-00627-7 (hbk)
ISBN: 978-1-032-00624-6 (pbk)
ISBN: 978-1-003-17495-0 (ebk)

DOI: 10.4324/9781003174950

Typeset in Adobe Caslon Pro
by Newgen Publishing UK

To my mother.
Carolina

To Milca, Agustín, my parents, and my Lord Jesus.
David

To my parents who have always been patient with me.
Toby

To Simone and my family, who are always my guide.
Brendan

Contents

FIGURES

Boxes

FOREWORD

The Covid-19 pandemic is without precedent in living memory. It has shaken people's lives around the world, causing a severe health, social and economic crisis. This shattering disruption has been partially mitigated by tailored policies and government interventions. While international investment has to be a key component of a resilient, sustainable and inclusive economic recovery, the context of uncertainty and declining flows makes investment facilitation and retention a central area of focus. Retaining firms and ensuring they operate in a favourable environment have become more important considerations than ever for investment policymakers and practitioners.

This is where investment promotion agencies (IPAs) have a unique role to play at the intersection of government and business. IPAs have already expanded their aftercare activities in the past year by scaling up services to existing investors to help their governments fight the pandemic.

Aftercare is about providing continuous responses to investor needs and challenges. It seeks to maintain an environment of trust through a constructive and mutually beneficial dialogue. OECD research shows that Aftercare can influence whether companies decide to maintain or expand their operations and that it supports broader investment climate reforms through policy advocacy and institutional coherence. Aftercare initiatives can also help maximise the benefits foreign investors bring to host countries. These initiatives include better anchoring of companies in the local economy and creating linkages with domestic firms, preventing potential disputes with the government or local communities, and promoting responsible business conduct and encouraging investors to adopt sustainable practices in their business operations.

Today's recovery policies will shape economic and social prospects for the coming decade. International cooperation initiatives, such as the OECD IPA Network, can support peer-learning and exchanges of best practices, including on Aftercare. While the OECD has always highlighted the key role of Aftercare in investment facilitation and business environment reforms, the Covid-19 pandemic has given it heightened impetus. Going forward, governments need to put further emphasis on investor retention and expansion in their medium to long-term investment promotion strategies. IPAs have to strengthen their Aftercare initiatives to support their governments in building resilient, sustainable and inclusive economies.

This makes the publication of *Investment Aftercare Explained: A Guide for FDI Practitioners and Policymakers on How to Grow and Retain Investors* particularly timely and topical. I am confident that this book will help practitioners better understand and use Aftercare through informative case studies and practical guidance.

Ana Novik, Head of Investment Division
The Organisation for Economic Co-operation
and Development, OECD
Link: http://www.oecd.org/investment/investment-promotion-and-facilitation.htm

February 2021

ABBREVIATIONS

Organisations

EURADA	European Association of Development Agencies
FAO	Food and Agriculture Organisation (United Nations)
IADB	Interamerican Development Bank
IsDB	Islamic Development Bank
ICSID	International Centre for Settlement of Investment Disputes
IISD	International Institute for Sustainable Development
IEDC	International Economic Development Council
IFIP	Inclusive Forum for Indigenous Peoples (World Bank Group)
IFC	International Finance Corporation (World Bank Group)
ILO	International Labour Organisation
IMF	International Monetary Fund
OECD	Organisation for Economic Cooperation and Development
OHCHR	United Nations' Office of the High Commissioner for Human Rights
UN	United Nations
UNCITRAL	United Nations Commission on International Trade Law
UNCTAD	United Nations Conference on Trade and Development

UNESCAP	United Nations Economic and Social Commission for Asia and the Pacific
UNPFII	United Nations Permanent Forum on Indigenous Issues
WAIPA	World Association of Investment Promotion Agencies
WBG	World Bank Group
WEF	World Economic Forum
WTO	World Trade Organisation

Acronyms

ADR	Alternative Dispute Resolution
AI	Artificial Intelligence
BIT	Bilateral Investment Treaty
BRE	Business Retention and Expansion
CISF	Comprehensive Investor Services Framework
CLV	Customer Life-time Value
CREED	Consolidate, Retain, Embed, Expand and Diversify
CRM	Customer Relationship Management
CSR	Corporate and Social Responsibility
DA	Development Agency
DPP	Dispute prevention policies
DSB	Dispute Settlement Body
DTT	Double Taxation Treaties
EDO	Economic Development Organisation
FDI	Foreign Direct Investment
FET	Fair and Equitable Treatment
FPIC	Free, Prior and Informed Consent
FTA	Free Trade Agreement
FTE	Full Time Equivalent
FTZ	Free Trade Zone
GSER	Global S Ecosystem Report
HQ	Headquarters
HQ2	Second Headquarters
ICS	investment court system
IIA	International Investment Agreement
IIS	Investor Information System
ILV	Investor Life-Time Value

IPA	International Promotional Agency or Investment Promotional Agency
IPO	Initial Public Offering
IPP	Investment Policy and Promotion (term used by the World Bank Group)
ISD	Investor-State Dispute
ISDS	Investor-state dispute settlement
IT	Information Technology
JV	Joint Venture
KPI	Key Performance Indicators
M&A	Mergers and Acquisition
MNC	Multinational Companies
MNE	Multinational Enterprises
MOU	Memorandum of Understanding
NEM	Non-Equity Modes
R&D	Research and Development
RDA	Regional Development Agency
RTA	Regional Trade Agreement
SDGs	Sustainable Development Goals
SEE	Support, Equip and Empower
SEZ	Special Economic Zone
SIRM	Systemic Investment Response Mechanism
TNC	Transnational Companies
TSR	Total Shareholder Return
UNDRIP	United Nations Declaration on the Rights of Indigenous Peoples
VC	Venture Capital

GLOSSARY

IPA used as an umbrella term to refer to IPAs, EDOs, DAs and RDAs collectively.

Host economy and location used as umbrella terms to refer to nations, countries, cities, territories, or areas that are served by an IPA.

Benchmark point of reference against which things may be compared.

Control Group the standard group of subjects (people, firms, countries, etc.) to which comparisons are made in an experiment.

Treatment Group the group of subjects (people, firms, countries, etc.) that receives a treatment in an experiment.

Counterfactual it measures what would have happened to the subjects in an experiment in the absence of the intervention.

Econometrics the branch of economics concerned with the use of mathematical methods (especially statistics) in describing economic systems.

Intervention the act of interfering with the outcome or course of a process.

Variable a factor in a scientific experiment that may be subject to change.

Acknowledgements

The path to writing this book was inspired by many FDI leaders. Special thanks go to Jeff Finkle from IEDC for being an industry pathfinder during uncertain times. To the 2007 UNCTAD team: Nazha Benabbes Taarji-Aschenbrenner, James Zhan, Paul Wessendorp and Jan Smit (UNCTAD consultant) for being pioneers with their "Aftercare a core function" paper. To Karl P. Sauvant from Columbia University, for being a beacon of light in the FDI industry. To Esteban Pelayo from EURADA for always welcoming enquiries and requests. To Bostjan Skalar and Ismail Ersahin from WAIPA for encouraging us to contribute to the development of stronger IPAs. To Armando Heilbron and Alex Sanchiz from the World Bank Group for the exchange of ideas.

A special thanks to Ana Novik and her team at the OECD for strongly endorsing Aftercare as quintessential part of FDI and for writing the foreword. In addition, we would like to thank Ana Arias Uriones, from the Inter-American Development Bank, for her invitation to write about Aftercare, and also to her colleague Christian Volpe Martinicus for encouraging us to write and promote proper methods to evaluate the impact of IPAs' actions. And to Pilar Moreno de Barreda, independent FDI consultant, for her support when researching for this book.

Many people shared their experience and insight for the book. In particular, we would like to thank the many investment promotional agencies, economic development agencies, policymakers and academics who generously shared their knowledge and resources. While listing them all here is not possible, we would like to mention: the team at Think London / London & Partners, Cristian Rodriguez and Vanessa Severin from InvestChile, Pilar Madrigal, Vanessa Gibson from CINDE Costa Rica, King Chung Lam and Andrew Davies from Invest Hong Kong, Michael Charlton from the Department of International Trade in the United Kingdom, Anne Have Kjærholm from Copenhagen Capacity, Ken Messina from the Rapid Response team at the State of Massachusetts, Kelvin Uwaibi from the Edo State Investment Promotion Office in Nigeria for suggesting including community engagement with indigenous communities in the book, Michael Darger from the University of Minnesota for introducing us to Routledge, Nicolás Vergara from the Faculty of Economics and Business at the University of Chile, Chris Fair from Resonance Consultancy, Susanne Lambregts-Winters for sharing her master's thesis and those who peer-reviewed the text.

Carolina would particularly like to thank her co-authors David Coble, Toby X. Li and Brendan Lewis for joining her on an uncertain journey and the unstinting efforts they put in to complete this book. Special thanks go to Rob Dean who helped edit this book, and without his friendship and support it would simply not exist. Thanks also go to the team at Routledge, led by Emily Ross and Hannah Rich, for believing in our proposal and their continuous support, and to Mazbahul Ismail for designing the diagrams.

Covid-19 arrived while we were working on one of the drafts of the text, and while it led us to rewrite several sections, it also reassured us of the need for this knowledge. We trust that this book will help readers better understand the relevance of Aftercare. It has never been more important.

Carolina Arriagada Peters, David Coble,
Toby X. Li and Brendan Lewis

AUTHOR PHOTOS

Carolina Arriagada Peters

David Coble

Toby X. Li

Brendan Lewis

INTRODUCTION

At the time of this book going to print, "Covid-19 has triggered global uncertainty like no other – a global health crisis that, in addition to an enormous human toll, is leading to the deepest global recession since the Second World War."[1] While the full impact of the pandemic will only be known in years to come, the World Bank has already identified that the crisis has pushed at least 88 million people into extreme poverty, that servicing significantly higher levels of national debt will impose a heavy burden for years to come and that the pandemic slowdown has deeply impacted businesses and jobs globally.[2]

The Covid-19 pandemic not only evidenced the fragility of global value chains, which represent the foundation upon which the internationalisation of business is built, it posed a stress-test to both foreign companies and host economies alike. Sequoia, a leading investment firm, called CEOs to move to business survival mode, quoting Darwin, surmising that those who survive "are not the strongest or the most intelligent, but the most adaptable to change."[3] Foreign investors know this, as do International Promotional Agencies (IPAs). IPAs are also aware that "a proportion of the foreign investors they worked so hard to attract in the first place are likely to leave, downsize or divest."[4]

UNCTAD, or the United Nations Conference on Trade and Development, reported that foreign direct investment (FDI) declined by

DOI: 10.4324/9781003174950-1

42% in 2020, hitting developed economies the hardest, which saw a decline of 69% compared to 2019.[5] The response from international organisations such as the World Bank and the OECD was unambiguous: "IPAs should immediately prioritise retention of strategic and anchor investors to mitigate the effects of the pandemic upon them, secure supply chains of essential products and services, and support a quick recovery."[6] The premise is that multinational enterprises (MNE) "tend to be larger, more productive, and R&D-intensive than purely domestic firms. As such, they are well-positioned to help governments deal with the effects of the pandemic."[7] However, these corporations are being hit hard.[8] Some have "carefully crafted distributed production strategies that allowed them to take advantages of a series of local competitive advantages, that collectively made them strong corporate players."[9] Some of these advantages have not withstood the crisis. As for business, corporates are reassessing their value chain strategies and looking at alternatives such as nearshoring and remote working. Host economies are not standing still either, mobilising whatever resources they have at hand for recovery. International organisations are carefully analysing data and publishing research papers to guide the FDI industry. In essence, the whole FDI industry is adjusting, evolving and acting.

The impact of Covid-19 provides an unprecedented opportunity to look at and leverage the role that established foreign investors play, not just in uncertain times, but in building and shaping local economic development generally. Against this backdrop, Aftercare, the function that focuses on growing, "retaining, expanding, and linking productive private investment"[10] is set to move to centre-stage. Unfortunately, Aftercare has previously only received limited attention, leaving many host economies ill-prepared to work alongside established investors to minimise the effects of the pandemic. Indeed, by neglecting Aftercare, host economies risk losing more jobs than they otherwise would have, and risk creating fewer new jobs in those sectors that have boomed during the pandemic. They also "disregard the positive externalities foreign investors bring to their locations. As a result, they unconsciously impoverish the communities they serve. Correcting this oversight should become a priority for the FDI industry."[11]

UNCTAD's Secretary-General Mukhisa Kituyi notes that the major transformation underway in international production will profoundly impact economies over the coming decade. This may call for a major policy rethink.[12] This book proposes that a long-term perspective on foreign investment should be included in that rethink. It also invites practitioners and policy makers to embrace Aftercare as an integral part of their economic development toolkits.

I.1 The book

I.1.1 Why we wrote this book

We wrote this book in response to the growing demand from the government and business communities to better understand post-investment – the why, the what and the how of attracting, growing and retaining foreign direct investments. In our conversations with policy makers, executives, managers and consultants involved with FDI, we observed a lack of an integrated perspective into the space of post-investment, a topic which is often perceived to be somewhat opaque. We noted there was no roadmap or framework that explained the interconnections between Aftercare, Policy Advocacy and the interaction with the local ecosystem or placemaking efforts. Our book responds to that need by gathering our collective experience and knowledge to comprehensively cover the key topics in a single book.

We also wrote this book because we believe that if FDI practitioners and policy makers are better informed about how to work for and with established foreign investors, the world would be a better place. We look around and see lots of serious challenges that need solving. Neither the public nor the private sector can solve them alone. Foreign investors attract a lot of smart people who are not only prepared, but often also ready to join forces. "The challenge facing them both is to connect with each other more efficiently."[13] Post-investment offers an opportunity to bring them together and to amplify their work by galvanising the support from local stakeholders.

We also wrote this book as a response to global trade polarisation in an increasingly connected society that moves at an ever-accelerating pace. Irrespective of the increase in trade-barriers, established foreign investors are an asset no location can afford to continue to ignore. Established investors represent an underutilised asset with the potential to counterbalance the loss of new FDI flow. There is societal value to be created when working with them and the hope is that readers are inspired by the examples in this book, that they see the glass half full and that they get mobilised for action. Because the worst Aftercare is the one that is not done.

The journey in writing this book was started by the lead author, Carolina Arriagada Peters, who is one of the first international consultants to specialise in Aftercare provision and the post-investment stage. Back when she was an FDI practitioner, Carolina experienced first-hand how public funding often prioritises attracting FDI, while sacrificing funding for post-investments services. While the 2008 financial crisis put the focus back on investor development and retention, such enthusiasm was short lived. This ongoing change puzzled her. A few years later, she was asked by an international organisation to prepare training material for an Aftercare course. While she could find hundreds of publications on attracting new investment, it was difficult to find more than a handful of publications that covered Aftercare, indicating a clear knowledge gap in the FDI value chain. Such an absence of serious research effort on Aftercare is surprising, especially considering UNCTAD's 2007 paper urging the industry to look after established investors.

The years of research, data collection and interviews with industry insiders by Carolina about Aftercare and post-investment helped build the foundations of this book. That insight was then unpacked, organised and systematised, resulting in knowledge building blocks and in the design of post-investment frameworks that bring clarity to the world of post-investment. Along the way, she invited co-authors economist David Coble, assistant professor of business Toby Li and foreign investor Brendan Lewis to contribute their expertise to the writing of this book.

Writing the first book on Aftercare required not only a bit of naivety, but also courage and endurance. It has been a bumpy journey given the fragmentation of the knowledge and the polyvalent nature of post-investment. In start-up lingo, we had to go from zero to one, which is the most difficult part of any journey. We are glad we did. While post-investment and Aftercare have often been pushed into the conversation of linkages, or project facilitation, our book demonstrates how post-investment is so much more.

Investment Aftercare Explained: A Guide for FDI Practitioners and Policymakers on How to Grow and Retain Investors reaches the bookshelves in a new era, one where governments across the world are asking themselves how to stand tall after the economic devastation wreaked by Covid-19. This book, based on years of experience and full of practical ideas and examples, offers a path that can help those economies create value by working closely with their foreign investors.

The ultimate ambition of this book is to move post-investment into mainstream FDI. And for that change to happen, Aftercare needs to capture the imagination of IPAs, foreign investors and stakeholders alike. So far, *Aftercare* has only attracted limited attention, *Policy Advocacy* is left to the public sector, *Ecosystem* growth is left to chance and *Place* is seen as only a marketing effort. This needs to change. And change needs to start with leaders thinking and acting differently.

The first step is to recognise that foreign investors are assets. Looking after these assets should be an essential part of all FDI-related policy making. Ideally it should be a national government-led initiative (orchestrated by the IPA) that calls for a long-term commitment and mutual ongoing collaboration between government departments, the private sector and civil society. Otherwise "there is no hope in hell of ever moving the needle"[14] on post-investment in general, and on Aftercare in particular.

The second step is to look after established foreign investors as you would look after a car. Once it is no longer the shiny new toy on the street, it still needs to be regularly cleaned, polished and serviced in order to perform reliably and for a long time. Foreign investors need to be serviced regularly if they are to bring long-term benefit to the host economy. This is where some IPAs fall down, whether it be due to an incorrect strategy, or the lack of one, or a lack of funding. Many neglect their established investors or assume that they can take care of themselves. However, investors who are not looked after are likely, sooner or later, to focus their attention elsewhere. And this is when this lack of responsibility becomes a loss for the host economy. An investor that leaves the country is unlikely to ever come back.

The third step is for the understanding and appreciation of post-investment to reach critical mass. The more IPAs embrace Aftercare, the more evident it will be that those who do not embrace it are doing so at their peril. However, such knowledge diffusion will not happen by chance, it needs to be driven by intentional policy design – international organisations and national governments must make extra efforts to encourage and support Aftercare until it becomes a mainstream practice.

This book provides a roadmap on how to do it.

I.1.2 Core principles that underpin this book

We wrote this book to provide IPAs and Aftercare practitioners with a comprehensive toolkit to support foreign investors. Specifically, the following core principles underpin this book:

- **Practitioner-led**: we wanted to give practical tools and street-level concepts to front-line practitioners and policy makers so that they can be more successful. As such, we have used plain language and tried to minimise the use of technical terms and academic jargon wherever possible. In seeking to make this book as real and practical as possible we have examples from over 80 countries. In particular, the later chapters of the book provide a "how to" guide on the delivery of Aftercare services, and also on how to articulate their benefit to the host economy and bring the business ecosystem together to support foreign investors. For front-line practitioners, consultants and executives seeking to add to their knowledge toolbox – this book has been written for you.
- **Policymaker minded**: while writing this book we asked ourselves what is it that policymakers need to know to effectively play their role in supporting FDI? This resulted in the inclusion of quotes and references from over 500 sources. The early chapters should be of particular interest to policy makers and those seeking to better understand what post-investment is all about. For policy makers and their advisers seeking to increase the return on investment of their FDI operation, and of course on tax-payer's money, this is your book.
- **Research-provoking**: while this book is the first attempt to bring together and systematise the huge topic of post-investment, academics, researchers and statisticians will most likely wish to have seen more data. On this occasion we believed that comprehensively covering post-investment was more important. Producing new data is work for another day. Nonetheless, we hope this book provides a sufficiently comprehensive overview of post-investment and that others will be inspired to cover specific topics in more depth at some point in the future. Perhaps the impact of the Covid-19 pandemic on FDI will make this happen sooner rather than later.

- **Knowledge-organising**: one of the main roles of this book is to provide a framework for post-investment, one which organises and unifies the disparate information produced by practitioners, policymakers and researchers. We focused on collecting, organising and reflecting on the knowledge we gathered about the key areas of Aftercare, which were often highly fragmented, with the aim of presenting them, for the first time, in a comprehensible, comprehensive, logical and above all practical manner.
- **Ecosystem-thinking**: we strongly believe that IPAs and investors benefit from looking at their own roles as "pro-investment ecosystem builders." Aftercare provides a platform to not only work with investors, but also to co-create with the FDI Ecosystem the economic foundations of tomorrow's society. We hope that professionals dedicated to adjacent roles, such as Policy Advocacy, Ecosystem development, community building, image-building and placemaking, use this book to expand their understanding of FDI and the role they play within the post-investment scene.

In essence, our book helps bring together the post-investment Ecosystem around Aftercare so that it can function and perform better for the benefit of both investor and host economies.

I.1.3 The research method

This book draws on the authors' collective experiences in post-investment practice, Ecosystem building, place development, Policy Advocacy and research to provide a comprehensive overview of the post-investment industry. We started the journey focusing on Aftercare, only to realise that, in order to fully understand how to grow and retain investors, it was necessary to also understand how to advocate for the best investment climate and how to support linkages and connectedness among local players so that the host economy is not only attractive and welcoming, but also fertile ground in which to invest and grow. We reflected on this carefully and consulted with many front-line practitioners. The message was clear – only a few understood the big picture of post-investment and how all the pieces fitted together, while the majority could only outline small parts of how the industry works. Consequently, we are considering writing a series of books that explore each of the pillars of post-investment, placing particular importance on how each one supports the other and how together they thrive. The next book in the series will be *Policy Advocacy Explained*, which will provide a comprehensive review of how to create the best investment climate to attract, grow and retain foreign investors.

The models, descriptions and recommendations that we offer in this book come from three primary sources:

1) A review of the existing literature, which is mainly produced by international organisations and academic journals. The authors hope is that this book builds on their work and contributes to the ongoing conversation about post-investment services.
2) Interviews conducted with almost 100 professionals working in IPAs, economic development organisations (EDOs), international organisations, academia, consultants and other FDI professionals covering some of the largest organisations in the industry, as well as some small ones.
3) The lead author draws on her deep experience working as a practitioner and consultant in the FDI industry for over 15 years, to share lessons from what she has learnt, first working at an IPA, and later from clients of her post-investment consulting practice. The other co-authors – an economist serving as a central banker, another as a professor of business and the third one as an international investor – bring critical policy, economic and business expertise.

I.1.4 What the book covers

Responding to the growing demand for Aftercare, which has been accelerated by the Covid-19 pandemic, this book covers topics that IPA professionals will be familiar but hope to better understand.

Part I – The why: starts by briefly explaining why FDI is critical for economic development. We make the case for why a well thought post-investment policy is necessary as part of a complete IPA strategy. The text starts out discussing well-established facts about the impact and importance of FDI attraction, positive externalities and virtuous cycles of technological improvement, more and better jobs, permanent increases in trade, all of which lead to economic growth and higher welfare in local economies. We highlight the fact that while governments in some countries devote substantial resources to attracting FDI, they have a mixed record when it comes to supporting foreign investors once they have arrived on their shores. Then we explain how post-investment – introduced as the 4 pillars of post-investment: Investor Services, Place, Ecosystem and Policy Advocacy – can provide the support required to help foreign investors grow, which in turn can create more local opportunities and contribute to the host economy. We then take a deep dive into what Aftercare is, and how practitioners serve foreign investors – irrespective of what label they use. We present a model of the 4 stages of maturity of Aftercare and discuss why Aftercare requires the support of the whole Ecosystem to be effective and impactful. Part I provides a framework to help policymakers and national, regional and local governments better understand the importance of Aftercare and the benefits of embracing it.

Part II – The what: is designed to be a detailed guide for policy makers and practitioners who seek to effectively provide Aftercare to foreign investors, and ultimately to develop the local economy. It focuses on three of the pillars, namely Investor Services, Place and Ecosystem.

Investor Services presents a framework to better understand how to serve foreign investors, including descriptions of the types of services involved, the types of projects delivered and what the typical service models are – these include administrative, operational and strategic services. It explores newer type of services, such as those related to value chains, sustainability and good governance. This is followed by an Investor Services Catalogue that provides examples of best practices from all over the world. The next chapter looks at negative post-investment experiences, investor dissatisfaction and investor grievances and what options investors have when they are not satisfied. It closes with a chapter on divestments, and what happens when investors leave or are distressed.

Place and Ecosystem explores how local economies can provide a welcoming environment for established investors. It explores what the links between place branding, place marketing, placemaking, cluster development and global connectedness have to do with developing vibrant communities where foreign investors can grow and thrive. It explores the basic building blocks of Place and Ecosystem. It then presents examples of programmes from all over the world that create value that directly or indirectly benefits investor's growth.

Part III – The how: covers the many factors practitioners need to consider when setting up post-investment units. It starts with a post-investment framework to explain what it takes to set up and run an Aftercare unit. It is intended to serve both as a handbook for IPAs and to provide guidance when it comes to putting together a case for why they should offer services, outlining what type of value they can create and how they can both design and deliver these services. This part also includes a chapter about impact evaluation and presents a novel approach to measuring the impact of post-investment.

I.1.5 How to use the content

This book aims to equip front-line practitioners, policy makers, consultants and business executives with the knowledge and tools to effectively address the main challenges in providing Aftercare services. The content of this book can be used in a number of different ways and for a range of purposes, such as:

- To support post-investment practitioners and to make their lives easier, as they can "use the book to authoritatively explain to their superiors and stakeholders what it is that they do and why their jobs are so challenging,"[15] as well as to strengthen their institutions' post-investment function. This is true for Aftercare professionals, but also for those working in stakeholder engagement.
- To help policymakers understand how post-investment can be a key component of a national, supranational or local economic development strategy, and how they can support post-investment.
- To support post-investment planning, budgeting and the deployment of resources, as well as attracting funding from private sources.
- To help stakeholders understand the complexities of post-investment, and how they can pull their weight, as well as how they can benefit.
- To help place makers develop common ground and a language that allows them to work with foreign investors and collaborate with the IPA.
- To provide evaluation and impact measurement professionals with a framework that allows them to assess the impact of post-investment activities.

- To help policy advocates work effectively with IPAs and to collaborate on joint activities.
- To support international organisations in their quest to provide practical support to IPAs.
- To support foreign investors in their dealing with IPAs, as well as the public affairs officers of foreign investors seeking to better understand the role of the IPA within the host economy.
- To support post-investment training and academic courses, as well as autonomous learning – readers can use this book as a standalone learning tool to build understanding of the key principles of Aftercare theory and its challenges.
- To support scholars in their research and also to encourage them to further build the knowledge base around post-investment.
- To encourage further collaboration between professionals in the post-investment industry, as they now have a framework that clarifies the different roles of the many different professions that make Aftercare such a rich industry.

I.1.6 The future

We hope that our book will lead to more research into various parts of post-investment. We have identified at least three areas that ought to be examined in greater depth: the long-term impact of looking after foreign investors, the causality between intervention and short / medium-term change, as well as the cumulative effect of working collaboratively with the FDI ecosystem. The hope is that other Aftercare advocates join our journey and contribute with new knowledge, data and resources and help the whole Aftercare industry to raise its game.

International organisations need to give a clear signal to IPAs and to encourage them to embrace Aftercare, increase their local capacity and provide more resources to do so, as well as to lead global initiatives to exchange best practices that could help increase the return of investment of FDI.

By providing a comprehensive overview of the major topics in post-investment, we also hope that this book will better connect those in academia and think tanks with each other's work. One of the goals of this book is to encourage academics to reflect the interconnectedness of post-investment.

The next call goes to IPAs to get creative, daring and ambitious. What location will become the next South Korea, Costa Rica, United Kingdom, Ireland or Holland when it comes to investor retention, customer care and joint-value creation?

The final call goes to professionals in the FDI industry who, irrespective of their role, contribute to making FDI a fundamental building block of the global economy. Post-investment is a platform that can bring host economies many rewards, but it requires laying the foundations first, and giving relationships and projects the time they need to mature. Funders need to have a long-term view of post-investment if they are to reap its benefits. Stakeholders need to find their role and become active co-creators of strong and vibrant local FDI Ecosystems that welcome foreign investors in their role of shaping societies. In an increasingly connected world, one that faces shared challenges such as climate change, food insecurity and natural disasters, FDI professionals can't focus solely on winning the next big project, doing whatever is necessary to attract an investor in the face of fierce competition, in what is a winner takes all game. The call is to revisit this approach to attracting and retaining investors that the FDI industry is so well-known for, and raise the game towards a more collaborative, integrated and stakeholder-driven approach, one that drives sustainable economic recovery and builds more cohesive, resilient and connected societies. Aftercare provides an effective platform for a wide range of interested stakeholders to get together to create new value, with a view that foreign investors become transformational champions of better societies.

The hope is that readers will now take the baton, embrace Aftercare and make their own mark. The stakes are high. The roadmap is ready. It is time to act.

Notes

1 World Bank, 2020. *COVID-19 to Plunge Global Economy into Worst Recession since World War II* [online]. Available at: https://www.worldbank.org/en/news/press-release/2020/06/08/covid-19-to-plunge-global-economy-into-worst-recession-since-world-war-ii.

2 Blake, P. and Wadhwa, D. 2020. *2020 Year in Review: The Impact of COVID-19 in 12 Charts* [online]. Available at: https://blogs.worldbank.org/voices/2020-year-review-impact-covid-19-12-charts.

3 Sequioa, 2020. *Coronavirus: The Black Swan of 2020* [online]. Available at: https://medium.com/sequoia-capital/coronavirus-the-black-swan-of-2020-7c 72bdeb9753.

4 Arriagada Peters, C. 2020. *FDI Aftercare & COVID19 – What to Do about That Mix* [online]. Available at: https://www.linkedin.com/pulse/fdi-aftercare-covid19-what-do-mix-carolina-arriagada-peters/.

5 UNCTAD, 2021. *Investment Trends Monitor.* New York & Geneva, Issue 38.

6 World Bank, 2020. *The Initial Responses of Investment Promotion Agencies to Covid-19 and Some Observed Effects on FDI* [online]. Available at: http://pubdocs.worldbank.org/en/917561588958415090/WBG-IPA-Response-to-COVID-19.pdf.

7 OECD, 2020. *Investment Promotion Agencies in the Time of Covid-19* [online]. Available at: http://www.oecd.org/coronavirus/policy-responses/investment-promotion-agencies-in-the-time-of-covid-19-50f79678/.

8 Qiang, C.Z., Liu, Y. Paganini, M. and Steenbergen, V. 2020. *Foreign Direct Investment and Global Value Chains in the Wake of COVID-19* [online]. Available at: https://blogs.worldbank.org/psd/foreign-direct-investment-and-global-value-chains-wake-covid-19.

9 Ibid.

10 Heilbron, A. and Aranda-Larrey, Y. 2020. *Strengthening Service Delivery of Investment Promotion Agencies: The Comprehensive Investor Services Framework.* Investment Promotion for Impact Series. Finance, Competitiveness, and Innovation In Focus. World Bank, Washington, DC [online]. Available at: http://documents1.worldbank.org/curated/en/375281584479055974/pdf/Strengthening-Service-Delivery-of-Investment-Promotion-Agencies-The-Comprehensive-Investor-Services-Framework.pdf.

11 Arriagada Peters, C. 2017. *Module 5 Aftercare and Policy Advocacy*, s.l: Course: Towards the next generation of IPAs by Inter-American Development Bank – Inter-American Development Bank (IDB).

12 UNCTAD, 2020. *COVID-19 Will Likely Transform Global Production, Says UN Report* [online]. Available at: https://unctad.org/news/covid-19-will-likely-transform-global-production-says-un-report.

13 McMakin, T. and Fletcher, D. 2018. *How Clients Buy: A Practical Guide to Business Development for Consulting and Professional Services.* 1st edn. Hoboken, NJ: Wiley.

14 Govers, R. 2018. *Imaginative Communities: Admired Cities, Regions and Countries.* 1st edn. Antwerp, Belgium: Reputo Press.

15 Ibid.

Part I
The why

1

UNDERSTANDING POST-INVESTMENT

Chapter highlights

- FDI is an important economic driver for developing a host country's economy, both locally and nationally.
- Different to new investment, that is unidirectional, growing and retaining foreign investments requires an eco-systemic approach, which has its own challenges and opportunities.
- Host governments have an inconsistent record when it comes to providing post-investment support to foreign companies.
- There are important economic benefits for a location from providing post-investment services to foreign companies.

1.1 Introduction

> If a project was worth securing as an inward investor,
> it must be worth supporting as an established investor.
>
> (Central government policy maker)

To better understand the relevance of foreign investment attraction, it is necessary to start with a basic definition of foreign direct investment (FDI). The United Nations Conference on Trade and Development (UNCTAD) defines FDI as "an investment involving a long-term relationship and reflecting a lasting interest and control by a resident entity in one economy

DOI: 10.4324/9781003174950-3

(foreign direct investor or parent enterprise) in an enterprise resident in an economy other than that of the foreign direct investor (FDI enterprise or affiliate enterprise or foreign affiliate)."[1] The most common form of FDI, and the one that is the focus of this book, involves an investor either establishing new operations overseas or acquiring business assets in another country. FDI is associated with a productive-type investment, where the investor is an active owner/manager, unlike a portfolio investment where an investor passively holds stocks of foreign-based companies. Thus, FDI is typically a long-term investment for the investor, which may involve them expanding further in the future.

The benefits that FDI bring to a host country's economy, either by a foreign company or its local subsidiary,[2] are well established. In particular, FDI has a positive impact on the host economy in the form of positive externalities, which include more and better employment opportunities, new technology, innovative practices, additional capital investment and more international trade. As a consequence, the local economy benefits from income growth and, most importantly, economic development.

According to UNCTAD, "for each foreign investment dollar attracted, the local economy generates another one, and exports [an]other two dollars."[3] For every job directly created by FDI, UNCTAD estimates that between one and two more jobs are created locally.[4] Meanwhile the international economists Stehrer and Woerz (2009) have found evidence that a 10% increase in FDI translates into a 1.2% increase in economic growth.[5] This is especially beneficial when foreign investment complements host country investment – particularly in technologically less developed countries – as it increases the development effect of FDI (De Mello, 1999).[6] Consequently, countries around the world have prioritised attracting FDI and have devoted considerable resources to it.

When knowledge is transferable, it becomes a public good. In other words, when a foreign firm invests in a country, the expertise it brings with it creates returns that are recognised beyond the firm as other parties benefit from its operation at no cost to themselves. A good example of this is the impact on labour markets. There are at least four ways FDI helps increase skill levels and job creation in the host country. First, foreign investment brings new processes and new ways of working. Over time, employees will leave the foreign subsidiary and take their newly acquired knowledge and skills to local firms, from where this knowledge spreads further into the local economy. Second, local suppliers will acquire the knowledge required to meet the needs and standards of their foreign customer. Third, to attract more and better FDI, countries invest in their labour force to ensure they have the latest skills and knowledge. Many of these new skills would not otherwise be acquired by the local workforce, and hence this is a clear positive benefit of foreign investment. Furthermore, foreign companies often bring with them new technology and innovative processes, which are key drivers of economic growth. Indeed, foreign investment enhances capital formation within an economy and enables output to increase. For example, research shows that technological spillovers from FDI to intra-country firms are a major driver of productivity growth in China.[7] Technology transfers from foreign companies also enable an economy to become more robust, stronger and more diversified.

Fourth, FDI increases exports from recipient countries as foreign investors typically seek to export to neighbouring markets. This not only increases the market for local firms, but also increases local companies' awareness of global market opportunities. As the Organization for Economic Cooperation and Development (OECD) says, FDI is "an integral part of an open and effective international economic system and a major catalyst to development."[8]

Given these benefits, attracting FDI is an economic policy priority in many developed and developing countries. To support public and private sector efforts to attract foreign investors, governments around the world have created investment promotion agencies (IPAs) or allocated the function to a local economic development organisation (EDOs). Their objectives include: promoting the country, region or city as a suitable destination for investment; raising awareness of available investment opportunities; attracting investors that can foster job creation and productivity growth; improving the investment climate; and then once an investor has arrived, facilitating their landing in the host country. Governments also work closely with international organisations to identify best practices to attract foreign investors. Such inter-organisational endeavours include the World Bank's efforts to share knowledge of investment promotion through the publication of reports such as "Institutions for FDI Investment", "Establishing a High-Performing Institutional Framework for Foreign Direct investment", "Strengthening Service Delivery of Investment Promotion Agencies", "The Comprehensive Investor Services Framework", "State of Investment

Promotion Agencies", "Evidence from WAIPA-WBG's Joint Global Survey" and a recent initiative by the UN Enhanced Integrated Framework to increase capacity in "least developed countries – LDCs".[9]

1.2 Considerations about the benefits of FDI

While foreign direct investment brings benefits to the host country, the extent of these benefits is dependent on many factors, including the governance of FDI programs, the range and quality of local institutions, the political status of the host country, the level of market concentration of competition, international market conditions for the industry's attracted, etc. For example, if a foreign company enters a country with the intention of competing with existing local businesses, then these local businesses may reduce in size or even disappear. Alternatively, if a foreign company repatriates all the profits it makes, rather than reinvesting some of them locally, the benefits of FDI are likely to be reduced. Meanwhile, there are export and trade agencies, such as Australia's Austrade, offering incentives to retain high value jobs in Australia, policies that look to ringfence valuable companies from foreign FDI efforts. Many of these issues may lead to foreign firms having excessive market power, which in turn may impact local employment and wages, disadvantage local enterprises and result in lower tax revenues for the host countries. Further, focussing excessively on economic growth risks attracting companies that undertake environmentally risky activities, or that have lower environmental standards, which could have an undesirable impact on social welfare.

Several assumptions about the benefits of FDI have been disproved by recent research published by the London School of Economics (LSE).[10] For example, there is a belief that the most desirable investors are the big tech firms, such as Amazon, Google or Microsoft. However, the LSE found that the big tech firms are less likely to hire local workers and that innovations are kept in-house and aggressively protected by confidentiality agreements. Moreover, due to limited, if any, collaboration with local firms, there is less spillover. In contrast, small and medium-sized tech firms have been found to have a greater impact on local economies in terms of creating innovation hubs. These firms tend to leverage the local workforce more, create more linkages with local enterprises and more actively promote the exchange of ideas.

A second misconception is that FDI is an optimal way to recover from recessions. In other words, that foreign investment should be a substitute for domestic investment. At first glance this sounds reasonable, but the reality is that it depends on which industry the foreign investment is allocated to. Economists Crescenzi and Ganau (2020) have shown that European countries that received more FDI recovered faster from the 2008 Great Recession, but only when these new investments went to mature and robust industries, while service industries have been shown to have a greater impact on driving recovery than manufacturing, which is what EU policies are currently focussed on.[11]

A third misconception is that greenfield investment is always better than brownfield investment. An idea based on the premise that a new investment, such as the construction of a brand-new factory, is better than buying an existing firm or installation. Economist Alexander Jaax indicated that this is not always the case. He found that while in Brazil and Mexico greenfield investment improved local innovation, in Colombia multinational companies acquiring local firms *actually improved* local innovation, noting that Colombia's level of technological development and international integration was less advanced than the other two countries. Apparently, brownfield investment has a greater impact than expected in countries that show a lower level of global integration.[12]

In summary, while the overall benefits of foreign investment to local economies are not in dispute, the effect and impact of FDI vary from place to place, from industry to industry, and vary in the different parts of the FDI value, and hence FDI practitioners and policy makers need to take these considerations into account.

1.3 The importance of post-investment support

Once a foreign company has made the decision to invest in a location, it will require significant support in order to get up and running quickly and to operate effectively in its new environment at each stage of its investment. For example, they may need legal assistance regarding local employment laws and environmental regulations, or assistance identifying suitable suppliers. This support is usually referred to as investment facilitation or (soft) landing. IPAs are generally good at providing these sorts of services to newly arrived foreign companies.

Once foreign companies are well established, the challenge becomes how countries can retain foreign investors in the long run. Post-arrival, foreign companies still require support, for example, assistance in adapting to changes in the local business environment, such as new regulations, or when they face abrupt market changes that challenge the viability of local jobs, such as the market shifts caused by the Covid-19 pandemic. In addition, established companies' focus on their own businesses may mean they are not well-informed about other opportunities in the local market, and so they may need help to address this asymmetry of information when it comes to accessing these opportunities.

The World Association of International Promotion Agencies (WAIPA) observes that "the most important aspect of investment promotion [we] drive home is that aftercare and follow-up service delivery matters just as much as initial investment attraction."[13] There has been much debate about the number of new jobs created and the level of new investment that comes from established foreign investors. UNESCAP's 2017 handbook estimates that reinvestment represents 32% of all FDI flow.[14] These figures relate to developing economies, as in developed economies reinvestment can be as high as 70% of total FDI.[15] WAIPA concluded that in 2016 that "more than 50% of new investments come from already established satisfied investors."[16]

Post-investment has a silver lining with clearly defined stages, as can be seen in Figure 1.1. In the pre-investment phase, the investor is typically considering a number of locations. Once it makes the decision to enter a new host economy, it will have to get to know the local environment. Landing services are helpful at this stage. As time passes, the subsidiary

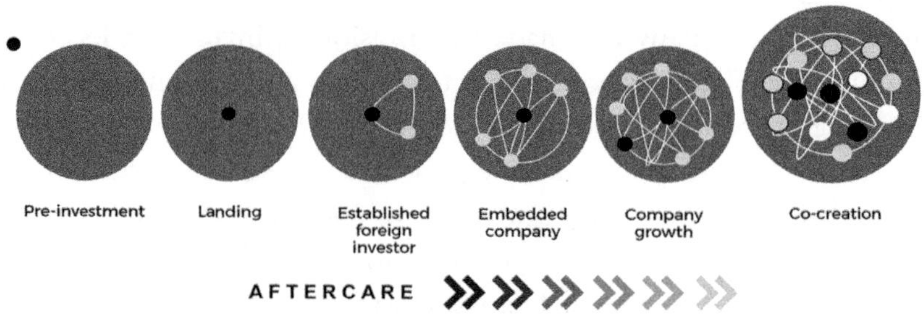

Figure 1.1 The foreign investor's growth path. © *Investment Aftercare Explained: A Guide for FDI Practitioners and Policymakers on How to Grow and Retain Investors.*

should become well-established in the locality and be operating as required by their head-office. Post-investment services can help embed the company locally, help it grow, thereby growing the host-economy to the benefit of many local actors.

1.4 Inconsistent record on post-investment support

1.4.1 Neglect existing investors at your peril

Most countries go to great lengths to attract new foreign investors – there are thousands of IPAs trying to portray their region as the best place to invest; many even use the same messaging! Consequently, many governments dedicate a significant proportion of their budget to trying to attract FDI, and may also receive international funds from development banks, such as the Asian Development Bank or the Inter-American Development Bank, to support these efforts. Despite all this up-front investment, in many host countries there is a substantial opportunity to improve the support provided to established foreign investors to help them with their on-going post-investment needs. According to an OECD study in 2018,[17] only 36% of OECD IPAs performed Aftercare, compared with 59% that provided investment facilitation services. The same study commented that, among the 36% of IPAs that do provide Aftercare services, "there are wide disparities from one national agency to another in the different activities covered under this function. In France, for example, investor services are provided by local autonomous agencies, who cooperate with national level to offer an end-to-end service to investors."[18] The OECD study also notes that there is a wide variety of service delivery models that are not well captured by statistics. For example, they indicate that the Aftercare function is sometimes deployed among different local and regional institutions with which the IPA collaborates. As such, "the fact that a national IPA does not provide facilitation and aftercare services is not so much an indication of the existence of such services in a country as it is a characteristic of its overarching institutional setting for investment promotion and facilitation."[19] The 2020 State of Investment Promotion Agencies – Evidence from WAIPA-WBG's Joint Global Survey of IPAs confirmed the point and found that IPAs focused more on the provision of services at attraction, than at entry and establishment. The range and level of services offered tends to decline at the retention and expansion stage, and especially at the linkages and spillovers stage, functions that only half of IPA members offer.[20]

As for those IPAs that deliver aftercare services under the banner of Aftercare, their efforts often look weak when compared with what could be done to support mobilising FDI to change local economic structures. UNESCAP's 2017 handbook notes that IPAs devote less than 10% of their resources to servicing established investors, while an OECD 2018 study arrived at a similar figure, finding that investment facilitation received 24% of resources available, more than double what post-investment services receives. And yet "84% of IPAs state that such post-investment support has a higher, or equal, priority than other activities with respect to generating reinvestment or expansion of existing activities."[21]

The primary reason for the poor attention that post-investment services receive is that host governments dedicate insufficient resources to supporting foreign companies post-landing. It appears that insights into post-investment's importance and delivery options are not readily available, and that politicians are not well-informed about the benefits of retaining investors, which in turn weakens Policy Advocacy efforts.

The perception that new foreign investment is the most important contribution a foreign company makes to a host economy is unfortunately often supported by a series of decision points in the FDI value chain. It starts with policy makers who might not understand what post-investment is, nor its contribution to the overall economic development toolkit. The same priority (or lack of priority of post-investment) is reflected in the budgets IPAs receive from their funders. IPAs might understand why post-investment is important, but nevertheless focus on delivering what they have been resourced to do, leaving post-investment services neglected. For example, in a recent World Bank publication, the authors mention that "IPAs focus mostly on the attraction stage and that a considerable percentage of IPAs leave the investor unattended after an investment decision has been made."[22] The same article emphasises that a long-standing, mutually beneficial relationship with stakeholders in the host economy attracts productive foreign investors. The key element in this alliance is IPAs providing relevant post-investment services that flexibly adapt to investors' needs.

Think-tanks and academia are also not highlighting this lack of focus on post-investment as there is too little research and data available to equip them with arguments that could result in white papers that would pass peer-review. And while international organisations recognise the information gap, they tend to be risk-adverse and are restricted by their budgets or by their priorities, which are usually dictated by their funders or members. This lack of insight into the benefits of Aftercare is holding back post-investment.

And yet post-investment services are not new. The capability and focus within IPAs have existed for decades, which limits industry advocates' ability to gain traction or secure sponsorship for post-investment-related proposals with the argument that this has been tried before with little benefit, or that research on that topic has no PR value. The result is a lukewarm response from a wide set of players in the extremely competitive FDI industry, which is pre-occupied with many other equally important priorities. For instance, in 2019 the World Bank published a document making this point. On the one hand, it seems logical for host governments to have policies that ensure that foreign investors are retained and expanded. On the other hand, most governments do not have the basic tools to monitor how many foreign investors are cancelling expansions, or why this is happening.[23] To the outsider, it would appear that the ugly duckling of post-investment services has little chance to become a swan. Supporting that transformation is at the core of this book.

The result is a neglect of the later stages of the FDI value chain. This is unfortunate as, at a micro level, it risks existing and substantial investors being taken for granted, underserved or receiving little support, which hinders further reinvestment. At a macro level, it lowers the return on investment on money spent attracting FDI, it misses an opportunity to strengthen the local business fabric, which in turn diminishes the resilience of the whole business economy, a topic that will be explored later in the book.

The coronavirus pandemic has somehow turned the tables when it comes to post-investment. Due to the unexpected nature of the Covid-19 pandemic, post-investment services are obtaining an unprecedented level of attention. UNCTAD reported that FDI flows plummeted by 42% in 2020, falling from US$1.5 trillion in 2019 to US$859 billion in 2020. This figure is 30% lower than the trough after the global financial crisis in 2009.[24] The contraction is due to the severe disruption in global value chains, the fast emergence of new technologies and the high level of uncertainty in international markets. As these changes do not appear to be transitory, they are likely to affect foreign investment flows negatively in a more permanent way.[25] In another report published during the first months of the pandemic, the World Bank mentions that due to this unexpected shock to the global economy, governments and IPAs should create "a predictable, business-friendly regulatory environment [that] goes beyond the rules on the books," and that forces them to implement new ways to satisfy foreign investors' needs.[26] In this new business landscape, it seems that post-investment activities will play an increasingly strategic and relevant role for IPAs.

1.5 The pillars of post-investment

Effective post-investment support builds upon the work of location competitiveness, investment attraction and investment facilitation. It is centred around four distinctive activities: Investor Services, Investment Climate, Ecosystem and Place – referred to collectively here as the Pillars of Post-Investment, as shown in Figure 1.2. Continuing with the building metaphor, all four pillars are required to create a stable solution. These pillars are interactive, feeding each other in a way that optimises their effectiveness for investors, the public sector, IPAs boards and the many players in the FDI ecosystem and the local constituency.

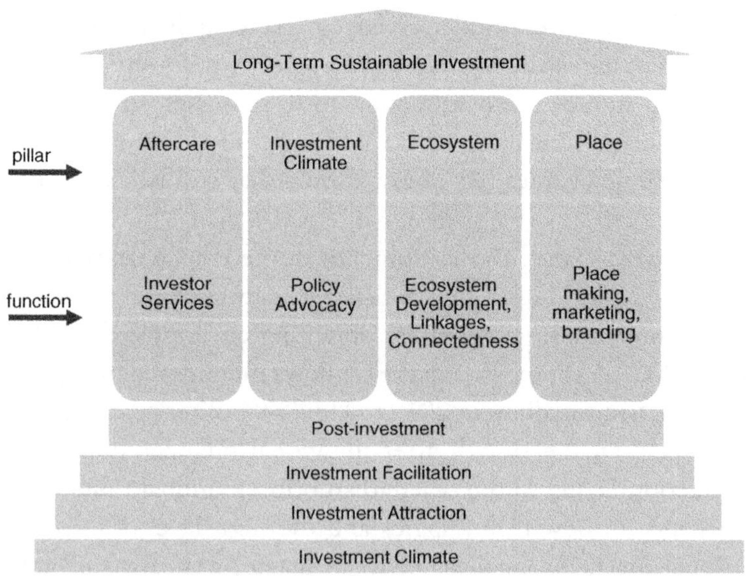

Figure 1.2 The pillars and functions of post-investment. © *Investment Aftercare Explained: A Guide for FDI Practitioners and Policymakers on How to Grow and Retain Investors.*

The four pillars and functions, are summarised below:

Aftercare: the main objective of Aftercare is to support foreign investors by responding to their needs. It encompasses all client-facing activity in the post-investment phase, usually referred to as **Investor Services** or, simply, facilitation. Broadly speaking, Aftercare covers a wide range of services driven by investor need and the corresponding back-office support required to help the investor grow and expand locally.

Investment Climate: according to the International Finance Corporation (IFC) "the rate and nature of private sector growth in a country is affected by many factors, including macroeconomic and political stability, traditions and culture, physical infrastructure, availability of capital, and human resources."[27] They add that, "institutional policy and regulatory factors also play an important role. They are often grouped together under the title 'investment climate'."[28] And the investment climate matters, as "substantial research literature has established an association between the characteristics of the business regulatory environment and the performance of firms, and thence to macroeconomic outcomes."[29] The function that influences the investment climate is **Policy Advocacy**, which seeks to foster a dialogue between government, regulators, business and the community with the aim of improving the business environment for foreign investors.

Ecosystem: ecosystems are systems that collaborate, compete and define the way different entities interact with each other with the aim of capturing the benefits of agglomeration and inter-connectedness and articulating the way in which this benefit is distributed. Sometimes referred to simply as the local business community, recent studies confirm that local business ecosystems strongly influence company growth, and therefore post-investment. Ecosystem includes the work of local subnational economic development agencies (EDOs) who need to maintain "proper, systematic and productive relationships"[30] with these local businesses, foreign investors and the FDI community. Ecosystem also includes network linkages, connectedness and clusters, which are bundled under greater **Ecosystem Development** – sometimes also referred to as ecosystem engagement or ecosystem affairs.

Place: foreign investment has, at its core, a human element. Staff need to live and thrive in their new environments. Places have identities people relate to. Together they create a sense of place. Location-wide collaborative efforts that reimagine and reshape the notion of the place of a host economy so that it becomes a more welcoming and desirable place to live, to visit and to invest, are key to post-investment. There are different functions that perform Place-related services such as **placemaking, place branding** and **place marketing**.

It is worth noting that during the pandemic, a 5th function emerged. Many IPAs reported being tasked to work with other public offices to deliver pandemic-specific programmes. For example, some IPAs saw themselves, for the first time, processing visa applications for foreign investors or supporting distribution of financial relief to domestic firms. It is still early days and there is no clarity about whether those services will remain after the pandemic. As such, they have not been included as a specific service pillar in this book.

At the same time as we were writing this book, the authors Armando Heilbron and Yago Aranda-Larrey, from the World Bank, developed a similar framework for investment promotion as seen from an integrated perspective. Their 2020 report titled "Strengthening Service Delivery of Investment Promotion Agencies: The Comprehensive Investor Services Framework"[31] provides a useful model to support IPAs looking to rethink the way they design and deliver investment services. They observe that "investor services alone cannot attract or retain investors; therefore, an IPA's services must build on the location's attractiveness as an investment destination. This includes providing advocacy services to continuously improve it."[32]

The more experts that support the notion that FDI needs to go beyond new investment, to meet investors' needs and to address the various stages of the investment lifecycle, the more likely it is that IPAs will focus a higher proportion of their resources on Aftercare – to the ultimate benefit of their economies. The Comprehensive Investor Services Framework (CISF) framework helps governments and their IPAs understand the "importance of providing services to investors at every stage of the investment life cycle, beyond the first stage of attracting them to invest in the country (the attraction stage), by providing a more comprehensive, service-oriented, and investor-centric approach that would benefit all IPAs, regardless of their level of development."[33] In their model, the World Bank identifies 4 service categories that broadly match the categories in this book: *marketing*, which corresponds in this book to place-making; *advocacy*, as in this book; *information and assistance*, covered here under Investor Services; and while the World Bank does not have a direct equivalent for ecosystem development, it does include *linkages* as part of value creation.

These functions also correspond to three economic cycles that are broadly consistent with the core FDI functions defined by Louis T. Wells and Alvin

G. Wint, professors in business management, who wrote one of the first texts about investment retention back in 2000.[34] Each cycle has distinctive characteristics:

- The business cycle of the foreign investor corresponds to Aftercare.
- The economic cycle of the host economy in which the foreign business has invested is the area that Policy Advocacy seeks to influence.
- While the dynamics of the local business community, how they cooperate and compete, and together sell the location correspond to Place and Ecosystem.

These three cycles influence each other and are deeply intertwined. Together they aim to realise the potential that foreign investors bring, namely the development of a more productive, integrated and sustainable Place to do business to the benefit of all parties involved. Viewed in this way, *post-investment becomes a set of value propositions, policy strategies and value creation methodologies that increase the return on investment (ROI) of the multiple resources invested by different actors in the FDI industry for the benefit of all stakeholders involved.*

Post-investment offers a methodology to capture the value derived from the presence of a foreign investor in the host economy, as well as an opportunity to create new value. Understanding this duality is key to effective post-investment services, advocacy and collaboration. Ultimately, post-investment is what local leaders make of it, that is to say, how they use FDI as a tool for economic growth, how they allocate resources, how they define priorities and their ability to develop collaboration frameworks that enable value creation. Or put another way, *post-investment is a multi-purpose, multi-stakeholder, multi-benefit value creation engine centred on maximising the presence of foreign investors in a host economy for the benefit of all stakeholders.* The latter definition injects dynamism, the notion of relativity, the convergence of different agendas and the importance of a specific space/time context to post-investment, where the different societal players have a stake in the presence of that foreign investor in the host economy. Thus far, these three topics have been the subject of too little discussion and research.

While the approach to attracting new investment corresponds to a step-by-step linear model that connects attraction, promotion and facilitation, understanding the nature of post-investment demands a different mindset. Figure 1.3 introduces the notion of a virtuous post-investment triangle. As with new investment, attraction and promotion lead to facilitation, which,

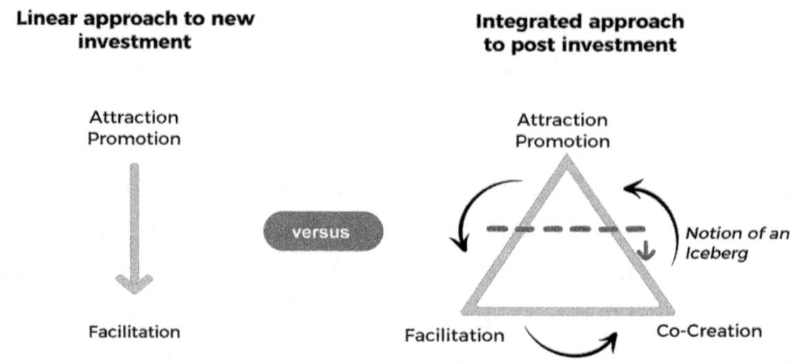

Figure 1.3 The post-investment virtuous triangle. © *Investment Aftercare Explained: A Guide for FDI Practitioners and Policymakers on How to Grow and Retain Investors.*

supported by continuous dialogue and value creation mind-sets, provide an opportunity for investors and public and private stakeholders to provide input and share insight as to how they can better collaborate, how they can work together to improve the local investment climate and how they can jointly create value that ultimately results in the co-creation of a vibrant, magnetic and thriving investment destination. In essence, this is like an iceberg; industry insiders will understand the depth of facilitation and co-creation needed for a host economy to become a destination. This in turn increases competitiveness, which results in attracting more investment. An economy that can effectively leverage the post-investment virtuous triangle approach will maximise value for all those with a stake in the FDI agenda.

In closing, the benefits that FDI brings to local economies are well-established. Consequently, both developed and developing countries have put a lot of their energy into attracting foreign investors. Unfortunately, the focus on new investment attraction sometimes comes at the expense of already-established foreign companies, many of which are neglected. This chapter has made the case for redressing this often damaging imbalance. This is particularly relevant today, as rising nationalism in many parts of the globe threatens to weaken global trade. Moreover, with the current global Covid-19 pandemic, many global value chains have been broken and new FDI has fallen sharply, and so post-investment policies should become much more of a priority. The framework presented in this and later chapters attempts to create an opportunity for IPAs to develop a robust post-investment strategy, an endeavour much needed in these times.

Notes

1 UNCTAD, 2007. *World Investment Report 2007* [online]. Available at: https://unctad.org/system/files/official-document/wir2007_en.pdf.

2 According to the OECD's Glossary of Statistical Terms, "a subsidiary is a company controlled by another company. Control occurs when the controlling company owns more than 50 per cent of the common shares. When the parent owns 100 per cent of the common shares, the subsidiary is said to be wholly owned. When the subsidiary operates in a different country, it is called a foreign subsidiary." However, foreign direct investment goes beyond the concept of a subsidiary and includes other types of ownership. The OECD definition of a foreign company is one where 10% or more of an entity is registered outside of the jurisdiction.

Defining a foreign-owned company to be one "where ownership ranges between 10% and 100% results in a broad range of foreign investors and hence of foreign investment." OECD, 2020. *Glossary of Statistical Terms* [online]. Available at: https://stats.oecd.org/glossary/.

3 UNCTAD, 2018. *World Investment Report* [online]. Available at: https://unctad.org/webflyer/world-investment-report-2018.

4 Ibid.

5 Stehrer, R. and Woerz, J. 2009. "Attract FDI! A universal golden rule? Empirical evidence for OECD and selected non-OECD countries". *European Journal of Development Research*, 21(1), pp. 95–111.

6 De Mello, L. 1999. "Foreign direct investment-led growth: evidence from time series and panel data". *Oxford Economic Papers*, 51(1), pp. 133–151.

7 Fu, X. and Gong, Y. 2009. "International and intranational technological spillovers and productivity growth in China". *Asian Economic Papers*, 8(2), pp. 1–23.

8 OECD, 2002. *Foreign Direct Investment for Development: Maximising Benefits, Minimising Costs* [online]. Available at: https://www.oecd.org/investment/investmentfordevelopment/foreigndirectinvestmentfordevelopmentmaximisingbenefitsminimisingcosts.htm.

9 WAIPA, 2020. *WAIPA Launches EIF Co-funded Project to Build Capacity on Investment Promotion in LDCs* [online]. Available at: https://waipa.org/announcements/waipa-launches-eif-co-funded-project-to-build-capacity-on-investment-promotion-in-ldcs/.

10 Crescenzi, R., Dyevre, A. and Neffke, F. 2020. *Innovation Catalysts: How Multinationals Reshape the Global Geography of Innovation*. London: LSE Research Online Documents on Economics 105684.

11 Crescenzi, R. and Ganau, R. 2020. *Inward FDI and Regional Performance in Europe after the Crisis*. London, UK: Institute of Global Affairs, London School of Economics and Political Science.

12 Jaax, A. 2016. *"Essays on Disparities in Innovative Performance and Economic Development in Emerging Countries: A Regional and Firm-level Investigation"*. London, UK, PhD thesis, The London School of Economics and Political Science (LSE).

13 Taken from a 2016 speech in Vienna by WAIPA, CEO Bostjan Skalar, UNIDO Vienna Investment Conference: Quality FDI, Growth and Development.

14 UNESCAP, 2017. *Handbook on Policies, Promotion and Facilitation of Foreign Direct Investment for Sustainable Development in Asia and the Pacific* [online]. Available at: https://www.unescap.org/resources/handbook-policies-promotion-and-facilitation-foreign-direct-investment-sustainable-0#.

15 UNCTAD, 2007. *Aftercare: A Core Function in Investment Promotion* [online]. Available at: https://unctad.org/system/files/official-document/iteipc20071_en.pdf.

16 Taken from a 2016 speech in Vienna by WAIPA, CEO Bostjan Skalar, UNIDO Vienna Investment Conference: Quality FDI, Growth and Development

17 OECD, 2018. *Mapping of Investment Promotion Agencies in OECD Countries* [online]. Available at: http://www.oecd.org/investment/Mapping-of-Investment-Promotion-Agencies-in-OECD-Countries.htm.

18 Ibid.

19 Ibid.

20 Sanchiz, A. and Omic, A. 2020. *State of Investment Promotion Agencies: Evidence from WAIPA-WBG's Joint Global Survey*. World Bank, Washington, DC. WAIPA (World Association of Investment Promotion Agencies), Geneva [online]. Available at: http://documents1.worldbank.org/curated/en/499971594008431029/pdf/State-of-Investment-Promotion-Agencies-Evidence-from-WAIPA-WBG-s-Joint-Global-Survey.pdf.

21 UNESCAP, 2017. *Handbook on Policies, Promotion and Facilitation of Foreign Direct Investment for Sustainable Development in Asia and the Pacific* [online]. Available at: https://www.unescap.org/resources/handbook-policies-promotion-and-facilitation-foreign-direct-investment-sustainable-0#.

22 Heilbron, A. and Aranda-Larrey, Y. 2020. *Strengthening Service Delivery of Investment Promotion Agencies: The Comprehensive Investor Services Framework. Finance, Competitiveness and Innovation in Focus*. World Bank, Washington, DC [online]. Available at: https://openknowledge.worldbank.org/handle/10986/33498.

23 Ibid.

24 UNCTAD, 2021. *Investment Trends Monitor*. New York & Geneva, Issue 38.

25 Sanchiz, A. and Omic, A. 2020. *State of Investment Promotion Agencies: Evidence from WAIPA-WBG's Joint Global Survey*. World Bank, Washington, DC. WAIPA (World Association of Investment Promotion Agencies), Geneva [online]. Available at: http://documents1.worldbank.org/curated/en/499971594008431029/pdf/State-of-Investment-Promotion-Agencies-Evidence-from-WAIPA-WBG-s-Joint-Global-Survey.pdf.

26 World Bank, 2020. *Global Investment Competitiveness Report 2019–2020: Rebuilding Investor Confidence in Times of Uncertainty* [online]. Available at: https://www.worldbank.org/en/topic/competitiveness/publication/global-investment-competitiveness-report-2019-2020.

27 International Finance Corporation (World Bank Group), 2016. *The Investment Climate* [online]. Available at: https://www.un.org/esa/ffd/wp-content/uploads/2016/01/The-Investment-Climate_IFC-World-Bank-Group_IATF-Issue-Brief.pdf.

28 Ibid.

29 Ibid.

30 Sanchiz, A. and Omic, A. 2020. *State of Investment Promotion Agencies: Evidence from WAIPA-WBG's Joint Global Survey*. World Bank, Washington, DC. WAIPA (World Association of Investment Promotion Agencies), Geneva [online]. Available at: http://documents1.worldbank.org/curated/en/499971594008431029/pdf/State-of-Investment-Promotion-Agencies-Evidence-from-WAIPA-WBG-s-Joint-Global-Survey.pdf.

31 Heilbron, A. and Aranda-Larrey, Y. 2020. *Strengthening Service Delivery of Investment Promotion Agencies: The Comprehensive Investor Services Framework. Finance, Competitiveness and Innovation in Focus*. World Bank, Washington, DC [online]. Available at: https://openknowledge.worldbank.org/handle/10986/33498.

32 Ibid.

33 Sanchiz, A. and Omic, A. 2020. *State of Investment Promotion Agencies: Evidence from WAIPA-WBG's Joint Global Survey*. World Bank, Washington, DC. WAIPA (World Association of Investment Promotion Agencies), Geneva [online]. Available at: http://documents1.worldbank.org/curated/en/499971594008431029/pdf/State-of-Investment-Promotion-Agencies-Evidence-from-WAIPA-WBG-s-Joint-Global-Survey.pdf.

34 Wells, L.T. and Wint, A.G. 2000. *Marketing a Country: Promotion as a Tool for Attracting Foreign Investment*. Revised edn. Washington, DC: World Bank Publications.

2
UNDERSTANDING AFTERCARE

Chapter highlights

- There are different definitions of Aftercare currently in use worldwide, this chapter offers a definition the authors believe should be used by the FDI industry.
- Effective Aftercare brings many benefits to a host economy and seeks to build a long-term relationship with the foreign investor to maximise the benefit FDI brings to the host economy.
- Post-investment has 4 distinctive target groups that need to be considered: the foreign investor, the board, the FDI support Ecosystem and the constituency. Understanding their different needs is key to designing effective post-investment services.
- The main objectives of Aftercare are to help foreign investors grow, to champion local opportunities, and to further develop the host economy.
- There is a business case, an economic development case and good governance arguments in favour of embracing Aftercare.

DOI: 10.4324/9781003174950-4

2.1 What is Aftercare

The word Aftercare is too small; it does not reflect the function.
(Practitioner – national IPA)

The previous chapter introduced the concept of post-investment, defining it as the value to a host economy that comes from the interaction of the four post-investment pillars: Aftercare, Place, Ecosystem and Policy Advocacy. This chapter explores Aftercare.

In 2007 UNCTAD defined Aftercare as the "range of activities from post-establishment facilitation services through to development support to retain investment, encourage follow-on investment and achieve greater local economic impact."[1] It also noted that Aftercare "means many different things to IPAs,"[2] a perception that was confirmed during the research for this book. Not only are there many different terms in use for Aftercare, but there are also many different interpretations of what these words (and by extension Aftercare services) mean. Hence the first step is to discuss the terminology and the definitions in more detail.

Aftercare is the most common term used to refer to client-facing services for investors. Interestingly, the word is used to convey different meanings.

The first meaning, commonly used in academic circles, by consultants and international organisations, centres on a specific part of the portfolio of investor-facing, post-investment services that focuses on helping investors to grow locally. For example, at UNESCAP's 2017 "Investment Facilitation through the investment cycle. Promotion and Facilitation of Foreign Direct Investment for Sustainable Development" workshop, they used the term Aftercare to describe a "re-active management of existing investors,"[3] in contrast to the term "Investor Development," which they used to "relate to pro-actively helping existing companies to grow."[4]

The second use of Aftercare is as an umbrella term that covers all investor-facing post-investment services. In other words, Aftercare is to long-term investment what facilitation is to new investment. The term is used as a synonym for Investor Services. This use is common amongst IPAs that have an Aftercare unit or Aftercare team that supports investors, irrespective of the type of support the investors need.

The third use of Aftercare is to describe the sum of Investor Services plus the local collaboration needed to generate value to match investor's needs. This use is common amongst IPAs that have a one-stop-shop, have wider mandates (and support, for example, national companies or entrepreneurs) and those in the private sector, who conceive Aftercare as a type of ongoing customer services.

Figure 2.1 presents how these different Aftercare terms relate to each other. It includes a fourth use of the term, which is explained later in the chapter.

In addition to the different uses of the term, there are different words used. For example, the term *post-investment services* is used as an umbrella term, and sometimes as a synonym, and is the meaning given by practitioners. Other terms used include *retention*, to convey specialised services to manage the risk of losing jobs, *expansion*, to describe services dedicated to identifying further projects at the parent company, and more generic words such as *business growth*, *investor care*, *investor development*, *business support services*, *reinvestment services*, *investor services* and *customer care*. Meanwhile in the USA, they use the term Business Retention and Expansion (BRE). Others favour the term "Investor Relations" on the basis that FDI is no different from capital investment, and that IPAs owe their stakeholders regular reporting in the same way that companies report back to their shareholders. And there are also a few professionals who deliver Aftercare services without giving them a specific name, as they consider them to be part of facilitation.

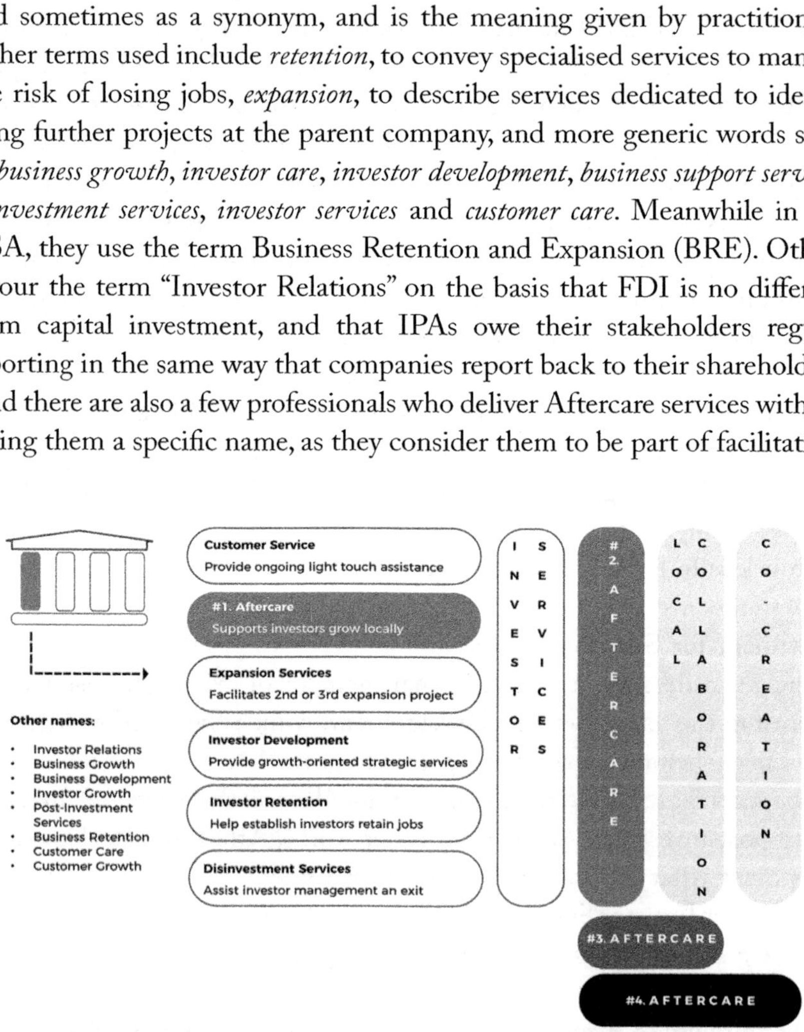

Figure 2.1 Most common use of the word Aftercare. © *Investment Aftercare Explained: A Guide for FDI Practitioners and Policymakers on How to Grow and Retain Investors.*

In the lead author's experience, the lack of agreement on terminology and the polyvalency of the terms, i.e. that the word has various definitions simultaneously, may help explain, at least in part, why supporting investors is a space that is so poorly understood. But what if there is a logic to the inconsistency? Careful consideration of the different uses of the term Aftercare, the lack of use of it, input from consultancy projects and interviews with practitioners and policy makes, have provided insight into what actually are different stages of the function, as can be seen in Figure 2.2 below.

The first stage is one where practitioners and policy makers new to post-investment will most likely read academic papers, receive support from international organisations and are likely to use the first definition, i.e. supporting investors to grow locally. This will usually correspond with small, client-friendly units that have a reactive approach to enquiries from investors.

The second stage demands that the host economy acquires more experience of supporting investors and develops local capacity and capability. The use of the term Aftercare evolves to describe a portfolio of Investor Services that covers the whole lifecycle of the investors. At this stage IPAs are likely to have dedicated Aftercare teams.

The third stage requires that the function secures a strong local Aftercare infrastructure to orchestrate services that support investors, which are

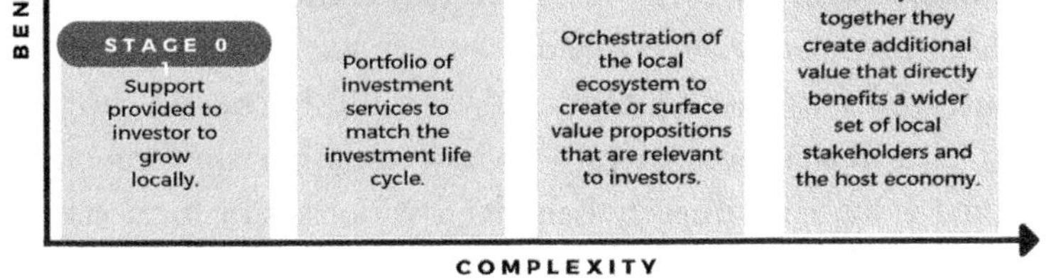

Figure 2.2 Four stages in Aftercare maturity. © *Investment Aftercare Explained: A Guide for FDI Practitioners and Policymakers on How to Grow and Retain Investors.*

provided throughout the whole local FDI Ecosystem. The term Aftercare starts merging into post-investment, conveying the notion of an umbrella concept that combines the front and back-office efforts needed to deliver those services. IPAs might have inter-organisation project teams dedicated to serve the function.

The fourth stage applies to very few IPAs. At this stage, the word Aftercare features less often as the function is usually referred to as long-term FDI, sustainable FDI, FDI as a tool for economic development or maximising the presence of foreign investors in the host economy. By this point, looking after investors becomes a synonym to post-investment that is intrinsically linked to Policy Advocacy, Place and Ecosystem, and it incorporates the symbiotic relationship between a host location and an international investor, where together they co-create additional value that directly benefits a wider set of local stakeholders.

When Aftercare reaches this fourth stage, it levers foreign investors to strengthen a host economy's attractiveness, increasing competitiveness, productivity and connectedness. This is the fourth use of the term Aftercare showed in Figure 2.1.

To summarise, Aftercare, as defined in this book, has 4 understandings of the term (see Figure 2.1), has 4 maturity stages (see Figure 2.2) and all these components shape an Aftercare definition as can be seen in Figure 2.3.

In summary, Aftercare:

- Refers to client-facing post-investment support to help foreign investors grow;
- It describes a portfolio of Investor Services that matches every stage of the FDI life cycle, both growth and contraction;
- It concerns the collaboration with local stakeholders and the capacity to orchestrate the local Ecosystem to create or surface value propositions that are relevant to investors (i.e. the back office required to deliver Investor Services); and
- It incorporates the symbiotic relationship between a host location and an international investor, where together they co-create additional value that directly benefits a wider set of local stakeholders and that shapes the host economy.

In simple terms, Aftercare is a growth mindset.

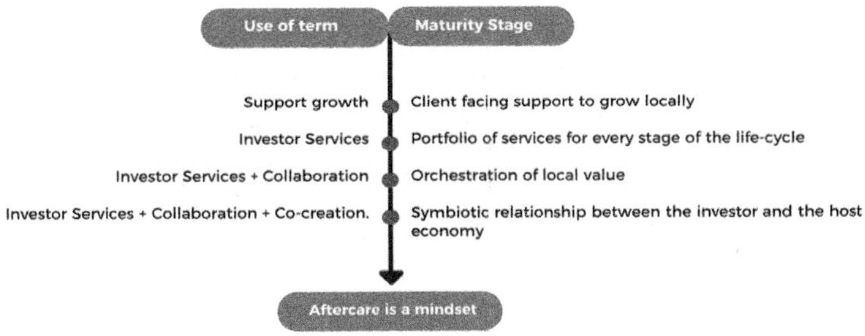

Figure 2.3 Aftercare is a mindset. © *Investment Aftercare Explained: A Guide for FDI Practitioners and Policymakers on How to Grow and Retain Investors.*

2.2 The benefits of Aftercare

Some locations aftercare, some after-think and some do not care.[5]

In a 2018 study performed by the Inter-American Development Bank, Aftercare services were found to be one of the 12 most effective activities for attracting and retaining FDI.[6] A further study by the World Bank, which reviewed around 30,000 high-value-added FDI projects, showed that post-investment assistance, including information provided by IPAs, greatly influenced decisions made by foreign companies to continue to re-invest in a host country's economy.[7] In addition, in a survey of executives responsible for selecting investment locations, 83% stated that they normally consult directly with IPAs throughout their investment decision process, and "consider the provided Aftercare services to be important in their consideration."[8] For these reasons, Loewendahl concludes that "to maximise the long-term benefits from inward FDI, Aftercare activity should form a major component of investment promotion activities."[9] So, while it is important to attract investments, it is arguably even more important to retain this investment once it has landed in the country.

When Aftercare is effectively implemented, there is a direct positive impact on the local foreign company and, more importantly, there are positive externalities for the local and national economy of the host country. The research and interviews conducted for this book identified three primary benefits of Aftercare: growth of foreign investors, an increase in local opportunities and the further development of the host economy. It is strongly influenced by the study by Dr Ana Arias, "The importance of aftercare in attracting foreign direct investment. The case of the Caribbean region."[10]

The first benefit of Aftercare is that it helps foreign investors' investments grow. As previously mentioned, these post-investor services help deliver the investor's project, manage expectations, embed the investor in the local Ecosystem and remove barriers to growth. The objective for the IPA being that these gains for the foreign investor will encourage and support further reinvestment.

The second main benefit of increasing local opportunities includes the immediate impact for the local economy created by supporting foreign investors. By helping foreign companies better integrate into the local economy, Aftercare helps facilitate the transfer of knowledge and skills to the local population. This includes, for example, upskilling the labour force who may then move on to other companies and take that knowledge with them, or by introducing sophisticated supply chain standards that local suppliers upgrade to and by doing so become more competitive.

The further development of the host economy comes about as a result of the interaction of the foreign investor with the Ecosystem and with its value chain, which has a multiplying effect beyond the initial value of the FDI. In essence, Aftercare becomes an economic development tool as it increases the level of connectedness between local and national stakeholders.

Figure 2.4 illustrates how Aftercare positively impacts the economy. The initial beneficiary of Aftercare is the foreign company, these benefits then ripple through the local Ecosystem and then on into the local economy. These benefits are all considered before any reinvestment activity by the foreign investor. Over the last 20 years, several international organisations have sought to estimate the levels of reinvestment:

- UNCTAD's 2007 paper estimated that reinvestment linked to the existing investment base can peak at up to 70% in developed countries, albeit it is significantly lower in developing economies.[11]
- The World Association of Investment Promotion Agencies (WAIPA) 2006 survey, which mainly covered developing economies, found that on average 32% of inward FDI came from reinvestment. The survey concluded that "it is possible that developing countries are not yet using this opportunity to the same extent as developed countries."[12]

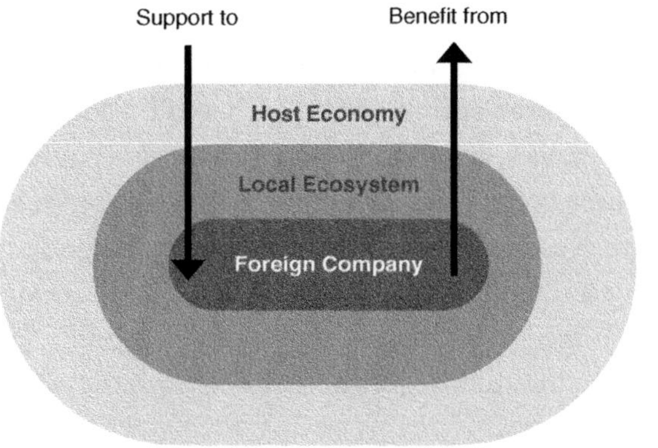

Figure 2.4 Sphere of influence of Aftercare. © *Investment Aftercare Explained: A Guide for FDI Practitioners and Policymakers on How to Grow and Retain Investors.*

- The World Bank's Multilateral Investment Guarantee Agency (MIGA) reported back in 2003 that "expansion investment to account for 42% of total global FDI."[13]
- The UNCTAD 2017 World Investment Report stated that for LAC (Latin America and Caribbean Countries), Russia and Kazakhstan, 30%, 47% and 55% respectively of their 2016 FDI inflows are from reinvested earnings in foreign affiliates.[14]
- The World Bank's Global Investment Competitiveness Report 2017/18 indicates that 30% of FDI inflows every year are reinvestment from investors already in the country.[15]

The OECD FDI figures in the April 2018[16] report calculated that reinvestment of earnings represented 60% of total OECD area outflows, compared to 46% in 2016, 38% in 2015 and 66% in 2014. Earnings reinvested by US parents in their foreign affiliates abroad increased by 15% in 2017, reaching their highest level since 2005 (at US$345 billion). They accounted for 54% of the total earnings reinvested by OECD area parents in their foreign affiliates. Reinvestment of earnings by parent companies in Japan, Canada, the United Kingdom and Germany accounted for an additional 20% of the total. In other countries, parent companies in Belgium, France, Ireland and Sweden reinvested more than US$10 billion of earnings in their foreign affiliates. Private sector consultancies have also studied initial investment and reinvestment levels by foreign companies in host countries. FDI

Markets 2017 FDI Reinvestment Ranking analysed data for initial investment and re-investment by foreign companies from 2006 to 2016. They found that the top three sectors expanding and co-locating globally were software and IT services, automotive components and industrial machinery and tools. The three companies making the largest overseas investments in the ranking were Nestlé, Toyota and Volkswagen. Regionally, China, India and the US gained the largest number of new jobs from expansion and co-location, while Singapore, London (UK) and Bangalore (India) were the three cities that secured the largest number of expansion projects.[17]

2.3 Who are the target groups for Aftercare?

Aftercare is by nature a facilitator function and, in particular, is intersectional, interdisciplinary and brings together public and private efforts. The primary beneficiary of its efforts is, of course, the foreign investor. Nevertheless, IPAs also need to take account of the views of, and impact on, other stakeholders such as the boards of directors or decision-makers who are ultimately responsible for an IPA (this can include both funders and influencers), the local community and other stakeholders who live and work in a location. In this section, we explore the different groups Aftercare professionals need to consider, and explain why an IPA should consider the impact of its actions on them.

In the interviews for this book, it became evident that use of the term *client* to refer to these different groups could be confusing, as different IPAs use the word "clients" differently (this is discussed in more depth in Chapter 9, The How of Investor Services). The word "stakeholder" did not meet the requirements either, as some IPAs associate the word to community engagement. In the absence of a better word, the authors use the term "target group" to refer to groups that have a stake in the success of the IPA, and to whom the IPA holds some level of responsibility.

Investor as an target group: a foreign company with a local expansion project is the primary focus and beneficiary of an Aftercare team's activities. Investors are looking for a business-friendly environment in which to operate. When an IPA supports an investor's investment journey, the unspoken agreement is that investor support services are provided in exchange for an investor's continued commitment to a location, including creating new jobs and paying taxes locally.

Board as a target group: ultimately IPAs serve their boards, which can have representatives from any or all of the public sector, business, academia and the local community. These different stakeholders may have (very) different views on what constitutes success, and hence are likely to define return on investment in different ways, thereby placing different demands on an IPA. Or as a publicly-funded IPA that asked not to be named put it, "Aftercare is the area of FDI where supporting the government's political agenda comes at the forefront. The Aftercare programmes become (one of the) vehicles through which government delivers better jobs, more sustainability and more opportunities for their voters."

For example, a public funder of Aftercare services is normally looking for economic growth in the form of jobs created, taxes paid and/or other local benefits, such as new roads or schools. On the back of this economic growth, they typically seek to generate political capital in the form of positive media coverage, support for their political agenda and ultimately votes. In addition, they are seeking input from the private sector on how to make their location even more business friendly, and for support to further internationalise their location. International funders are typically looking for a broadly-based economic uplift in the location they are supporting, with performance indicators aligned to global initiatives such as the UN Social Development Goals (SDGs).

Private funders of Aftercare services, unsurprisingly, want to generate business for themselves and their members. For example, a law firm might fund a local IPA to gain preferential access to potential investors who could become future clients, while a chamber of commerce might want to gain increased exposure to investors, seeking to recruit them as members or to gain access to government bodies for their members.

Academic institutions are more likely to be interested in the ideas, principles and policies that underpin Aftercare. Other stakeholders, such as think tanks and brand agencies, might seek to improve their profile and reputation both in the local Ecosystem and also internationally.

Irrespective of the composition of the board of the IPA, the IPA's executive team must understand the board's vision and how it defines success. Without the board's support, it is unlikely that the IPA can successfully deliver its Aftercare mandate.

Investment Support Ecosystem as a target group. IPAs do not deliver Aftercare services alone – they rely on the support of many partners and collaborators both in the public and private sphere. These include commercial partners with whom they deliver services, such as accountancy firms that can advise investors on tax issues, academic institutions regarding the sourcing of talent, bilateral chambers of commerce that support companies linked to a particular country of origin, or local supply chains with the potential to collaborate with a foreign multinational. While the investment support Ecosystem rarely has a position on, or interacts with, the board of an IPA, they are still a group to consider when it comes to target groups to serve, particularly as they can add significant value to foreign investors and can amplify the work of an IPA. The investment support Ecosystem brings expertise, networks and resources that complement the value offer of an IPA. In return, they want to be part of the FDI support Ecosystem and have exposure to its players.

Constituency as a target group: publicly-funded IPAs are ultimately responsible to the local (taxpaying) population who live, work and play locally, and therefore have a vested interest in the future of their location. Taxes paid by a foreign company are often a key asset as they provide a boost to the local economy, while reinvestment brings new jobs (which in turn generates more tax receipts), more business for the local supply base, more linkages to global supply chains and often a shift towards higher value activities through technology transfer and research and development investment. However, investment projects that adversely affect these interests may lead to taxpayers expressing their dissatisfaction when voting in local elections or for public officials, by demonstrating or via social media.

It is also important to remember that IPAs may not be the only entity supporting foreign investors. As a 2004 survey undertaken by the World Bank noted, "52 percent of IPAs indicate the existence of other entities charged with the promotion of FDI in their country. A variety of both private (such as chambers of commerce) and public sector entities typically share the common objective."[18] Consequently, IPAs should make themselves aware of any organisations that support foreign investors and ensure that, as far as possible, all efforts are co-ordinated to ensure that investors receive a seamless service, there is clarity about who is doing what, there is no duplication of effort and there is minimal friction between delivery organisations.

Figure 2.5 summarises the four different constituencies of post-investment, what they are looking to achieve through engaging in

Figure 2.5 The different target groups of post-investment. © *Investment Aftercare Explained: A Guide for FDI Practitioners and Policymakers on How to Grow and Retain Investors.*

post-investment activity and what they can offer a location. Understanding each of these target groups, their different needs, agendas and priorities, is increasingly important for any IPA looking to satisfy its stakeholders.

A word about language. These different target groups might also use different words in their interaction with FDI. As can be seen in Figure 2.6, government will speak about jobs, capital investment, investment stock and, in general, about the contribution of investors to economic development. In parallel, there are at least two additional terminologies to keep in mind. IPAs speak about promotion and attraction, provide facilitation and landing services, and may or may not, as discussed before, use the word Aftercare. At the same time, investors use a complete different set of terms. For them, it is about being aware of market opportunities in another country and starting to trade, whether by importing, exporting or visiting the country. If conditions are right and expectations of growth and return on investment

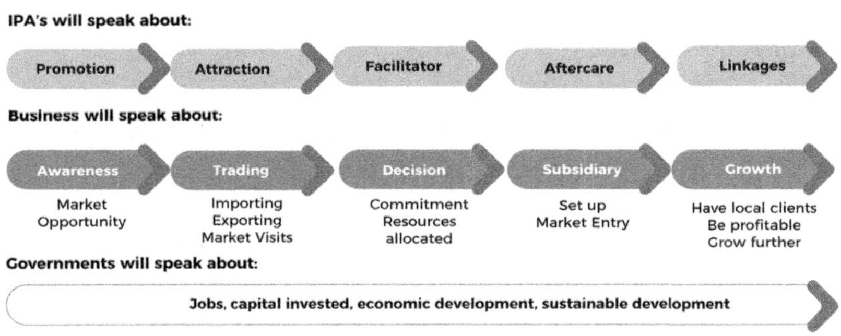

Figure 2.6 Differences in use of language. © *Investment Aftercare Explained: A Guide for FDI Practitioners and Policymakers on How to Grow and Retain Investors.*

exceed the cost in time and resources to serve that market, companies will make the decision and commit to a location with formal resources to open a subsidiary. This marks the start of their presence in the local market, which is followed by a pursuit of growth, where they have local clients, are profitable and find further opportunities to expand their businesses. During this process, they will engage with a number of other stakeholders in the local FDI Ecosystem, who might each have their own terminology.

2.4 FDI and post-investment behaviour

Most vendors want their customers to be happy with their purchase, ideally to such an extent that in the future they will purchase from them again and, ultimately, that they become advocates of the vendor. Of course, there are occasions when customers are dissatisfied with the product or service they receive – how the vendor responds to any dissatisfied customers can have a major impact on the future of the business.

This is no different for FDI, as it bears many similarities to making a purchase, as the investor "buys into" a location.

2.4.1 Post-investment satisfaction

Unsurprisingly, positive post-investment behaviour is closely linked with satisfaction, namely how closely the investor's expectations of the products and services it received compare with the *perceived* performance of the location.[19] When an investor has a positive view of an investment decision, and by extension of the host economy, they are more likely to display behaviour that benefits the location, a key objective of Aftercare.

There are five common positive post-investment behaviours, as shown in Figure 2.7.

A happy investor will:

1. **Invest again**: a happy investor is more likely to further invest in a location, thereby creating more jobs and giving another boost to the local economy.
2. **Engage more with the local economy**: a satisfied investor is likely to engage more with the local economy by, for example, collaborating with local colleges to hire their graduates, or by sourcing more products from local suppliers, thereby further increasing the economic benefit to the local economy.

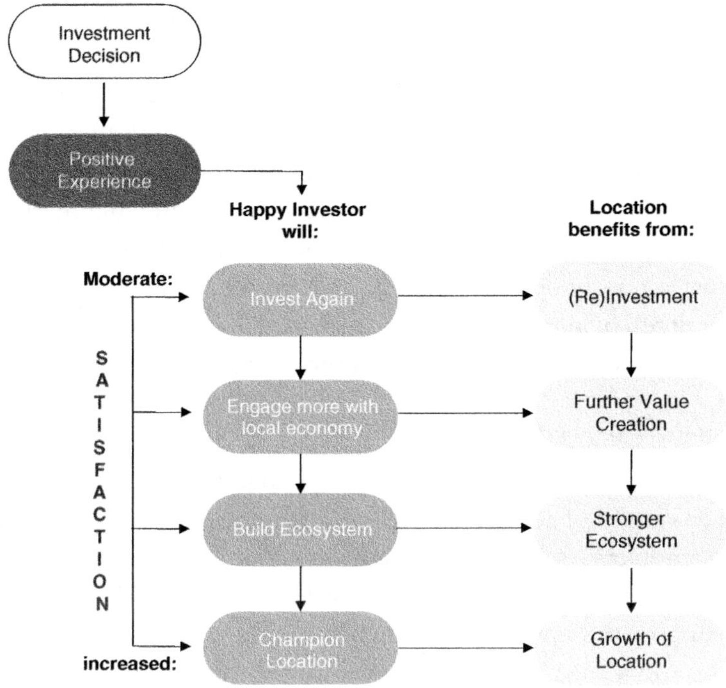

Figure 2.7 FDI and positive post-investment behaviour. © *Investment Aftercare Explained: A Guide for FDI Practitioners and Policymakers on How to Grow and Retain Investors.*

3. **Commit to the location**: satisfied investors will commit to the location and embed themselves further in the host economy, therefore making disinvestment less likely.
4. **Help build the Ecosystem**: satisfied consumers often (proudly) display their purchase and may also participate in a community of fellow buyers. For FDI, this means the IPA gaining "a friend." Satisfied investors are therefore more likely to recommend potential new investors open operations locally, link with local companies and participate in activities organised by the IPA.
5. **Champion the location**: the holy grail of Aftercare, where foreign investors are not only loyal to the location, but also take an active role in further developing the location. Whether it be helping to strengthen the local Ecosystem, persuading other investors to come to the location or leading an Ecosystem activity that increases local connectedness.

James L. Heskett, Professor Emeritus of the Harvard Business School, observes that "loyalty is a direct result of customer satisfaction. Customer satisfaction is largely influenced by the value of service provided to customers."[20] Clients that are loyal and satisfied become apostles, "customers so satisfied that they convert the uninitiated to a product or service."[21] Dissatisfied customers, by contrast, won't be loyal and might turn into terrorists, a term used to describe "customers so unhappy that they speak out against a poorly delivered service at every opportunity. Terrorists can reach hundreds of potential customers. In some instances, they can even discourage acquaintances from trying a service or product."[22]

2.4.2 Post-investment dissonance

Sometimes an investor has a bad post-investment experience. This can be for a wide variety of reasons including difficulty in finding suitable local suppliers, problems sourcing appropriate talent or simply a mistrust in the local investment climate. In some of these situations the IPA will be able to support the investor, in others it won't – indeed the IPA may not even be aware of the challenges the investor was facing. The result is post-investment dissonance, defined as when an investor is unsatisfied or unsure of their investment decision, usually due to a discrepancy between their expectations of the location they invested in and their post-investment experience.

There are five main actions a dissatisfied investor may take in post-investment, as shown in Figure 2.8. These are:

- **Early exit post-entry**: an investor may reconsider and decide to abandon their initial investment project shortly after landing in the new host location. They may simply have changed their view of a location once their feet were on the ground, reassessed and chosen to invest in a different location, or not to invest at all.
- **Quiet exit**: regardless of how long ago an investment decision was made, astute investors are always monitoring the local business environment for changes that may affect their investment. Where any changes put their existing investment at risk, the investor may quietly exit the project without contacting the local IPA. Common examples include an election that leads to a change in the

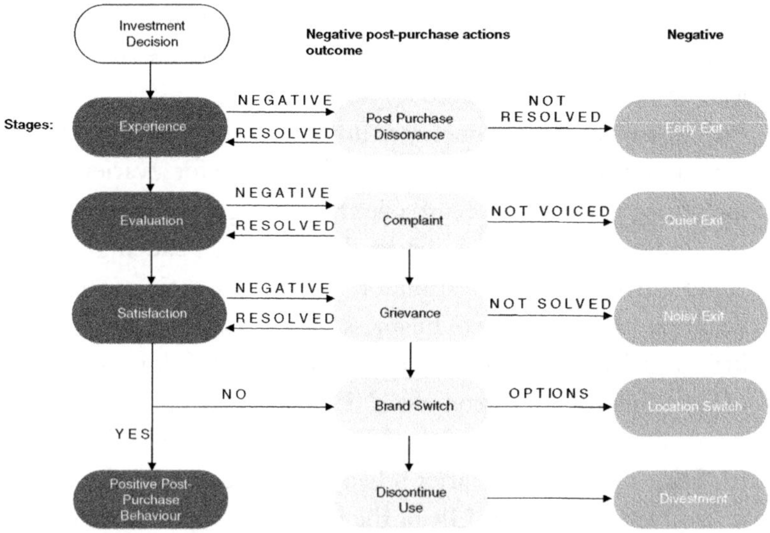

Figure 2.8 FDI and negative post-purchase behaviour. © *Investment Aftercare Explained: A Guide for FDI Practitioners and Policymakers on How to Grow and Retain Investors.*

host-economy's political climate, or operational challenges at the parent company.

- **Noisy exit**: where an investor does not believe it has received the support it was promised, they usually raise their concerns with the local IPA. However, where any issues are not resolved to their satisfaction, and while some investors may choose to remain silent, other investors will choose to make their disappointment public. A disappointed investor may give a negative review of the location to potential future investors, speak adversely about the IPA to the local authority, discuss their grievances in the media or, in the worst-case scenario, go to court. And significant disputes do happen – around 70 FDI related cases are filed each year at the International Centre for Settlement of Investment Disputes (ICSID), which is run by the World Bank. (See Chapter 5, Investor Aid and Grievances).
- **Location switch**: there are occasions where an investor is not considering exiting a location, it's just that they are not convinced that their current location can help them grow (even) further, and hence they choose to locate a new project elsewhere, or that another location made them an offer they could not refuse. This is potentially

a lost opportunity for a location or an IPA, particularly if they were unaware of the investor's thinking or the existence of the new project, and hence were unable to pitch for it.

- **Full disinvestment**: sometimes investors simply become dissatisfied with a location and choose to exit. This can be for a variety of reasons including a failure to secure clients in a highly competitive market, the ending of incentives or tax-breaks thus reducing the relative competitiveness of a location, or simply that their parent company decides to exit that line of business. At such a late stage there is often little an IPA can do to change the investor's decision. As an example of post-investment dissonance, Nissan announced in early 2019 that it was abandoning plans to build its X-Trail model in Sunderland (in the UK) only two years after it had publicly committed to expanding its Sunderland facility. Given the uncertainty surrounding Brexit at the time, Nissan chose to keep production of the X-Trail in Japan because "keeping production there would reduce upfront investment costs."[23] Another example is the retail chain Carrefour leaving India "after the government failed to convince states to open up the multi-brand segment to overseas players."[24]

IPAs have an important role to play regarding positively influencing an investor's post-investment behaviour. While adverse actions from foreign investors are always a risk, and are part of any investment cycle, a well-managed Aftercare program can minimise these risks and mitigate its effects. Chapter 6, Disinvestment, discusses the details of corporate exits and how to manage disinvestment.

2.5 The objectives of Aftercare

In the experience of the authors, a common request in Aftercare consultancy projects relates to the objectives of Aftercare. As discussed earlier, Aftercare should be considered in the specific context in which an IPA operates. The following pages present guidance for the three main objectives:

- To help foreign investors grow;
- To champion local opportunities; and
- To further develop the host economy.

Each of these objectives has different components that oftentimes relate to each other. These objectives are arranged in this form to make it more understandable to the reader.

2.5.1 Objective one: help foreign investors grow

The first objective of Aftercare is the growth of foreign investors. The responsibility for this usually rests with the IPA, but it will most likely involve many external collaborations. There are seven key components:[25]

1. **Help deliver an investment project**: IPAs sell their locations by emphasising their commitment to support investors throughout their investment journeys. This reassurance "can be a critical factor in winning an investment, especially for areas with weaknesses in their 'offer'." Investors buy in to that promise, and therefore, once an investor has made a commitment to a location, it is the IPA's responsibility to deliver on that promise. When working with (relatively recently established) investors, the point where investment facilitation ends and Aftercare begins is often unclear; nevertheless, the objective is to provide a delivery platform that meets that promise. However, a surprisingly high number of established investors do not have contact with the local IPA, as was unveiled by the study "The importance [of] Aftercare in attracting foreign direct investment. The case of the Caribbean region," where Dr Ana Arias studied 16 countries and established that 44% of existing investors had not heard of the host country IPA, and that there "appears to be a mismatch between the FDI opportunities and the services that the IPAs provide to convert these ones into tangible projects."[26]
2. **Minimise over-optimism**: investors are often over-optimistic when it comes to estimating the number of new jobs they think they are going to create. Where a proportion of planned jobs do not materialise, this is commonly referred to as "projects with a low implementation rate." Aftercare can reduce the level of over-optimism by working with foreign investors to implement job creation plans (for more details see Chapter 9, The How of Investor Services). It can also "create greater 'embeddedness' of the foreign

investor into the country making them less likely to relocate or downsize."[27]

3. **Help to embed a company in the local Ecosystem**: terminology has changed since 2001 when Henry Loewendahl back then at UNCTAD, talked about "helping to 'embed' TNCs," but the sentiment remains the same. Companies, both local and foreign, perform better when they are well connected to their customers, suppliers, competitors, centres of excellence, innovation centres, start-ups, etc. These connections are sometimes referred to as "linkages."
4. **Remove blockages to growth**: growing a company in a foreign country is rarely straightforward. Foreign investors are likely to face challenges along their growth journey, such as problems obtaining permits, a lack of bandwidth to address a particular question, a disconnect with the public sector regarding the compliance requirements to meet local legislation, a lack of understanding of how the local economy works or operational bottlenecks that require attention. IPAs should play an important role in helping the investor overcome these blockages to growth.
5. **Support re-investment and expansions:** IPAs aim to encourage further re-investment in the form of expansions, new divisions, opening a second office, increased production capacity, etc. The reassurance that the IPA will provide effective support in resolving any problems or challenges the investor faces as and when they arrive is key to helping secure these additional projects.
6. **Reduce risk of disinvestment and closure**: international companies close or relocate businesses for a variety of reasons, including relative labour costs, automation or changes in local macroeconomic conditions. Whilst some of these factors are beyond the control of an IPA, there are others, such as local talent and real estate acquisition, that an IPA can influence in order to minimise the risk of a company downsizing or closing its operations. The focus here should be on risk management to safeguard existing local jobs.
7. **Identify needs for new IPA services**: while IPAs work with investors in supporting them with all the previously mentioned objectives, they also learn first-hand what investors need and can

turn this insight into new value propositions. The focus here is to keep the IPAs services aligned with the evolving needs of foreign investors.

2.5.2 Objective two: champion local opportunities

Aftercare's second objective focuses on strengthening and encouraging linkages between the local players and the Ecosystem. In such a capacity, Aftercare becomes a driver for collaboration and value co-creation. There are five different ways championing local opportunities can be achieved.

1. **Identify local initiatives that add value to established foreign companies**: here IPAs play at least three roles: they scan the Ecosystem to identify value-adding initiatives and organisations; they work with local organisations to articulate their offer in a way that is relevant to foreign investors; and they equip these organisations with the tools and methodologies they need to engage with foreign investors.
2. **Identify foreign investor's initiatives that add value to the location**: foreign investors bring capabilities, processes and resources with them. In many cases, they keep them for themselves, not because they are not interested in sharing them, but because their primary focus when landing in a new country is to "find their feet." However, this changes with time, and once the company is well-established, long-term investors tend to open-up to the local community, with some of them making significant efforts to establish themselves as collaborative, sustainable and responsible investors. Examples include transferring new skills and bringing global, corporate and social initiatives to the local economy. IPAs play a key role in identifying these opportunities and channelling them appropriately.
3. **Generate new leads for IPA**: as UNIDO noted in its 2011 Africa Report, "most foreign investors – between 60 and 70% – state that their decisions for investment in a particular location are primarily based on information obtained from existing investors in those locations."[28] This is a key part of a potential investor's due diligence, and hence existing investors will often be aware of potential new

projects at an early stage in their development. Therefore, by staying close to existing investors, an IPA can identify new leads.
In addition, Aftercare can raise awareness about additional services established investors routinely are eligible for, and thereby generate another "sale" of the IPA's services.

4. **Identify new opportunities for partners**: of particular relevance to locations that have a strong collaboration culture, or that have policies in place that favour collaboration between different organisations, is the ability to identify new opportunities for the IPA's partners. In the public sector, for example, IPAs can help other public offices to identify candidates for newly launched support programmes (for example a women-in-business programme launched by the Ministry of Social Development in Chile welcomes working with a foreign IT company that already has a women-in-engineering programme in place). As for private IPAs that are funded by membership fees, they need to find opportunities for their members to justify membership charges. An example of this is introducing a foreign investor to a consultant, who is a member of the IPA, who values early exposure to potential future clients.
5. **Join forces with local initiatives that promote the location**: articulating the local story is a role that many different organisations perform in any given location. From tourism boards to start-up hubs, sector associations, place marketers, property developers and universities, Aftercare provides an excellent platform for collaboration for and with "storytellers" to amplify initiatives that help create a sense of vibrancy in the local community. For more details see Chapter 7, Place and Ecosystem.

2.5.3 Objective three: further develop the host economy

The last group of Aftercare objectives is focused on maximising value creation in the host economy. It goes beyond the investor-centric objective of supporting reinvestment and expansion, and the partner-centric objective of championing local opportunities to consider the host economy as a whole. It includes:

1. **Increasing the value of an investment to the host economy**: here IPAs work with investors to maximise spillovers, for example

helping to up-skill the local workforce with nation-wide skills development programmes, working with local suppliers, introducing new production practices and working with or donating to local charities and voluntary organisations.

2. **Strengthening the local Ecosystem**: foreign investors can create location-centric societal value when they champion collaboration, introduce new ways of bringing a community together or create online and offline platforms that unleash growth. They essentially help amalgamate foreign and local knowledge, skills and resources. For example, Google, with its many Google Campuses[29] throughout the world, and Alibaba, through the role it plays in South East Asia creating international marketing reach for small local firms,[30] provide insightful case studies as to how a foreign investor can play a crucial role in injecting dynamism into a region or a cluster, thereby making it more competitive.
3. **Increasing connectedness**: global and local connectedness is often a differentiator when it comes to economic growth, a topic that will be discussed in more depth in Chapter 7, Place and Ecosystem. In brief, the links between a local economy and cross-border markets, networks, capital and talent are assets locations can foster. IPAs and foreign investors both have a role to play in developing these connections. For example, Bosch, a German company that has expanded into India, provides support to the Indian government's accelerator programme in Delhi by providing Indian start-ups with access to Bosch's global knowhow, engineers and labs.[31]
4. **Improving the investment climate**: usually linked to Policy Advocacy and the work to revise regulations and practices that are not conducive to business, improving the investment climate can be a key outcome of Aftercare. The investment climate is also linked to location competitiveness and is an area both governments and international donors monitor closely. Client-facing activities essential to Aftercare enable the capturing of insight that is critical to improving the work of policy advocates to better the investment climate. For example, the collation of feedback from foreign investors by the Polish IPA led to a number of changes to the labour laws, thereby making Poland a more attractive destination for foreign investment.[32]

5. **Maximising stakeholder value**: from a stakeholder value perspective, Aftercare has a role to play when it comes to building sustainable and inclusive societies. The objective here is for both a foreign investor and its host economy to address growth from a holistic standpoint, moving away from a company-centric shareholder view and towards a society-centric stakeholder view. The focus is on co-creation, where every party contributes their skills and assets to help create the best conditions for mutual and long-term societal benefit. Stakeholders include not only investors, government and those who benefit from the newly generated jobs, but all other societal parties such as local communities, the organisations tasked with taking care of the environment and thinktanks who shed light on how to shape the future of a location and what type of opportunities it is seeking to create. In summary, maximising stakeholder value is about tapping into the power of long-term foreign investment to create inclusive societies that leave no one behind.

Figure 2.9 provides an overview of the three principal objectives of Aftercare featuring: (1) removing institutional obstacles to help foreign investors grow; (2) championing business opportunities in the local economy; and (3) strengthening the local Ecosystem to improve the investment climate and further develop host economy.

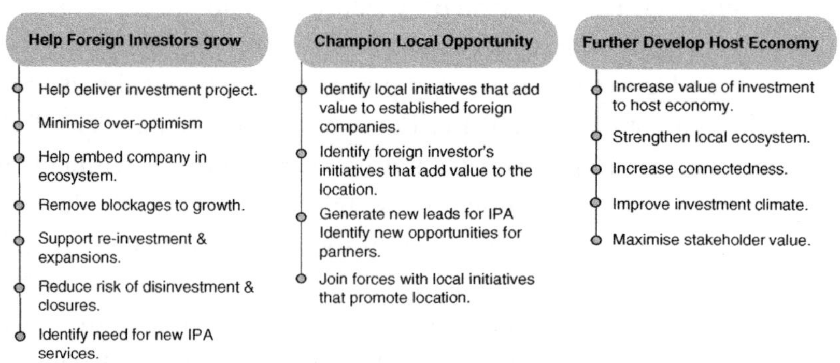

Figure 2.9 Objectives of Aftercare. © *Investment Aftercare Explained: A Guide for FDI Practitioners and Policymakers on How to Grow and Retain Investors.*

Box 2.1 Presents an extract from a speech from WAIPA that illustrates the wide range of positive outcomes of effective Aftercare.

Box 2.1 The importance of Aftercare to South Korea's economy

"When we speak of FDI around the world, the importance of Korea for promoting Global FDI cannot be missed. Given the changes brought forth by the globalizing world economy, the Korean government has recently pursued an FDI policy regime very different from that of the previous 'compressed industrialization' era. As a result, Foreign Direct Investment in South Korea increased multifold in 2016. Korean firms were able to assimilate imported embodied technology so rapidly that they managed to achieve subsequent expansion while upgrading industrial structure to emerge as global brands like Samsung, Hyundai and LG. Korea moved from an agrarian economy to a mature economy in just three decades. This model of economic uplift is what inspires other IPAs and therefore, the investment promotion example set by Korea shows us that Aftercare and follow-up service delivery matters just as much as initial investment attraction."

Reproduced with kind permission from the World Association of Investment Promotion Agencies – WAIPA: www.waipa.org.

2.6 The case for Aftercare

This section answers the question: why is it a good idea to assign resources to Aftercare? It also aims to help IPAs put a compelling case for allocating funding support to Aftercare activities and seeks to equip policy makers with arguments that justify why Aftercare should have resources allocated to it, and hence why it must be included in the area's economic development toolkit. In brief, there is a business and an economic development case to perform the function, together with a strong governance argument in favour of Aftercare, as can be seen in Figure 2.10.

2.6.1 The business case

There are several reasons why allocating resources to Aftercare is a good investment: it is cost effective, it lowers risks and it is an efficient use of resources.

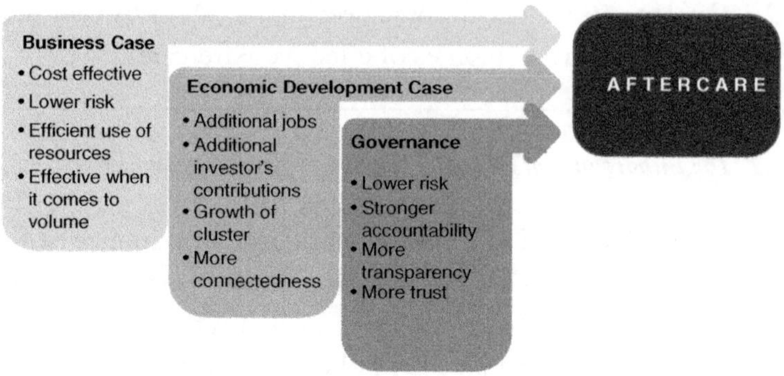

Figure 2.10 The case for Aftercare. © *Investment Aftercare Explained: A Guide for FDI Practitioners and Policymakers on How to Grow and Retain Investors.*

1. **Cost effectiveness**: when a foreign investor makes a long-term investment in a location, over time they increase their knowledge of how to do business in that location and learn how to build strong(er) relationships with key stakeholders across both the public and private sectors. IPAs can leverage these relationships and enter into a dialogue with these companies that goes beyond a soft landing that, as they become more established, should make it easier to encourage further investment. Consequently, it should be (significantly) cheaper as the company has already bought into the location, and hence fewer promotion and attraction resources should be required than would be the case to attract a new investor. Nevertheless, while long term foreign investors are, to some extent, a "captive audience," they should not be taken for granted.

   Commercially the importance of customer retention over winning new customers is well established. As the Harvard Business Review states, "depending on which study you believe, and what industry you are in, acquiring a new customer is anywhere from 5 to 25 times more expensive than retaining an existing one."[33] The maths is simple: existing investors do not require investment to find them or to convert them into clients, all of which provides important savings when compared to finding a new client from scratch. Further research by Fred Reichheld of Bain & Co shows that increasing customer retention rates by 5% increases profits by 25% to 95%.[34] Whilst there are no studies that replicate this research in the FDI and Aftercare arena, the same logic surely applies: supporting existing investors is likely cheaper than attracting new ones, and increases the likelihood that an investor will stay and make follow-on investments.

2. **Lower risk**: "Existing foreign investors have already proven their adaptability to the local conditions."[35] They have developed the knowledge required to operate in the local environment, and hence are more likely to thrive than a newcomer. As such, an additional job promised by an existing foreign investor is more likely to materialise and to endure than one promised by a new investor. Hence there is a strong argument for allocating some of an IPA's resources to Aftercare, rather than using them all to try and attract new investment.
3. **Efficiency**: a significant proportion of Aftercare services are delivered in collaboration with external partners and stakeholders. These partners have resources that the IPA can leverage, that is to say, more can be achieved with the same resources. For example, a local private company may produce industry insights that highlight the opportunities offered by their location. These reports can form part of an IPA's marketing materials for a location at little or no cost. By tapping into external resources an IPA not only enables other stakeholders to contribute to the development of a location, but by using (or reusing) resources that had originally been created for other purposes, also creates value at very little extra cost. Moreover, when foreign investors become ambassadors for their host location, they perform an "unpaid marketing function."
4. **Effectiveness**: the impact of foreign investment on a host economy is cumulative year after year. New investors and expansion projects build on what is already there and widen the scope of influence. Indeed, Microsoft estimates that for every one person it employs, 30 new jobs are created in the local economy.[36] Aftercare provides a framework through which to keep investors locally engaged long term, and which keeps that virtuous circle growing and contributing to co-create new local value. This does not happen by chance; it requires a carefully designed strategy that is applied consistently in the long term. Aftercare is the platform to do this.

Successful global trade and investment initiatives, first and foremost, require IPAs to become experts on their own economies and firms. This expertise is acquired largely through a robust regional Aftercare program, "which is anchored by on-going engagement with targeted local firms and industry clusters."[37]

2.6.2 The economic development case

According to the Cambridge Dictionary, economic development is "the process in which an economy grows or changes and becomes more advanced, especially when both economic and social conditions are improved."[38] Aftercare has a role in such a process. Among the most important economic development factors that support the case for Aftercare are:

1. **It creates local jobs**: the most visible and headline-grabbing benefit is the creation of jobs, which stem from the opening of new subsidiaries, the building of new facilities or the setting up of an additional production line.
2. **It increases an investor's contribution to the local economy**: while new investors are focussed on establishing their businesses locally, long-term foreign investors are better positioned to contribute to the local business community. Tangible benefits can include skillset development, better integration of the local economy into global value chains and resilience in times of uncertainly.
3. **It grows clusters**: when companies from the same sector are located close together, they are all more likely to grow faster, collaborate more and generate more growth in the region. This results in a stronger business sector, higher quality local talent, better partnerships and hence a more dynamic Ecosystem. This is the well-established cluster effect, of which Silicon Valley is probably the most famous example.
4. **It fosters connectedness**: based on the increasing importance of cities, and their role in generating economic growth, in 2013 the Brookings Institutive and JPMorgan Chase set up a comprehensive programme to support cities looking to enhance their global presence. Unsurprisingly, foreign companies are a key component in this global presence, and hence working closely with them is critical to strengthening both local and international connectedness.

Research conducted by the Global Cities Initiative[39] came to similar conclusions. Chapter 7, covering Place and Ecosystem, explores the concept of connectedness in detail.

5. **It creates local capacity**: supporting (existing) investors is a job that never ends. Moreover, "locations that embrace Aftercare also learn how to collaborate better, how to ignite local innovation and how to instil a location-wide drive for growth."[40]

2.6.3 Governance

Over the last decade the importance of robust governance, across both the public and private sectors, has increased. This also applies to FDI and, by extension, to Aftercare. While governance is a supporting function, and hence not a case for Aftercare per se, good governance can help ensure that the objectives of Aftercare are achieved. Aftercare supports the good governance of FDI in four areas:

1. **Risk management**: a well-thought-out Aftercare proposition signals to local stakeholders that tax-payers' money is being used both to retain existing investors and also to secure additional jobs. Similar to an insurance policy, a robust Aftercare proposition helps mitigate or manage potential risks of disinvestment and any related political risk.
2. **Accountability**: most locations describe themselves as investor-friendly. However, only a few deliver on that promise once a company has landed. IPAs are the de-facto responsible agency when it comes to delivering against any commitment as they have the role of ensuring that a location meets the expectations of an investor. Hence, Aftercare teams are also the accountable party investors engage with when they feel they have not received the support that was promised.
3. **Transparency**: Aftercare fosters transparency in at least three ways. First, in the context of international trade agreements that guarantee foreign companies are not discriminated against, Aftercare programmes provide clarity to stakeholders as to how foreign investors are supported. Second, where local stakeholders may have a negative view of a foreign investor, Aftercare can help manage any negative sentiment by helping to implement reporting policies and/

or community engagement practices that address local concerns. Third, in the case of IPAs that depend on public funding, Aftercare programmes with strong impact evaluation measurements and reporting mechanisms can reassure funders and the public that they are making good use of tax-payers' money.[41]

4. **Trust**: funders often demand regular reporting, including an audit trail and appropriate impact measurements, as a condition of providing support. Good Aftercare programmes verify the positive impact generated by the investments they make, the incentives they grant and any other stakeholder funds they are able to secure. This is key. The 2017 Edelman Trust Barometer[42] reported that trust levels in public, private and not for profit businesses and government have declined significantly since 2012. Their 2020 Report confirmed this, underlining "a growing sense of inequality undermining trust"[43] that exists in all sectors of society. When trust is in short supply, governance holds an even more important role. Aftercare can and should help the delivery of governance objectives.

In closing, understanding Aftercare is a crucial part of the work of an IPA. As seen in this chapter, Aftercare activities bring benefits and reach a variety of objectives that allow IPAs to build long-term relationships, understand investors' needs and their behaviour, and appreciate how these connections ignite a virtuous cycle that has an impact on the local economy. These effects go beyond pure economic benefits, as they also support improvement of the business climate and help create more economic value, which further increases society's welfare.

Notes

1 UNCTAD, 2007. *Aftercare: A Core Function in Investment Promotion* [online]. Available at: https://unctad.org/system/files/official-document/iteipc20071_en.pdf.

2 Ibid.

3 UNESCAP, 2017. *Investment Facilitation through the Investment Cycle* [online]. Available at: https://www.unescap.org/sites/default/files/UNESCAP-Uzbekistan-Session%209-Investment%20facilitation-Project%20establishment%20and%20after-care-December%202017_0.pdf.

4 Ibid.

5 Arriagada Peters, C. 2017. *Module 5 Aftercare and Policy Advocacy*, s.l: Course: Towards the next generation of IPAs by Inter-American Development Bank – Inter-American Development Bank (IDB).

6 Loewendahl, H. 2018. *Innovations in Foreign Direct Investment Attraction* [online]. Available at: http://dx.doi.org/10.18235/0001442.

7 Hornberger, K., Battat, J. and Kusek, P. 2011. *Attractive FDI: How Much Does Investment Climate Matter?* [online]. Available at: https://openknowledge.worldbank.org/handle/10986/11060.

8 Development Counsellors International, 2011. *A View from Corporate America: Winning Strategies in Economic Development Marketing* [online]. Available at: http://www.aboutdci.com/winning-strategies/.

9 Loewendahl, H. 2001. "A framework for FDI promotion". *Transnational Corporations*, 10(1), pp. 1–42.

10 Arias, A. 2017. *The Importance of Aftercare in Attracting Foreign Direct Investment: The Case of the Caribbean Region*. Madrid, Spain, Doctoral Thesis. Universidad Camilo José Cela.

11 UNCTAD, 2007. *Aftercare: A Core Function in Investment Promotion* [online]. Available at: https://unctad.org/system/files/official-document/iteipc20071_en.pdf.

12 WAIPA 2006 survey on IPA Aftercare is referred to as "survey on Aftercare".

13 MIGA, 2003. *Benchmarking FDI Competitiveness in Asia* [online]. Available at: https://www.hse.ru/data/588/897/1235/FDI_asia.pdf.

14 UNCTAD, 2017. *World Investment Report 2017* [online]. Available at: https://unctad.org/webflyer/world-investment-report-2017.

15 World Bank Group, 2018. *Global Investment Competitiveness Report 2017/2018* [online] Available at: https://openknowledge.worldbank.org/handle/10986/28493.

16 OECD, 2018. *FDI in Figures* [online]. Available at: http://www.oecd.org/industry/inv/investment-policy/FDI-in-Figures-April-2018.pdf.

17 FDI Markets, 2018. *FDI Reinvestment Ranking 2018* [online]. Available at: https://www.fdiintelligence.com/content/download/71002/2026169/file/fDi%20Reinvestment%20Ranking%202018.pdf.

18 World Bank, 2004. *World Development Report 2005: A Better Investment Climate for Everyone* [online]. Available at: https://openknowledge.worldbank.org/handle/10986/5987.

19 Kotler, P. 1998. *Marketing Management*. The Millennium edn. Upper Saddle River, NJ: Prentice Hall.

20 Heskett, J.L. et al. 2008. *Putting the Service-Profit Chain to Work* [online]. Available at: https://hbr.org/2008/07/putting-the-service-profit-chain-to-work.

21 Ibid.

22 Ibid.

23 Jones, R. and Sabbagh, D. 2019. *Nissan Warns of Brexit Concerns as U-turn at Sunderland Confirmed* [online]. Available at: https://www.theguardian.com/business/2019/feb/03/nissan-confirms-new-x-trail-will-not-be-built-in-sunderlan.

24 *The Times of India*, 2014. *Carrefour to Shut Shop, Exit India* [online]. Available at: https://timesofindia.indiatimes.com/business/india-business/carrefour-to-shut-shop-exit-india/articleshowprint/34558683.cms.

25 Loewendahl, H. 2001. "A framework for FDI promotion". *Transnational Corporations*, 10(1), pp. 1–42.

26 Arias, A. 2017. "The Importance of Aftercare in Attracting Foreign Direct Investment: The Case of the Caribbean Region". Madrid, Spain, Doctoral Thesis. Universidad Camilo José Cela.

27 Ibid.

28 UNIDO, 2012. *Africa Investor Report 2011: Towards Evidence-based Investment Promotion Strategies* [online]. Available at: https://doi.org/10.18356/07c88761-en.

29 See Google Campuses: https://www.campus.co/.

30 Both examples are described in detail in Part II of this book.

31 See http://www.boschaccelerator.in/.

32 See https://www.paih.gov.pl/our_services/investor_package/business_advocacy.

33 Gallo, A., 2014. *The Value of Keeping the Right Customers* [online]. Available at: https://hbr.org/2014/10/the-value-of-keeping-the-right-customers.

34 Reichheld, F. 2001. *Loyalty Rules! How Ttoday's Leaders Build Lasting Relationships*, Harvard Business Press.

35 Manasoe, B and Mears, R. 2011. *Aftercare of Inward Foreign Direct Investment: A Case Study of South Africa* [online]. Available at: https://econrsa.org/publications/working-papers/Aftercare-inward-foreign-direct-investment-case-study-south-africa.

36 McDarman, B. and Donahue, R. 2015. *The 10 Lessons from Global Trade and Investment Planning in U.S. Metro Areas* [online]. Available at: https://www.brookings.edu/research/the-10-lessons-from-global-trade-and-investment-planning-in-u-s-metro-areas/.

37 Ibid.

38 See Cambridge Dictionary https://dictionary.cambridge.org/dictionary/english/economic-development.

39 See https://www.jpmorganchase.com/corporate/Corporate-Responsibility/globalcities.htm.

40 Arriagada, C. 2018. *Investment Promotion: The Road to Maturity* [online]. Available at: https://www.citynationplace.com/investment-promotion-the-road-to-maturity.

41 For more information, see Chapter 10, Impact Evaluation, later in this book.

42 Edelman, 2017. *2017 Edelman Trust Barometer* [online]. Available at: https://www.edelman.com/trust/2017-trust-barometer.

43 Edelman, 2020. *2020 Edelman Trust Baromenter* [online]. Available at: https://www.edelman.com/trust/2020-trust-barometer.

PART II
THE WHAT

3

FRAMEWORK FOR INVESTOR SERVICES

Chapter highlights

- There are two distinctive business cycle frameworks that affect business; the economic cycle and the corporate life cycle.
- Combining them with a typical approach to international expansion introduces the concept of the foreign investment life cycle, which has four distinctive stages.
- Investor Services supports an investor's needs during all four stages. These services are classified into 7 different categories.

3.1 Introduction

"The driving seat of Aftercare is reserved for the foreign investor."
Pilar Madrigal, Head of Investment Promotion and Aftercare,
CINDE – Costa Rica

A customer-centric approach is the key to success in any modern business. FDI is no exception to this. Consequently, IPAs dedicate significant insight and resources to understanding, designing and deploying services that investors need, welcome and take up. This chapter outlines a framework behind Investor Services. It looks at economic cycles and business life cycles and how these define a company's ambition to open a subsidiary abroad, and therefore how these result in different types of Investor Services.

DOI: 10.4324/9781003174950-6

3.2 Economic cycles

Economies go through cycles. A period of growth is followed by a typically shorter period of economic stagnation or decline, followed by a further period of growth. For example, looking at the US economy since 1980, periods of growth have typically lasted from 5–10 years and been followed by a period of economic contraction of typically 6–18 months.[1] In India, this cycle is estimated to last 12 years on average.[2] The economic cycle impacts the majority of businesses as they grow as the economy grows, and retrench or contract as the economy stagnates or goes into recession. Of course, some businesses thrive during economic downturns, but the fortune of the majority of businesses is somewhat correlated to the economic cycle.

Understanding economic cycles and their impact on business is important for IPAs as businesses require different types of support at different stages of the economic cycle. Successful IPAs adapt the services they offer to investors depending on where they are in the economic cycle. The US state of Massachusetts has taken account of the business cycle in designing its offer to investors, as shown in Figure 3.1, kindly shared by Massachusetts's Rapid Response Team, Mass BizWorks. The figure shows the type of services that companies need at each stage of the business cycle. Looking at talent, for example, its shows that during the growth phase companies

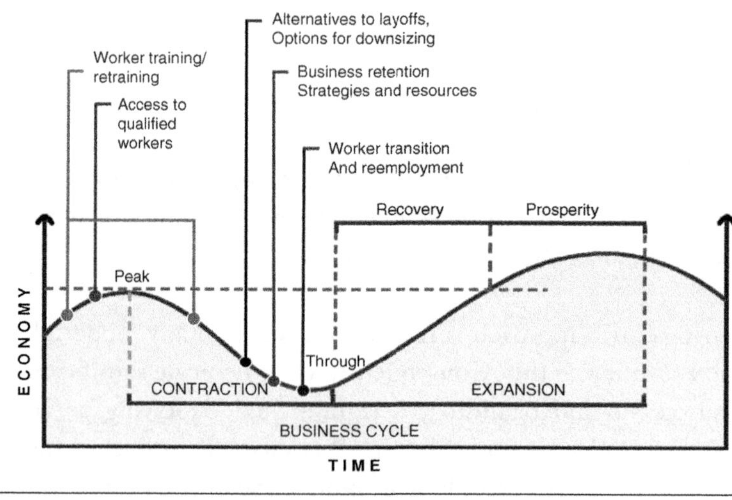

Figure 3.1 Mass BizWorks – providing services throughout the business cycle.

Source: Reproduced with kind permission from MassBizWorks state of Massachusetts.

require support identifying and developing talent, whereas during the contraction phase companies require support to help retain talent and avoid layoffs.

Mass BizWorks makes an important point when they say that "our aim at the Rapid Response Team is to build [a] relationship with companies when they are healthy, so we can help them grow; understanding this will help us to help them when they go through bad times."[3] Mr. Messina also noted that the Rapid Response Team's main role is "to understand what services could benefit companies in the different business life stages, as well as to articulate an offer that responds to the different phases of economic business cycles."[4] This approach helps them build a comprehensive service offer as outlined in Box 3.1.

Box 3.1 Service Offer from the State of Massachusetts

Service Offer from the State of Massachusetts – Mass BizWorks

Mass BizWorks is designed to enhance and align services for Massachusetts businesses. Mass BizWorks connects businesses to state and federal resources to help businesses through different business cycles. Over the years, thousands of companies in Massachusetts have taken advantage of our programs and services.

Resources for business growth or expansion

Congratulations on the continued growth of your company. Even as your company is growing and expanding, we have programs and services to help further enhance your company's growth and bottom line. Please contact us to access any of the following programs.

No Cost Job Posting: JobQuest provides employers with free job posting and job matching services. You can also search for qualified candidates registered on JobQuest.

Recruitment and Hiring Support: Staff at the One-Stop Career Centres can assist employers with recruiting and screening of candidates.

Registered Apprenticeship: Registered apprenticeships help employers build a dynamic, self-empowered workforce into the future.

Training Grants: Several types of grants are available for small, medium to large companies. The grants can be used to train incumbent workers to upgrade their skills.

Safety Grant: Grants up to $25,000 are available to help companies fund workplace safety training. Additionally, free on-site consultation is available to help companies meet OSHA requirements.

On-the-Job Training: On-the-Job Training (OJT) Program assists employers with the cost of hiring and training a new employee.

Tax Credit for Hiring: If you hire employees from certain target populations, you may be eligible for tax credit incentives.

Tax Incentive Program: Businesses seeking to locate or expand may be eligible for state and local tax incentives in exchange for job creation and investment commitments.

Economic Growth Support: Mass Development offers a wide range of finance and real estate development services to support businesses that are investing in Massachusetts.

Resources for Business Maintenance

If you do not anticipate changes to your workforce or business, you may still want to look into programs that could help you stay competitive or enhance your bottom line. And you may have to replace staff who leave or retire.

The list of services is the same as for business growth and expansion with one further addition:

Training Grants: Several types of grants are available for small, medium to large companies. The grants can be used to train incumbent workers to upgrade their skills.

Resources for business downsizing

Unfortunately, businesses get caught in a down cycle due to many unforeseen circumstances. Before you make that difficult decision to close a facility or lay off employees, please contact us to see if any of the following services can help avert the drastic action.

Rapid Response Program: The Rapid Response team can offer alternatives to closing a facility and laying off employees. If layoffs are inevitable, measures can be taken to lessen the impact on the company and workforce.

WorkShare Program: If you are experiencing a temporary slowdown in your business, WorkShare can help you reduce your payroll costs and maintain your valued workforce.

Unemployment Insurance For Workers: Unemployment Insurance provides Massachusetts workers with a temporary income, training and support during periods of unemployment.

Safety Grant: Grants up to $25,000 are available to help companies fund workplace safety training. Additionally, free on-site consultations are available to help companies meet OSHA requirements.

Note: content reviewed at time of publication, however programs are likely to change and evolve over time. Please visit website for further details.

Reproduced with kind permission from the State of Massachusetts: www.mass.gov.

Link: https://www.mass.gov/service-details/learn-about-masshire-bizworks.

3.3 Corporate life cycles

"Similar to how people grow and mature; the business life cycle shows businesses maturing from infancy through adolescence to adulthood and eventually, old age."[5] The vast majority of businesses, irrespective of what sector they are in or what country they are from, follow a similar trajectory, albeit at different speeds. These stages are, according to Forbes, "start-up, growth, maturity and renewal/decline,"[6] as can be seen in Figure 3.2.

Harvard Business Review contributors Neil C. Churchill and Virginia L. Lewis provide an overview of what companies face during each stage of the business life cycle.[7] During the start-up phase, businesses are primarily focussed on creating something potential customers want to pay for, winning customers and then delivering what was promised. Sooner or later, they shift from mere existence to managing revenues and expenses. As the company moves into the growth phase, it is able to solidify its stance in the

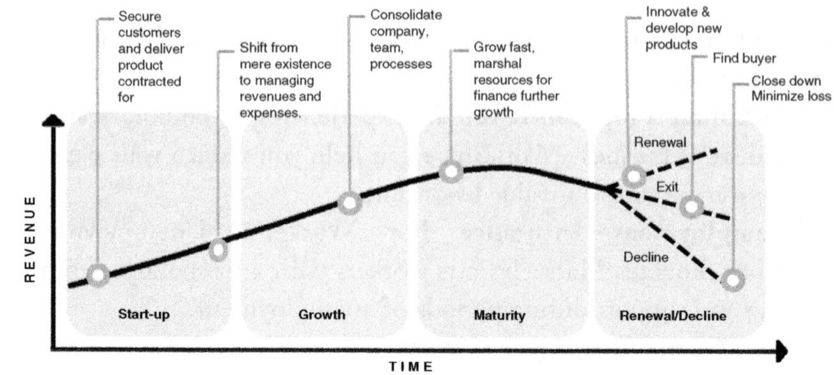

Figure 3.2 Corporate life cycle. © *Investment Aftercare Explained: A Guide for FDI Practitioners and Policymakers on How to Grow and Retain Investors.*

market and focus on consolidating the company, strengthening the team and streamlining processes. The next phase is maturity, where the company knows its business well, has a steady flow of clients and is focused on growing fast and marshalling resources to finance further growth. Eventually the company will reach a point where the market is saturated or market conditions change. At this point they either innovate and develop new products and enter a phase of renewal, or they enter the decline phase, ultimately exiting the business, downsizing or closing operations.

The parallels with FDI are clear. When a company lands, it is akin to a start-up that needs to find talent, customers and suppliers to help it deliver on its promise. If things go well, the priority in the growth phase is to consolidate the subsidiary and become a local player well versed in the local market. The maturity phase is very similar to a non-FDI business, and then it is a question of how the investor approaches the renewal/decline phase. The parent company can choose to expand and take advantage of new business opportunities, or it can stagnate and eventually decline and contract, ultimately leading to disinvestment.

Figure 3.3 shows the foreign investment life cycle, which is similar to the corporate life cycle, and illustrates the four stages a foreign investor goes through when investing in a new country, as well as the changing priorities it faces while it grows which require it to adjust both to local market conditions, and to the strategy of its overseas parent company.

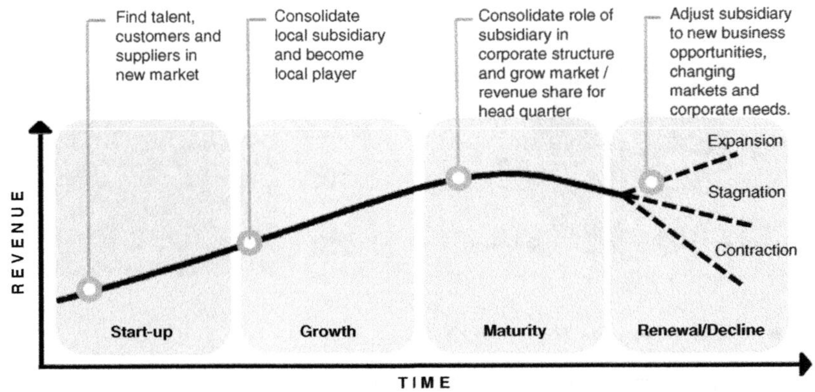

Figure 3.3 Foreign investment life cycle. © *Investment Aftercare Explained: A Guide for FDI Practitioners and Policymakers on How to Grow and Retain Investors.*

The key point that IPAs need to be aware of is that different divisions of a local affiliate of an overseas investor might be at different stages of the corporate life cycle, and hence require different services.

The corporate life cycle explained here coincides with the model presented by authors Armando Heilbron and Yago Aranda-Larrey from the World Bank Group in their report "Strengthening Service of Investment Promotion Agencies: The Comprehensive Investor Services Framework" published in December 2020. The model, titled CISF, observes that "many investment promotion programs – typically labelled promotion, facilitation, and aftercare – leave important service gaps"[8] and proposes a framework to help "governments and IPAs understand the importance of providing relevant, standardised services to the investor at every stage of the investment cycle (attraction, entry and establishment, retention and expansion, and linkages and spillovers)."[9] Figure 3.4 represents the different stages of how they approach the investment cycle and the 4 host country investment stages.

Columbia University professor Karl P. Sauvant, a leading international consultant fostering the adoption of guiding principles on investment facilitation for sustainable development in G-20 countries, also advocates integrating Investor Services throughout the investment lifecycle, moving away from the industry practice of only prioritising new investment. His latest policy paper outlines 5 stages in the FDI lifecycle: development of an FDI

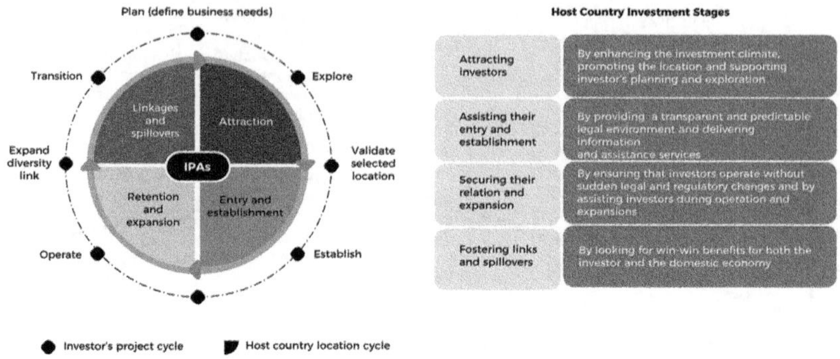

Figure 3.4 The World Bank's Comprehensive Investor Services Framework.

Source: Heilbron, A. and Aranda-Larrey, Y. 2020. *Strengthening Service Delivery of Investment Promotion Agencies: The Comprehensive Investor Services Framework. Finance, Competitiveness and Innovation in Focus.* World Bank, Washington.

vision or strategy; FDI attraction; FDI entry and establishment; retention of FDI, including dispute prevention; and fostering linkages between foreign and domestic firms to increase the benefits of FDI. He observes that "until now, discussions about investment facilitation have principally focused on stage 3, the host economy's policies and procedures regarding the entry and establishment of foreign investment and have paid less attention to the importance of facilitation at the post-establishment stage and beyond."[10]

3.4 Services that match the investor life cycle

The foreign investment life cycle provides a good framework around which to design Investor Services. Broadly speaking, there are 7 types of Investor Services: facilitation; customer services; business growth; retention; safeguarding; mergers and acquisitions (M&A) and disinvestment, which match, somewhat unevenly, with the 4 foreign investment lifecycle stages.

The seven Investor Services are:

1. **Facilitation services**: these are the most common Investor Services, and all IPAs provide them as they are an essential part of the mandate to attract foreign investment. Facilitation Services usually focus on *market entry*, and they become part of the post-investment services offer when established investors decide to expand, or to bring new divisions into the country. Examples include briefing

documents on the local jurisdiction's compliance requirements, especially around visas, real estate guidance and data provision.

2. **Customer services**: here, IPAs offer on-going support to investors, irrespective of how long their companies have been established in the host economy. Customer services, sometimes referred to as investor relations, focus on *troubleshooting*, signposting, networking, etc. They often either work closely with, or are responsible for, the one-stop-shop service (discussed in detail in Chapter 4, Portfolio of Investor Services).
3. **Business growth services** (also called expansion services): there are 5 different ways IPAs can help investors grow and expand:
   a) Scaling: when a company is in a growth phase and is ready, willing and able to invest additional resources to increase local capacity, their focus is on *scaling*, securing additional revenues or increasing local capacity to service the increase in revenues. In this scenario, the IPA's attention should be on helping to accelerate that growth and to make it bigger, better and faster. A typical example of business growth services is when IPAs help investors consolidate relationships, moving from a transactional to a partnership approach that gives them access to new growth-centred conversations.
   b) When a business is in the renewal stage, the company often has a bullish attitude towards the market and is positive about its ability to take advantage of the opportunity. This might lead to the investor choosing to bring an additional business unit to the host location. Irrespective of whether such a project may be initiated by a parent company or by the local subsidiary, IPAs' services may include market insights to help *land the new division*. Where an investor is looking to expand by *acquiring new assets*, help may focus on better integrating the new asset into the local value chain (see merger and acquisition services below).
   c) Alternatively, the company might be seeking to improve existing products or develop new ones. In this scenario an IPA's services may focus on *helping the company to innovate* by connecting them with the local start-up scene or by facilitating partnerships with research centres.

d) Where the company is facing stagnation or decline, an IPA's focus should be on *helping them to find new opportunities*, as this may be critical to the future presence of the company in that location. The IPA might refine a business case for the local economy from a generic template and identify what other local assets, resources or connections can benefit the investor, and hence help them swing their business towards expansion. Many IPAs work closely with local affiliates to send a coordinated message to the affiliate's parent company as to the benefits of increasing their presence in the area.

4. **Retention services**: as investment cycles become shorter, and competition between locations increases, investment decisions are more frequently reviewed. There are many factors that lead to a *reassessment* of an investment, including technological changes that reduce the viability of an existing location, shortage of suitable talent, insufficient incentives, mobility of leadership, etc. A retention project is "a type of investment where a foreign investor agrees to make an additional investment into an existing foreign direct enterprise with the purpose of preventing the enterprise from reduction or closure."[11] Services are focussed on retaining the investor locally (rather than seeing them relocate elsewhere) by, for example, preparing a business case that articulates how and why the investor would benefit from remaining in the current location.
5. **Safeguarding services**: when an investor is considering *downsizing* its operations or reducing its presence in a location, support focuses on ensuring that any contraction is as small as possible. This can be achieved by proposing alternative options that preserve jobs, such as exploring incentive schemes currently not being accessed by the investor, identifying alternative premises that are more cost-effective or reviewing the company's business case for downsizing or exiting a location to ensure they have taken account of all the costs and possible implications, as this is not always the case. These situations are sometimes referred to as safeguard(ing) projects, as (more) jobs would be lost without the IPA's intervention.
6. **Merger and acquisitions (M&A) services**: a merger occurs when two or more companies agree to merge into a new single company "rather than remain separated for creating business synergies."[12] An

acquisition, in contrast, is a "transaction between two companies by which the acquiring company purchases the existing assets and liabilities of the target company. M&As are a common mechanism for entering a new market and are usually followed by new additional investments."[13] There is no consensus on whether or not M&A services are part of FDI, and consequently whether or not IPAs should support M&A activity, whether in the expansion or the contraction phase. M&A services, during the contraction phase, focus on helping the local affiliate find a buyer, support buy-out readiness and make the new owner (if a foreign investor) feel welcome. Those IPAs that do support M&A activity often, and should, monitor the strategy of these new owners, as the outcome of the transaction often commences with downsizing as a prelude to growth.

7. **Divestment services**: when circumstances change, companies sometimes need to *close operations*. This is a normal part of the business cycle. However, such events can have serious implications for a location. Despite the best efforts of an IPA, and an investor having a positive opinion of a location, there are times when business drivers make disinvestment the logical business option. In these situations, an IPA's focus should be on minimising the loss to all stakeholders. While investors may benefit from specialised support, the priority here is to develop contingency plans that minimise any negative impact, to support alternative employment options for affected staff and to manage the associated political risk. Types of service can include advice on crisis management, public relations, support with employment relationships, (re)training programs for affected staff and relocation assistance. Chapter 6, Divestment, explores this topic in detail.

In closing, where in the foreign investment life cycle a company finds itself will determine the type of support it requires and, based on this information, how IPAs should design their services to be investor centric. The 2020 World Bank Group and WAIPA joint report, "State of Investment Promotion Agencies", also advocates for an integrated approach to services as a demand-led service design allows IPAs to "tackle a greater number of investors' needs and issues, thus increasing the probability that the location will successfully harness the investment it wants."[14]

In this chapter, the type of services businesses require through the economic and business cycles have been presented, as well as an overview of the 7 types of service IPAs offer to meet this demand. Understanding the type of services businesses require through the economic and business cycles, as well as the 7 different types of service, will help IPAs develop services to meet investor demand. This arrangement also helps the reader to better comprehend the scope of the catalogue of Investors Services, which is explained in detail in the next chapter.

3.5 Services that respond to investor needs

UNCTAD's seminal 2007 paper, "Aftercare: A Core Function in Investment Promotion", proposed that foreign investors require three types of services: administrative, operational and strategic,[15] as can be seen in Figure 3.5.

1. **Administrative services**: they support operational activities and may include support obtaining permits and authorisations to trade, finding a new office or assistance with staff relocation.
2. **Operational services**: they help ensure the successful operation of a transnational business and cover areas such as finding suppliers, training and development support, and export assistance.
3. **Strategic services**: they support the higher-level investor goals so that the subsidiary can meet its corporate mandate successfully – whether it be agendas, such as becoming a local leader, a centre of

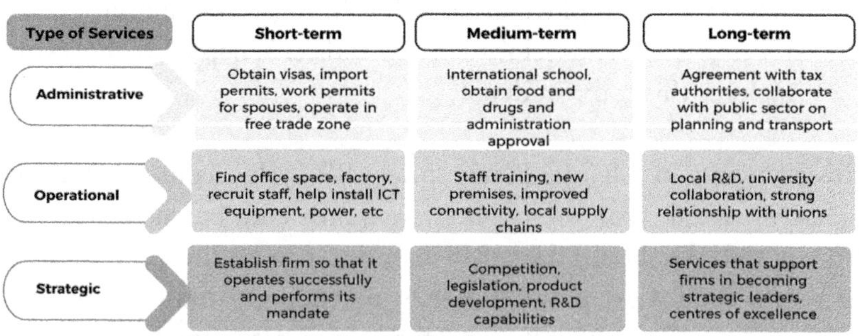

Figure 3.5 Type of Aftercare services according to UNCTAD.

Source: Author's own design using data from: UNCTAD (2007, p. 16). "Aftercare: A Core Function in Investment Promotion". Investment Advisory Series (A), No. 1. New York: United Nations.

excellence, or a strategic player for their parent company. Strategic services have three components:

- *Information*: where the IPA brings insight and opportunities to the attention of an investor. In this scenario, the IPA is an "information broker" for strategic opportunities.
- *Skills development*: for decision makers, and the provision of tools to help better assess market opportunities and threats.
- *Innovation*: where an IPA supports innovation within the foreign company. This can include providing exposure to new research, cutting edge and disruptive technologies, and introductions to trend-spotters and futurologists who can help investors establish the likely future of their markets, society and therefore their business.

As the global economy and political and social priorities have changed since 2007, the authors observe that two further categories of services are required to describe a service portfolio and these are value chain services and sustainability services.

3.6 Value chain services

The word "linkages" is commonly used in the FDI industry to describe interactions, connections and relationships that facilitate doing business. Linkages play a key role in helping to embed foreign investors in an Ecosystem. The exact definition describes them as "explicit and/or implicit connections that a firm creates with critical entities of its supply chain in order to manage the flow and/or quality of inputs from suppliers into the firm and of outputs from the firm to customers."[16] Linkages are important to the host economy, as the OECD observes that "spill-overs arise largely through linkages between foreign investors and local firms."[17]

With the professionalisation of logistics and procurement, two more concepts emerged, namely supply chains and value chains. Supply chains "involves all parties in fulfilling a customer request and leading to customer satisfaction".[18] They are basically the steps required to get the product to the customer. In contrast, value chains are processes in "which a company adds value to its raw materials to produce products eventually sold to consumers."[19] In technical terms, "a value chain is a set of interrelated activities a company uses to create a competitive advantage."[20]

Linkages, supply chains and value chains are referred to collectively in this book as value chains. UNCTAD included them as part of strategic services in 2007, but the increasingly integrated nature of the global economy means that value chain services now need to be viewed as a separate category.

The Covid-19 pandemic illustrated all too clearly the fragility of many businesses value chains and, as a consequence, many businesses are reassessing their value chains and considering alternative locations and suppliers in order to assure business continuity. According to the World Bank, the "COVID-19 pandemic has posed an unprecedented challenge to global value chains (GVCs), hampering the supply of raw materials, intermediate inputs, and final goods."[21] Major manufacturing hubs such as Germany, China, USA, Japan were severely affected – indeed, countries all over the world were impacted by weakened or even broken supply chains. Along the same lines, the OECD observed that companies are likely to rethink their supply chains in the medium and long run and reassess risk management and exposure as a result of the pandemic. "The direction of changes will depend on how companies will balance risk-mitigation with cost-efficiency."[22] In a post-pandemic world, value chain decisions may result in disinvestment in some locations and expansion in others. Possible outcomes include shortening of global value chains, geographic diversification as a means of hedging supply risk and reshoring and nearshoring on the basis that shorter distances reduce risks. The OECD adds that "nearshoring and reshoring are likely to affect more developing countries."[23]

3.7 Sustainability services

The impact of climate change together with sociodemographic changes and rising concerns around social inequality have put sustainability higher up the agenda in many countries and global forums. The United Nations 2030 agenda combines private and public interests and seeks wide-spanning collaborations to address societies' most pressing challenges. Concern around sustainability, in the broadest sense, means it is now on the agenda of organisations both large and small, as well as local and national governments. The result is that sustainability has become mainstream, with investors increasingly referring to it in their business plans and annual reports. Governments have committed to it via the UN's Social Development Goals (SDGs), and locations are benchmarked by a variety of interested agencies such as global commercial real estate firms and law firms. The driver behind this is the notion that environmental and economic agendas are aligned. From social inclusion to reducing the carbon footprint, from staff health and wellbeing to more environmentally friendly cities, the challenges are many and varied and require effective public-private partnerships to deliver innovative solutions.

All 5 services have the objective of ensuring that a foreign business not only remains in the host territory, but also that it grows and thrives. As ever, one size doesn't fit all, so when Investor Services offers are being designed and delivered, programs should be adapted to meet the needs of both the investors and the location. In other words, the services provided need to be customer-driven, rather than offered without any thought as to the services investors actually require. Experienced practitioners suggest starting with administrative services and then developing operational, value chain, sustainability and strategic offers as investors become more established – typically over the next two to four years. In essence, the aim is to follow and support the investor's business as it grows. Investors usually start by demanding simple troubleshooting support, which over time develops into a need for more complex strategic services.

The following chapter presents examples of Investor Services from across the world that are either delivered directly by IPAs, or facilitated by them.

Notes

1 NBER, 2020. *US Business Cycle Expansions and Contractions* [online]. Available at: https://www.nber.org/research/data/us-business-cycle-expansions-and-contractions.

2 Rajadhyaksha, N. 2019. *A Close Examination of Indian Financial and Business Cycles* [online]. Available at: https://www.livemint.com/opinion/columns/opinion-the-mystery-of-financial-cycles-and-business-cycles-in-india-1562666433331.html.

3 Insight gathered by this book's research team – interview 2019.

4 Ibid.

5 Nexcess, 2021. *Understanding the Business Life Cycle* [online]. Available at: https://www.nexcess.net/woocommerce-resource/business-life-cycle/.

6 Dempsey, B. 2018. *Business Life Cycle Spectrum: Where Are You?* [online]. Available at: https://www.forbes.com/sites/theyec/2018/01/11/business-life-cycle-spectrum-where-are-you/?sh=17444bafef5e.

7 Churchill, N.C. and Lewis, V.L. 1983. "The five stages of small business growth". *Harvard Business Review*, Volume May.

8 Heilbron, A. and Aranda-Larrey, Y. 2020. *Strengthening Service Delivery of Investment Promotion Agencies: The Comprehensive Investor Services Framework. Finance, Competitiveness and Innovation in Focus. World Bank, Washington, DC* [online]. Available at: https://openknowledge.worldbank.org/handle/10986/33498.

9 Ibid.

10 Sauvant, K.P. et al. 2019. *Towards G20 Guiding Principles on Investment Facilitation for Sustainable Development* [online]. Available at: https://www.g20-insights.org/policy_briefs/towards-g20-guiding-principles-on-investment-facilitation-for-sustainable-development/.

11 Department for International Trade of the United Kingdom, 2018. *Inward Investment Results 2017–18 Technical Annex* [online]. Available at: https://assets.publishing.service.gov.uk/government/uploads/system/uploads/attachment_data/file/718902/Inward_Investment_Results_2017-18_Technical_Annex.pdf.

12 Business Sweden, 2020. *Start a Company in Sweden – Mergers and Acquisitions in Sweden* [online]. Available at: https://www.business-sweden.com/globalassets/services/learning-center/establishment-guides/mergers-and-acquisitions-in-sweden.pdf.

13 Ibid.

14 Sanchiz, A. and Omic, A. 2020. *State of Investment Promotion Agencies: Evidence from WAIPA-WBG's Joint Global Survey*. World Bank, Washington, DC. WAIPA (World Association of Investment Promotion Agencies), Geneva [online]. Available at: http://documents1.worldbank.org/curated/en/499971594008431029/pdf/State-of-Investment-Promotion-Agencies-Evidence-from-WAIPA-WBG-s-Joint-Global-Survey.pdf.

15 UNCTAD, 2007. *Aftercare: A Core Function in Investment Promotion* [online]. Available at: https://unctad.org/system/files/official-document/iteipc20071_en.pdf

16 Rungtusanatham, M., Salvador, F., Forza, C. and Choi, T. 2003. "Supply-chain linkages and operational performance: A resource-based-view perspective". *International Journal of Operations & Production Management*, 23(9), pp. 1084–1099.

17 OECD, 2011. *Policy Framework for Investment. User's Toolkit Chapter 2: Investment Promotion and Facilitation* [online]. Available at: https://www.oecd.org/investment/toolkit/policyareas/investmentpromotionfacilitation/41246119.pdf.

18 Tarver, E. 2020. *Value Chain vs. Supply Chain: What's the Difference?* [online]. Available at: https://www.investopedia.com/ask/answers/043015/what-difference-between-value-chain-and-supply-chain.asp.

19 Ibid.

20 Ibid.

21 Qiang, C.Z., Liu, Y., Paganini, M. and Steenbergen, V. 2020. *Foreign Direct Investment and Global Value Chains in the Wake of COVID-19* [Online] Available at: https://blogs.worldbank.org/psd/foreign-direct-investment-and-global-value-chains-wake-covid-19

22 OECD, 2020. *Investment Promotion Agencies in the Time of COVID-19* [online]. Available at: http://www.oecd.org/coronavirus/policy-responses/investment-promotion-agencies-in-the-time-of-covid-19-50f79678/.

23 Ibid.

4
PORTFOLIO OF INVESTOR SERVICES

Chapter highlights

- This chapter provides examples of the 5 different types of Investor Services.
- Administrative services include introductions to service providers, working with regulators and immigration services.
- Operational services include support to find new premises, export support services, workforce development and access to finance.
- Strategic services include business case services, mentoring and innovation.
- Linkages, supply chain and value chain offerings include match-making services, non-equity modes of investment and joint ventures.
- Sustainable services include leaner and greener practices, driving the gender agenda, philanthropic activities and engaging with indigenous communities.

4.1 Introduction

Putting a service portfolio together is both an art and a science.
It must address real needs and provide practical solutions,
while at the same time make investors feel confident, ambitious,
and equipped.

DOI: 10.4324/9781003174950-7

The 2018 OECD study, "Mapping of Investment Promotion Agencies in OECD Countries,"[1] provides a good overview of the services currently being provided by IPAs. Their first observation is that "investment facilitation and retention, together with policy advocacy, is the most heterogeneous of the four core functions across OECD IPAs, as there are wide disparities from one national agency to another in the different activities covered under this function."[2] The study goes on to say that OECD IPAs conduct more investment facilitation than Aftercare activities but that the "categorisation somewhat simplifies the reality, as some of these activities can sometimes overlap with both the facilitation and aftercare sub-categories (e.g. an IPA can support an established business with immigration procedures)."[3] On average, for every 5 facilitation services delivered, IPAs provide three Aftercare services. The report explains that IPAs that provide a high number of facilitation services often provide a high number of Aftercare services, "but this is not a systematic trend. Conversely, some IPAs that provide a comparatively low number of facilitation services offer a high(er) number of aftercare services than the average, as is the case of Innovation Norway."[4] The same study unveiled that the most common facilitation and Aftercare services provided by OECD IPAs are arranging site visits, providing information about local suppliers and customers, and facilitating working meetings with local stakeholders, such as local officials or local suppliers. The most commonly delivered Investor Services are structured troubleshooting discussions with individual investors on recognised blockages to the success of an investment, support finding appropriate suppliers via providing databases, and matchmaking services that enable investors to find local suppliers and customers, and vice versa.

The 2020 WAIPA-WBG joint study came to a similar conclusion and adds that "communication with investors to gather information about grievances related to government conduct, the provision of tailored responses to questions asked by investors, the facilitation and coordination of initiatives and events that provide networking opportunities in the local ecosystem at the linkages and spillovers stage"[5] are the most commonly provided services by WAIPA members.

This chapter provides examples of those services and explores a total of 32 different types of Investor Services currently being delivered by IPAs both large and small, and in both developed and developing economies. They are split into the five categories, as explained previously, namely administrative, operational, strategic, value chain and sustainability services, noting that the categories are not exclusive, and that some services could appear in more than one category. These services are presented in the format developed by FDI consultant Dr. Ashraf A. Mahate,[6] and cover 4 topics: description, main beneficiary, implementation and intended outcome.

This chapter illustrates the wide range of Investor services IPAs across the world are currently offering to investors, and can be used as a source of inspiration for IPAs looking to expand their own range of services.

4.2 Administrative services

When starting in Aftercare, IPAs will usually offer administrative services in response to enquiries from established investors. The following examples provide an overview of the most commonly delivered services.

4.2.1 Introduction to service providers

IPAs are expected to be well-connected with the local business community and to be able to provide foreign investors with introductions to key service providers as required.

- **Description**: IPAs facilitate introductions to carefully selected service providers such as banks, accountants and lawyers that have expertise in helping international investors grow.
- **Main beneficiaries**: foreign investors seeking to grow their business looking for advisers specialised in helping foreign companies. The service providers also gain access to potential new clients.
- **Implementation**: IPAs prepare a list of service providers who have proven expertise in working with international investors, and who adhere to the IPA's code of practice. These service providers often offer free consultancy services, typically a few hours, to foreign investors as part of their agreement with the IPA.

  IPAs should consult with their legal department about the legal implications of listing service providers. Some IPAs (such as Costa Rica, below) have a disclaimer, clearly stating the role they play in providing this information. Other IPAs, particularly publicly funded ones, are wary of offering introductions due to governance concerns, notably how to ensure that all qualified service providers have an equal opportunity to offer their services to investors. Ensuring fairness can be cumbersome and expensive, requiring public tenders and the publishing of supplier selection criteria. This explains why some IPAs choose not to offer introductions to service providers.

- **Intended outcome**: foreign investors receive high quality advice from appropriately qualified experts, thereby enabling them to make better decisions.

The example features in Box 4.1 comes from award-winning IPA CINDE.

Box 4.1 Costa Rica offer to find the right corporate service provider

"We bring you a directory of companies to help you in almost all areas regarding setting [up] a business in Costa Rica. With these right (sic) partners, you'll be in the best hands.

Select one category below to see its matching providers: Telecom, Insurance Companies, Immigration Law firms, Labour Law, Banks, Logistics, IT Services & Data Centres, Consulting Services, Environmental Validation & Regulatory Consulting, Energy Efficiency & Industrial Recycling, Relocation / Housing, Construction, Architecture & Design, Cafeteria Admin, Office Furniture, Project Management, Industrial & Packaged Gases.

Disclaimer: All service providers included in this Directory have fulfilled the eligibility and competence requirements established by CINDE. Any contractual relation(s) established between a client and any of the service providers within this Directory are the responsibility of both parties and not CINDE's. Therefore, CINDE accepts no liability nor does it give any guarantee on the matter."

Note: The website adds additional information about the service provider, such as company description, the type of service they provide, [and] a list of existing clients and contact details.

Reproduced with kind permission from CINDE: www.cinde.org.

4.2.2 Working with regulators

Investors often require support when dealing with government departments or regulators, as they "don't know how things work" in that particular location.

- **Description**: where regulatory authorities have a key role to play in granting expansion approvals or managing incentives, some IPAs not only help educate investors about the process involved, challenges they are likely to face and what they can expect when engaging with government departments, they also arrange introductions as and when required.
- **Main beneficiaries**: foreign investors needing to engage with local regulators as well as regulators who rely on, and expect, IPAs to ensure timely engagement with potential new investors.
- **Implementation**: firstly, an IPA should develop strong relationships with the relevant regulatory departments, establish engagement processes that address the most frequently asked questions and train its staff in how to navigate these institutions. When an issue arises, the IPA can arrange a meeting between the investor and the appropriate regulatory authority. Depending on the needs and capability of the investor, the IPA can then "handhold" them through the regulatory process as required.
- **Intended outcome**: investors are able to obtain the necessary regulatory approvals in a quick and pain-free manner.

An example of what how SelectUSA works with regulators can be seen in Box 4.2.

Box 4.2 SelectUSA: assistance with navigating the regulatory environment

SelectUSA offers information and data that help businesses move investments forward.

Familiarity with the U.S. economic, political, and regulatory environment is critical for business leaders to make informed decisions about their investments. As "America's Data Agency," the U.S. Department of Commerce produces the most comprehensive and credible data on the U.S. economy and population. SelectUSA investment specialists help companies find the most relevant, geographically neutral information for businesses individual investment project needs. This information covers a wide range of topics – from the overall economy and investment trends through industry overviews and information about consumers, the workforce, supply chains, and available federal resources.

The United States is recognized for its ease of doing business and FDI attractiveness – SelectUSA can make the investment process even easier.

SelectUSA works with companies to address issues or questions involving federal regulations, programs, or activities related to existing and potential investments. Working with SelectUSA, investors can develop a better understanding of how to navigate the U.S. regulatory environment.

Reproduce with kind permission from SelectUSA: www.selectusa.gov.

4.2.3 Incentives: love or loathe?

Incentives are a key part of FDI. Indeed, many investors actively ask what incentives are available. And while some may argue that incentives introduce an element of unfair competition, they are here to stay as investors' "heads are turned" by locations offering incentives, and hence other locations feel the need to compete, which risks creating a vicious circle of ever-increasing incentives.

Typically, incentives are offered in the areas of favourable tax treatments, grants, vouchers and preferential access to certain facilities and assets, and often a country may offer particularly favourable terms should a company choose to set up in an economically deprived area. However, the nature and range of incentives offered to potential investors is only limited by the creativity of the relevant authorities. Nevertheless, irrespective of one's views on incentives, they are a key component of most countries FDI strategy, both for new investments and for Aftercare. Arguments about the ethics of incentives are unlikely to end any time soon.

There are three instances where investors might need help with incentives: when the investor is not aware the incentive is available, where there is a business case to submit an application for an incentive and once the application has been approved, there is the paperwork to actually make use of the incentive.

The FDI industry has different views as to whether providing incentive-related services is a role the IPA should play. Arguments in favour of providing services to help an investor with the paperwork associated with incentives centre around reducing paperwork, simplicity and efficiency. For example, incentive documents are often complex, are worded in legal terms and may refer to local considerations an investor is unlikely to be aware of. Another example is where IPAs help investors navigate what may be an incentive minefield. Incentives are most likely managed by an independent government department and the IPA can liaise with that department on behalf of the investor. A third example is typical of locations with significant bureaucracy, or that feature low on international investment rankings or benchmarks, who might want to compensate for a less-than-optimum regulatory environment. They are aware that if the investor is not helped this may hinder an expansion. They will want to reassure the investor that the benefit of the incentives outweighs its cost.

Arguments against providing services to deal with incentives paperwork centre around influence, discrimination and governance. For example, it is typical that incentives are managed by a government department or funder the IPA has little influence over. Investors might have unreasonable expectations of what the IPA can actually achieve, which in turn may erode the IPA's authority in the eyes of the investor. A second example relates to the notion that incentives are granted on a competitive basis. There is an unfair competition argument if IPAs help some foreign investors prepare a business case for an incentive while other businesses receive no support when making their applications. A case of governance, for example, arises out of the dual role of applying for grant while at the same time controlling it. Most organisations that offer grants will have processes to control their use. If the IPA gets involved, it might end up delivering a sort of outsourced compliance role on behalf of the granting organisation. This can put the IPA in an uncomfortable position, where they are both representing the investor and providing customer-care services to the private sector, and they are also working on behalf of the granting authority and playing a "watchdog" role for the public sector. Playing both these roles can have a negative effect on an IPA's Policy Advocacy work as it reduces their authority or legitimacy as a conduit for investor feedback. Smart IPAs and their funders put good-governance measures in place to avoid any conflict of interest when it comes to services relating to incentives.

- **Description**: to help investors learn, access and benefit from incentives, including helping them complete any necessary administrative procedures.
- **Main beneficiaries**: the primary beneficiary is the foreign investor. The second beneficiary is the granting authority, which is likely to benefit from good candidates for their incentive programmes and a smoother application process. The third beneficiary is the IPA, which by supporting the investor through the incentive application process will strengthen its relationship with the investor and meets its objectives.
- **Implementation**: different IPAs provide different levels of support. Some IPAs only offer information and signposting services, while others help investors complete the often complicated paperwork involved in applying for grants and incentives. For large-scale investments such as for utilities, infrastructure or mining projects, IPAs may have a team of fulltime professionals on site, some of whom may come from the corresponding ministry. For major projects, it is not unusual for teams to be based at the client's premises, particularly when a number of different grant applications are being made and permits are required.
- **Intended outcome**: simplify the administrative burden of managing incentives and increase speed of doing so. It also will provide an IPA with oversight of how incentives are actually used by their investor clients.

The following two examples show a wide range of incentives that the Kenyan Revenue Authority offers (see Box 4.3); and how Invest Nigeria (see Box 4.4) articulates and promote incentives provided by government agencies.

Box 4.3 Incentives offered by the Kenyan Revenue Authority

Incentives available to investors in Kenya

"**Capital allowances**: These are tax incentives offered for capital expenditures.

They include wear and tear allowances, industrial building deduction, investment deduction and farm-works deductions.

Wear and tear allowances: The wear and tear allowances are charged on capital expenditure on machinery and equipment where they are classified into five classes all of which are offered the allowances at different rates.

Investment deduction: An investor who incurs capital expenditure on building and/or machinery used for manufacture is entitled to an investment deduction equal to 100% of the cost. For capital expenditures on building and/or machinery exceeding a threshold if the investment is outside Nairobi special rates apply

Industrial Building Deduction: This is an allowance granted to an investor who incurs capital expenditure on a building used as an industrial building at the rate of 10% of the cost

Public expenditures: Expenditures of a capital nature incurred in that year of income (with the prior approval by the Minister) by the person on the construction of a public school, hospital, road or any similar infrastructure will be an allowable deduction.

Telecommunication sector: An investor in the telecoms industry who incurs capital expenditure on telecommunications equipment purchased and used by him in business is entitled to a straight-line deduction at the rate of 20% of such cost.

Computer software: An investor who incurs capital expenditure on the purchase of the right to use a computer software used by him in business is entitled to a straight-line deduction at the rate of 20% of such cost.

Farm Works Deductions: This deduction is a capital allowance granted to a farmer who incurs capital expenditure on the construction of farm works at the rate of 100% of the cost. A farm work is any structure constructed to enhance the operations of a farm.

Special Economic Zones: Capital expenditure on buildings and machinery for use in a Special Economic Zone shall be entitled to Investment deduction equal to one hundred percent of the capital expenditure. Corporate taxation at rate of 10% for first 10 years and 15%for the next 10 years Withholding tax rates on payments made to non-residents (royalties, interest, management fees) 5%; Dividends paid to non- residents by the SEZ entity, exempt from tax.

Export Processing Zones Incentives: A 10-year corporate income tax holiday is available to certain designated enterprises that undertake activities consisting of the manufacture of goods for exports only (under the Export Processing Zones) and a 25% tax rate for a further 10 years

10 year withholding tax holiday on dividends and other remittances to non-resident parties (except for EPZ commercial licence enterprises)

100% investment deduction on new investment in EPZ buildings and machinery.

Incentives for Newly Listed Companies: For newly listed companies, there are preferential corporate tax rates dependent on the percentage of listed shares.

Incentives through Double Tax Agreement: Where there are negotiated Double tax agreement between Kenya and any other state, there are usually concessionary tax rates on various categories of payments.

Medical incentives: In the case of a full-time employee including whole time service directors, the value of medical services provided by the employer or medical insurance provided by an insurance provider approved by the Commissioner and paid for by the employer on behalf of a full-time employee.

Insurance relief: With effect from 2003, any life insurance cover taken by an individual on self, spouse or child will qualify for relief at rate 15% of premium paid up to up to a maximum of KShs 60,000/ = per year. An education policy with a maturity period of at least 10 years shall also qualify for relief in a similar manner.

Mortgage relief: Any person who borrows money from a registered financial institution to purchase a home or to improve a home as long as he/she occupies the home, will be entitled to a interest deduction of up to a maximum of KShs 300,000/= per annum of interest paid to the approved and registered financial institutions.

Home Ownership Savings Plan (Hosp): An individual will be entitled to relief/deductions on funds deposited under a registered Home Ownership Savings Plan subject to a maximum of KShs 8,000/ = per month or KShs 96,000/= per year for 10 years. Any interest income earned by a depositor on deposits of up to a maximum of KShs 3 million shall be exempt from tax.

Housing bonds: Any individual who purchases housing bonds will be granted tax exemption on interest accruing on housing bonds up to a maximum of KShs 300,000/=.

Retirement Benefits Savings: Contributions into a registered retirement benefits scheme is tax deductible to a maximum of ksh 20000 pm or ksh 240000 pa. First ksh 600000 of lumpsum upon withdrawal of benefits and ksh 25000 monthly pension received from such scheme is tax free. **Collective investment schemes** (Unit Trusts, Real Estate Investment Trusts, Employee Share Ownership Plans). Collective Investment schemes registered with Commissioner are exempt from tax on their incomes except for payment of withholding tax on dividends or interest paid to unit holders who are not tax exempt.

Exemptions on VAT: This is granted to Donor Funded project upon recommendation by National Treasury, Diplomats (DA 1s) upon recommendation by CS for Foreign affairs, and privileged persons e.g. KDF."

Note: content reviewed at time of publication, however programs are likely to change and evolve over time. Please visit website for updated details.

Reproduced with kind permission from KenInvest, Kenya Investment Authority: www.invest.go.ke.

Link: https://kra.go.ke/en/ngos/incentives-investors-certificate/investing-in-kenya/incentives-investors.

Box 4.4 Nigeria's Compendium of Incentives

Nigeria has come a long way in offering incentives to foreign investors. The Nigerian Investment Promotion Commission together with the Federal Inland Revenue Service produced a Compendium of Investment Incentives in Nigeria, released in October 2017. It lists tax-based incentives, sector specific incentives, tariff incentives, export incentives and incentives of special economic zones. The Compendium is aimed at raising awareness of investment incentives in Nigeria, the relevant agencies involved and provides guide for investor decision-making.

Reproduced with kind permission from the Nigerian Investment Promotion Commission: www.nipc.gov.ng.

A further example of incentives can be found at the end of this chapter where the incentives offered by literally hundreds of locations seeking to attract Amazon's HQ2 are discussed.

4.2.4 Immigration support services

Understandably investors want to recruit the best possible talent, irrespective of where it is from. However, in a world with increasing immigration controls, and where migration is politically charged, this can be a cumbersome endeavour. Governments all over the world, guided by political perspectives or under pressure from their voters, are taking an increasingly protectionist stance.

Prior to arrival there is the increasingly sensitive subject of immigration, and in particular work visas – a version of the "taking local jobs" argument. Consequently, some IPAs support investors' visa applications, while others have made the decision not to get involved.

For those IPAs that support applications, visas are a delicate matter. For example, when a company wants to bring a highly skilled employee to a new location, but the person in question is refused a visa or work permit, investors are likely to request help from the IPA. If the application is not resolved in the investor's favour, this may impact the opinion the investor has of the IPA, and may even impact their current and future investment decisions. For example, on large infrastructure projects it is not unusual for investors to, as a condition of their investment, insist that the host economy grant work visas to the investor's staff working on the project. Some Chinese companies have, on occasion, relocated hundreds and even thousands of their workers – in 2016 there were more than 260,000 Chinese workers involved in such projects in Africa.[7] In some African countries, tension between the investor (and its migrant staff) and the local community have emerged,[8] and hence is something IPAs need to be aware of when offering visa support services.

- **Description**: a fast-track service for obtaining visas or work permits. Immigration support services are usually designed to attract highly skilled talent and high net worth individuals.

  Permits are usually granted for a specific length of time, with either a maximum term of stay, say two years, or a minimum term of stay, when, for example, visas are granted to talent that is in short supply locally. The situation is different when visas are linked to investment, and are contingent on the applicant investing a minimum sum in local properties or businesses.
- **Main beneficiaries**: foreign employees, entrepreneurs with skills that are in high demand locally and foreign investors who bring capital.
- **Implementation**: a specific helpline to guide applicants on how to fill in papers and/or a priority desk to assist, on a preferential basis, those individuals who meet the necessary criteria. Services may be delivered by the IPA or by fast-track service lanes at the Visa Office.
- **Intended outcome**: minimise the time and effort required to obtain permits to enter, work and invest in a foreign country, and therefore make a location more attractive to highly skilled workers, high net worth individuals, as well as the HR teams of the foreign company.

The following example comes from Catalonia who has developed a programme to expedite visas for skilled worders as can be seen in Box 4.5.

Box 4.5 Catalonia's fast-track visa system

New fast-track visa system for highly skilled workers or international entrepreneurs

"The new legislation on visa and residence authorizations accelerates permit procedures for investors, entrepreneurs and highly qualified professionals, improving the business climate and making Catalonia more attractive to foreign investors.

This new framework facilitates the entry of investment and talent in order to foster economic growth and job creation in the following categories:

- Investors: investments in the purchase of property (€>500,000); €1M in equities and shares in Spanish companies; €2M in Spanish government bonds; €1M bank deposit.
- Entrepreneurs: innovative business plans that could be of special economic interest to Catalonia.
- Highly skilled workers: a higher education qualification and a salary greater than €28,000 as the national employment situation is no longer taken into account.
- Intra-company transfers: migrant workers relocated to Catalonia, having worked in the company for a minimum of 3 months (if they maintain their employment relationship and are paid their salary in their country of origin). A higher education qualification or 3 years' work experience is required.
- Training and R&D + Innovation: ideal for researchers, scientific and technological staff and teachers of universities and business schools.

The main benefits are:

Applications are streamlined: Visas are processed and approved in 10 working days. Residence permits are processed in 20 working days.

- Single residence and work permit.
- The national employment situation does not apply (i.e., workers in the domestic market who meet the requirements of a job profile do not have priority over foreigners).

- Joint applications for residence permits and/or visas for spouses and children.
- Applications for permits may be submitted to any public register.
- Freedom of movement within the Schengen member states."

Reproduced with kind permission from Catalonia Trade & Investment: www.catalonia.com.

4.2.5 Relocation services

Relocation services focus on the practical, on-the-ground aspects of helping employees move from one location to another. The need stems from investors bringing in highly skilled workers to help start, and later to grow, an investment. These highly skilled workers, who may come from head office, a subsidiary in another country or be a new but not local hire, will need support to relocate to the host economy.

- **Description**: relocation services are aimed at helping directors, employees and their families to quickly settle in a new location. Other terms used to describe these services include executive soft-landing services or executive concierge services. Typical services include help with:
  - Obtaining national identity cards
  - Registering with local tax authorities
  - Registering with local doctors
  - Opening bank accounts, which may require the provision of a support letter and help meeting any anti-money laundering requirements
  - Finding a home
  - Finding and applying for school or childcare places
  - Integrating into the international community through leisure and cultural activities, networking events and charitable or volunteering events
- **Main beneficiaries**: foreign employees and their families. The company also benefits from not having to divert resources to predominantly administrative and bureaucratic matters.

- **Implementation**: relocation services typically cover a wide range of activities, procedures and processes an employee and the company need to deal with quickly in order to settle in a location. These services may be provided in-house by the IPA or be outsourced to a specialist relocation company.
- **Intended outcome**: foreign companies' employees and their families quickly settle into a location and therefore become productive quicker.

The following soft-landing example comes from Spain (see Box 4.6).

Box 4.6 Invest in Andalucia's soft landing for investors

Invest in Andalucia made a concerted effort to strengthen its relationships with foreign investors. In particular, they launched a pilot scheme focussed on the provision of specialist relocation services to help multinational employees and their families integrate quicker into the region.

The scheme was a success, and in its first year Invest in Andalucia helped 321 employees from large corporations integrate into the area. In addition, Invest in Andalucia organised 14 networking events connecting new and existing investors with relevant contacts in the local business community.

Reproduced with kind permission from Invest in Andalucia: www.investinandalucia.es.

Services provided by Agencia de Innovación y Desarrollo de Andalucía (Agencia IDEA).

4.2.6 Recruitment services

According to McKinsey, a consultancy firm, "superior talent is up to eight times more productive."[9] The availability or shortage of talent depends on many variables including economic cycles, as discussed in the previous chapter, the pipeline of graduates studying in local institutions, job rotation, seasonality, etc. Moreover, as innovation and technology development increase, the demand for highly skilled workers also increases. Covid-19 has further accelerated the embracing of digital products and services. Hence skill shortages in certain sectors, particularly those that are growing fast, are likely to remain for some time.

- **Description**: help companies attract the right candidates.
- **Main beneficiaries**: foreign-invested companies who can more rapidly recruit appropriate candidates, and the jobseeker who can more easily find a (quality) job.
- **Implementation**: this will vary from basic signposting to talent portals to sophisticated programmes IPAs deliver together with external providers.
- **Intended outcome**: reduce the time it takes for foreign investors to become fully operational, create a vibrant local job market and increase a location's competitiveness.

The following examples come from award-winning IPAs: CINDE in Costa Rica (Box 4.7) and London & Partners (Box 4.8) in the UK.

Box 4.7 CINDE's recruitment fair

Some recruitment fairs have a particular focus, such as the annual fair organised by CINDE in Costa Rica that focusses on the recruitment of multilingual personnel, as this is the number one requirement to work in an international company, and is a skill that foreign investors have struggled with.

Over 50 leading companies, as well as academic institutions, participate, with an average of 6,000 attendees. In 2018 they also offered an online fair that attracted 15,000 participants who had the option to test their level proficiency in English, Portuguese and French. The language assessment proved valuable to participating foreign companies. The 2020 fair filled around 3,000 positions and attracted 8,500 attendees.

Participating companies: Amazon, SYKES, IBM, BAC Credomatic, Abbott, Accenture, Bayer, Brightstar, Citrix, Creganna Medical, CWT, EQUIFAX, Evonik, HP INC, Intertec, Kareo, Prodigious, Roche,

Smith & Nephew, Stryker, Tech Data, Thomson Reuters, Western Union, Align Technology, OTSI, Akamai, Auxis, BAXTER, Bimbo Global Services, BuildCR, Cardinal Health, Curtis Wright, Eurofinds IT, EY, GSK, Infosys, Infotree Global Solutions, Johnson Controls, Lion Resources, National Instruments, Neustar, Refinitiv, Lightstorm, Fujitsu, British American Tobacco, Cloudera, Teleperformance, Acuity, Knowledge Partners, Concentrix, Universidad Cenfotec and Health Prime.

Reproduced with kind permission from CINDE: www.cinde.org.

Other types of recruitment support include customised support for companies looking to recruit on a large-scale (over 100 roles). For example, Invest Korea offers support in producing PR content and holding consulting sessions and job interviews.[10] They also have an online recruitment support system that provides guidance to foreign invested enterprises about labour regulations in Korea, and run information sessions for foreign-invested companies to help them raise their profile and brand awareness.

Finally, London & Partner's efforts to provide quality information, signposting and introductions to carefully selected organisations has been praised as a talent one-stop-shop.

Box 4.8 London & Partners' Job and Talent Toolkit

"Find London's world-class talent in unexpected places, keep your best people and get guidance on employing people from overseas. Our Jobs and Talent Toolkit will help you hire, recruit and retain your workforce.

Explore the toolkit:

- **Visas and citizenship**: Find out about employing staff, how to become a visa sponsor and applying for citizenship. [The site provides further links to information]
- **Recruiting talent**: explore some of the key resources of hiring digital specialists graduates and apprenticeships. There's no better place in the world for growth than London, because

there's no better talent than the London workforce. Highly skilled, motivated, and with an international mindset, London's talent is ready to build your business. Explore some of the key resources for hiring digital specialists, graduates and apprentices. [The site provides links to recruitment sites, graduate recruitment, digital skills, apprenticeships, and how to get help from their expert recruitment partners.]

- **Recruiting multilingual talent**: London has a thriving international community, so it's no surprise that you can find a wide range of languages spoken in its talent pool. There are plenty of resources to help you access these foreign language skills should your business require them in its London offices. [The site provides links to Specific language recruitment, Multilingual recruitment agencies, Universities, Chambers of Commerce offering recruitment services]
- **Unexpected places to recruit**: think outside the box and hire exceptional individuals through unusual avenues. Tap into London's diverse talent pool to hire a strong and varied workforce. From committed ex-military personnel and hard-working former athletes, to underrepresented tech superstars and passionate returners, the capital is full of skilled people to recruit. To ensure your company is inclusive, consider working with a diversity recruitment. Take satisfaction in knowing that your new hires benefit the community as well as your business by working with charities and social enterprises. Work with specialist agencies to find individuals with the specific skillsets your business needs. Hire professional workers returning after a career break, who are passionate to get back into work. Find determined candidates who know the value of hard work by hiring a current or former professional athlete. Professional bodies are an excellent source of advice on reaching experts in particular fields, and many include specialist recruitment services. [the site provides links]
- **Universities**: London is famous for its higher education, with four of the world's top 40 universities among its offering (2019 Times Higher Education World University Rankings).

However, there are many more top-quality institutions in the capital, ranging from large multi-faculty universities to smaller specialists focused on business, law or finance. All of these are keen to work with employers to ensure their graduates get the best possible job opportunities. Visit StudyLondon for a list of London's principal university level institutions. A selection of graduate recruitment websites can be found on our recruiting talent page.

- **Developing Talent**: take advantage of the training workshops, mentoring and events in London: Getting your team together is key. You can find the right people in London, and you'll need to build on their skills and support them as your business evolves. When it comes to professional development, London has all you need, from formal training to workshops, mentoring and events. [The site provides links to further resources]."

Reproduced with kind permission from London & Partners: www.londonandpartners.com.

Link: https://business.london/invest/jobs-and-talent.

4.2.7 Spousal employment services

Spousal employment or engagement in the location is critically important when it comes to attracting talent, and yet is often overlooked. According to Talent Wars,[11] a quarterly report prepared by North American based DCI consultants, job opportunities for spouses are amongst the top 5 most important considerations in relocation decisions. Joann Lublin, a writer on business and management issues for the *Wall Street Journal*, says that "it's important for the *leading* spouse to find an equally significant career opportunity for the *trailing* spouse in their new location."[12] Lublin goes on to say that "over the course of a relationship between two ambitious people, it's worth noting, the leading spouse will alternate."[13] Indeed, some companies, particularly those in highly competitive industries, also help spouses to find work. This represents an opportunity for IPAs to further support companies seeking to attract talent, and can be a key differentiator.

- **Description**: provide job hunting support for the *trailing* spouse.
- **Main beneficiaries**: the relocating couple, the foreign investor, the employer that hires the trailing spouse and, ultimately, the location.
- **Implementation**: there are a number of ways to support the trailing spouse, including a partnership with a head-hunter, referral to job sites, support putting a CV together appropriate to the local market and introductions to networking events.
- **Intended outcome**: a location is more attractive to highly skilled workers and their partners.

The feature in Box 4.9 comes from the British social enterprise Recruit for Spouses. While they are not supported by or work with IPAs currently, they provide a blueprint of how IPAs could design spousal services.

Box 4.9 Recruit for Spouses

Recruit for Spouses helps military spouses find a job or start a business. They explain that their work "is not just about finding a job. It's about spouses re-establishing their identity and independence – building a fulfilling life that benefits them, their partners and their families." Launched in 2012, Recruit for Spouses helps around a thousand military spouses a year, partnering with companies such as Deloitte or Airbus, local SMEs and charities that support diversity in the workforce. Support includes writing CVs, interview training and skills development. While Recruit for Spouses only works with the Armed Forces, their approach offers lessons that others can learn from and build on.

Reproduced with kind permission from Recruit for Spouses: www.recruitforspouses.co.uk.

4.2.8 One-stop-shop

One-stop-shops, sometimes called single window or virtual shops, are exactly what they say: a single person or address an investor needs to go to that consolidates various services. There are two types. The *Letterbox*, where an IPA receives an investor's information requests and completed forms, sends them to the relevant government departments, collates the responses and sends them back to the investor, and the *Single-Point-of-Contact*, where a case manager is responsible for ensuring that an investor's documents are directed to the relevant departments and institutions and that responses are received.

- **Description**: a single point of contact, which can be physical or digital, from which investors interested in launching or expanding a business can obtain key documents, or to which they can submit applications for permits, registrations, planning permits, foreign investment certificates (if applicable), etc.
- **Main beneficiaries**: foreign companies expanding their business in a location, and public offices who benefit from faster, more streamlined applications.
- **Implementation**: care needs to be taken to ensure that the one-stop-shop does not become a "one-more-stop."[14] To avoid the creation of a new office with staff from a number of government departments, some IPAs choose a "virtual one-stop-shop," a single online interface where all required information is collected, and which then shares it with the relevant government departments, thereby significantly reducing registration times. To be effective, IPAs often need support from the highest levels of government to ensure frictionless coordination between different government departments.

  While the one-stop-shop approach does simplify matters for an investor, there are detractors who are concerned that staff seconded or transferred to a one-stop-shop risk losing their connection with their original department, thereby reducing their effectiveness. UNESCAP adds that there is also a "risk of building [a] massive and expensive bureaucratic super-agency undermining efficiency and [the] ability for rapid response."[15] Though UNESCAP also cites examples of where a one-stop-shop approach works well, such as the Economic Development Board (EDB) of Singapore, the Malaysian Industrial Development Authority (MIDA) and the Industrial Development Authority (IDA) of Ireland.

- **Intended Outcome**: the administrative burden on investors is reduced, therefore enabling them to enact their growth plans more quickly.

The next three examples provide a range of options of how to formulate a one stop shop. While Taiwan (see Box 4.10) offers a dedicated case manager, Yokohama (see Box 4.11) places emphasis on 24/7 accessibility, while Malaysia (see Box 4.12) focuses on post-investment facilitation for approved projects.

Box 4.10 One-stop-shop Invest Taiwan Service Center

In order to provide a more business-friendly investment service, and to attract international firms to invest in Taiwan, the Invest Taiwan Service Center (ITSC) offers a single point of contact for investors in the form of a "project-oriented, dedicated case manager with specific responsibilities, and customized start-to-finish service" approach to assisting investing firms. Once an investor's requirements are understood, the ITSC provides services to an investor throughout its investment journey, while also taking advantage of the administrative coordination mechanisms of various agencies and city and county governments to jointly assist firms in eliminating obstacles to investment, thereby accelerating the completion of investment projects in Taiwan.

The assistance offered is post-investment and is focussed on enabling investors to quickly and smoothly invest in Taiwan. Support includes:

- Help with overcoming obstacles, expanding operations and investing in start-ups.
- The Ministry of Economic Affairs (MOEA) assigns a dedicated project manager to investments of over NT$500 million.
- 24-hour response to any enquiry with customised information relevant to the investor.
- MOEA convenes inter-agency meetings to help resolve any relevant issues. Any problems that are not resolved by these

meetings are handled via the Executive Yuan's inter-agency, helping to speed up the investment project involved.

There is an extensive list of success stories on the ITSC's website, including their investment experience and operating practice.

Reproduced with kind permission from Invest Taiwan: www.investtaiwan.nat.gov.tw.

Link: https://investtaiwan.nat.gov.tw/showPage?lang=eng&search=serviceCenter_01.

Box 4.11 One-stop-shop Yokohama World Business Hotline

The City of Yokohama established the "Yokohama World Business Hotline," a 24/7 phone line acting as a one-stop-shop service, to address the wide variety of questions that established foreign investors have, as well as "making the human connection more relevant." This service offers a comprehensive signposting service and helps investors navigate the city.

Reproduced with kind permission form the City of Yokohama: www.ywbc.org.

Box 4.12 Malaysia's post-investment and infrastructure support division

Project Acceleration and Coordination Unit (PACU), a recently established unit in MIDA, provides end-to-end facilitation for all projects approved. PACU ensures a more accelerated process from the approval of projects right up to its implementation. The status of projects can be monitored and tracked in real-time through MIDA's digitalised system.

PACU assists and accelerates submitted applications and tracks the status of approval. Applications via e-Manufacturing License will be approved within two working days for non-sensitive industries.

PACU monitors the progress of project implementation (within 12 months from approval) through the implementation and monitoring system (ITMS).

PACU identifies and facilitates issues and challenges faced by companies in implementing their project and propose appropriate solutions.

PACU collaborates with federal and state government, service providers, investment promotions agencies, technical agencies and other related stakeholders.

The functions:

- To provide end-to-end facilitation including handholding services for all projects approved by the National Committee of Investment (NCI) through its Project Acceleration and Coordination Unit (PACU).
- To ensure acceleration from approvals of projects to its implementation through working closely with State Authorities, utility & telecommunication providers, Customs and environmental agencies.
- Responsible for managing the Upgrading of Existing Industrial Estate Infrastructure (INFRA) Fund.
- Undertakes periodic reviews of issues and formulate appropriate solutions for the smooth implementation and operation of projects.
- To provide dedicated assistance to investors.

Reproduced with kind permission from the Malaysian Investment Development Authority (MIDA): www.mida.gov.my.

4.3 Operational services

IPAs also offer a wide range of operational support services to investors, including human resources, production, facilities management, finances and sales. The following pages present 8 examples of operational services.

4.3.1 Support to find new premises

While the private sector often works closely with investors to help them find new premises, IPAs may be aware of sites not available on the open market, or of public regeneration programmes that could be of particular interest to investors.

- **Description**: providing information to foreign investors about available real estate, including new property developments, brownfield locations, office space and business parks. This can tie in with providing information on available grants.
- **Main beneficiaries**: foreign companies seeking to expand, and owners of available real estate assets.
- **Implementation**: IPAs have several options here. From introductions to property agents to partnering with data providers to leverage in-house databases. When it comes to data, relevant information includes cost, accessibility, use (industrial, commercial, residential, etc.), local amenities, lengths of lease, terms, access and costs to utilities, transport links, etc. Some locations have incorporated interactive online benchmarking tools to enable comparisons between different locations. This can be of particular benefit when working with local authorities or other local experts who can provide a level of detail sometimes not available to national IPAs. In addition, and in part thanks to the Covid-19 pandemic, locations are increasingly using technology, such as virtual reality tours and drone flyovers, to enable investors to assess potential sites from their home countries.
- **Intended outcome**: foreign investors are able to easily and quickly identify and assess potential locations to expand their businesses, and also to promote real estate opportunities.

The next two examples present two different approaches. The first one, from the Czech Republic (see Box 4.13), helps identify potential locations linked to economic development plans.

Box 4.13 CzechInvest helps investors find new premises

CzechInvest provides access to a selection of suitable locations and properties (including office space) nation-wide. CzechInvest operates through a network of regional offices that provide information on brownfield investment sites for more than 2,350 locations as part of the national Brownfield Regeneration Strategy.

Source: http://czechinvest.org/en/brownfields.

The second example, from Berlin (see Box 4.14), uses technology, notably 3D tools, to provide a better client experience.

Box 4.14 Berlin Economic Atlas: a 3D source of local data

The Economic Atlas shows Berlin in three different map views and provides comprehensive information about businesses, research institutes, planning regulations, co-working places, and other information in the surroundings of any selected address. By providing these different information types in the context of a three-dimensional model of the city, the Berlin Business Atlas makes it easy to find the perfect location for new or growing businesses. Use the search or the filter window to retrieve selected industry-specific and infrastructure information about spaces throughout the city of Berlin. Use it, for example, to quickly find out about nearby scientific institutions or which day care centres and schools are located in the vicinity.

You can choose between a 2D map view, an image-based 3D surface model, high-resolution oblique aerial images, and a planning view which shows important planning projects based on a 3D model from the Senate of Urban Development and Housing. To produce the Berlin Economic Atlas, the entire city area, including the BER airport, was photographed from the air in 2018 and a state-of-the art 3D model was calculated from the aerial images. This 3D meshmodel is enriched with more than 10,000 points-of-interests including companies, institutes, government agencies, business centre, and many more.

This model was created for non-commercial purposes, and it is not based on any commercially available 3D models. Rather, it was created on behalf of the Land of Berlin by the Senate Administration for Urban Development and Housing (Senatsverwaltung für Stadtentwicklung und Wohnen) and the Senate Administration for Economics, Energy and Public Enterprises (Senatsverwaltung für Wirtschaft, Energie und Betriebe) as well as Berlin Partner for Business and Technology.

Reproduced with kind permission from Berlin Partner for Business and Technology: www.berlin-partner.de/en.

Link: www.businesslocationcenter.de/en.

4.3.2 Export support services

Export support services are a well-established tool in economic development, and many governments make significant efforts to help local companies looking to export their products and services. Indeed, there have been situations where the provision of export support services has been a key reason why an investor chose to move to a location, for example Singaporean bases to address the Chinese market.

- **Description**: some IPAs, particularly those that cover both trade and investment, help foreign-owned companies participate in the export promotion programmes that are available to domestic companies.
- **Main beneficiaries**: foreign companies seeking to export their products or services.
- **Implementation**: most countries have established export promotion programmes, many of them supported by international organisations. IPAs introduce foreign investors to these programmes, and in some cases also endorse applications or secure places on these programmes for an investor.
- **Intended outcome**: foreign investors grow more rapidly due to faster export growth. Where growth does accelerate, this can have the additional benefit that should demand exceed (production) capacity, the investor may consider an expansion project in the location.

The following example comes from Hungary (see Box 4.15) where the IPA takes an active role in helping foreign investors export.

Box 4.15 Hungary's efforts to support investors to export to Slovakia

In March 2018, The Hungarian Investment Promotion Agency (HIPA) organised a suppliers' day for KIA whose purchasing department is based in Slovakia. 12 Hungarian companies took part, all hoping that in the future they would become part of Hyundai-KIA's supply chain.

In addition to serving the needs of large foreign investors, one of HIPA's key goals is to increase the revenue of Hungarian SMEs focussed on supplying foreign companies. This is particularly important in the automotive industry, where the major vehicle manufacturers are constantly asking their suppliers to play an ever-increasing role in the development of new vehicles. In order to promote and facilitate this growth, HIPA provides supplier training, professional advice and intermediary assistance between the foreign investor and the manufacturer free of charge.

Reproduced with kind permission from Hungarian Investment Promotion Agency: HIPA www.hipa.hu.

4.3.3 Support for regional expansion

It is quite common for an investor, once it has settled in a location, to seek to expand in the same geographical area, though not necessarily in the same country. This represents an opportunity for the local IPA to work with the investor and IPAs elsewhere in the country to ensure they maximise the chances that any expansion project stays in the country.

- **Description**: helping investors expand beyond their immediate location and into parts of the country that are the responsibility of other IPAs. Competition among locations to attract the initial FDI is normally fierce and is often a zero-sum game with only one winner. However, circumstances can change when an investor seeks to expand beyond its initial location. When this is the case, the first location may be in a position to advise an investor, suggesting other possible locations for further expansion. Conversely, the local IPA can also provide IPAs elsewhere in the country with insight about the investor, subject to any confidentiality agreements agreed with the investor, thereby increasing their chances of landing a further expansion project.

- **Main beneficiaries**: other locations in the country, and to a lesser extent the investor.
- **Implementation**: for an investor to receive high quality support from a second location, the regions and IPAs need to work together in a transparent and coordinated manner. Typically, a Memorandum of Understanding (MoU) is agreed between the respective IPAs (whether national to regional or between regional IPAs) to ensure alignment and clear communication.
- **Intended outcome**: an investor seeking to expand its operations chooses to do so in the same country. The investor also benefits from a seamless service from the IPA in the new location, as well as continuing to benefit from the service from the "original" IPA. A further benefit is to reduce the time to market for the second project, as the "sponsoring IPA" can help the "receiving IPA" reduce the time and cost of servicing their common client.

The next two examples provide insight into different approaches to regional expansions. The first example comes from Japan (see Box 4.16) where the national IPA works with local IPAs across the country to jointly support expansion by foreign investors.

Box 4.16 Japan's support for regional expansions

Japan External Trade Organization (JETRO) is a government-affiliated organisation that promotes trade and investment between Japan and the rest of the world.

One of the services provided by JETRO to locally-established foreign investors is help to expand within Japan. "Indeed, Jetro has launched a new division specifically to assist foreign-affiliated companies already operating in Japan who are looking to further invest.

This new division works with the 47 regional prefectures across Japan who can support an enterprise looking to expand its operations in the country."[16]

Source: https://www.jetro.go.jp/en/invest/foreign-affiliate_support/.

The second example shows international collaboration, albeit in a regional context. Here, the government of South Africa is helping neighbouring countries to attract investment from investors already established in locally (see Box 4.17).

Box 4.17 South Africa's role in aiding regional economic development

The Republic of South Africa takes a leadership role when it comes to "aiding the economic development of neighbouring countries."[17] The Department for Trade and industry helps locally based businesses to enter foreign countries. They do so by directing investors to peer agencies in neighbouring countries, arranging introductions to local IPAs, making sure investors are well networked locally and even providing support so that foreign investment projects secure funding via adequate deal structuring with financial institutions.

Source: www.thedti.gov.za.

4.3.4 Workforce development

It is well established that increasing the skills of the labour force is a key driver in accelerating economic growth and a pillar for investment attraction. Consequently, governments across the world develop and deploy programmes aimed at increasing the skills of the local workforce. Moreover, workforce development is important during all phases of the economic cycle. For example, the *New York Times* reported in 2017, the "lack of workers, not work, weighs on the [US] nation's economy."[18] The problem is particularly acute in Utah where labour shortages are slowing economic growth and, as the president of the Utah Manufacturers Association explained, "3.1 per cent unemployment is fabulous unless you're looking to hire people. [Their members] could grow faster, could produce more product, if [they] had the workers."[19] By the autumn of 2018 labour shortages had become even more acute in the US as the unemployment rate hit a 50-year low of 3.7%. This all changed abruptly with the Covid-19 pandemic, not only for the US, but globally. The International Labour Organisation (ILO) estimates a loss of "495 million full-time equivalent (FTE) jobs"[20] globally over 2020. The main priority in a phase of economic contraction is to generate new jobs, retain existing jobs, retraining and talent development to match new needs. Interestingly, according to the 2021 Deloitte Global Human Capital Trends survey, the top 5 outcomes that company executives seek to achieve with their work transformation efforts are improving the customer experience, increasing innovation, reducing costs, improving quality and doing new work.[21]

- **Description**: helping investors learn about, access and benefit from the various talent support schemes available locally, which may include tax benefits or vouchers to pay for skill conversion programmes. In addition, well-designed skills development programmes and training schemes can improve the viability of expansion projects where specialist or scarce skills are required; while in a situation where an investor is considering downsizing, restructuring, or even closing an operation, offering retraining support to affected employees can reduce the impact on a location.
- **Main beneficiaries**: foreign companies, their employees and the local workforce.
- **Implementation**: there are several ways an IPA can assist an investor:
  - By introducing investors to organisations that have talent development programmes in place, such as academic institutions, training centres and recruitment agencies;
  - By directing investors to providers of training grants or providing help with talent development funding applications; and
  - By designing and/or financing specialised training courses.
- **Intended outcome**: support foreign companies seeking to adapt their workforce development plans in response to both economic and business cycles. This includes attracting, developing and retaining higher quality employees, and deploying large-scale workforce

upskilling programmes. All efforts are geared towards helping foreign companies recruit and develop the talent they need, to become more productive, which by extension raises the competitiveness of the local workforce.

The following example presents Ontario's talent-related offer (see Box 4.18).

Box 4.18 Invest in Ontario's training offer

From advanced manufacturing to medical technology, financial services to forestry, Ontario companies have access to a robust pipeline of talent through the province's 44 colleges and universities that produce workforce-ready graduates at all skill levels, including nearly 50,000 STEM graduates annually. To complement their steady supply of talent, Ontario layers on employment programs and tax credits to further assist businesses to access new talent and upskill or reskill their existing workforce – critical factors to compete successfully in the global marketplace.

- Co-operative Education Tax Credit: hire business-ready undergrad, master's and PhD talent from Ontario universities and colleges with help from this 25–30% refundable tax credit (to a max of $3,000 per placement).
- IRAP Youth Employment Program: companies looking to develop new products are eligible to hire an intern to work on R&D innovation products.
- Canada-Ontario Job Grant: receive one-sixth of eligible training costs, to a max of $10,000 per person to train new or existing employees in Ontario.
- Northern Ontario Internship Program: the program provides recent graduates interested in launching and building their careers in Northern Ontario access to internships.
- Mitacs: an internship program for Ontario R&D projects covering 50% up to $15,000 and a postdoctoral fellowship program for companies looking to develop an in-house R&D team covering 50% of the $60,000 stipend per fellow per year.

Note: content reviewed at time of publication, but programs are likely to change and evolve over time. Please visit website for further details.

Reproduced with kind permission from Invest Ontario: www.investontario.com.

Link: https://www.investinontario.com/incentive-programs-and-services.

4.3.5 Raising an investor's profile

Investors always want to be well thought of by the locations and countries they invest in. In particular they want to maximise the positive PR they receive when they announce new investments and expansions. An example is provided in Box 4.19.

- **Description**: the local IPA helps a foreign company raise its profile in the local business community, particularly at the time of a significant event, such as the announcement of a new investment, the opening of a new facility, the expansion of an existing facility or the creation of new jobs.
- **Main beneficiaries**: the foreign investor, media companies as this type of support produces news, advertorials and content. This also strengthens a location's brand.
- **Implementation**: an IPA will, for example, organise launch events, secure VIP participation, support the opening of a new plant, provide social media support, connect the company with local journalists, etc.
- **Intended outcome**: investors and their affiliates have a higher and more positive profile in the local business community and, by extension, the profile of the location also increases.

Box 4.19 AzPromo support to help raise an investor's profile

AzPromo, the Azerbaijan Export & Investment Promotion Foundation, offers marketing support to foreign investors, by "establishing contacts with local advertising agencies and organising various business events aimed at establishing and developing cooperation between businesspeople."[22]

Source: http://azpromo.az/investments/our-services.

4.3.6 Saving costs

Foreign direct investment is by nature a capital-intensive endeavour. The foreign investor needs to cover the cost of opening a new office, hiring additional staff, increase administrative workload, buying machinery, just to name a few. Some IPAs look to reduce the costs investors encounter, consolidating different options that are available to local companies in a one single offer to raise awareness of these products among foreign investors.

- **Description**: help the investor access different cost saving options available locally. This can include signposting and help with applications
- **Main beneficiaries**: the foreign investor is the primary beneficiary of the cost savings.
- **Implementation**: identify possible cost saving programmes that are available locally, articulate their value and raise awareness of the benefit for foreign investors.
- **Intended outcome**: that foreign investors who qualify for the benefit takes up the programme.

The following examples comes from Ontario (see Box 4.20), IPA that prepared a cost saving offer to address energy costs.

Box 4.20 Supporting business costs in Ontario

Businesses operating in Ontario can tap into incentives and usage optimization programs for "cost of doing business" items such as utilities and capital investments.

Save-ON-Energy: a program to help industrial consumers manage and conserve their energy usage better.

Industrial Conservation Initiative (ICI): an initiative that supports large electricity consumers by charging global adjustments based on their contribution to the top 5 peak demand hours in a year, rather than on the total volume of electricity consumed.

Northern Industrial Electricity Rate Program (NIER): a program that assists Northern Ontario's largest industrial electricity consumers to reduce energy costs and sustain jobs. This program provides electricity rebates to qualifying participants that commit to the development and implementation of a comprehensive energy management plan and work to achieve energy efficiency and conservation targets.

Natural Gas: a program to help natural gas industrial consumers manage and conserve their energy usage better.

Capital Cost Allowance: businesses in Ontario can free up more capital for investments in business growth, innovation and productivity by writing-off a larger share of their capital costs in the investment year.

Note: content reviewed at time of publication, however programs are likely to change and evolve over time. Please visit website for further details.

Reproduced with kind permission from Invest Ontario: www.investontario.com

https://www.investinontario.com/incentive-programs-and-services.

4.3.7 Access to finance

New projects and expansions nearly always require funding. While large multinationals often use their own resources to finance their expansion plans, some companies require their subsidiaries to seek local funding to finance any expansion, invest in new equipment or simply to fund working capital. While some IPAs avoid this area, others play a broker role or even secure public funds, which they administer and distribute to the various beneficiaries. These IPAs are operating on the basis that if an investor can secure additional funding, it may result in further local jobs or in retaining local jobs.

- **Description**: make foreign investors aware of available grants, incentives, special loans and other financial products they can access to support the development of their operations in a location.
- **Main beneficiaries**: foreign companies considering changing the size of their existing operations through expansion or injecting additional capital to continue in operation.
- **Implementation**: some IPAs take a light-touch approach; they create a database containing information on available grants, incentives, soft loans, tax credits, etc. Other IPAs take a more "hand-holding" approach and support investors in meetings with funding providers, such as government agencies, local authorities, national agencies or international organisations (such as development banks), and may even help investors with the application process.
- **Intended outcome**: foreign investors secure additional financial support, thereby increasing the likelihood that an investor expands or remains in a location.

The following example from Hong Kong (see Box 4.21) shows the type of financial support they offer to both local SMEs and foreign investors.

Box 4.21 Examples of support to companies operating in Hong Kong

Examples of financial resources and policies to support companies operating in Hong Kong:

- Financial aid for equipment and marketing: the SME Loan Guarantee Scheme (SGS) secures loans of up to HK$6 million for companies that need working equipment or business capital, for up to 5 years.
- SME Export Marketing Fund (EMF) helps companies participate in overseas exhibitions and business missions and to place B2B advertising. It can fund up to 50% of approved expenditure, up to HK$100,000 per application, whichever is less, up to a cumulative total of HK$800,000 per enterprise.
- The SME Financing Guarantee Scheme can provide guarantee coverage of 50–100% depending on loans amounts, up to a maximum of HK$12 million.

- The CreateSmart Initiative provides financial support to SMEs in the creative industries, funding them to build their brand through participation in overseas exhibitions and competitions.
- For innovation and technology: the Innovation and Technology Fund (ITF) supports companies to upgrade their technology and inject innovative ideas into their business. Funding schemes include: the Enterprise Support Scheme (ESS), which provides 1-to-1 dollar matching of up to HK$10 million per project; R&D Cash Rebate Scheme (CRS), which provides a 40% cash return for a company's eligible expenditure in R&D; and the Enhanced Tax Deduction for R&D Expenditure allows 300% for the first HK$2 million in eligible R&D expenditure and 200% thereafter, with no cap.

The above are examples of funding and policy initiatives to help companies in targeted areas. The information is correct as of the time of going to press. There are over 40 such programmes and initiatives supporting companies operating in Hong Kong, and each is regularly reviewed and enhanced as needed. For the most up-to-date information, please visit: https://www.investhk.gov.hk/en/resource-centre.html.

Reproduced with kind permission from Invest Hong Kong: www.investhkk.gov.hk.

European IPAs often offer support services to investors for both public and private sources of funding. Services focused on providing information and access to public sources of funding include:

- Providing information on available incentives, grants and aid (national, regional and local).
- Inviting companies to apply to public sector programmes, such as innovation competitions, which provide funding to implement a proposed solution.
- Setting up a fund tailored to foreign investors. For example, Sodena, the financial arm of the Government of Navarra in Spain, supports

both local and foreign businesses established in Navarra with venture capital.[23]
- Facilitating access to export financing aid support, which foreign investors sometimes don't realise they are eligible for.
- Supporting applications to international funds, such as the regional development programmes managed by the European Bank for Reconstruction and Development (EBRD).

Services focussed on private sector sources of funding include:

- Making introductions to banks, local cooperatives and foundations.
- Providing introductions to investment funds, for example in London the local IPA has set up the VC Club, which is only available to established foreign investors.[24]
- Encouraging participation at pitching opportunities, such as the Amsterdam Capital Week (see Box 4.22), to support fundraising for start-ups.
- Making introductions to locally based business angels and to high-net worth individuals.
- Providing introductions to local diaspora who are interested in building financial connections with their homeland.[25]
- Supporting crowdfunding initiatives. While a relatively new form of finance, crowdfunding is being studied by the European Crowdfunding Network (ECN), in collaboration with the European Association of Regional Development Agencies (EURADA), as a tool to support company growth. In their 2017 paper, Promoting the Benefits of Civic Crowdfunding, they report that "most of the European Regional Development Agencies (RDAs) are already promoting loans, guarantee schemes and venture capital to contribute to financing private investment. Implementation of a matching fund tool can amplify the impact of these funds."[26] They observe that crowdfunding is "an effective tool to engage citizens, [and] enhance overall transparency while [also] boosting capital efficacy."[27]

Important though funding or funding support often is to securing investment, it is a complex and sensitive area, and so managing expectations is key. This is particularly true of public sector funding. While investors are keen to gain access to public funding, particularly grants or incentives, they are unlikely to estimate correctly the workload required to access these funds – funds that may have very specific objectives. Hence, funding applications often fail because they don't, or don't articulate how they do, meet the requirements necessary to access these funds. For example, only 14% of applications to Horizon 2020, a European Business support Programme funded by the European Union, succeed.[28]

Similar outcomes have been seen in the private sector, with some VCs reporting success rates of less than 10%, while those VCs active in more competitive sectors report success rates closer to 1%. Venture capital funding is relevant for FDI, as many companies rely on VC funding to execute their expansion projects. Expansion fuelled by VC funding includes disruptors like Uber or AirBnB, and most recently Cornershop.[29] This Chilean-Mexican grocery delivery start-up is already present in 7 countries including Canada, Mexico and Colombia, backed with funds from ALLVP, a Mexican VC firm, and has a long queue of prospective buyers, including Walmart and Uber, seeking to help it enter the USA and Brazil,[30] moving the company to unicorn status in less than 4 years.

Providing fundraising support services is often time-consuming, resource-intensive and requires sector expertise. Hence some IPAs hire staff with experience of managing funds or in investment banking, while others partner with third parties to whom they channel funding requests. A further group choose to partner-up with private sector initiatives, as Amsterdam does, while some IPAs have chosen not to provide any funding support to investors.

Box 4.22 Amsterdam Capital Week

Amsterdam Capital Week is a private sector initiative, supported by Dutch business support organisations, which seeks to channel investment capital towards start-ups.

The perfect opportunity to explore the Amsterdam start-up and capital ecosystem and connect to other investors is during Amsterdam Capital Week. The week is held annually in Amsterdam in the last week of September. For 5 days, there is an intense focus on capital, creating exceptional opportunity for start-ups, scale-ups and investors.

The week features high-level events covering capital for the various phases of start-ups and scale-ups. Amsterdam Capital Week is about two-way connections: all participants – start-ups and investors – get to pitch, meet and learn to inspire new investments and long-term partnerships.

After 5 years of growing Amsterdam Capital Week (connecting around 3,000 startups & scale-ups with 500+ investors annually) and helping shape the Dutch start-up ecosystem, the organisation has now evolved into Amsterdam Capital House. Focusing on connecting purpose-driven founders, building a closer ecosystem and creating meaningful connections with capital (human, social and financial capital).

Reproduced with kind permission from Capital Week Amsterdam: www.capitalweek.amsterdam.

4.3.8 Expanding investors' local networks

Connectedness is one of the pillars of both company growth and economic development. Sophisticated foreign investors often commit significant time and resources to developing strong networks as this helps them become both more agile and more resilient.

- **Description**: carefully selected introductions to networks and individuals who can support an investor in their growth journey and provide support and advice, and also invitations to appropriate events and conferences.
- **Main beneficiaries**: foreign affiliates.
- **Implementation**: match-make investors with other local stakeholders who have similar or complimentary agendas. IPAs should also build and maintain a database of people and organisations who can support a foreign investor at different stages of their journey. This includes, for example, identifying key connections within export programmes that investors can connect with, programmes that many IPAs run in parallel to FDI.

- **Intended outcome**: connectedness on a local scale where foreign investors develop strong business and social networks in the local area and vice versa.

The following examples provide different approaches to networking: Turkey (see Box 4.23) offers support with public sector, while Invest in Bavaria (see Box 4.24) promotes their global networks.

Box 4.23 Expand your network in the public sector in Turkey

"One of the essential services provided by the Investment Office to newcomers and the existing investor community in Turkey is the coordination and maintenance of relationships with governmental bodies, local authorities, business associations, and other stakeholders such as universities, service providers, and non-governmental organizations. The Investment Office plays a key role in facilitation of organizing ad-hoc B2B and B2G meetings, functioning as a bridge between the government, private sector, and investors. In order to provide smooth entry into Turkey, the Investment Office assists with the initial introductory connections and meetings with potential suppliers, customers, and service providers based upon the needs of the related investment project and investors."

Reproduced with kind permission from the Investment Office of the Presidency of the Republic of Turkey | T.C. Cumhurbaşkanlığı Yatırım Ofisi: www.invest.gov.tr.

Box 4.24 Expand your network worldwide with Invest in Bavaria

Our Services: Growing in Bavaria

- A worldwide network of Bavarian representatives abroad, whose work will benefit your plans for possible internationalisation

- Brokering contacts for foreign companies to communities, institutions and organisations from your home country in Bavaria (if required).
- Information about useful company databases and sector networks which serve your purposes.
- Invitations to networking events and information about events held by our partners."

Reproduced with kind permission from Invest in Bavaria: www.invest-in-bavaria.com.

Link: https://www.invest-in-bavaria.com/en/how-we-can-help/our-service.html.

4.3.9 Enabling public procurements

The World Trade Organization estimates that on average public procurement accounts for 10–15% of a country's Gross Domestic Product (GDP).[31] Public, a UK-based venture capitalist firm and the founders of GovTechSummit, observes that "for the modern state, there are few policy priorities as important as how it buys."[32] Indeed, public services face multiple challenges as "citizens want better services. Officials want to be able to use better technologies. Politicians want better outcomes at lower prices." Public procurement is, at the same time, at the very heart of these challenges as well as the opportunities for improvement and innovation through its purchasing power.

- **Description**: facilitate access to government procurement opportunities at local, federal, regional and national level.
- **Main beneficiaries**: foreign investors seeking to secure a client and public procurement offices looking for quality suppliers and innovation.
- **Implementation**: these services vary in depth and can start with signposting to online procurement portals and the provision of information about the public procurement process. Some IPAs, for example, facilitate introductions to procurement officers, broker

opportunities, encourage suppliers to consider working with the government and support training to obtain supplier certifications. These services are usually provided as a programme, with activities scheduled for the whole year.

- **Intended outcome**: the best possible procurement options for public buyers, in particular maximising options to win business, while minimising the time and resources spent in the process. At the same time, it fosters public-private collaboration and innovation.

The following example comes from Business Sweden (see Box 4.25), who offer specialised services to help clients better engage with the public sector not only in Sweden, but internationally.

Box 4.25 Business Sweden enables public procurements

"Do you mainly do business with the public sector in international markets? If so, our Business to Government services can help you succeed and grow sales globally.

How we can help: The relation[ship] to government representatives and other public sector stakeholders can be a make-or-break factor for success. Thanks to our dual public and private ownership, we have connections that give maximum value from public partnerships abroad.

Our services: By analysing the public sector in your markets, we can help you navigate complex regulations and create a targeted strategy. We can also provide access to and aid communication with stakeholders at all levels of state-owned organisations and departments.

What you can expect: Our services save you time and effort to understand complex regulations, taking the shortest route to market. You will also increase your chances of winning public deals and minimise the risk associated with global expansion significantly.

All our services are tailor-made. Here is a selection of common questions about global B2G-strategies and how we can help.

Can you help me create an international B2G strategy?

Absolutely! Creating a solid strategy that takes local conditions into account can make a huge difference and set you on the right track from the start. This is how we can help:

- Develop a tailor-made growth strategy and tactical plan.
- Keep you updated on regulatory changes in the local market.
- Solve regulatory challenges that may arise if you offer innovative solutions or a new business model.

How do I find and get access to relevant stakeholders?

We understand that it is a challenge for many companies to identify who the relevant government stakeholders are, let alone shape a message that suits them – especially in an international market where the cultural values are new to the company. And yet it is so important to develop good working relations with government representatives for a successful business venture within the public sector. This is how we can help:

- Identify key contacts, explain the role they play and how they interact with each other.
- Help you to complete proposals and submit tenders.
- Give advice on the opportunities of partners and alliances.

I'd like to streamline my communications for the public sector in a new market. Can you help?

Getting a company's message across in a remote market is a delicate affair. It must be adapted to the local market context and placed in channels where the intended recipients will consume the message. This requires deep knowledge not only of the local stakeholders and media channels, but also of your offering, company culture and communication style. This is how we can help:

- Plan and create an effective communication strategy.
- Use our networks, media contacts, and international meeting arenas to support your communication efforts.
- Tailor your marketing messages to the local context and key stakeholders, ensuring that you reach the intended audience effectively.
- Lower policy hurdles and increase public-sector demand.

I have contacts in the public sector but would like to improve our work relations. What can I do?

We know that it can be hard to develop good work relations between your company and the government representatives in a market with a different culture. Business Sweden's business developers are well aware of the local business climate and understand that a well-crafted tactical approach is needed for a successful public sector business venture. This is how we can help:

- Use our extended contact network to identify important stakeholders.
- Create settings and forums that aid transparent communication.
- Bridge cultural differences and help you to get your message across in the right context."

Reproduced with kind permission from Business Sweden: www.business-sweden.com.

Link: https://www.business-sweden.com/services/business-to-government/.

4.3.10 International treaties and the foreign investor

As noted by the OECD, "the quality of a country's investment environment is also strongly influenced by its international investment related commitments."[33] Providing information about international treaties, bilateral and free trade agreements to investors, and also insight into how these agreements are relevant to them, is a service that is growing in importance. This is because few foreign investors are familiar with the details of topics such as double taxation, foreign ownership restrictions, customs duties and immigration rules, and in particular how they will affect their business.

- **Description**: information services about these treaties not only seek to overcome the asymmetry of information, but also to encourage the take up of opportunities created by international treaties.

- **Main beneficiaries**: foreign affiliates and the regulatory bodies that oversee these treaties.
- **Implementation**: the first step is to provide up-to-date information on the key parts of any trade agreements, whether on paper or online. The second step is to advise investors as to how they can best exploit these treaties and agreements.
- **Intended outcome**: raise awareness about the opportunities provided by investment treaties, and that these opportunities are then exploited by investors.

The examples of help with treaties comes from Ecuador as can be seen in Box 4.26.

Box 4.26 Help with conventions and international treaties signed by Ecuador

Ecuador has trade agreements that offer access to markets totalling more than 1,000 million people across ALADI, the Andean Community and the European Union.

Existing agreements: The Cartagena Agreement (CAN), EU (28), ECA 59 MERCOSUR, PSA 29 Mexico, PSA 42 Guatemala, ECA 65 Chile, PSA 46 Cuba, Nicaragua, El Salvador, CEPA EFTA, United Kingdom.

Agreements under negotiation: Mexico, Pacific Alliance.

The Ministry of Production, Foreign Trade, Investments and Fisheries provides information about these treaties and advises investors how the treaties can benefit them.

Reproduced with kind permission from the Ministry of Production, Foreign Trade, Investments and Fisheries from Ecuador and ProEcuador. www.proecuador.gob.ec

4.4 Strategic services

Strategic services are aimed at encouraging and supporting the development of higher value-added products and services for foreign investors. Strategic services are typically delivered in partnership with a wide variety of stakeholders, and are often aligned with a government's sectorial, geographic or economic strategy in order to maximise their impact. Given the cost and complexity of providing these services, they may only be offered to a few clients. The following pages explore some examples of strategic services from around the world.

4.4.1 High-level networking

A business can become established more quickly, and also generate more local support, by developing strong networks, particularly with influential people in the local, and where appropriate national, business community, and also with other important stakeholders such as local politicians and community leaders. Therefore, IPAs need to understand the requirements and ambitions of foreign companies so that they can facilitate the most appropriate introductions.

- **Description**: introducing the senior management team of a foreign affiliate to high-level private sector networks, national policy advisers, international organisations and thought leaders, which may be of benefit both to the investing company and the local organisations.
- **Main beneficiaries**: the foreign investor and prospective partners.
- **Implementation**: introducing a company's leaders to relevant parties and organisations requires a thorough understanding of the needs and strategic direction of a company. As a consequence, this service needs to be tailored to each individual company. In support of this, IPAs need to maintain a relevant and up-to-date knowledge base of opportunities. A word of caution: IPAs are advised to check their local lobby regulations and make sure they have the right protocols in place to comply with potential requests of disclosure of these introductions.
- **Intended outcome**: help a foreign investor develop strong networks in a location that enable it to grow more quickly, keep up-to-date with the latest developments in a location and be in a position to influence developments where appropriate.

4.4.2 Brokering of major investment opportunities

Foreign investors may consider investing in a location in areas unrelated to their initial investment, sometimes with profits they are unable or unwilling to repatriate. IPAs are well-positioned to introduce investment opportunities to foreign companies, particularly where they relate to government programmes, notably infrastructure development.

- **Description**: introduce foreign investors seeking to diversify or invest surplus cash to investment opportunities related to the development of infrastructure or the regeneration of local areas. This could include investment in industrial parks, roads, bridges, the construction of fibre optic networks, etc.
- **Main beneficiaries**: local projects, which become (better) funded, while the foreign company benefits from access to an investment opportunity.
- **Implementation**: due to the size of infrastructure projects, specialist expertise is often required to articulate an opportunity to investors. While some major infrastructure projects are promoted and developed by governments, many locations partner with private real estate consultants, infrastructure companies and other advisers to present opportunities to investors, and then to negotiate the associated contracts.
- **Intended outcome**: foreign investors invest in local infrastructure projects, thereby accelerating the development of the local economy.

The following example is from Mexico (see Box 4.27), which has built a website that consolidates major investment opportunities in infrastructure and energy investment across the country.

Box 4.27 Mexico Project Hub

The Mexico Project Hub is a Federal Government initiative that provides information on the country's most important infrastructure and energy projects seeking support from the private sector. The platform is operated by Banobras (Banco Nacional de Obras y Servicios Publicos) and provides information about more than 400 investment opportunities, including details of each project, the organisations involved, the government department that manages the project, timelines and the likely procurement model.

Reproduced with kind permission from the Mexico Project Hub.

Link: http://www.proyectosmexico.gob.mx/en/home/.

4.4.3 Business case services

Foreign investors regularly reassess their overseas investments and subsidiaries to establish whether or not they are still aligned with the group's strategy, and hence whether they should be expanded, shrunk or closed. IPAs can help a local subsidiary by providing research data and insights into markets and locations of interest to the investor, and also into the supply chain effectiveness of the foreign investor.

- **Description**: provision of consultancy services that help foreign investors to assess the opportunity for them to upgrade their presence in their host country by bringing in new products and higher added value services, to benchmark the current location against an alternative location or to assess the cost of exiting.
- **Main beneficiaries**: foreign affiliates, particularly those competing for expansion funds with sibling affiliates (located in other countries) and companies in distress.
- **Implementation**: IPAs help foreign investors to prepare business plans to be presented to their parent companies. Support might include identifying potential areas of improvement in the company's value chain, or benchmarking costs against another location the investor may be considering. In such a scenario, IPAs should seek to provide detailed information about supply chain costs, competitors, local suppliers and any other relevant data that could support the case for investment or retention.
- **Intended outcome**: foreign affiliates upgrade or expand their local operations, or, where they were originally considering downsizing or closing a facility, retain it.

The following example comes from Copenhagen Capacity (see Box 4.28), who offer as part of their value proposition help for investors wishing to consolidate Nordic operations in the Danish capital.

Box 4.28 Upgrading products in Copenhagen

"Our business is to grow yours

Build a strong business case to prove the value of your investment or business set-up in Greater Copenhagen.

Before you establish or expand your business in Greater Copenhagen, you need to create a strong, convincing business case that will prove the value of your investment.

Our business consultants can:

- Benchmark the performance cost/quality wise of your potential set-up whether it is European headquarters, R&D center, Center of Excellence or a shared services centre against other European or worldwide city regions.
- Give you industry insights and connect you to potential partners, research institutions, business network etc. relevant for you to build relations to.
- Identify potential new business opportunities for you in Greater Copenhagen.
- Provide information on legal and financial framework conditions to optimise the performance of your set-up.

Is your set-up in Greater Copenhagen being challenged by Headquarters, or do you have an opportunity to expand your present set-up with more business functions or responsibility?

If you are already located in Greater Copenhagen, and your company's strategy are [is] changing in a way that could affect your corporate structure, we can assist you in building a strong convincing business case for retaining and expanding your set-up in Greater Copenhagen.

It will be based on the same argumentation as above, as these fact-based and neutral benchmarks and comparisons are as equally important whether you have to justify your presence in Greater Copenhagen or experience an opportunity to attract new business functions."

Reproduced with kind permission from Copenhagen Capacity.

Link: https://www.copcap.com/how-we-help/aftercare.

4.4.4 Mentoring programme

Being the CEO is often a lonely job. The job may be even more lonely in a foreign country, foreign culture and foreign business environment. A local business mentor can help a leader navigate many challenges, thereby increasing the likelihood that the leader, and by extension the business they are leading, will succeed.

- **Description**: foreign business leaders of local affiliates are introduced to experienced business mentors who have the ability to support and guide them as they seek to establish and grow their business, and in particular when they may face particular challenges. Funding for this type of programme may come from the IPA or another government department such as the department for innovation or SME Support. A foreign investor might also be eligible to access any leadership skills incentives programmes run either locally or by international organisations focused on increasing local business capability. IPAs usually play a brokering role.
- **Main beneficiaries**: the senior management team of the local affiliate.
- **Implementation**: these services are often outsourced to consultancies or developed in partnership with academic institutions.
- **Intended outcome**: leaders of local affiliates become better leaders, run their business more effectively, thus accelerating the development of their companies.

The example comes from Ireland, an IPA that is well-known for working closely with local stakeholders (see Box 4.29).

Box 4.29 Mentoring programmes in Ireland

IDA Ireland offers, in partnership with Enterprise Ireland, a unique mentoring scheme with the "purpose is to support leaders to identify and overcome obstacles to the development and growth of their activities in Ireland. Mentors in our network can provide tailored advice, guidance and support, to help you accelerate growth and build management capability."[34]

This programme, originally designed for domestic firms, has been extended to foreign investors. In their service brochure they explain that "mentors are senior executives, drawn from the private sector, with a proven track record in business. They act as a confidential sounding board, advising you as the Mentee on key operational and strategic issues."[35]

The programmes make every effort to match business needs with mentors' expertise and to do so, they have support from an extensive network of "CEOs and senior executives with high levels of achievement and with proven skills in marketing, strategic development, organisation development, R&D, funding, building corporate relationship and influencing across the global footprint. Mentors come from a variety of sectors such as software, services, life sciences, environment, engineering and consumer products."[36] Companies apply to the programme and, once approved, a shortlist of qualified mentors is presented to the company.

Source: Brochure IDA Ireland Mentor Programme https://www.idaireland.com/IDAIreland/media/HowWeHelp/IDA_Mentor_Programme.pdf.

4.4.5 Benchmarking services

Understanding the relative competitiveness of a business is a key part of understanding the opportunities a business has for improvement and growth. A few IPAs, such as Ireland, help investors benchmark the performance of their local affiliates with other companies, both local and international.

- **Description**: provide training and tools to measure a company's performance against national and international competition. This service often includes a gap analysis as well as potential areas for improvement for the business to consider.
- **Main beneficiaries**: the foreign investor.
- **Implementation**: benchmarking services are often performed by an external organisation, such as a university or a private sector

consultancy. In order to benchmark a company, the appropriate key performance indicators (KPIs) to measure need to be provided by the investor for their company. These KPIs are then compared with industry standards.

- **Intended outcome**: foreign investors are equipped with insights that can help them become more competitive.

The following box comes from Ireland (see Box 4.30), where the national IPA offers a pioneering benchmark analysis.

Box 4.30 IDA Ireland's competitiveness benchmark

IDA Ireland offers a competitive benchmark analysis in partnership with Enterprise Ireland.

"A Competitiveness Benchmark will measure a company's performance compared to its competition, identify strengths and weaknesses of the company and be a springboard for improving competitiveness and growing the business."[37] The goal is to "improve a company's competitive position and help target business areas for further improvement, in order to deliver best in class products or services."[38]

The programme is carried out in three stages, with the assistance of a trained facilitator, and seeks to establish "the company's competitiveness against international standards/companies. It includes a summary of the company's strengths and weaknesses under six business areas namely: Strategy and Productivity, Finance, Marketing, Operations, Innovation and Human Resources, Company Commitment/Cost."[39]

Source: Brochure IDA Ireland Competitive Benchmark – Measuring Company Competitiveness: https://www.idaireland.com/IDAIreland/media/HowWeHelp/IDA_Competitiveness_Benchmark.pdf.

4.4.6 Working with academia

Academia can and does make a significant contribution to business. However, many businesses overlook, or don't make the effort to explore, the opportunities that collaborating with academia can bring to their business, particularly those businesses seeking to innovate.

According to the Confederation of British Industry (CBI), which speaks for more than 195,000 UK businesses, academia plays a vital role in igniting business growth. In their 2015 report, "Best of Both Worlds: guide to business-university collaboration", the CBI noted that there was a need to help "businesses understand how to get the best from the opportunities universities offer, whether it be collaboration on research, innovation or skills."[40] IPAs can facilitate this by bringing these sometimes "distant" parties closer together. The report also noted that "there is a burgeoning community of interest in new forms of business-university collaboration for skills development, and a dynamic marketplace in 'learn-while-you-earn' models of study which enable students to support their study and career development by remaining in work or building links with the workplace."[41] The report continues, indicating that "more and more businesses are working with universities in a variety of ways to build a competitive edge around the skills of their current and future employees."[42] The CBI identified 4 key benefits for companies from working with academia:

- Links with universities can help give firms gain a *competitive edge* by giving them early access to innovation.
- Universities play a vital part in the *innovation ecosystem*. They can develop partnerships with both small and large businesses, and are well placed to lead on knowledge transfer initiatives that can result in further innovation. Universities are also always on the lookout for new ideas and can provide early warning of potential new opportunities or threats (from, for example, a new technology that might replace an existing one).
- By their very nature, universities have access to an unrivalled list of research topics and can also provide introductions to unusual or difficult to access innovation hubs. Companies, even those with significant resources, sometimes struggle to keep up with the pace of innovation, and hence connecting with academia can offer opportunities as it is ideally placed to triangulate partnerships and collaboration with the private sector.
- Collaboration can also help win the "war for talent" by helping to develop skills, improve capabilities and raise profiles in order to attract the best talent.

Expenditure on research and development (R&D) in OECD higher education institutions is huge, about $160 billion per annum, and hence businesses "that don't work with universities may be missing opportunities of significant proportions."[43] IPAs can play a role in articulating the benefits of partnerships with local education centres and build on the many benefits university-business partnerships bring to a local economy.

- **Description**: provision of services that connect academia with business. This is likely to be primarily in the area of R&D.
- **Main beneficiaries**: both the company and the innovation team at the university.
- **Implementation**: these programmes may be offered by academic institutions and can be highly tailored to business needs. The IPA will require a deep understanding of local academic capabilities and the ambitions of local companies in order to be in a position to arrange valuable introductions.
- **Intended outcome**: strengthen joint innovation capability, increase the transfer of knowledge, accelerate the rate that innovation is brought to market and support the development of a specific industry sector.

An example of working with academia is provided by CINDE Costa Rica (see Box 4.31).

Box 4.31 CINDE's collaboration with academia

CINDE, the Costa Rican IPA, works closely with the National Training Institute (INA) to connect foreign investors with INA's training programmes. These training programmes are funded by the employer payroll tax, and are therefore free for investors. INA also designs tailored training programmes to meet specific investor needs that are not met by their normal programs under what they call "Academic Collaboration Models". Furthermore, INA has signed partnerships with international universities, such as one for medical devices with the University of Minnesota, and one with the bioengineering faculty at Rice University in Texas, as a means of securing high-quality research and access to experts in topics and sectors that are important to investors.

CINDE's efforts do incorporate the INA (Training Institute) but go beyond this institution to create national and international academic alliances with centres such as University of Minnesota, Rice, Texas Tech, Fraunhofer Institute in Germany or a more recent alliance with Coursera and its global workforce recovery skills development programme, launched during the pandemic.

Reproduced with kind permission from CINDE: www.cinde.org.

4.4.7 Supporting innovation

According to the 2007 OECD report, "Innovation and Growth Rationale for an Innovation Strategy", "undoubtedly the capability to innovate and to bring innovation successfully to market will be a crucial determinant of the global competitiveness of nations over the coming decade."[44] This is likely to continue to be the case in the medium term. The study also outlined similarities between FDI and innovation, notably that increases in R&D and innovation are driven by two factors related to foreign investors. The first is "a low level of restrictions on foreign direct investment, which can improve cross-border knowledge transfers,"[45] in other words, making it easier to invest in a location is likely to increase investment in innovation. The second factor is "openness to foreign R&D, which is associated with higher productivity growth, especially when domestic R&D investment and domestic capabilities are also high."[46] By working to strengthen the links between foreign investors and local innovation centres, IPAs can help increase the amount of R&D an investor performs locally.

Another OECD study, the "2008 Open Innovation in Global Networks,"[47] found that for open innovation (innovation that embraces external cooperation) the principal reason for locating a R&D facility abroad is the proximity of large and growing markets – customers and suppliers are the most sought-after innovation partners. Other important factors include the availability of engineers and researchers, and the company's proximity to other activities (production, sales). While universities and public research institutes are generally considered an important source of knowledge for companies' innovation activities, especially in the more upstream areas of research and exploration, in reality they represent only a small proportion of innovation collaborations. The OECD study also confirmed that proximity matters, as companies, unsurprisingly, prefer innovation partners who are geographically close. These factors are all in the sweet spot of what many IPAs already do, and hence improving connectedness amongst these parties should be a logical extension of the work of an IPA.

Academics Emilia Rovira Nordman and Daniel Tolstoy from the Stockholm School of Economics studied what impact the connectedness of Swedish SMEs acting in foreign markets had on innovation. They observed that companies require a higher level of connectedness "to convert opportunities into innovative outcome(s) when acting in foreign market(s) compared to doing the same in their home market"."[48] They go on to say that "when opportunities become increasingly contextually remote, the importance of collaborative business relationships increases."[49] This suggests that IPAs have a role to play in helping established foreign SMEs become more connected locally, and hence to increase the likelihood that their innovations will be successful.

Michael Olabisi, an assistant professor in Community and Sustainability at Michigan State University, studied the impact of exporting and foreign direct investment on innovation at Chinese manufacturers between 2005 and 2007.[50] He found that exporters are more likely to be exposed to the challenges their clients face and to focus their efforts on finding solutions to those challenges. He further notes that the mere fact of exporting is likely to lead to innovation. This process, referred to as "learning-by-exporting" is a strong predictor of product innovation. The study revealed that 20% of exporters developed new products, whereas only 14% of non-exporters innovated. "Firms that receive foreign capital investment also tend to engage in more product innovation, but not at the same level as the firms that export."[51] Moreover, Olabisi's analysis showed that when it comes to new product development the relationship is reversed, with development occurring at a level of only "19% for Chinese-owned firms innovating from scratch, while only 13% of majority foreign-owned firms did."[52] This suggests that when it comes to inventing something completely new, it is local linkages that matter most, but when it comes to improving existing products, it is global connectedness which makes a difference.

Another study by academics Luong et al,[53] titled "How Do Foreign Institutional Investors Enhance Firm Innovation?" examined the effect of foreign institutional investors on firm innovation. Using data from 26 non-U.S. economies between 2000 and 2010, it found that foreign institutional ownership has a positive, causal effect on firm innovation. The paper explored underlying mechanisms through which foreign institutions affect firm innovation, and identified that foreign investors "promote innovation by acting as active monitors, by providing insurance against innovation failures to firm managers with career or reputational concerns, and by promoting knowledge spill-overs from high innovation countries."[54]

Several other studies have also explored the link between foreign investment and innovation. Many of them outline the link between innovation and connectedness and provide insights that can help the design of innovation support programmes. Moreover, most of the factors that drive innovation are in areas where many IPAs are already active, including availability of talent, introductions to suppliers, connections with universities and local linkages. Aftercare teams are therefore well placed to facilitate linkages and to support an innovation agenda. It is therefore no surprise that 56% of OECD IPAs have an innovation mandate.[55] Irrespective of whether or not the innovation function is inhouse, close collaboration between the innovation team of the foreign investor and the IPA can result in significant benefits.

- **Description**: to support innovation and facilitate access to innovation that develops new products or processes, improves existing ones and increases local competitiveness.
- **Main beneficiaries**: innovation is usually a cooperative effort. The first beneficiary of innovation services are the innovators, who may be local or foreign, and may be a private company or a research institute looking to commercialise their research. In this situation the support tends to follow an Ecosystem logic where the focus is not on who the innovator is, but on how they add value to another player in the Ecosystem and what type of connections are needed to develop the innovation into a commercial proposition, and later to scale. As such, the role a foreign investor plays will vary, as it can be either the innovator, the supporter of innovation, the beneficiary of the innovation or even the buyer.
- **Implementation**: innovation services can be varied in nature and will most likely be tailored to a specific investor. Some services will focus on sourcing and ensuring new technology visibility, while others will

focus on introducing businesses that would benefit from innovation (support) to innovators and product development experts, by enabling access to R&D facilities and capabilities or by providing support with patents and registrations of intellectual property.
- **Intended outcome**: to increase the likelihood that an innovation happens, is developed and to reduce the time to market.

The following example (see Box 4.32) comes from Scottish Development International, the Scottish IPA, where they help local companies (including foreign investors) address challenges and find innovators who can help them find solutions for local challenges.

Box 4.32 Scotland's Open Innovation Marketplace

"Solving your business challenges through the Open Innovation Marketplace connects you to a global network of inventive organisations and offers an unrivalled opportunity for company growth. You'll work together to produce a solution and share risk and reward along the way.

How does the marketplace work? We match Scottish and global companies to help them find the lightbulb moments in business that solve challenges and make business growth a reality.

Support and funding options. There's a wealth of great support and funding out there to encourage an exciting ecosystem of open innovation business collaboration partnerships.

Post a challenge and get it solved. If you've got a company conundrum that your everyday business strategies can't get a handle on, here's where you post that challenge to a wider innovation audience.

Find a challenge and solve it. If you think you've got the answers when it comes to solving business obstacles explore our list of company challenges that are calling for innovative approaches."

Reproduced with kind permission from Scottish Development International: www.sdi.co.uk.

Link: https://www.scottish-enterprise.com/support-for-businesses/develop-products-and-services/scotlands-open-innovation-marketplace.

The Innovation and Development Agency of Andalusia, Spain (see Box 4.33), also provides innovation support services to investors.

Box 4.33 Innovation and development in Andalusia

"The Innovation and Development Agency of Andalusia (IDEA Agency) is the Andalusian Government's agency for regional development. Their mission is to contribute to the region's economic and social development. The agency aims to foster entrepreneurship, innovation and cooperation in the science-technology-business system and also to improve competitiveness. The priority is the establishment of collaborative networks, as well as the participation [in regional activities to promote] innovation [at] regional, national and international level and the foreign direct investment promotion.

General Services offered:

- Technological Watch (Technological information Search)
- R&D Information and Advice
- Patents, trademarks and industrial design
- Cooperation and Technology Transfer including innovation diagnosis, search for partners, dissemination of opportunities and help with securing investment.

Foreign Direct Investment Promotion Services:

- Information and contacts related to investment planning and implementation of the investment
- Softlanding services
- Aftercare
- Promotion of Industrial Warehouses. This program works collaboratively with local councils to provide access to warehouses and experimentation space at affordable prices."

Reproduced with kind permission from Invest Andalucia: www.investinandalucia.es.

Link: https://juntadeandalucia.es/organismos/transformacioneconomicaindustriaconocimientoyuniversidades/idea/areas.html.

The next example comes from the state of Alabama (see Box 4.34), one of the pioneers in business retention and expansion in the USA.

Box 4.34 Alabama's Research Capabilities Interactive Map

Business can quickly explore relevant research being conducted at Alabama universities and research organisations thanks to a new interactive map designed to catalogue research capabilities in the state. Companies can use the tool to connect with researchers who could assist in product development, testing, and other functions. The map was developed by the Alabama Experimental Program to Stimulate Competitive Research (Alabama EPSCoR).

Reproduced with kind permission from Made in Alabama.

Link: https://www.madeinalabama.com/business-development/recruitment-and-retention/.

4.5 Linkages, supply chain and value chain services

When investors arrive in a new location they are rarely, if ever, self-supporting. They look for and need (local) suppliers and (local) customers. Indeed, the presence of these local suppliers and customers is often a major reason why they chose that location in the first place. Hence, companies looking to grow typically spend significant amounts of time analysing a country's value chain for their industry and, in particular, identifying potential suppliers and customers, preferably companies with whom they can build long-term collaborative relationships.

Value chain services are complex in nature and require extensive resources to deliver them. Moreover, the need for these services has increased as a result of the Covid-19 pandemic as the disruption to value chains has impacted business continuity and so many IPAs have stepped in to help foreign investors adapt to the new circumstances. The World Bank reiterates that "efforts in the current crisis should focus on assisting systematically strategic multinational corporations and their suppliers to preserve the value chains."[56] They researched actions taken by IPAs to assist foreign investors and identified a focus on "fastening foreign exchange approvals, and advocacy for urgent government actions to solve these companies' grievance issues more systematically and benefit other similar investors." Other examples include specific support to export-oriented industrial parks and helping foreign investors to expand "new production lines as part of the country's strategic re-orientation to in-demand products and services in light of Covid-19."[57]

With linkages, supplier and value chain programmes now present in many markets, the OECD identified a need for guidelines on how to implement value chain match-making programmes. The OECD Investment Promotion Facilitation Toolkit,[58] published in 2011, makes suggestions on how to improve linkages, including:

- **Sound environment**: linkage promotion should complement, not substitute for, active efforts to establish a sound investment environment. For instance, open trade and investment regimes combined with a strong competition policy provide a fertile environment for the transfer of technology.
- **Absorptive capacity**: close linkages can also be promoted through government efforts to develop human resources through investments in education, training and public health, which can all improve the capacity of a country to absorb foreign technology.
- **Linkages requirements**: while some investment contracts include an obligation on the investor to encourage linkages or technology transfers between foreign affiliates and local enterprises, the OECD recommendation is for this to be done on a voluntary basis, as "obligations can have a perverse effect on linkages. Not only might they discourage investment in the first place, they also might imply a lower quantity and quality of technology transferred from the parent to its foreign affiliate in the host country."[59]
- **Targeted approaches**: rather than focusing on investment incentives, which can be expensive and sometimes result in poor quality investments, countries may generate more jobs and more technological benefits by encouraging large anchor industrial investors to purchase from local suppliers, and by designing support services to increase local capacity.

The following examples look at value chain services from different perspectives, including support to tap into new markets, non-equity investment, join-venture services and mergers and acquisitions. It should be noted that some of these services could also be included under strategic services.

4.5.1 Supply chain matchmaking services

While most of the value chain analysis is performed by the companies themselves, IPAs can help accelerate the process by matching foreign affiliates and suppliers. Indeed, the OECD notes that "the most common linkage services are information exchange networks."[60] Deep knowledge of the local business environment helps IPAs engage with, and add value to, a foreign investor.

- **Description**: connecting investors with local businesses that could form part of their supply chain.
- **Main beneficiaries**: foreign affiliates and local suppliers.
- **Implementation**: having first understood the type of suppliers an investor's business requires, the next stage is to facilitate introductions. This may involve the use of online matchmaking tools where foreign companies can showcase their products and services to potential local suppliers, or the organisation of "meet the buyer" events. A thorough knowledge of the local business Ecosystem, including links to organisations such as sector associations, research centres, technology parks and academia, is key to providing an effective service.
- **Intended outcome**: investors source as much business as possible from local suppliers. The follow-on strengthening of the local supply base and associated knowledge transfer makes a location more attractive to other investors, particularly those in the same industry sector.

The following three examples explore different ways IPAs have deployed supply chain matchmaking. The first one is from Belize (Box 4.35) who signed an MOU with neighbouring country Mexico to access their supply chain. The second one is from Hong Kong, where the local government makes a proactive effort to involve foreign investors in their supply chain (see Box 4.36). The third example is from Invest in Africa, a private initiative to support pan-African access to supply chain (see Box 4.37).

Box 4.35 Belize's Supply Chain Offer

A Memorandum of Understanding (MOU) was signed between Belize and Mexico with the aim of establishing a practical framework for the development of stronger business relations between both countries. As part of the MOU, both Belize Trade and Investment Development Service (BELTRAIDE) and ProMexico will exchange publicly available information on investment policies, rules, regulations, procedures, incentives and opportunities, and general updates on statistics and business data on Belize and Mexico.

One of the areas covered in the MOU is access to open business databases, which allow Beltraide to identify Mexican suppliers that can provide industrial consumables to local and foreign business based in Belize.

Reproduced with kind permission form Belize Trade and Investment Development Service. Beltraide. http://www.belizeinvest.org.bz/, http://www.belizeinvest.org.bz/.

Link: https://belizeinvest.net/2015/09/29/belize-and-mexico-sign-a-memorandum-of-understanding/.

Box 4.36 Hong Kong's one-stop procurement online tool

Hong Kong has a one-stop online tool where they announce public procurement activities and make significant efforts to explain to foreign companies how they can register to become public sector suppliers, and therefore gain access to public sector procurement opportunities.

Link: www.gov.hk.

Box 4.37 Invest in Africa Portal

In Ghana, Invest in Africa[61] introduced a two-pronged approach to working with supply chains. The "African Partner Pool" brings businesses together by connecting companies across different sectors with the best local partners for their requirements. As a consequence, African businesses can easily promote their products, making it more straightforward for foreign businesses to find the local suppliers they need. The "Business Linkage Program", which is partly funded by the African Development Bank, is a skills-based training programme offering mentoring and coaching from local and international consultants with the objective of helping local companies to become more competitive, and therefore more likely to win orders from larger companies. Both initiatives began in 2015, and by the end of 2016 had confirmed 79 contracts totalling US$11.7 million of which an estimated 72% ($8.5m) was won by local suppliers.

Reproduced with kind permission from Invest in Africa: www.investinafrica.com.

When it comes to linkages, an area that requires particular attention is partnering readiness, especially when it comes to SMEs. In many cases, SMEs may be unfamiliar with the quality, technical or sanitary standards required by foreign firms, and therefore have difficulty entering supply chain agreements with them. Training can be a valuable way to not only encourage linkages, but also to increase the likelihood of success. In some cases, local suppliers may be individually too small to provide the needed volumes on a regular, secure basis, but efforts to create production cooperatives can assist SMEs in fulfilling the needs of larger firms. Particularly in tourism and other service industries, training and facilitation can assist larger companies in sourcing supplies and labour from local communities, and can also assist in preventing labour or community disputes, for example, over water rights. Larger companies can also play a role by sharing their material and service-sector purchasing requirements with smaller local firms in advance, so that these firms have time to adapt to any specific requirements.

Linkages programmes must be tailored to the specific investor and SME needs, "[as] a one-size-fits-all approach is unlikely to work. Programmes should be carefully designed with input from both investors and SMEs and should be built around regular dialogue to ensure that problems are identified and quickly corrected."[62]

These activities are relevant to all businesses, and by taking advantage of them foreign firms will increase their chances of securing local contracts. There is ample scope for IPAs to direct foreign investors towards linkages opportunities, including inviting speakers to outline opportunities, arranging supplier days and fostering local capacity building.

4.5.2 Tapping into value chain shifts

Sudden market changes generate uncertainty, but they also create opportunities for businesses that are ready, willing and able to exploit them. For example, Covid-19 has disrupted many value chains, thereby creating opportunities for companies to fill the gaps created, and it has also significantly increased demand for other products and services, such as masks and home delivery. IPAs, and other public and private players, can help foreign investors tap into these new business opportunities.

- **Description**: services that facilitate access to global value chains, helping established companies use existing infrastructure to win new business in emerging market segments.
- **Main beneficiaries**: the foreign investor who can exploit new business opportunities, and employees whose jobs might otherwise have been at risk.
- **Implementation**: delivery will vary from IPA to IPA as it's likely that a variety of different services may be required. Some IPAs choose to partner with universities or sector associations to deliver these services, other IPAs appoint sector experts to work directly with clients, while a further group of IPAs seeks to secure supply or purchasing contracts with other agencies that they open up for tender among local companies, including investors. Programmes of this nature will require the participation of an extended group of participants, and IPAs might have different roles in the programme, from coordinators to programme designers, etc.
- **Intended outcome**: help local investors win new business, secure jobs at risk, grow export capacity and upskill an industry.

The following examples comes from Ethiopia (see Box 4.38), a country with a leather and textile manufacturing sector that found itself with excess production capacity due to the value chain disruption caused by Covid-19.

Box 4.38 Covid19 manufacturing task force in Ethiopia

The Ethiopian Investment Commission (EIC) established a manufacturing task force to provide targeted support for manufacturers that "have or are planning to re-purpose their operations to supply personal protective equipment." The task force focuses on the demand side by linking manufactures to buyers, and on the supply side, by helping companies procure raw material, provide financial support, offer technical advice on operations while keeping productivity high by providing tailored support for employee (re)training.

Reproduced with kind permission from the Ethiopian Investment Commission EIC: www.investethiopia.gov.

Link: http://www.investethiopia.gov.et/index.php/covid-19/support-for-ppe-manufacturing.html.

4.5.3 Non-equity modes of investment

Sometimes foreign businesses establish operations in a country without investing their own money. These operations are referred to as non-equity modes (NEMs) of investment and include, according to UNCTAD, "contract manufacturing, services outsourcing, contract farming, franchising, licensing, management contracts and other types of contractual relationships through which TNCs [trans-national companies] coordinate activities in their global value chains and influence the management of host-country firms without owning an equity stake in those firms."[63] The foreign business will typically encourage local investors to establish an operation by providing long term contracts to manufacturers and back-office sub-contractors, and marketing support to businesses such as hotels and restaurants. For example, Apple sub-contracts the assembly of its iPhones to companies like Foxconn, while many major corporations outsource their back-office functions, such as IT and HR, to third parties. NEM partnerships present an opportunity for host countries to integrate into global value chains. "A key advantage of NEMs is that they are flexible arrangements with local firms, with a built-in motive for TNCs to invest in the viability of their partners through dissemination of knowledge, technology and skills." The "2020 State of Investment Promotion Agencies" report, from WAIPA and the World Bank, confirms that NEMs are growing in importance and that 53% of IPAs are considering NEMs as part of their service portfolio. From those IPAs that included NEMs offerings, the most common approaches include service outsourcing (34% of IPAs), contract manufacturing (30%), contract farming (20%), licensing (15%), franchising (14%) and management contracts (9%).[64]

4.5.4 Joint venture services

Joint ventures (JVs) are strategic alliances where two or more parties form a partnership to share markets, intellectual property, assets, knowledge and, of course, profits. A joint venture differs from a merger in the sense that there is no transfer of ownership in the deal. They bring a variety of benefits to the signing parties including access to new markets and distribution networks, increased production capacity, sharing of risks and costs, access to new knowledge and expertise, and access to greater resources such as technology and finance.

- **Description**: services are geared first towards identifying partners with complementary skillsets and who are willing to enter into a partnership, and then in helping them make the JV a success. Services then move to supporting the crafting of JV contracts that provide an appropriate framework under which a local company and a foreign company can work together for the benefit of all parties involved.
- **Main beneficiaries**: foreign company and local business through leveraging each other's skills, knowledge and capabilities.
- **Implementation**: some IPAs partner with consultants who specialise in providing this type of service and who will help a foreign investor to find an appropriate JV partner. Others focus on creating online databases, often in collaboration with other public agencies, where foreign investors can find potential JV partners, and vice versa, and encourage both local and foreign companies to use the database. A word of caution: JVs agreements can be complex and need extensive legal contracts that require specialised skills to draft. For this

reason, many investors commission specialist consultancies to help in the sourcing, matching, negotiating and document crafting necessary for a successful JV.

- **Intended outcome**: foreign investors and local companies achieve a variety of benefits, including revenue growth, increased production capacity, sharing of risks and costs, access to new knowledge and expertise, and access to greater resources such as technology and finance.

The following example comes from the Malaysian Investment Development Authority (MIDA), which focuses on the manufacturing and services sectors (see Box 4.39).

Box 4.39 Sourcing joint venture partners in Malaysia

Can MIDA help on sourcing for a joint venture partner (domestic or foreign)?

MIDA has established an online facility, e-BizMatch (formerly known as Enterprise Connect or E-Connect), to assist and facilitate business matching services. e-BizMatch is an online business matching service connecting businesses worldwide. This web-based facility will help connect with international business partners.

The e-BizMatch provides an opportunity for local and foreign investors seeking joint-venture partners in Malaysia, undertaking contract manufacturing or technical collaboration. Registered members will be able to conduct customised searches for business partners based on their specific requirements that match their interest. The registration is free of charge. To be a member of the e-BizMatch, the applicant is required to submit the application online. In addition to e-BizMatch, MIDA will also assist in proposing relevant companies/investors.

Reproduced with kind permission from the Malaysian Investment Development Authority: MIDA. www.mida.gov.my.

Link: http://matriix.mida.gov.my:9080/Promotion/userLogin.do.

4.5.5 Mergers and acquisitions services

Foreign investors often look to buy local companies to accelerate their growth or to increase their control of their value chain. M&A is an acronym for mergers and acquisitions. In broad terms, M&A is about the acquisition of companies and the merging of companies, and the processes that surround such transactions. Some IPAs stay clear of M&As and do not consider M&A to be part of FDI. Others don't make that difference and offer a comprehensive set of services.

- **Description**: help foreign investors identify companies they could potentially acquire or merge with, or in the case of disinvestment, companies they could potentially sell their operations to. As such, M&A plays a role in two stages of the corporate life cycle. When companies find themselves in the growth stage, some might choose to accelerate growth by incorporating into their portfolio new products or skills, or by acquiring market share. They might decide not to repatriate profits, but to re-invest them locally by buying a local company. However, when the business is going through a decline phase and the investor is considering exiting the business, they may look for a buyer for the local subsidiary (or part thereof). When such a transaction takes place and those funds are repatriated, rather than being reinvested in the growth of the remaining local subsidiary, it effectively becomes a disinvestment.
- **Main beneficiaries**: foreign investors seeking opportunities to rapidly grow in new markets, to expand market share in an existing market or to exit a location.
- **Implementation**: Relatively few IPAs have M&A advisory and matchmaking services inhouse due to the highly specialised and expensive expertise required. Some IPAs outsource this service to professional M&A advisory firms. Others maintain a database of potential target companies within their region, which they share with parties interested in M&A. Where IPAs are involved, it is mainly in a matchmaking role and they generally step aside once introductions have been made and contracts need to be drafted.
- **Intended outcome**: foreign investors merge with or acquire businesses in the host economy resulting in a further capital injection, technology transfer, retention of jobs, etc., or successfully sell their operations to a third party, thereby retaining local jobs.

One IPA that offers M&A services is Invest in Sweden as can be seen in Box 4.40.

Box 4.40 Business Sweden's M&A services

Attractive business opportunities, high transparency and uncomplicated legal and regulatory procedures underpin Sweden's attractiveness to companies seeking business opportunities. This information aims to provide a brief overview of the market as well as information on the process for mergers and acquisitions.

Business opportunities: small and medium sized enterprises in Sweden host a rich diversity of advanced technology that presents unique opportunities for international companies seeking to enter the Swedish market, expand their footprint or develop new know-how.

Advanced technology: sustained investment in higher education and core research, an array of homegrown research-intensive multinationals and a commitment to top scientific infrastructure have made Sweden a leading supplier of innovative solutions and products to international business. A proven ability to work across disciplines and bridge corporate and academic research environments makes Sweden eminently placed to deliver results. The capacity to develop and integrate complex systems is evident in Sweden's advanced industrial sectors.

Family controlled businesses: family-owned or controlled businesses have historically been a pillar of the Swedish enterprise landscape. Demographics are now coming into play as the baby boomers who built many of these companies look to retire. Many of them will be seeking to hand over their businesses to the next generation. But equally, many are contemplating new external owners.

Firm framework for M&A activity: in many countries, the process of acquiring a company is often seen as complex and time-consuming. This is not the case in Sweden, where a culture of openness and transparency avoids bureaucracy and red tape and facilitates business dynamism. Legal agreements are relatively simple by international standards. Information on a target company's shares, articles of association, real property or floating charges is easily available in publicly available registers.

Note: The document also provides step-by-step guidance on how to undertake M&As in Sweden as well as valuable information for a prospective buyer.

Source: https://www.business-sweden.se/globalassets/invest-new/reports-and-documents/mergers-and-acquisitions---process-overview.pdf

4.6 Services that foster sustainability

The sustainability agenda touches every stage of the investment cycle, from promotion to attraction, market entry, establishment and further local growth. With the UN's SDG agenda permeating all economic activity, sustainability is becoming an increasingly important part of Investor Services.

Indeed, some IPAs are helping companies address social development goals (SDGs) by providing assistance in gaining sustainability certification and access to information and financial incentives. The following examples show how some IPAs are doing this.

4.6.1 Leaner and greener practices

Sustainability is a journey of continuous improvement, where companies continuously review their practices and upgrade how they create value for society. It usually starts with preventing physical waste, increasing energy efficiency or improving resource productivity, which in turn results in cost-efficiency, improved profitability and enhanced competitiveness. "Lean means doing more with less. That's why lean thinking supports green and vice versa."[65]

- **Description**: provision of services that seek to support leaner and greener practices.
- **Main beneficiaries**: the foreign company as it acquires new insight and skills. Employees of that company who benefit from improved company performance and a sense of mission. Local stakeholders who are keen to protect the planet.
- **Implementation**: these services usually require specialist knowledge, long term planning, plant upgrades and often certification. As such, IPAs often partner with academia and private sector consultancies, or partner with state agencies to deliver the large variety of sustainability

programmes such as improving lighting energy efficiency, upgrading buildings or facilitating the certification of products. Given the value add of these services, some IPAs charge for them, while others offer subsidies to companies that participate.

- **Intended outcome**: better equipped investors who support the overall green agenda by embracing sustainability practices.

Once again, leading IPA IDA Ireland offers a one-of-a-kind service to help drive the sustainability agenda as show in Box 4.41.

Box 4.41 Ireland's lean/green offer

As one of the leading IPAs worldwide, IDA Ireland has embraced sustainability and is "keen to support its client companies to develop their operations in Ireland and to introduce good environment management practices."[66] They offer a unique service "to encourage clients to adopt Lean business principles to increase performance and competitiveness that will help sustain and grow their Irish operations," as they observe that those tools build the "capability to identify problems and take an innovative approach to improvements in operations and services as well as understand the importance of building environmental best practices into the workplace."[67]

IDA Ireland offers this service in collaboration with Enterprise Ireland, particularly targeting companies engaged in both manufacturing and service activities.

The first step is to introduce the foreign investor to "[l]ean principles, environmental best practices, agile processes including the completion of a specific cost reduction project."[68]

The second step is to identify a "medium-scale business process improvement project with an external business development consultant, which will result in sustained use by the company of Lean techniques and related methodologies and will achieve significant measurable gains in company capabilities and competitiveness."[69]

The third step is to explore "company transformation programme with an external consultancy team of international reputation. It will embed the culture and competences necessary for on-going competitiveness gains, sustainable continuous improvement and business transformation across the business and its supply chain."[70] This step looks to roll out bigger lean/green projects throughout the organisation.

The complete project last for several years and is eligible for some funding support.

Source: https://www.idaireland.com/IDAIreland/media/HowWeHelp/Green_Business_Offer.pdf.

4.6.2 Working with refugees

The United Nations Global Compact for Refugees, ratified in 2019, marked "a major conceptual shift among the global community by recognizing that displacement is usually not temporary. In fact, it can last around two decades on average. It could and should be considered an emerging issue for IPAs to consider, especially if they need to deal with an evolving workforce. Sadly, there aren't relevant reference services in the market to highlight or investigate as yet."[71] According to UNHCR, the UN Refugee Agency, there were 79.5 million displaced people as of the end of 2019.[72] Jobs are a key route to self-reliance and easing the pressure on host countries. In some cases, governments have encouraged their IPAs to work with foreign investors to find solutions to tackle this global crisis. Meanwhile the private sector, together with charities, has in some countries stepped up. Some IPAs have responded to the circumstances and have taken an active role in bringing public and private sector together to jointly address the crisis.

- **Description**: help refugees get established in a country including finding a place to live, integration, job seeking and even entrepreneurship.
- **Main beneficiaries**: direct beneficiaries will vary depending on the programme, but, on the whole, beneficiaries include the refugee who finds a job, the company that recruits a skilled and employee,
- **Implementation**: it is difficult to describe implementation as the support varies significantly from location to location. However, the most important aspect is that different players collaborate and

hammer-out proposals that incorporate displaced people in the building of societies.
- **Intended outcome**: offer opportunities to newcomers and increase local productivity by incorporating that labour force into the market.

The following two examples show how three foreign investors, coffee chain Starbucks, high-street fashion retailer H&M (see Box 4.42) and online media and recruitment platform LinkedIn (see Box 4.43) got involved in activities to integrate refugees.

Box 4.42 The Tent Partnership for Refugees

"The Tent Partnership for Refugees is a non-profit organization launched in 2016 to mobilize the global business community to include refugees. Today, we are a network of over 100 multinational companies committed to integrating refugees in the many locations where they are present. Two of their programmes seek to provide employment for refugees via supporting hiring and training and by leveraging supply chain.

Hiring & Training: Refugees often face increased barriers to accessing jobs in their new host communities. Companies can play a vital role in creating jobs for refugees, by training them and hiring them directly into their workforce. For example, North American coffee chain Starbucks' operation in Canada has committed to employing 1,000 refugees by 2022. This is part of Starbucks's global effort to hire refugees around the world.

Supply chain programme: Companies can encourage their suppliers and vendors to hire refugees, or commit to sourcing from businesses which employ refugees. This may be especially relevant for companies who have suppliers in large refugee-hosting countries, such as Turkey and Colombia. In these markets, refugees often face increased barriers to work - and are more vulnerable to forced labour – making it even more critical for companies to take proactive efforts to advance refugees' economic integration. For example: Swedish textile mogul H&M works with 20 suppliers employing about 500 refugees. By 2025, H&M has committed to doubling the number of suppliers it works with on this effort from 20 to 40, to create jobs for at least 2,000 refugees in Turkey."

Reproduced with kind permission from the Tent Partnership www.tent.org.

Link: https://www.tent.org/.

Box 4.43 LinkedIn's Welcome Talent programme in Sweden

"Helping newly settled refugees find economic opportunity in Sweden

By Lisa Gunnarsson

LinkedIn's vision is to create economic opportunity for every member of the global workforce. It's this vision that makes me proud to work for LinkedIn, especially when it can help an important global issue: the refugee crisis.

Last October, a friend who works at the Swedish Migration Board shared with me some of the challenges refugees face as they enter the country and look for employment. These challenges include no local professional network, a language barrier, the nuances of a new culture, and of course, knowing where to find a job. We quickly realized that LinkedIn had a unique opportunity to leverage what our company does best: connect these individuals – many of whom are highly skilled – with opportunity.

On a per capita basis, Sweden has received more refugees than any other European country. In addition, many of these refugees have skills that the Swedish economy can benefit. According to a recent article, a quarter of refugees in 2014 had higher education – up almost 5% on the previous year. More than two-thirds of them had skills that matched graduate job vacancies.

Today, we are very proud to launch Welcome Talent, a new initiative that aims to help refugees in Sweden find opportunities created specifically for them and their unique circumstances. The site includes resources in both Arabic and English, including potential opportunities and information on how to create an effective LinkedIn profile.

There is also a section for employers that explains how to to post internships and jobs on LinkedIn, at no cost, for refugees. Employers simply mark their internships and job opportunities with a special hashtag, #welcometalent, so they can be easily discovered by refugees. To date there are more than 150 opportunities from companies such as Spotify, Proffice, 3 and Happyr.

If you work in Sweden, please consider joining us by posting an opportunity. If you're a newly settled refugee, either in Sweden or anywhere in the world, create a LinkedIn profile to help find opportunity, no matter where you are."

Reproduced with kind permission from LinkedIn Sweden.

Link: https://blog.linkedin.com/2016/02/15/helping-newly-settled-refugees-find-economic-opportunity-in-sweden.

4.6.3 Driving the gender agenda

A 2015 McKinsey report suggested that advancing women's equality could add US$12 trillion to global growth. "Gender inequality is not only a pressing moral and social issue but also a critical economic challenge. If women – who account for half the world's working-age population – do not achieve their full economic potential, the global economy will suffer."[73] Significant progress in improving gender equality has been made all over the world, though a lot still remains to be done in companies, as "narrowing the global gender gap in work would not only be equitable in the broadest sense but could double the contribution of women to global GDP growth between 2014 and 2025." Public and private sector organisations across the world see the benefit of driving a gender agenda. While there is solid academic research about the link between economic growth and gender, with international campaigns such as #SheTrades or tailored export support programmes for female-led companies, the question of gender and FDI has only recently been studied. Some IPAs have embraced a pro-gender career development approach, looking to introduce gender parity in their operations. However, the topic is broader as it raises the question of what the impact of FDI is on gender advancement in the host location.

Services that support gender equality are relatively new, and there are very few examples.

- **Description**: services that support women's advancement including career development within foreign investors, as well as the empowerment of women in other sectors of society.
- **Main beneficiaries**: the direct beneficiaries of these programmes are women, but achieving gender balance benefits society as a whole.
- **Implementation**: most gender balance programmes are organised by third parties. IPAs take a broker role encouraging foreign investors to enrol. In other cases, they might fund these programmes.
- **Intended outcome**: women advancement and support of a societal agenda.

The following examples comes from New York (see Box 4.44), which recognises that women's advancement is key to creating the future they envision for themselves.

Box 4.44 Women.nyc

"New York City is committed to being the best place in the world for women to succeed."[74] To achieve this, the New York City Economic Development Corporation NYCEDC designed a pioneering programme to "make sure the city remains the best place in the world for women of all backgrounds, ages, abilities and identities to thrive in their careers, run businesses and launch start-ups."[75] Women.nyc works with local organisations "to financially empower women" and by "leveraging all the tools the city has to offer, Women.nyc has rolled out groundbreaking programmes that have a real impact: from free tech classes and career training to investment and crowdfunding, job connections, legal advice from the city's most respected law firms and more."[76]

Women.nyc provides access to networks to women of all abilities, identities and background, to help them connect and advance. They do so by "fostering equitable NYC workplaces that create paths for diverse women to advance"[77] and by advocating for women-friendly policies.

Source: https://women.nyc/about/.

4.6.4 Civic and philanthropic footprint of foreign investors

While civic engagement and philanthropy are not often associated with foreign investors, some multinationals make significant philanthropic contributions and also make efforts to strengthen the links their foreign associates have with local communities.

Economist Dan Ikenson, director of the Herbert Stiefel Centre for Trade Policy Studies at the Cato Institute, conducted research into the relationship between global investment and civic connection, which was published on the Global Business Alliance website. He found that in the last decade, US FDI companies increased their charitable spending by 127%, compared with an economy-wide average of just 19%.[78] This significant difference in charitable giving reflects not only the substantial financial support foreign businesses often give to their host communities, but also the untapped potential that could be unleashed by putting the right mechanisms in place to maximise the social good. Indeed, foreign investors who are members of the Global Business Alliance "score an impressive 117.2 percent higher than the average U.S. company in terms of reducing their product carbon emissions."[79]

Few IPAs take a strategic approach to maximising the civic footprint of their foreign investors. This may be a missed opportunity, as the skills IPAs possess could not only be used to attract new businesses, but also to bring any social responsibility programmes a foreign investor is already performing elsewhere to the local area.

IPAs with a corporate and social responsibility (CSR) value proposition could help a foreign company unlock further social good benefits for the benefit of the local community. The range of activities could include patronage of the arts, volunteering of staff in schools, support for charities, fundraising for good causes, donation of pro-bono skills to social enterprises, sponsorship of events relevant to the community, engagement with disadvantaged communities, supporting minorities and much more.

- **Description**: facilitation services that create societal value by helping a foreign investor roll out CRS programmes, or in implementing the social good ambitions of the foreign investors.
- **Main beneficiaries**: the foreign investor is the direct beneficiary of the services; however, the programme will impact the local community.

- **Implementation**: very varied in nature and will depend on each case. It may be as simple as small players, such as Australian RealThing Ai underwriting the use of their technology with visually impaired users in foreign markets, through to behemoths, such as Microsoft providing grants for local players to develop accessible technologies on their platforms.
- **Intended outcome**: unlock CSR activities led by the investor for the benefit of the local community.

The following example (see Box 4.45) comes from the city of Malaga, in the Costa del Sol of Spain, where the local IPA has supported North American foreign investor Oracle in the CSR activities of their employees.

Box 4.45 City of Málaga support to CSR activities from investors

Since 2013, the City of Málaga has supported the annual evening-concert organised by volunteers from the Oracle Málaga office to raise funds for the non-governmental organisation (NGO) Pozos Sin Fronteras (PSF). This event takes place in an outdoor amphitheatre within the historic Castillo Gibralfaro. By facilitating the use of this public space, the support is considered as an "aftercare" service to international companies. It is considered that this action is good to promote the positive integration of the international community, especially foreign workers, their spouses and relatives. The funds raised, through the sale of tickets (€15 adults – €10 children/senior) and drinks, go entirely to the NGO.

Organisers: Pozos Sin Fronteras (PSF) (or Wells Without Borders in English) is a is a non-profit organisation born in Málaga and whose main mission is to provide people and local communities with water, as a basic tool, to get out of poverty, promoting education and agricultural training as priority instruments of development. PSF has been working since 2003 in countries such as Morocco, Burkina Faso and Peru.

Oracle Ibérica SL is one of the largest software companies in the world. Oracle's trajectory in Málaga began in 2007, with the opening of a consulting centre, and was reinforced in 2010 with a European sales centre.

Reproduced with kind permission from the City of Málaga: www.malaga.eu.

According to their 2019 company report, Oracle gifted US$21 million to 4,800 non-profits globally and donated 124,932 employee volunteer hours in 48 countries.[80] That's almost half a million US dollars donated to 100 grass-root organisations and 2,600 volunteering hours donated per country. This might seem small numbers per country, but when added to the amounts donated by other hundreds and sometimes even thousands of foreign investors established locally, the amounts become relevant, making a significant difference to the NGOs that received the funds and in building more cohesive societies.

As can be seen in the examples above, sustainability is a common feature of Investor Services. Many IPAs, particularly those in the public sector who are based within ministries, regional or local government, broker activities organised in-house to drive a sustainable and inclusive programme. The same is true of IPAs funded by the private sector, as many companies look for member organisations to help them amplify and expand their sustainability activities. While it is still early days when it comes to Investor Services specialised in sustainability, IPAs can expect this area to become an increasingly important part of their work.

4.6.5 Engagement with indigenous communities

With indigenous communities accounting for 5% of the world's population and living in over 90 countries, they are fundamental partners in the development of their role as stewards of 25% of the world's water and land.[81] The United Nations' Office of the High Commissioner for Human Rights (OHCHR) recognises the rights of indigenous people for self-determination, which comes down to their right to have a say in interventions that may affect their lives. From that perspective, they are an important stakeholder in FDI activities that "may affect their lives", such as investment in mining, forestry and agriculture.

The UN recognises that "public attention is increasingly focusing on indigenous people's issues for a variety of reasons."[82] They observe that, on one hand, their territories and livelihoods are seriously threatened by the world's demographic pressure, compounded by the extractive industries' appetite for resources. And on the other hand, "scientists increasingly recognize what indigenous peoples have been voicing for decades: while holding much of the world's diversity in terms of culture, language and spirituality, indigenous peoples are also the stewards of natural resources and guardians of biodiversity."[83] The latter has resulted in international organisations, foundations and activists taking an interest in the life and rights of indigenous peoples, in the view that they "hold some of today's answers to tomorrow's challenges."[84]

In 2015, the UN issued guidelines for **F**ree, **P**rior and **I**nformed **C**onsent (FPIC). Rights to FPIC stem from the notion that "all peoples have the right to freely pursue their economic, social and cultural development."[85] FPIC is backed by the United Nations Declaration on the Rights of Indigenous Peoples (UNDRIP), the Convention on Biological Diversity and the International Labour Organization (ILO) Convention 169, which "are the most powerful and comprehensive international instruments that recognize the plights of Indigenous Peoples and defend their rights."[86]

In light of the natural overlap between the food industry, agriculture and indigenous communities, the United Nations Food and Agriculture Organisation (FAO) issued an FPIC manual titled "Free Prior and Informed Consent. An indigenous peoples' right and a good practice for local communities", which provides information about the right to FPIC and how it can be applied on the ground. The FAO notes that rights to FPIC include "granting or denying consent, but only after the indigenous community received the information about the intervention, well in advance, in a culturally appropriate manner and prior to authorising or starting any activity."[87] The manual seeks to facilitate a common approach to FPIC to follow along the lifecycle of any projects that involves indigenous communities and suggests 6 steps, namely identification, participatory mapping, communication planning, reach consent, monitoring and evaluating, and lessons learnt. These steps ensure that equal consideration is given to all members of the local community and that "indigenous peoples collectively decide, free of coercion, violence and manipulation, knowing that if consent is given, it can also be withdrawn at any stage. FPIC ensures that the voices from indigenous women, men and elders are also heard, respected and considered and enables indigenous people to participate in negotiating conditions under which interventions are designed, implemented, monitored and evaluated."[88] The FAO observes that implementing FPCIs from the beginning of any local intervention "improves understanding of Indigenous Communities, builds trust, and ensures sustainability and ownership,"[89] which in turn increases engagement, resilience and positive impact. Box 4.46 provides further information about FPIC implementation provided by the FAO.

Box 4.46 Key elements in Free, Prior and Informed Consent

Extracts from the manual written by the UN Food and Agriculture Organisation (FAO) titled "Free Prior and Informed Consent – An Indigenous Peoples' right and a good practice for local communities" (2016).

"All elements within FPIC are interlinked, and they should not be treated as separate elements. The first three elements (free, prior and informed) qualify and set the conditions of consent as a decision-making process. In short, consent should be sought before any project, plan or action takes place (prior), it should be independently decided upon (free) and based on accurate, timely and sufficient information provided in a culturally appropriate way (informed) for it to be considered a valid result or outcome of a collective decision-making process.

The definitions below build on the elements of a common understanding of free, prior and informed consent endorsed by the United Nations Permanent Forum on Indigenous Issues (UNPFII) at its Fourth Session in 2005, and from the UNREDD Programme Guidelines on Free, Prior and Informed Consent.

FREE: refers to a consent given voluntarily and without coercion, intimidation or manipulation. It also refers to a process that is self-directed by the community from whom consent is being sought, unencumbered by coercion, expectations or timelines that are externally imposed. More specifically:

- Rights-holders determine the process, timeline and decision-making structure.
- Information is offered transparently and objectively at the request of the rights-holders.
- The process is free from coercion, bias, conditions, bribery or rewards.
- Meetings and decisions take place at locations and times and in languages and formats determined by the rights-holders. And

- All community members are free to participate regardless of gender, age or standing.

PRIOR: means that consent is sought sufficiently in advance of any authorisation or commencement of activities, at the early stages of a development or investment plan, and not only when the need arises to obtain approval from the community. It should be noted that:

- Prior implies that time is provided to understand, access, and analyse information on the proposed activity. The amount of time required will depend on the decision-making processes of the rights-holders.
- Information must be provided before activities can be initiated, at the beginning or initiation of an activity, process or phase of implementation, including conceptualisation, design, proposal, information, execution, and following evaluation. And
- The decision-making timeline established by the rights-holders must be respected, as it reflects the time needed to understand, analyse, and evaluate the activities under consideration in accordance with their own customs.

INFORMED: refers mainly to the nature of the engagement and type of information that should be provided prior to seeking consent and also as part of the ongoing consent process. Information should be:

- Accessible, clear, consistent, accurate, and transparent.
- Delivered in the local language and in a culturally appropriate format (including radio, traditional/local media, video, graphics, documentaries, photos, oral presentations, or new media); Objective, covering both the positive and negative potential of the proposed activities and consequences of giving or withholding consent.
- Complete, including a preliminary assessment of the possible economic, social, cultural and environmental impacts, including potential risks and benefits.

- Complete, including the nature, size, pace, duration, reversibility and scope of any proposed project, its purpose and the location of areas that will be affected.
- Delivered by culturally appropriate personnel, in culturally appropriate locations, and include capacity building of indigenous or local trainers;
- Delivered with sufficient time to be understood and verified.
- Accessible to the most remote, rural communities, including youth, women, the elderly and persons with disabilities, who are sometimes neglected; and
- Provided in an ongoing and continuous basis throughout the FPIC process, with a view to enhancing local communication and decision-making processes.

CONSENT: refers to the collective decision made by the rights-holders and reached through the customary decision-making processes of the affected Indigenous Peoples or communities. Consent must be sought and granted or withheld according to the unique formal or informal political-administrative dynamic of each community. Indigenous peoples and local communities must be able to participate through their own freely chosen representatives, while ensuring the participation of youth, women, the elderly and persons with disabilities as much as possible. In particular consent is:

- A freely given decision that may be a '"Yes"', a '"No"', or a '"Yes with conditions"', including the option to reconsider if the proposed activities change or if new information relevant to the proposed activities emerges.
- A collective decision (e.g. through consensus or majority) determined by the affected peoples in accordance with their own customs and traditions.
- The expression of rights (to self-determination, lands, resources and territories, culture). And
- Given or withheld in phases, over specific periods of time for distinct stages or phases of the project activities. It is not a one-off process.

An example of bad practice

After a flood, the Government asked an organisation to provide emergency assistance in the form of tools, seeds, and livelihood support to the affected areas. One of these areas was inhabited by Indigenous Peoples. When officers in the technical division requested FPIC implementation, the project manager replied that it had been already completed as they had the agreement by the administrative authority in the region. The technical officers explained to the project manager that this was exactly the opposite of FPIC, and that the letter by one administrative authority was not a substitute of FPIC. A true FPIC process meant disclosing the terms of the project in the local language with the community, involving the youth, women, the elderly and persons with disabilities, and allowing sufficient time for them to discuss in their local language. It also meant allowing for the Indigenous community to revert back to the project manager with a consolidated consent or withheld consent to the proposed interventions, and proposals of how they would participate during the implementation of the project."

Source: FAO, 2016. "Free Prior and Informed Consent – An Indigenous Peoples' right and a good practice for local communities" [online]. Available at: http://www.fao.org/3/i6190e/i6190e.pdf.

Foreign investors, particularly in extractive industries, are aware of the need to undertake community consultations as part of their operation. Many have well-equipped and skilled community engagement teams, PR agencies and consultation project skills, the use of which often results in consent being granted by the community to the project. Many investors approach the consultation process with professionalism and purpose, seeking to generate economic and sustainable development for all. There are also investors who see community consultation as a necessary and unpleasant step in the long due diligence process required to get project approval. They face the consultation with a transaction mentality and restrict the relationship with communities to a CSR negotiation exercise, where consent is secured in exchanged for charitable benefits awarded to local communities. Indigenous Communities often hold different views about FDI; while some groups and tribal leaders engage in conversations of co-creation and mutual benefit, others see the foreign investor as the exploiter, who represents centuries of colonialism. This attitude does not help either. Against that background, FPIC is a tool to augment the consultation process with indigenous communities to introduce transparency, accountability and to seek to level the field.

International stakeholders watch this space carefully. In fact, the United Nations Permanent Forum on Indigenous Issues (UNPFII) "receives complaints from hundreds of indigenous communities,"[90] many of these cases affecting foreign investors. They observe that "it is obvious that indigenous peoples have not benefited from these businesses or state initiatives." The UNPFI reports of "greater distrust among the global indigenous leaders on the intentions of politicians and businessmen on projects in their territories, and thus complicates the relationship between indigenous peoples, states and private companies."[91] The UN has a role dedicated to the topic, the Special Rapporteur on the rights of indigenous peoples, whose function is to respond to individual complaints, conduct studies, provide advice on technical cooperation and undertake country visits. These Special Rapporteurs are independent experts appointed by the UN Human Rights Council with the mandate to monitor, advise and publicly report on human rights situations in specific country or mandates or thematic mandates,[92] which also include "cases of alleged violations of indigenous peoples' rights."[93] For example, in February 2021, the Special Rapporteur called for halt to a tourism resort planned in Bangladesh – a five-star tourism project that "would require an extensive network of buildings, roads, drainage and sewage systems which would pollute and harm the biodiversity in the area. Some 10,000 people will be at risk of eviction due to construction."[94]

At the very heart of investor-community relationships in the exploration of natural resources are investment contracts. These contracts draw together interest not only from states and investors, but also many other local stakeholders including indigenous communities. Natural resource contracts define the rights and responsibilities of the parties involved and capture the very concept of sovereignty, ownership and consent. Box 4.47 provides some background about how these three concepts, embedded in legal frameworks, influence the relationships between state, investors and communities.

Box 4.47 Natural resource contracts

Extracts from chapter, "Reconsidering Sovereignty, Ownership and Consent in Natural Resource Contracts" from *Concepts to Practice*, written by Lorenzo Cotula (2018).

"In broad terms, Natural Resource Contracts are contracts that 'involve the allocation of resource exploration and/or development rights to an investor, in exchange for considerations such as revenues, employment or infrastructure development.'" Many times, these large-scale natural resource projects have often been accompanied by reports of social conflict and environmental degradation."

[The] "prominent place of investor-state contracts has underpinned what some scholars have called a 'transactional view' of investment relations, whereby legal arrangements are structured, at least in part, around a bargain between the investor and the state. However, the 'transaction' involves complex constellations of both commercial and non-commercial dimensions. In market-based economies, commercial viability provides the foundation of any investment activity. Contracts and contract renegotiations can affect the balance of risks and returns in any investment, and ultimately its profitability."

"In addition, contractual developments 'on the ground' have questioned traditional approaches that frame investment relations exclusively in terms of bilateral arrangements between investors and states. The need for investors to establish workable relations with local actors has fostered the negotiation of community-investor agreements aimed at channelling benefits to the local economy. Many companies have come to see these contractual arrangements as a strategy to promote support for the business, while some indigenous movements and non-governmental organisations (NGOs) have appropriated the language of partnerships to advance local claims to natural resources."

"Taken together, these evolutions have prompted renewed public reflection on multiple aspects of natural resource contracts. Some early explorations focused on specific clauses in investor-state contracts – such as stabilisation clauses, and environmental provisions. Over time, the interrelatedness of contractual clauses and the need to consider the role of local actors in investment contracting led to more holistic approaches to understanding both the content of the contract, and its parties and formation process. Significant developments have also occurred through the emergence of authoritative international guidance, including principles for addressing human rights issues in contracting processes, learning materials on how to implement the principles, and model contracts for natural resource projects."

"It is now clear that addressing the challenges associated with natural resource contracts involves not only ensuring that governments are in a position to get a fair deal in their negotiations with investors, but also reconsidering the fundamental parameters on which contracting rests. Yet these deeper-level parameters are still underexplored. Questions remain, for example, about legal arrangements to ensure that states exercise sovereignty in the interest of their people; about how contracting can operate in multi-layered resource ownership systems, including where socially legitimate resource rights enjoy little recognition under national law; and about who should have the right to manifest their consent, at which stage and under what conditions, in the distribution of decision-making authority that underpins natural resource contracting."

Kindly reproduced with permission from the author.

Source: Cotula L. (2018) Reconsidering Sovereignty, Ownership and Consent in Natural Resource Contracts: From Concepts to Practice. Published in: Bungenberg M., Krajewski M., Tams C., Terhechte J. and Ziegler A. (eds), *European Yearbook of International Economic Law 2018*, vol 9. Springer, Cham [online]. Available at: https://doi.org/10.1007/8165_2018_23.

While the topic of community engagement exceeds the scope of this book, IPAs from any of the 90 countries that host indigenous groups in their territories will be exposed to it either directly or indirectly. Therefore, it is important that they take a proactive role in learning and increasing capacity from both policy makers and practitioners of the context in which investor-contracts are designed, signed and implemented, as well as the community engagement processes and best practices that underpin them. Services that facilitate community engagement typically will be delivered by sub-national IPAs, as they are the ones who are closer to the local communities.

- **Description**: services oriented to facilitate investor-community engagement, in their various forms.
- **Main beneficiaries**: both the investor and the local community will benefit from these services.
- **Implementation**: important to facilitating relationships is holding an ongoing relationship with both the investor and the community, to understand their strength and pain points, as well as their expectations of what solutions could look like. Brokering this information in a culturally appropriate manner provides the context in which to overcome challenges and generate value for all parties involved.
- **Intended outcome**: streamline the way in which both parties interact, build trust among the parties so they can have open dialogue to address any challenges that might arise.

The following example comes from Nigeria (see Box 4.48), where the subnational IPA played an essential role in supporting the investor engage with local communities.

Box 4.48 Edo State in Nigeria facilitates community engagement

Historically, FPIC has only been applied to communities identified as indigenous peoples and continues to be required under international human rights law. However, more recently the right to FPIC has also been applied to local communities who are not identified as indigenous peoples and is now required under the governance of tenure technical guide of the Food and Agriculture Organization of the United Nations, IFAD investment projects, Round Table on Sustainable Palm Oil (RSPO), extractive industry and other numerous sector standards and best practices around the world, with countries like Peru, Australia and the Philippines including FPIC to its national law.

In the experience of Edo State Investment Promotion Office (ESIPO) in Nigeria, some established investors reported challenges with host communities, particularly those cases when, at the point of the original investments, the communities had not been involved in the investment project, nor had there been a proper consultation.

Kelvin Uwaibi, Managing Director of ESIPO highlighted that "it is important that host communities and investors live in harmony. It saves the investor important losses in time and resources and avoids possible conflict with the host community. Aftercare service provided the process for early detection and resolution."

An example of ESIPO's Aftercare work is the role they played to facilitate engagement between communities located in Ovia South-West LGA and Okomu Oil Palm Company Plc, a subsidiary of Socfin S.A Belgium. Initially, there was a challenge with a community accusing the investor of neglect, such as not supporting the community's fish and farm activities. By keeping an ongoing engagement with the communities ESIPO learnt about the local views and perception about existing investors. They brought knowledge of the territory, cultural sensitivity and insight of the power structure in play locally. This exposure to what was happening locally was a unique perspective the subnational IPAs brought to the case. ESIPO's swift intervention through its Aftercare services, helped find common ground and resolved the issue. They played a critical role in ensuring host communities and investors addressed the concerns and developed more positive relationships.

Okomu Oil Palm Company Plc recently achieved its Roundtable on Sustainable Palm Oil (RSPO) certification. RSPO ensure that oil palm is produced sustainably without causing harm to the environment and local community. Such certification would have not been possible without the support received from the IPA to improve their relationship with the local communities.

The experience in Edo State evidenced that their Aftercare model has saved investors resources that would otherwise have been spent on conflict as a result of crisis with the communities. In turn, frictionless operation facilitated further expansion of investments.

Reproduced with kind permission from the Edo State Investment Promotion Office (ESIPO), Nigeria: http://invest.edostate.gov.ng/.

4.7 The Amazon HQ2 case

This section covers the bidding war to host Amazon's HQ2 in the USA, one of the most competitive business expansion processes in history. It provides unique insight into how host economies understand what services to provide to investors, as well as how investors decide about where to invest.

In the summer of 2017, Amazon announced plans to build a second headquarters (HQ2) in North America. The call was simple: Amazon invited economic development organisations to participate in a "competitive site selection process and is considering metro regions in North America for its second corporate headquarters."[95] The tender document encouraged states, provinces and metro areas "to coordinate with relevant jurisdictions to submit one application per metropolitan statistical area, state/province, county, city and the relevant localities therein."

Suffice to say that Amazon created one of the most competitive business attraction processes in history. The estimates were that Amazon would invest over US$5 billion on developing HQ2, and generate as many as 50,000 high-paying jobs. Moreover, Amazon "expects HQ2 to generate a similar level of activity in the local economy as at its Seattle base. Its investment in Seattle from 2010 through 2016 contributed an additional $38 billion to the city's economy, with every dollar invested by Amazon generating an additional $1.40 from other parties."[96]

Amazon received 238 proposals from across the US, plus border states with partnerships with Mexico or Canada. Many offered millions of dollars, and some billions of dollars, of incentives. This illustrated both the appetite some corporates have for public money in their pursuit of growth, and also the willingness of some locations to spend big in order to attract businesses to their area. According to journalist Leanna Garfield from businesinsider.com, "it is unlikely that Amazon select[s] a city that doesn't offer it pretty substantial incentives, as that was a key requirement."[97] In fact they have used tax incentives as a driver to open local subsidiaries intensively; "from 2005 to 2014, the company received at least $613 million in local government subsidies to build warehouses, according to a 2016 report by the Institute for Local Self-Reliance."[98] The report also "found that Amazon received an additional $147 million in subsidies for its data centres."[99] The think tank advocates for local funding to be used for local community development as opposed to giving them away in the forms of incentives.

Twenty finalist cities for HQ2 were selected in January 2018 with 9 of these locations offering major economic incentives as part of their bids (see Box 4.49). Notably three locations, Austin in Texas, Boston and Toronto,[100] said they would not give Amazon any tax breaks. At the other extreme, Newark, New Jersey offered the largest incentive package – US$7 billion. With incentives at this level, it is no surprise that questions have been raised by the media, local authorities, think tanks, FDI consultants and taxpayers about the rules and ethics of the incentives game. Bid teams across the US justified offering such incentives with calculations of return of investment, and narratives of market failure, indicating that they were what was required in order to attract Amazon. Many people have also questioned the value for money a location would get from offering these huge incentives, and how else these funds could have been used. Moreover, a significant part of the debate centred around governance, and whether bidding teams had the authority to grant this level of incentives without prior public consultation. Journalist David Leonhardt, writing for the *New York Times*, captured the sentiment of many critics when he commented that "corporate-relocation subsidies are terrible policy. They do nothing to lift the country's economic growth – to create more cupcakes, as it were. The subsidies mostly redistribute income upward, from taxpayers to corporate shareholders."[101]

What is clear is that the bidding war for HQ2 is likely to have opened a new era in the way corporates, particularly really large ones, engage with locations in regards to expansion projects, and in how public opinion around corporate expansion evolves. Both factors are likely to influence political and public sentiment, and therefore responses to such calls will be subject to higher public scrutiny. The same is true for corporates, as many critics have raised concerns as to how companies manage expansions, whether opening these bidding wars is aligned with responsible business practices and many have particular concerns about how site selection processes are managed.

Box 4.49 Incentives offered by shortlisted candidate locations for Amazon's HQ2 Project

Denver, Colorado – US$100 million or more

The state's proposal named some possible incentives, including: the job growth tax credit; job training grants of up to US$1,200 per employee; enterprise zone program offering income-tax credits for companies locating in distressed areas; in-state tuition benefits for employees; and local city incentives. Incentives could be "in excess of $100 million."[102]

Wake County, Raleigh, North Carolina – US$277 million

Wake County was prepared to offer Amazon its largest-ever incentive package and one that could have been worth up to $277 million during a 15-year period, including a "customized training support," of between $1,800 and $2,000 per job.[103]

Atlanta, Georgia – US$1–2 billion

The offer included "Amazon Georgia Academy a state university-affiliated education program featuring 24-week boot camp programs for company employees; an exclusive lounge – with free parking – for Amazon executives at one of the busiest airports in the world"." It also considered the use of an addition of a car on city passenger train to help logistics of Amazon delivery.[104]

Chicago, Illinois – at least US$1.32 billion

Chicago offered Amazon Economic Development for a Growing Economy (EDGE) tax credits. This is the program in which the state essentially lets a corporation keep the income tax dollars that its employees would normally pay to the state.[105]

Philadelphia, Pennsylvania – US$4.6 billion

The state of Pennsylvania offered tax incentives for up to 25 years. It also offered another $100 million for transportation improvements.[106]

Newark, New Jersey – US$7 billion

New Jersey offered Amazon tax breaks worth $7 billion over the next decade if the company decided to build in Newark, according to Bloomberg. The plan would expand a subsidy program called Grow NJ, and provide economic incentives for companies (like Amazon) that launch "transformative projects" (like HQ2).[107]

Ultimately Amazon did not select a single new HQ2, but instead chose to award new developments to two locations: New York City and the Washington DC suburb of Arlington, Virginia, a decision that was made public in December 2018. According to Monica Nickelsburg, a journalist at GeekWire.com, "one of the most controversial aspects of Amazon's year-long search for a second headquarters was the request for government incentives."[108] Both Arlington and New York made very generous offers. In addition to New York and Arlington, Amazon announced opening an operations centre in Nashville, generating 5,000 new jobs for Tennessee city that offered US$102 million of performance-based incentives

As soon as the winning locations were announced, critics were incensed with the incentives offered, with New York under particular scrutiny. Winning the bidding war for Amazon's HQ2 "came with a steep price tag – $3.4 billion. That's the total amount in tax incentives and grants that state and local officials in New York and Virginia offered the e-commerce giant as part of their bids to house '"HQ2"' in Long Island City, N.Y., and Arlington County, Va., respectively."[109]

What at first seemed to be a reason for celebration for New York soon turned sour, as activists and politicians questioned the incentives package offered and asked what the alternative use of those funds could be. Opposition grew further on the back of Amazon's anti-union stance. The *New York Times* reported that "some unions supported the deal, and even those opposed had appeared willing to work with Amazon if the company agreed to not work against the unionisation of its employees in New York. An Amazon representative, during one council hearing, pointedly said the company would not agree to such terms."[110] This proved to be a dealbreaker when Amazon presented its plan for Long Island at City Council hearings. The *New York Times* added that "protesters filled the seats, unfurled banners and chanted against the company. Not a single council member spoke up in defence of the deal or the company."[111] Surprisingly, Amazon did not have New York based representatives who could join local discussions, as Amazon spokespeople travelled from Washington to New York to attend official meetings. The pressure in New York grew to such extend that only three months later "enough New Yorkers raised enough of a ruckus about the nearly $3 billion in tax breaks that the city and state were bestowing on Amazon that Amazon finally had enough. It announced that it would no longer be bringing 25,000 jobs to Queens."[112] The *New York Times* commented that "as much as Amazon wanted New York's talent, it was not worth facing years of opposition on broad swaths of issues."[113]

The Arlington site, in contrast, did not face this level of push back. According to Arlington's Economic Development Office, the RFP resulted in an opportunity to convene partners to co-create. "The City of Alexandria, Arlington County, Fairfax County, and Loudoun County chose to partner to respond as a region. This unprecedented collaboration amongst the four jurisdictions resulted in the creation of significant new data and assets that the communities used for the HQ2 pitch."[114] They believe that other winning factors included a pragmatic approach and a promise to double Virginia's Tech-Talent Pipeline with a contribution of "nearly $1 billion investment into the Commonwealth's tech talent pipeline, including the creation of innovation campuses for George Mason University and Virginia Tech in Northern Virginia."[115] The county's final "incentive package included a 15-year, estimated tax $23 million incentive if Amazon meets office space occupancy goals over the years."[116] It will be provided on a post-performance basis, paid out to Amazon annually based on effective job creation and wage levels. Overall, Arlington's Economic Development Office calculate that HQ2 will generate significant revenues through its job creation and capital investment. "For Virginia, the project is estimated to generate a 6-to-1 return on the state's incentive package and a 5-to-1 return on the County's incentive package."[117]

The company opted to go to an existing urban site and development in South Eads Street in Pentagon City, adjacent to Metropolitan Park. The application process for the new building took 7 months from submission to approval. According to ABC7/WJLA, a local online news website, Arlington County granted exceptions to zoning rules regarding building height, density and parking ratios. In exchange, Amazon negotiated a community benefits package with Arlington County staff before construction began that included "over two acres of public open space, a $20 million affordable housing contribution, two new public streets, sidewalk and streetscape improvements, protected bike lanes, floating bus islands with shelters, street-level retail space a shared underground parking garage and a contribution of $225,000 for public art."[118]

Amazon announced that, "as with our Seattle headquarters, we plan to invest in developing a new headquarters in Arlington that will grow alongside its neighbours, supporting local businesses, building new public spaces for all to enjoy, and integrating sustainable design features throughout our campus."[119] They plan to redevelop a block of vacant warehouses, convert it into a 22-story office tower, add new retail spaces for local businesses and plenty of open space. Amazon indicates that they "are looking to foster a sense of place for our teams and community residents."[120] Their urban campus will "allow our employees to think creatively, to be a part of the surrounding community, and to remain connected to the region's unique culture and environment."[121]

The HQ2 case offers an unprecedented insight into the particularities of corporate decision making around expansions, as well as how host economies respond to winning a tender highly dependent on incentives. Moreover, the New York situation provides insight into the type of local opposition companies can face when looking to move to a new location – FDI can be a highly political endeavour. The Arlington case illustrates how local authorities can successfully work together, be creative and jointly create value to secure a highly contested project, while at the same time representing the interests of their local communities.

4.8 Closing

This chapter presented a wide portfolio of services provided by IPAs today, covering the 5 different types of services. To deliver these services, many IPAs develop inhouse service propositions that address client's needs. They also collaborate with a wide range of private and public sector entities that offer value-adding programmes. This flexible and collaborative approach to service delivery enables an IPA to meet a wide range of investor's needs outside of budgetary constraints. It also confirms the value of curation; akin to art directors who carefully select outstanding paintings to exhibit in a museum, IPAs curate local value, which they take to investors.

Notes

1 OECD, 2018. *Mapping of Investment Promotion Agencies in OECD Countries* [online]. Available at: http://www.oecd.org/investment/Mapping-of-Investment-Promotion-Agencies-in-OECD-Countries.htm.

2 Ibid.

3 Ibid.

4 Ibid.

5 Sanchiz, A. and Omic, A. 2020. *State of Investment Promotion Agencies: Evidence from WAIPA-WBG's Joint Global Survey*. World Bank, Washington, DC. WAIPA (World Association of Investment Promotion Agencies), Geneva [online]. Available at: http://documents1.worldbank.org/curated/en/499971594008431029/pdf/State-of-Investment-Promotion-Agencies-Evidence-from-WAIPA-WBG-s-Joint-Global-Survey.pdf.

6 Ibid.

7 Oya, C. and Schaefer, F. 2019. *Chinese Firms and Employment Dynamics in Africa: A Comparative Analysis. IDCEA Research Synthesis Report, SOAS*. University of London [online]. Available at: https://www.soas.ac.uk/idcea/publications/reports/file141857.pdf.

8 French, H.W. 2010. *The Next Empire* [online]. Available at: https://www.theatlantic.com/magazine/archive/2010/05/the-next-empire/308018/.

9 Keller, S. and Meaney, M. 2017. *Attracting and Retaining the Right Talent* [online]. Available at: https://www.mckinsey.com/business-functions/organization/our-insights/attracting-and-retaining-the-right-talent.

10 InvestKorea, 2021. *Recruitment Support* [online]. Available at: http://www.investkorea.org/en/service/recruitment.do.

11 Development Counsellors International, 2017. *Talent Wars: What People Look for in Jobs and Locations* [online]. Available at: http://aboutdci.com/wp-content/uploads/2017/03/TalentWars2017.pdf.

12 Lublin, J.S. 2016. *Earning It: Hard-Won Lessons from Trailblazing Women at the Top of the Business World*. Broadway, NY: HarperCollins Publishers.

13 Ibid.

14 Attributed to economist Sanjaya Lall.

15 UNESCAP, 2017. *Investment Facilitation through the Investment Cycle* [online]. Available at: https://www.unescap.org/sites/default/files/UNESCAP-Uzbekistan-Session%209-Investment%20facilitation-Project%20establishment%20and%20aftercare-December%202017_0.pdf.

16 See https://www.jetro.go.jp/en/invest/foreign-affiliate_support/.

17 See: www.thedti.gov.za.

18 Appelbaum, B. 2017. *Lack of Workers, Not Work, Weighs on the Nation's Economy*. [online]. Available at: https://www.nytimes.com/2017/05/21/us/politics/utah-economy-jobs.html.

19 Ibid.

20 International Labour Organization, 2020. *ILO Monitor: COVID-19 and the World of Work. Sixth Edition. Updated Estimates and Analysis* [online]. Available at: https://www.ilo.org/wcmsp5/groups/public/@dgreports/@dcomm/documents/briefingnote/wcms_755910.pdf.

21 Deloitte, 2021. *2021 Global Human Capital Trends* [online]. Available at: https://www2.deloitte.com/us/en/insights/focus/human-capital-trends.html.

22 See http://azpromo.az/investments/our-services.

23 SODENA, 2014. *Venture Capital* [online]. Available at: https://www.sodena.com/index.php/en/capital-riesgo.html.

24 London & Partners, 2020. *Set Up in London* [online]. Available at: https://business.london/invest.

25 Rodríguez-Montemayor, E. 2012. "Diaspora Direct Investment Policy: Options for Development". *IADB Integration and Trade Sector. Policy Brief*, Volume IDB-PB-183.

26 Passeri, F. 2017. *Network (2017) by Francesca Passeri. The European Dimension of Civic Crowdfunding. The potential of crowdfunding for boosting the economic and social effectiveness of European Structural and Investment Funds* [online]. Available at: https://cdn.crowdfundinsider.com/wp-content/uploads/2017/12/Civic-Crowdfunding-and-ESF_Final.pdf.

27 Ibid.

28 European Commission, 2015. *Horizon 2020: First Results* [online]. Available at: https://ec.europa.eu/programmes/horizon2020/sites/horizon2020/files/horizon_2020_first_results.pdf.

29 HyperNoir, 2020. *Cornershop Enters United States, Plans to Expand Further in Brazil* [online]. Available at: https://hypernoir.com/en/cornershop-expands-grocery-delivery-united-states/.

30 LAVCA Venture Investors, 2018. *ALLVP Exits Delivery Startup Cornershop in US$225M Sale to Walmart* [online]. Available at: https://lavca.org/2018/09/14/allvp-exits-delivery-startup-cornershop-in-us225m-sale-to-walmart/.

31 World Trade Organization, 2020. *WTO and Government Procurement* [online]. Available at: https://www.wto.org/english/tratop_e/gproc_e/gproc_e.htm.

32 Hugill, J. and Puvinathan, R. 2019. *Buying into the Future Report. How to Deliver Innovation through Public Procurement* [online]. Available at: https://view.publitas.com/public-1/buying-into-the-future-how-to-deliver-innovation-through-public-procurement/page/1.

33 OECD, 2006. *Policy Framework for Investment: A Review of Good Practices* [online]. Available at: http://www.oecd.org/daf/inv/investment-policy/40287306.pdf.

34 See Brochure IDA Ireland Mentor Programme [online]. Available at: https://www.idaireland.com/IDAIreland/media/HowWeHelp/IDA_Mentor_Programme.pdf.

35 See Brochure IDA Ireland Mentor Programme [online]. Available at: https://www.idaireland.com/IDAIreland/media/HowWeHelp/IDA_Mentor_Programme.pdf.

36 See Brochure IDA Ireland Mentor Programme [online]. Available at: https://www.idaireland.com/IDAIreland/media/HowWeHelp/IDA_Mentor_Programme.pdf.

37 See Brochure IDA Ireland Competitive Benchmark – Measuring Company Competitiveness [online]. Available at: https://www.idaireland.com/IDAIreland/media/HowWeHelp/IDA_Competitiveness_Benchmark.pdf.

38 See Brochure IDA Ireland Competitive Benchmark – Measuring Company Competitiveness [online]. Available at: https://www.idaireland.com/IDAIreland/media/HowWeHelp/IDA_Competitiveness_Benchmark.pdf.

39 See Brochure IDA Ireland Competitive Benchmark – Measuring Company Competitiveness [online]. Available at: https://www.idaireland.com/IDAIreland/media/HowWeHelp/IDA_Competitiveness_Benchmark.pdf.

40 CBI, 2015. *Best of Both Worlds: Guide to Business-University Collaboration* [online]. Available at: https://www.ncub.co.uk/reports/cbi-best.html.

41 Ibid.

42 Ibid.

43 Perkmann, M. and Salter, A. 2012. *How to Create Productive Partnerships With Universities* [online]. Available at: https://sloanreview.mit.edu/article/how-to-create-productive-partnerships-with-universities/Figures calculated from OECD figures, according to which, in the OECD area, higher education expenditure on R&D (HERD) equaled 0.4% of GDP in 2009. See OECD, 2011. *OECD Science, Technology and Industry Scoreboard* [online]. Available at: https://doi.org/10.1787/20725345.

44 OECD, 2007. *Innovation and Growth: Rationale for an Innovation Strategy* [online]. Available at: https://www.oecd.org/sti/39374789.pdf.

45 Ibid.

46 Ibid.

47 OECD, 2008. *Open Innovation in Global Networks* [online]. Available at: https://doi.org/10.1787/9789264047693-en.

48 Nordman, E.R. and Tolstoy, D. 2016. "The impact of opportunity connectedness on innovation in SMEs' foreign-market relationships". *Technovation*, Vol. 57–58, pp. 47–57.

49 Ibid.

50 Olabisi, M. 2017. "The impact of exporting and Foreign Direct Investment on product innovation: Evidence from Chinese manufacturers". *Contemporary Economic Policy*, 35(4), pp. 735–750.

51 Ibid.

52 Ibid.

53 Luong, H. et al. 2017. "How do foreign institutional investors enhance firm innovation?" *Journal of Financial and Quantitative Analysis*, 52(4), pp. 1449–1490

54 Ibid.

55 OECD, 2018. *Mapping of Investment Promotion Agencies in OECD Countries* [online]. Available at: http://www.oecd.org/investment/Mapping-of-Investment-Promotion-Agencies-in-OECD-Countries.htm.

56 Amazon Jobs, n.d. *About Arlington Area* [online]. Available at: https://www.amazon.jobs/en/locations/arlington.

57 Ibid.

58 Ibid.

59 Ibid.

60 OECD, 2018. *Mapping of Investment Promotion Agencies in OECD Countries* [online]. Available at: http://www.oecd.org/investment/Mapping-of-Investment-Promotion-Agencies-in-OECD-Countries.htm.

61 See www.investinafrica.com.

62 OECD, 2011. *Policy Framework for Investment User's Toolkit – Chapter 2*, s.l: OECD.

63 UNCTAD, 2011. *World Investment Report 2011: Non-Equity Modes of International Production and Development*, s.l: United Nation Publications.

64 Sanchiz, A. and Omic, A. 2020. *State of Investment Promotion Agencies: Evidence from WAIPA-WBG's Joint Global Survey*. World Bank, Washington, DC. WAIPA (World Association of Investment Promotion Agencies), Geneva [online]. Available at: http://documents1.worldbank.org/curated/en/499971594008431029/pdf/State-of-Investment-Promotion-Agencies-Evidence-from-WAIPA-WBG-s-Joint-Global-Survey.pdf.

65 Partners, S., n.d. [online]. Available at: https://sapartners.com/creating-a-lean-and-green-business-system/.

66 See https://www.idaireland.com/IDAIreland/media/HowWeHelp/Green_Business_Offer.pdf.

67 See https://www.idaireland.com/IDAIreland/media/HowWeHelp/Green_Business_Offer.pdf.

68 See https://www.idaireland.com/IDAIreland/media/HowWeHelp/Green_Business_Offer.pdf.

69 See https://www.idaireland.com/IDAIreland/media/HowWeHelp/Green_Business_Offer.pdf.

70 See https://www.idaireland.com/IDAIreland/media/HowWeHelp/Green_Business_Offer.pdf.

71 Culbertson, S. and Kumar, K.B. 2019. *Jobs Can Improve the Lives of Syrian Refugees and Their Host Communities – and Support Stability in the Middle East* [online]. Available at: https://www.rand.org/blog/2019/03/jobs-can-improve-the-lives-of-syrian-refugees-and-their.html.

72 UNHCR, 2020. *1 Per Cent of Humanity Displaced: UNHCR Global Trends Report* [online]. Available at: https://www.unhcr.org/news/press/2020/6/5ee9db2e4/1-cent-humanity-displaced-unhcr-global-trends-report.html.

73 Woetzel, J. et al. 2015. "The Power of Parity: How advancing women's equality can add $ 12 trillion to global growth". *McKinsey.com*, 1 September, https://www.mckinsey.com/featured-insights/employment-and-growth/how-advancing-womens-equality-can-add-12-trillion-to-global-growth.

74 Source: www.women.nyc.

75 Source: www.women.nyc.

76 Ibid.

77 Ibid.

78 Source: www.globalbusiness.org.

79 Ibid.

80 See https://www.oracle.com/corporate/citizenship/.

81 Hall, G. and Gandolfo, A. 2016. *Poverty and Exclusion among Indigenous Peoples: The Global Evidence*. The World Bank blog [online]. Available aa: https://blogs.worldbank.org/voices/poverty-and-exclusion-among-indigenous-peoples-global-evidence?cid=EXT_WBBlogTweetableShare_D_EXT.

82 FAO. 2016. Free Prior and Informed Consent – An Indigenous Peoples' right and a good practice for local communities [online]. Available at: http://www.fao.org/3/i6190e/i6190e.pdf.

83 Ibid.

84 Ibid.

85 Ibid.

86 Ibid.

87 Ibid.

88 Ibid.

89 Ibid.

90 Ibid.

91 Ibid.

92 UN HROCH, *Special Rapporteur on the Rights of Indigenous Peoples* [online]. Available at: https://www.ohchr.org/en/issues/ipeoples/srindigenouspeoples/pages/sripeoplesindex.asps.

93 Ibid.

94 UN OROHC, 2021. *UN Experts Call for Halt to Contentious Tourism Resort in Bangladesh* [online]. Available at: https://www.ohchr.org/EN/NewsEvents/Pages/DisplayNews.aspx?NewsID=26733&LangID=E.

95 Amazon, 2017. *Amazon HQ2 Request for Proposal* [online]. Available at: https://images-na.ssl-images-amazon.com/images/G/01/Anything/test/images/usa/RFP_3._V516043504_.pdf.

96 Garfield, L. 2018. *Cities are Throwing Hundreds of Millions at Amazon to Land HQ2 – Here's How They Stack Up* [online]. Available at: https://www.businessinsider.com/amazon-hq2-cities-developers-economic-tax-incentives-2017-10?r=UK.

97 Ibid.

98 Ibid.

99 Ibid.

100 Hanbury, M. 2018. *Amazon Is Reportedly Revisiting HQ2 Contenders as It Prepares to Make Its Decision – Here's Who's Left in the Running* [online]. Available at: https://www.businessinsider.com/amazon-hq2-20-finalist-cities-revealed-2018-1.

101 Leonhardt, D. 2019. *New York Did Us All a Favor by Standing Up to Amazon* [online]. Available at: https://www.nytimes.com/2019/02/17/opinion/amazon-new-york.html.

102 Chuang, T. 2017. *Colorado Releases Its Proposal Pitching the Denver Area as Amazon's Second Headquarters* [online]. Available at https://www.denverpost.com/2017/11/16/colorado-releases-amazon-hq2-proposal-pitching-denver-area/.

103 Eanes, Z. 2018. *Wake County Was Prepared to pay Amazon a Record-setting Amount for HQ2* [online]. Available at https://www.newsobserver.com/news/business/article221710720.html.

104 Miranda, L. et al. 2018. *Here Are the Most Outrageous Incentives Cities Offered Amazon In Their HQ2 Bids* [online]. Available at https://www.buzzfeednews.com/article/leticiamiranda/amazon-hq2-finalist-cities-incentives-airport-lounge.

105 Joravsky, B. 2017. *Chicago's Amazon HQ2 Bid Offers Money for Nothing, TIFs for Free* [online]. Available at: https://www.chicagoreader.com/chicago/chicagos-amazon-hq2-bid-money-for-nothing-tifs-for-free/Content?oid=33535992.

106 Wagaman, A. 2018. *Pennsylvania Offered Amazon up to $4.6Billion over 25 Years* [online]. Available at: https://www.mcall.com/business/mc-biz-amazon-hq2-proposal-lehigh-pennsylvania-sidebar-20181113-story.html.

107 Garfield, L. 2018. *Cities are Throwing Hundreds of Millions at Amazon to Land HQ2 – Here's How They Stack Up* [online]. Available at: https://www.businessinsider.com/amazon-hq2-cities-developers-economic-tax-incentives-2017-10?r=UK.

108 Nickelsburg, M. 2018. *HQ2 Incentives Revealed: Here's What NYC and Virginia Gave Up to Get Amazon's New Headquarters* [online]. Available at: https://www.geekwire.com/2018/hq2-incentives-finally-revealed-heres-nyc-virginia-gave-get-amazons-new-headquarters/.

109 Passy, J. 2019. *This Is What Amazon's 'HQ2' Was Going to Cost New York Taxpayers* [online]. Available at: https://www.marketwatch.com/story/what-amazons-hq2-means-for-taxpayers-in-new-york-and-virginia-2018-11-14.

110 Goodman, D. 2019. *Amazon Pulls Out of Planned New York City Headquarters* [online]. Available at: https://www.nytimes.com/2019/02/14/nyregion/amazon-hq2-queens.html.

111 Ibid.

112 Leonhardt, D. 2019. *New York Did Us All a Favor by Standing Up to Amazon* [online]. Available at: https://www.nytimes.com/2019/02/17/opinion/amazon-new-york.html.

113 Goodman, D. 2019. *Amazon Pulls Out of Planned New York City Headquarters* [online]. Available at: https://www.nytimes.com/2019/02/14/nyregion/amazon-hq2-queens.html.

114 Arlington Economic Development Office, 2018. *Amazon HQ2: Then and Now* [online]. Available at: https://www.arlingtoneconomicdevelopment.com/why-arlington/amazon-hq2-then-and-now/.

115 Ibid.

116 DeVoe, J. 2020. *At Two-Year Mark, Amazon Says HQ2 is On Track for Construction and Hiring Goals* [online]. Available at: https://www.arlnow.com/2020/11/16/at-two-year-mark-amazon-says-hq2-is-on-track-for-construction-and-hiring-goals/.

117 Arlington Economic Development Office, 2018. *Amazon HQ2: Then and Now* [online]. Available at: https://www.arlingtoneconomicdevelopment.com/why-arlington/amazon-hq2-then-and-now/.

118 Graf, H. 2020. *It's Been Exactly 2 Years since Amazon Announced HQ2 Would Be Built in Arlington* [online]. Available at: https://wjla.com/news/local/its-been-exactly-2-years-since-amazon-announced-hq2-would-be-built-in-arlington.

119 Amazon Jobs, n.d. *About Arlington Area* [online]. Available at: https://www.amazon.jobs/en/locations/arlington.

120 Ibid.

121 Ibid.

5
INVESTOR AID AND GRIEVANCES

Chapter highlights

- Even the best post-investment efforts won't avoid conflict with investors. This is an inherent by-product of FDI, one which requires particular attention.
- Investor aid is a mechanism for resolving any conflicts in a fair and equitable manner. Alternatives include mediation, seeking help from an ombudsperson and investor-state grievances.
- Many international investment treaties include provisions for resolving investor-state disputes.

There are 9 common types of investor dissatisfaction. Understanding the nature and cause of any complaints or grievances helps IPAs and host economies introduce policy change that should minimise the risk of similar problems in the future.

5.1 Investor aid

The primary objective of post-investment activity is to help an investor grow. However, there are times when growth is not possible, and investors may even regret their investment decisions (see post-purchase dissonance in Chapter 3, Investor Services). Investors may also be dissatisfied with the level of support they received from the host economy, either directly from

DOI: 10.4324/9781003174950-8

the government, or from the IPA. Indeed, it is not unusual for investors to make complaints, which often focus on the belief that their expectations have not been met. This is where investor aid comes in to help investors find solutions to their needs.

The World Bank notes that "studies have consistently shown that each year, around 25 percent of foreign investors investing in developing countries totally withdraw or cancel planned expansion plans of their FDI projects."[1] In particular, the World Bank notes that FDI disinvestment is often in response to government action such as "expropriation, breach of contract, transfer and convertibility restrictions, and arbitrary or sudden regulatory changes and actions."[2] Moreover, some disgruntled investors take legal action, which has "significant monetary costs and political and economic implications derived from reputational damage and loss of jobs and FDI, among others."[3]

However, despite the potential adverse impact of disappointed or disgruntled investors, many IPAs do not systematically monitor complaints. According to a 2020 WAIPA study, in collaboration with the World Bank, titled "State of Investment Promotion Agencies: Evidence from WAIPA-WBG's Joint Global Survey", "64 percent of IPAs have systems in place for the collection of complaints from investors and 34 percent of them do not."[4] The study noted that the most common method of responding to complaints is proactive follow-up and ad hoc contact during events to respond to clients' needs. Unsurprisingly, detecting and addressing investor dissatisfaction at an early stage increases the likelihood of finding an amicable solution.

The most effective way to avoid investor conflict is to have a strong Aftercare value proposition centred around investor dialogue. In particular, IPAs equipped with action-driven resolution mechanisms that work closely with policy advocates are well-placed to find solutions to most investors' enquiries and complaints. In addition, IPAs can support the use of mediation services and work closely with the ombudsperson (should that role exist).

5.1.1 Mediation

Mediation is often used in business disputes as it is cheaper than going to court and has the added benefit of typically taking place behind closed doors, thereby avoiding generating adverse publicity for either party. According to

North American journalist Peter Lovenheim and employment lawyer Lisa Guerin, in their book *Mediation: The Six Stages*, the benefit of mediation is that it is "forward-looking; the goal is for all parties to work out a solution they can live with and trust. It focuses on solving problems, not uncovering the truth or imposing legal rules. This, of course, is a far different approach than courts take. In court, a judge or jury looks back to determine who was right and who was wrong, then imposes a penalty or award based on its decision."[5]

In mediation, the parties agree to work with a third party who "has no authority to impose a decision, [and therefore] nothing will be decided unless both parties agree to it."[6] And, in the event that no agreement is reached, both parties still have to ability to take each other to court.

A small number of IPAs, particularly those linked to high profile government departments, offer themselves as mediators to help resolve any conflicts a foreign investor may wish to raise. One such example is the Polish Investment and Trade Agency (PAIH), which states on its website that they "help clients to resolve current issues in their business in Poland. We offer mediation support, relations management, and intermediation in contacts with the central administration and local governments."[7]

Other mediation options include an independent, experienced and respected director or consultant, an active or retired diplomat or an industry champion who has the ability to act as an independent arbitrator. In this scenario there is no official process, just the willingness on the part of all parties to come to an amicable solution.

5.1.2 Ombudsperson

A more formal option, where it exists, is to use an ombudsperson to resolve any problem or dispute. An ombudsperson is an officially appointed, independent professional who is responsible for resolving disputes between the government of a location and foreign investors. The first country to introduce an ombudsperson was South Korea. After the Asian financial crisis in the late 1990s, Korea was asked by the IMF to introduce FDI-friendly initiatives. Korea adopted an Aftercare strategy as a way of attracting new investment. This included the creation of the Office of the Foreign Investment Ombudsman (OFIO), as well as the establishment of the Investment Aftercare Team. The Ombudsman is commissioned by the

President of the Republic of Korea on the recommendation of the Minister of Trade, Industry and Energy following discussions with the Foreign Investment Committee. The fact that the Ombudsman is unconnected to Korea's IPA is intended to give investors comfort that Korea will take any concerns they have seriously and independently.

Moreover, the OFIO and its grievance resolution body "collects and analyses information concerning the problems foreign firms experience, request cooperation from and recommend implementation thereof to relevant administrative agencies, propose new policies to improve the foreign investment promotion system, and carry out other necessary tasks to assist foreign-invested companies in resolving their grievances."[8]

The Korean Investment Aftercare Team is staffed with experts in the fields of finance, trade, law, taxation, customs, labour management and construction. These experts, also known as "home doctors," act as liaisons to help find solutions to grievances filed by foreign companies in consultation with relevant government institutions. By law, the ombudsman system ensures prompt cooperation from these agencies. Between 2013 and 2017 they dealt with 2,035 cases covering a wide range of issues, as is shown in Figure 5.1. The most common grievances related to taxation, investment procedures, incentives, visas and certification inspections.

The Korean Ombudsman Office is often cited as an example of best practice in the FDI industry and is regularly invited to participate in forums and conferences to share their approach. Their dispute resolution model has been acknowledged by investors as playing a key role in their decisions to expand their operations in Korea. In recognition of its excellence, WAIPA granted Korea the IPA Award at the World Investment Conference in 2007. The United Nations Conference on Trade and Development and Asia-Pacific Economic Cooperation have praised Korea's Foreign Investment Ombudsman system as being an effective way to prevent investor-state disputes. "Many countries are interested in benchmarking Korea's Foreign Investment Ombudsman system, including Russia, Kazakhstan, Brazil and Vietnam."[9]

5.2 Grievances

Unfortunately, sometimes things do go wrong and, despite everyone's best efforts, some investor complaints get escalated. In these situations, the investor should have access to impartial grievance procedures.

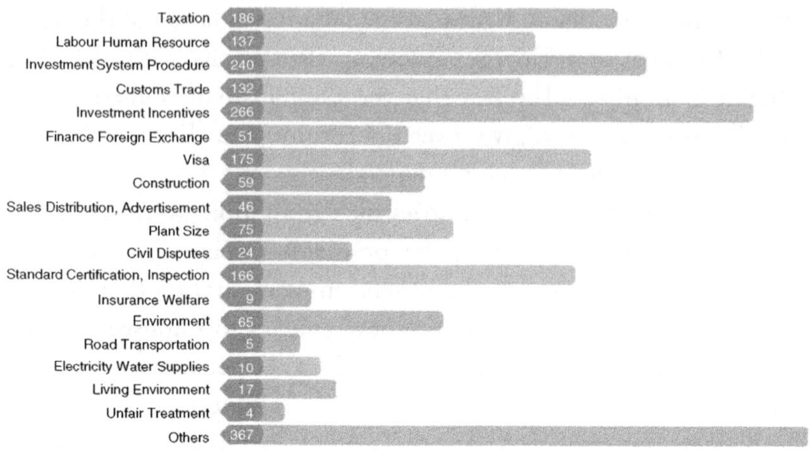

Figure 5.1 Cases resolved by the Korean Office of the Ombudsman.

Source: Authors' own design based on data from Ombudsman Kotra (http://ombudsman.kotra.or.kr/eng/au/act.do).

Grievance mechanisms "help avoid investor-state disputes by identifying and managing grievances between investors and public agencies proactively, especially those that are derived from government actions (such as sudden arbitrary and adverse regulatory changes, abuse of authority, breach of contract and expropriation)."[10]

When a dispute cannot be resolved within a country, investors have the option to take their grievance to an international investment court system (ICS) and file an investor-state dispute settlement (ISDS) at the International Centre for Settlement of Investment Disputes (ICSID), which is part of the World Bank Group. The ICSID is an independent, apolitical dispute resolution organisation backed by the 160 signatories of the Convention on the Settlement of Investment Disputes between States and Nationals of Other States. Judgments passed by ICSID are binding on both parties.

According to UNCTAD, of the more than 1,200 ISDS cases so far brought forward, close to 700 have been concluded, including the cases presented in Box 5.1. And while both states and investors have won cases, the fines where a state has been held liable can be significant and have "ranged from several millions to $8 billion."[11] There are added layers of complexity in international disputes, with UNCTAD noting that "the blurring of investor nationality has made the application of rules and regulations on foreign ownership more challenging."[12] The report goes on to say that "ownership chains of multinationals made with multiple cross-border links involving on average three jurisdictions"[13] are making disputes more complex and therefore the settlement of them more resource intensive.

Box 5.1 Examples of investor-state disputes

Name: *GSI v Canada*

Home state(s) of investor: United States of America

Details of investment: ownership of Geophysical Service Inc. (GSI), a company creating and licensing seismic data principally for use in oil and gas exploration.

Summary of the dispute: claims arising out of the government's alleged unilateral disclosure to third parties of proprietary marine seismic data created or acquired by the claimants' company GSI, without compensation for GSI or the possibility of recourse. According to the claimants, the government thereby confiscated GSI's intellectual property rights in the seismic data.

Arbitration rules: UNCITRAL

Applicable IIA: NAFTA (1992)

Claimed by investor: US$2,529.00 million

Outcome: case pending.

Case name: *Oschadbank v Russia*

Home state(s) of investor: Ukraine

Details of investment: ownership of a large number of properties in Crimea, including offices, apartment buildings and villas.

Summary of the dispute: claims arising out of the alleged expropriation of properties following the 2014 Russian annexation of Crimea.

Arbitration rules: UNCITRAL

Applicable IIA: Russian Federation – Ukraine BIT (1998)

Outcome: decided in favour of investor.

Claimed by investor: US$220.00 million. Awarded by tribunal: US$130.00 million.
IIA breaches alleged and found: direct expropriation.

Case name: *Kunsttrans v Serbia*

Home state(s) of investor: Austria

Details of investment: art storage contract concluded with the National Museum of Serbia.

Summary of the dispute: claims arising out of a contract signed in 2006 between the National Museum of Serbia and the claimant for the storage of the museum's art collection during a planned renovation. The museum allegedly failed to pay over €500,000 in rental fees for the use of the art storage facility that the claimant had constructed in 2007.

Arbitration rules: ICSID

Applicable IIA: Austria – Serbia BIT (2001)

Outcome: decided in favour of investor.

Claimed by investor: €9.00 million. Awarded by tribunal: €1.70 million.

IIA breaches alleged and found: fair and equitable treatment/minimum standard of treatment, including denial of justice claims.

Case name: *Seo v Korea*

Home state(s) of investor: United States of America

Details of investment: partial ownership (76%) of a residential property in Seoul.

Summary of the dispute: claims arising out of the allegedly insufficient amount of compensation set by the government for the claimant's real estate property that had been expropriated following the municipal government's designation of the relevant area for redevelopment.

Arbitration rules: UNCITRAL

Applicable IIA: Korea – US FTA (2007)

Administering institution: Hong Kong International Arbitration Centre (HKIAC)

Claimed by investor: US$3.00 million. Awarded by tribunal: data not available.

Outcome: decided in favour of the state.

IIA breaches alleged: direct expropriation Fair and equitable treatment/Minimum standard of treatment, including denial of justice claims.

IIA breaches found: None: jurisdiction declined.

Case name: *Itisaluna Iraq and others v Iraq*

Home state(s) of investor: Jordan

Applicable IIA: OIC Investment Agreement (1981)

Arbitration rules: ICSID

Investment: licence for telecommunications services.

Summary: claims arising out of the government's alleged impairment of the claimants' rights under a telecommunications licence and subsequent non-renewal of the licence.

Outcome: decided in favour of state.

IIA breaches alleged: full protection and security, direct or indirect expropriation.

IIA breaches found: none: jurisdiction declined.

Case name: *Cervin and Rhone v Costa Rica*

Home State(s) of investor: Switzerland

Applicable IIA: Costa Rica – Switzerland BIT (2000)

Arbitration Rules: ICSID

IIA breaches alleged: indirect expropriation, fair and equitable treatment/minimum standard of treatment, including denial of justice claims, full protection and security, or similar, umbrella clause, national treatment.

IIA breaches found: fair and equitable treatment/minimum standard of treatment, including denial of justice claims.

Outcome: decided in favour of neither party (liability found but no damages awarded).

Claimed by investor: US$75.00 million. Awarded by tribunal: US$0.00.

Data obtained from the Investment Dispute Settlement Navigator.

Link: https://investmentpolicy.unctad.org/investment-dispute-settlement.

Most international trade agreements, particularly those signed after 2000, have an Investor to State Dispute Settlement (ISDS) mechanism that allows signatory countries to resolve their differences directly. The 2020 World Investment Report noted that during 2019 there were 3,284 active international investment agreements (IIA) with an ISDS clause.[14] These dispute settlement mechanisms provide "guarantees to companies that their investments will be treated fairly and on an equal footing to national companies. By creating legal certainty and predictability for companies, investment protection is also a tool for states around the world to attract and maintain FDI to underpin their economy."[15] The ISDS mechanism also allows signatory countries of the treaties to use a dispute settlement mechanism specifically designed to deal with disputes arising under the trade agreement.

In a situation where the home country of an investor and the host country where the investment has been made have both signed a free trade agreement that contains ISDS disputes clauses, then the two countries have the ability to resolve the dispute themselves. In the large majority of cases, it is usually the host state that has violated the rights granted to the investor under the treaty, and it is the investor who has the option to bring the matter before a bilateral tribunal.

The World Trade Organisation (WTO) also provides a framework for resolving trade disputes, stating that "resolving trade disputes is one of the core activities of the WTO. A dispute arises when a member government believes another member government is violating an agreement or a commitment that it has made in the WTO."[16] The WTO has a Dispute Settlement Body (DSB) that has the "authority to establish dispute settlement panels, refer matters to arbitration, adopt panel, Appellate Body and arbitration reports, maintain surveillance over the implementation of recommendations and rulings contained in such reports, and authorise suspension of concessions in the event of non-compliance with those recommendations and rulings."[17] Since its inception in 1995, WTO members have opened 597 disputes. "Not all of these disputes have required formal rulings to resolve them. A mutually agreed solution is always the preferred outcome, and consultations among disputing members within the framework of WTO dispute settlement can often be sufficient to resolve the matter in dispute."[18] If the panel's report is not acceptable to either party, they can appeal to the WTO Appellate Body. If a member does not comply with the recommendations from a dispute settlement, then trade compensation or sanctions, for example in the form of increases in customs duties, can be applied. This is a bone of contention for several countries. Both governments and the FDI industry have voiced concerns "about the system's reliance on arbitrators, given its lack of transparency, issues over the predictability and consistency of their decisions, and the excessive costs involved."[19] In response, the United Nations Commission on International Trade Law (UNCITRAL) agreed in July 2017 to discuss possible multilateral approaches to address ISDS reform. A couple of months later, the European Union presented a proposal for a multilateral investment court, which it sees as the logical next step along the road to establishing a more transparent, coherent and fair system to deal with investor complaints under investment protection agreements. They suggest highly qualified, permanent and full-time judges, completely independent of investors and states. And in terms of funding, they are of the view that "like all other international organisations, the contracting parties would in principle finance the court."[20]

However, UNCITRAL's talks have progressed since 2017, "although states are eager to reform the ISDS system, the complexity of the issue is likely to require additional sessions before agreement can be reached."[21] Broadly speaking, current "proposals reflect two distinct approaches. Some states back the creation of tools – such as a code of conduct and/or an advisory body for smaller economies and small and medium-sized enterprises – to complement the current system. Others favour fundamental changes through the creation of a two-court system with appointed members."[22] The European Union, for example, advocates for what they call the "EU's goals with a multilateral investment court." These goals are twofold. First, to address the limitations of the existing ISDS system and presenting a "proposal to include in all EU trade and investment negotiations a permanent institution for resolving investment disputes. This new mechanism is known as the Investment Court System."[23] Second, to make the system more efficient. It suggests "it would be much more efficient to have just one multilateral institution to rule on investment disputes covered by all the bilateral agreements in place."[24] In addition, they suggest that judges are appointed dependant "on the number of participating countries and also on the number of cases the court will have to deal with."[25]

5.3 Conflict resolution in action

When conflict does occur, effective management of the situation can lead to early resolution and, in particular, before any conflict becomes too serious, thereby minimising the risk of FDI loss. Most of the cases are resolved within the mandate of the IPA, or at the government authority they report to. Indeed, the World Bank observes that "when problems arise, investors' first step is to engage in consultations with host governments, rather than turning to litigation."[26] They add that "data also shows that investors have a high degree of dissatisfaction with the effectiveness of this engagement."[27]

When an investor has an enquiry or a complaint, it usually falls into one of the following 9 types:

1. **Asymmetry of information**: this occurs when there is a gap in an investor's knowledge which negatively affects the operation of the investor. An IPA should be well-prepared for this type of situation. For example, an investor might be struggling to find a suitable supplier base. In the investor's view, the company has been misled into believing they were investing in a location with a thriving sector cluster, and hence that all the suppliers they would need would already be present in the location. The IPA can help address the asymmetry of information by introducing the investor to alternative sector networks, contacting providers directly or helping with disseminating a request for proposals, thereby addressing the asymmetry, and resolving the conflict.

2. **Questions where there are no clear-cut answers**: investors like definitive answers and can struggle with the non-committal political responses they sometimes receive from government departments. A common issue is whether or not exports are subject to sales taxes. In this situation, the IPA might also contact the tax authority and seek to obtain a definitive answer, only to receive the same answer the investor received. When a clear-cut answer is not possible and the source of the conflict is not addressable, then the best approach is to manage an investor's expectations. Ideally this is done early on in a project, prior to the investor making any significant financial commitments.
3. **Needs not previously anticipated**: this occurs when an investor has a requirement not covered by the current Aftercare service offer, but which can be met elsewhere in the local Ecosystem. For example, if a foreign investor is looking to introduce a sustainability best practice policy, and wants to understand local solutions, discovers that sustainability is not an integral part of the local regulatory system and desired solutions, such as recycling, are not on offer, this can have an impact on the company's commitment towards sustainability and therefore company reporting to their shareholders. The investor may then voice discontent, as well as the governance risk that operating in such an environment represents for the company. The IPA may be able to introduce the investor to other local companies that already have established sustainability practices in place, as well as looking at the need from a Policy Advocacy perspective.
4. **Service out of remit**: sometimes investors have needs that are beyond an IPA's remit, such as support in resolving a disagreement with a local authority. The IPA can escalate the case to other hierarchies where a more investor-friendly approach applies, and/or play a mediator role. At this point, as appropriate, the IPA can either close the project or handhold the investor through the relevant procedure.
5. **Gap in the service**: sometimes investors have needs that cannot be met by the IPA or by anyone else in the local Ecosystem. This can be problematic when the investor has received this particular service in another location and therefore expects to receive it elsewhere. An example is when a mining company has an expectation that the issue of a permit to explore a mine will automatically grant

the authority to build a private road, while the host economy has different authorities supervising the two different requirements. The investor might consider that the service provided locally does not fully meet the company's needs. This is another situation where managing client expectations is important, being aware as early as possible of what an investor's requirements are and not promising services that cannot be delivered. In this case the need is not met, and close monitoring is needed in order to avoid escalation.

6. **Depth of service**: sometimes investors have a different view of the level of service they were promised compared to the one they actually received. For example, local industry research may be offered, but the resultant report is simply a list of relevant websites for the foreign investor to review. This is often due to unclear terms of engagement, oversold services at the beginning of a project or a change in policy by the IPA. This again reiterates how important it is to properly manage expectations up front, in terms of what services can and cannot be delivered by the IPA and the local government. Level of service is a common source of discontent mentioned by investors.
7. **Quality of service**: investors, as with any other local business, expect professional and fair treatment, including transparency, due process, fair and equitable treatment, proportionality of fines, government conduct and adherence to commitments. With potentially hundreds of public bodies interacting with an investor on any given project, assuring a consistent level of service is sometimes a challenge for host economies. This is often a source of post-investment dissonance and can result in either disinvestment or an investor-state dispute.
8. **Difference in views and/or interpretation** of existing investment partnerships, agreements and collaborations. When a client expresses dissatisfaction with any services received that were subject to a contractual agreement, IPAs need to be careful how they respond. The investor may be unfamiliar with common practice locally, while the IPA might be unfamiliar with the services the investor receives in other jurisdictions. It is therefore key to first properly understand the reason for an investor's dissatisfaction prior to taking any action, particularly as this is a common cause of conflict escalation.

9. **Unfair or unequitable treatment**: investors expect fair and equitable treatment (FET), which the World Bank defines as "requiring that government action be transparent, coherent, reasonable, proportionate or consistent with the expectations of foreign investors arising from written commitments undertaken by governments through contracts of investment authorisations."[28] FETs such as "lack of transparency, predictability in dealing with public agencies and sudden adverse regulatory changes" are the most frequent forms of government conduct that result in negative post-investment behaviour by investors.[29]

Irrespective of the type of complaint an investor makes, IPAs should deal with any complaints as quickly as possible and keep records of all actions taken. When IPAs are unable to resolve an issue, or the dispute falls outside their area of influence, they should promptly make the relevant government departments aware of the situation. Some IPAs recognise the importance of swift response to conflict and have defined service protocols to provide an answer to investors. Others have consolidated all complaints and conflicts in their territories via a single digital grievance platform, as it is the case of Tamil Nadu, India's second largest economy, located on the south-eastern coast. As can be seen in Box 5.2 they provide an online help desk, BizBuddy, as well as a specific grievance tool.

Box 5.2 Guidance Tamil Nadu's online help desk and grievance portal

Biz Buddy – Online Help Desk

Tamil Nadu Biz Buddy is an electronic help desk portal dedicated for the industry to ensure time bound resolution of any help requests. It builds on real-time governance through feedback loops. Investors can submit any issue that has not been resolved for 5 days by the concerned government department through a "Help Call" on Biz Buddy. Help Calls are then taken up and monitored by Guidance and automatically escalated to the concerned Tamil Nadu Government Departments(s) in a time bound escalation matrix.

The requests can relate to incentives, clearances or any operational issues. Once the Help Call is submitted, a ticket number is generated to track the progress. Simultaneously, the concerned nodal officer in the government is alerted and the department has 30 working days to solve the issue. During this time, the officer can also get in touch with the applicant to get any additional information needed through the portal. So far, 129 help calls have been resolved within the timeframe with an 80% reduction in time of processing compared to the time of pendency.

Key features:

- Unique reference number to track Help Call submissions
- Applicants and government officials are notified electronically of the Help Call status changes in real-time
- Inbuilt escalation mechanism escalates Help Calls not resolved within a defined period across each level in the government department up to the Hon'ble Chief Minister
- Resolution of Help Calls is aimed at within 30 working days

Grievance Redressal – Online Portal

The Grievance Redressal [Online] Portal for industry is a unique initiative to boost the investors' confidence and improve the ease of doing business in the state.

Key features:

- Unique reference number to track grievance submissions
- Stakeholders are notified of the ticket status
- Ticket can be escalated if grievance is not resolved within given time
- Dashboard showcasing pending grievances, escalated issues, widget to sort
- Mechanism to acquire industry stakeholder's ideas and suggestions
- Resolution will be provided within 30 working days

Reproduced with kind permission from Guidance, Industries Department, Government of Tamil Nadu.

Link: https://www.bizbuddy.tn.gov.in/.

The World Bank provides guidance on how to effectively deal with investor enquiries and complaints, identifying 4 key elements to handling responses. These are: availability and contactability; responsiveness and handling; response quality; and ongoing customer care – with these operations working together in an integrated system that is continuously monitored for improvement.[30] In its 2009 briefing, "What sets the world's best investment facilitators apart from the rest", the World Bank outlined that "few things are more damaging to an IPA's image and actual performance than giving a first impression of being disinterested or incapable of providing a basic, professional response"[31] to a complaint. The World Bank also highlighted the need for detailed guidelines on the content, style, timeframe and quality assurance of inquiry responses.[32] This is important, as making an investor feel unwelcome can threaten an investment and generate adverse publicity about the local investment climate. Moreover, IPAs should have contingency plans in place in the (hopefully rare) event that an investor is dissatisfied. Such a plan should aim to minimise, and preferably eliminate, the possibility that a disappointed or dissatisfied investor shares their views with other parties and investors. Furthermore, when an IPA is unable to respond in detail, the investor's inquiry should still be acknowledged. To ensure a high quality and timely response to an inquiry, the best IPAs have written guidelines for content, quality control procedures and deadlines for submissions of replies to clients.

Professor and leading FDI adviser Karl P. Sauvant places particular importance on the role of facilitation to prevent investment disputes, "not only because these disputes can be costly in and of themselves, but also because they can discourage both reinvestment and new investment."[33] In his "G-20 Guiding Principles on Investment Facilitation for Sustainable Development" he encourages governments to "put in place mechanisms to identify and address investment irritants and complaints before they become formal disputes, and in so doing avoid the concomitant economic, reputational, and political costs."[34]

The World Bank has proposed that countries adopt what they call a Systemic Investment Response Mechanism (SIRM) in order to provide good public governance when responding to investor grievances. The WBG conceived the SIRM "as a practical solution package designed to enable governments to identify, track, and resolve, in a timely manner, investor-state grievances that put investment projects at risk,"[35] further noting that "some countries have started to focus attention on the beginning of the investor-state conflict continuum, addressing problems affecting investors at an early stage, before they have escalated to grievances. Other countries have focused on problems that place FDI at risk of withdrawal or cancellation."[36] SIRMs seek to gather data and establish public-sector collaboration and coordination protocols on how to deal with grievances, generate insight based on historic grievances and assess the need to advocate for reform. The WBG suggests appointing a single government agency to play that role. Thus far, the WBG has piloted the SIRM model in 9 countries, and found that only a small proportion of grievances are serious enough to put the investment at risk, and that adverse regulatory conduct is the grievance most likely to make an investor seek to take further action, thereby putting its investment at risk. "Specifically, abuse of authority, abuse of discretion when interpreting laws and regulations, and lack of transparency are the most common sources of grievances."[37] The advantage of using the SIRM mechanism can be seen in the number of investments retained, reinvestment retained and, most importantly, significant public cost savings derived from finding alternative solutions that dissuade investors ready to commence investor-state arbitration proceedings.

Sectors that feature more prominently in grievance procedures are the extractive industries, the service sector and manufacturing. Conflicts then generate from specialised and subnational regulatory agencies. The most common grievances include "taxation problems, breach of contract, cancellation of land leases and operation licenses, as well as fines imposed due to alleged regulatory infractions."[38]

In summary, host economies that focus on attraction, promotion and facilitation services while failing to create formal conflict resolution mechanisms risk higher levels of investor dissatisfaction. The cost of not having good conflict resolution mechanisms in place can be high. Conflict needs to be contained early and establishing mechanisms to do so are not only a fundamental part of good risk management, but they also help protect the local area's reputation, provide insight for policy improvement, are cost-effective and encourage long-term investment. Hence, conflict resolution should not be left to chance. To be effective, it requires an institutional infrastructure carefully designed and integrated into a host-economy's service offer.

Notes

1 World Bank, 2019. *Retention and Expansion of Foreign Direct Investment: Political Risk and Policy Responses*. Washington, DC: World Bank.

2 Ibid.

3 Ibid.

4 Sanchiz, A. and Omic, A. 2020. *State of Investment Promotion Agencies: Evidence from WAIPA-WBG's Joint Global Survey*. World Bank, Washington, DC. WAIPA (World Association of Investment Promotion Agencies), Geneva [online]. Available at: http://documents1.worldbank.org/curated/en/499971594008431029/pdf/State-of-Investment-Promotion-Agencies-Evidence-from-WAIPA-WBG-s-Joint-Global-Survey.pdf.

5 Lovenheim, P. and Guerin, L. 2004. *Mediate, Don't Litigate: Strategies for Successful Mediation*. Berkeley, CA: Nolo.

6 Ibid.

7 See https://www.paih.gov.pl/en.

8 Global Business' website: https://www.globalbusiness.org/.

9 InvestKorea, n.d. *Foreign Investment Ombudsman* [online]. Available at: http://www.investkorea.org/en/ik/ombusman.do.

10 Sanchiz, A. and Omic, A. 2020. *State of Investment Promotion Agencies: Evidence from WAIPA-WBG's Joint Global Survey*. World Bank, Washington, DC. WAIPA (World Association of Investment Promotion Agencies), Geneva [online]. Available at: http://documents1.worldbank.org/curated/en/499971594008431029/pdf/State-of-Investment-Promotion-Agencies-Evidence-from-WAIPA-WBG-s-Joint-Global-Survey.pdf.

11 UNCTAD, 2016. *World Investment Report 2016 – Investor Nationality: Policy Challenges* [online]. Available at: http://unctad.org/en/PublicationChapters/wir2016_KeyMessage_en.pdf.

12 Ibid.

13 Ibid.

14 UNCTAD, 2020. *World Investment Report 2020* [online]. Available at: https://unctad.org/webflyer/world-investment-report-2020.

15 Ibid.

16 World Trade Organization, 2017. *A Handbook on the WTO Dispute Settlement System*. 2nd edn. Cambridge: Cambridge University Press.

17 WTO, 2017. *Dispute Settlement Body* [online]. Available at: https://www.wto.org/english/tratop_e/dispu_e/dispu_body_e.htm.

18 Ibid.

19 Hallak, I. 2020. *Multilateral Investment Court: Overview of the reform proposals and prospects* [online]. Available at: https://www.europarl.europa.eu/RegData/etudes/BRIE/2020/646147/EPRS_BRI(2020)646147_EN.pdf.

20 Ibid.

21 Ibid.

22 Ibid.

23 Factsheet on the Multilateral Investment Court. 2017 [online]. Available at: http://trade.ec.europa.eu/doclib/docs/2017/september/tradoc_156042.pdf.

24 Ibid.

25 Ibid.

26 World Bank, 2019. *Retention and Expansion of Foreign Direct Investment: Political Risk and Policy Responses*. Washington, DC: World Bank.

27 Ibid.

28 Ibid.

29 Ibid.

30 Ortega, C. and Griffin, C. 2009. *Investment Promotion Essentials: What Sets the World's Best Investment Facilitators Apart From the Rest*. Investment Climate in Practice, Volume 6.

31 Ibid.

32 Ibid.

33 Sauvant, K.P. et al. 2019. *Towards G20 Guiding Principles on Investment Facilitation for Sustainable Development* [online]. Available at: https://www.g20-insights.org/policy_briefs/towards-g20-guiding-principles-on-investment-facilitation-for-sustainable-development/.

34 Ibid.

35 World Bank, 2019. *Retention and Expansion of Foreign Direct Investment: Political Risk and Policy Responses*. Washington, DC: World Bank.

36 Ibid.

37 Ibid.

38 Ibid.

6
DIVESTMENT

Lead author: Toby X. Li

Chapter highlights

- A company's decision to divest can be due to factors that are internal, external or a combination of the two.
- When businesses are in a decline phase, typically the parent company will arrange capital withdrawals and consider the sale, the downsizing or the closure of the subsidiary.
- While divestment decisions are made in the corporate boardroom, there are opportunities for practitioners and policymakers to pre-emptively address key issues for these investors before they reach a decision to exit.
- When host economies have no influence over divestment decisions, IPAs can still help manage the corporate exit or closure in a manner that is efficient, and that minimises the impact on the host economy.

6.1 Introduction

> Aftercare is a no-brainer.
> Why lose what you worked so hard to secure in the first place?
> (Copenhagen Capacity)

This chapter addresses the fourth phase of the investment cycle: divestment. This phase is often misunderstood, is not an area of focus and is sometimes

DOI: 10.4324/9781003174950-9

even ignored from an economic development perspective. This stage is, however, as important as any of the other stages, outlined in Chapter 3 (Framework for Investor Services) describing how foreign investment is affected by business cycles.

Divestment, or the selling and/or closing of a subsidiary, aims to maximise the value of the parent company. According to the OECD, divestment is "an adjustment in the firm ownership and business portfolio structure that involves the partial or full disposal of an asset or a business unit."[1] Divestment can be partial, as, for example, with a spin-off. Divestment can also be the liquidation of one division or of all the firm's divisions, as in the case of the closure of a business, sometimes described as an exit. Divestments are also known as *divestitures*. Another term often used in the FDI world is *disinvestment*. This last term is used specifically to refer to capital withdrawals, sometimes called *negative investment* or *reverse investment*.

A 2019 World Bank study found that investors divest from developing countries during a *normal* year at a rate of approximately 25%.[2] A similar study focusing on OECD countries found that 22% of investors leave each year.[3] Indeed, the likelihood of foreign investors divesting at least part of their business is higher and earlier than is often thought to be the case.[4] These figures have wide implications for the FDI industry. With about 1 in 4 companies leaving every year, the jobs that foreign investors create may be less stable or of a shorter nature than the host economy would like, which directly affects the return on efforts to attract FDI.

The 2020 OECD study "Divestment by Multinational Enterprises" analysed 62,000 affiliates between 2007 and 2014. It found that "34% of all total assets of foreign-owned firms in 2007, accounting for 17% of their sales and 23% of their employees, had been divested by 2014."[5] Divestments are therefore clearly just a normal part of business, and so IPAs need to be aware that "just as firms buy, build and expand their business operations, they also sell, downscale and close them down."[6]

It should be noted that net FDI investment can still be positive if resources are reallocated to other opportunities in the same country, for example, when an operation is closed in London but a new business is opened in Glasgow. These types of divestments might not appear in official records. Divestments also play a role in the reallocation of resources within a multinational corporation (MNC), as companies may choose to exit certain markets as they seek to restore their financial health by focussing on their core business.[7]

There can be severe consequences for the host country's economy when foreign investors choose to divest. Their actions not only impact the divested firms, but also the local communities and their stakeholders, as research by the OECD has found. Foreign investors that divest also affect their business affiliates and value chains, often directly hurting local partners – "these affiliates can suffer on average 28% lower sales, 24% lower value-added and 13% lower employment, compared to firms that stay foreign-owned."[8]

Foreign investors divesting can also affect local companies in other ways. When a divestment involves the sale of a subsidiary to a local company in the host country (known as a foreign-to-domestic change in ownership), research by academics Alex Mohr, Palitha Konara and Panagiotis Ganotakis has shown that in such situations the performance of the business sold often declines due to the loss of foreign expertise and related valuable resources.[9] However, where another foreign investor is the purchaser, research by Alexandros Ragoussis from the World Bank has found "that firms acquired by multinational enterprises not only perform better than the average domestic firm at the time of the acquisition but also improve their performance after acquisition faster than local firms."[10] Improvements include a higher likelihood to export, higher salaries, faster growth and a higher rate of creating new jobs when compared to local firms.

6.2 Why do foreign investors divest?

Reasons why foreign investors divest can be internal firm-specific factors and external factors, ranging from changing market conditions to abrupt changes in tax policies. Internally, the common justification made by foreign investors, at least publicly, is the financial challenge – where the company's investment returns do not meet the expectations of its shareholders. Disappointing investment returns can have many causes, but are generally presented as the subsidiary failing to achieve the desired profitability in the desired timeframe. This can be due to operational challenges, such as suppliers being more expensive than expected, difficulties in securing appropriate talent or unexpected local charges that increase operational costs. It could also be a function of poor forecasting or poor management.[11]

Another related internal factor is the firm's capacity to innovate, and hence its ability to deliver and maintain strong financial performance. This is often a critical determinant of divestment decisions. British academics Palitha Konara and Panagiotis Ganotakis analysed a large sample of foreign subsidiaries in Spain and found that "foreign subsidiaries are less likely to be sold off when they are characterized by high levels of product innovation performance, human capital or have introduced organizational innovations."[12] They note that those companies that orient their efforts towards exporting were "more likely to be divested to other foreign buyers whereas subsidiaries with domestic-market oriented capabilities were more likely to be divested to domestic buyers."[13] As mentioned in the introduction, the ownership of the buying company is relevant to the long term performance of the company, with foreign investor purchases producing better economic results for the host economy.

External factors can also play a significant role in any decision to divest. For instance, a study in the US asked MNCs operating abroad the reasons why they may divest and found that changing market conditions, such as exchange rate volatility,[14] featured high in the reasons to leave a country. In addition, institutional problems in the host country can hinder efficient economic transactions. For instance, the changes and development of political institutions in a host country can quickly alter the business environment in which firms make decisions about the scope and organisation of their foreign operations.[15]

Other reasons involve policy changes by the host government that make the business environment less attractive to foreign investors. Consider the case of China, which has, for decades, been a haven for foreign companies seeking access to low-cost labour. As the Chinese government has sought to shift its economy towards a more consumption-driven one, this has led to a significant increase in wages. Such a shift in public policy, and the consequent higher wages, has negatively affected FDI inflows and business retention across many Chinese provinces.[16] Furthermore, firms divest in response to political instability, institutional weaknesses and the ineffectiveness of intergovernmental organisations.[17] Interestingly, even when profits are strong in a host country, firms with foreign operations and subsidiaries are highly sensitive to non-economic conditions, such as the country's political environment. Indeed, these firms will even forego profits when the political situation in a host country is considered to be too unstable or too risky.[18]

Of course, these internal and external factors together affect a firm's FDI divestment decisions. Companies vary in their ability to manage environmental risks, especially when entering foreign markets that are different to their own or which are at different stages of economic development than their home market, as research by FDI and economics researchers Eric Tsang and Paul Yip has shown.[19] For instance, the OECD study "Divestment by Multinational Enterprises" found that foreign investors from "larger and more distant host markets are less prone to experience divestments, while those from more advanced economies (i.e. with higher levels of per capita income) experience higher divestment rates, all else being equal."[20] In addition, they identified 5 investment policies that correlate with divestment, as shown in Figure 6.1.

Specifically, the OECD study found that real exchange rate stability reduces the probability of divestment, while tax policy changes seem to have less of an influence on divestment, as was also the case with the quality of education and infrastructure. This is different when it comes to economic integration agreements. For instance, the existence of a single market or customs union between the investor's home country and its host country "reduces the probability of foreign divestment by 11% in OECD and G20

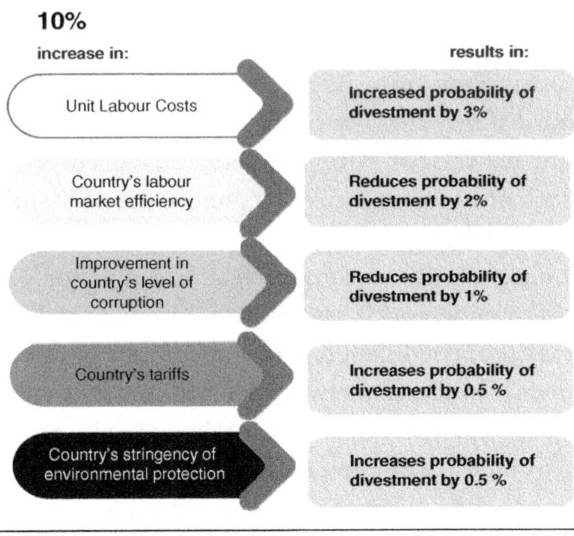

Figure 6.1 OEDC divestment factors.

Source: Author's own designed based on data from Borga, M., Ibarlucea-Flores, P. and Sztajerowska, M., 2020. *Disinvestments by Multinational Enterprises*. OECD, Paris.

economies and has a similar effect elsewhere."[21] The key message of the OECD study is that factors that drive FDI retention are different to those the investors responded to when making the decision to originally invest in the host economy.

Explaining investors' exits by simply highlighting poor market conditions, unhelpful policies and/or institutions misses a key cause of many divestment decisions. That is that investors' expectations do not meet reality on the ground, referred to as post-investment dissonance, which was discussed in Chapter 2, Understanding Aftercare. Any mismatch in expectations typically has two main sources: first, there is the investor's lack of knowledge about the local market, which can result in higher-than-expected operating costs. Second is where an investor's expectations are unrealistically high due to over-enthusiastic attraction and promotion efforts by the local government and/or IPA. For example, to attract these foreign investors in the first instance, some host governments promise to help facilitate these investors' business operations. Broadly, the promises of post-investment services or of changes to legal or regulatory frameworks are often used to "fill in the gaps" of weak institutions or the lack of available services. Promises may include providing additional intellectual property protection or help in navigating government and regulatory bureaucracies, such as how to obtain permits. Collectively, these promises of Investor Services and policy support are intended to reassure foreign investors who have concerns about investing in the host country. But the investor experiences can differ materially from what was promised. Inconsistent and substandard delivery of Aftercare services, stalled efforts at regulatory changes, lack of a vibrant Ecosystem and sense of identity within the locality can be the reality.

Investor discontent has two primary effects: the investor loses confidence in the host government, and it also reduces the financial forecasts of its subsidiary in that country. Taken together the investor may therefore scale back its investments in the country and look to invest elsewhere. Research in behavioural economics has shown that when executives make decisions about whether to increase or decrease their investment commitment, they are not concerned with uncertainty per se, they are primarily concerned with minimising the downside loss, known as loss aversion, rather than focussing on capturing any potential upside.[22]

6.3 Decision-making in the corporate boardroom

Understanding how executives make divestment decisions will help IPAs better target and tailor their post-investment efforts, as well as helping guide policy makers in the changes they need to make to retain investors. From the perspective of investors, when they encounter problems in their businesses their immediate response is to determine how much strategic agency they have for solutions. In other words, they conduct external and internal analyses to determine how much control they have when responding to external challenges. When factors are internal, they adjust management and operations as required. When factors are external, and so management considers they have less control of the situation, foreign investors have different options. First, they seek to influence external factors using grievance procedures and Policy Advocacy as appropriate. However, sometimes these approaches are not effective. Should that be the case, investors will be faced with other options, as can be seen in Figure 6.2. These are: 1) take no action and essentially continue operating under uncertain circumstances, which often seeds organisational decline; 2) capital withdrawals, which means that those funds are no longer invested locally; 3) sale of the subsidiary, which includes joint ventures, mergers and acquisition and spin-offs; and 4) to close operations.

Any business entering the decline phase of the business life cycle will be subject to close scrutiny in the corporate boardroom. To understand boardroom dynamics, the starting point is to recognise that most international

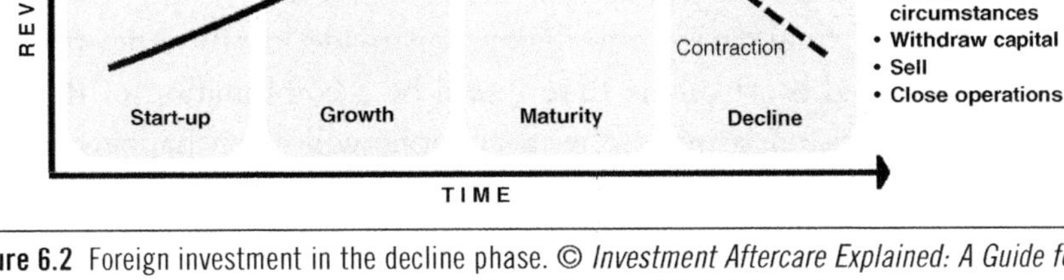

Figure 6.2 Foreign investment in the decline phase. © *Investment Aftercare Explained: A Guide for FDI Practitioners and Policymakers on How to Grow and Retain Investors.*

companies have a portfolio strategy; this includes an ongoing evaluation of what assets to grow and which ones to dispose of. Understanding that, as far as a foreign investor is concerned, a local subsidiary is just an asset in a bigger investment portfolio injects business thinking into FDI, and helps understand the forces in play. Indeed, a business's divestment-readiness is increasingly being factored into the growth strategies of MNCs. Such an approach, favoured by management consultancies and private equity firms advising or financing these foreign investors, gives both the parent company and the subsidiary the confidence and ability to act fast when the time is right. EY, a management consultancy, observes that 72% of companies believed that they held onto assets too long in 2020, up from 63% in 2019 and 56% in 2018.[23] Furthermore, investors that "did not hold onto assets for too long are twice as likely to secure a better price from the transaction."[24]

Boardrooms are likely to explore several options: turning the business around, perhaps under the leadership of new management, spinning off a part of the business, seeking a joint-venture partner, selling the subsidiary (but this may not be attractive due to concerns a competitor may gain access to a company's intellectual property) and finally closing the subsidiary.

The decision of whether or not to close a location is typically a strategic one, and will consider questions such as: does the company still want to want to make this product or provide this service? Is the market still attractive, and will it continue to produce acceptable returns? Does this location continue to fit the investor's overall strategy? Is it cost-competitive? Is there another location that better suits its current and future corporate needs? Can a loss-making or under-performing subsidiary be turned around? And if so, is it worth committing the time and effort to do so? Are there other business units that bring better results, or are of greater strategic value to the group? What is the alternative use of the funds invested?

Sometimes the final decision to disinvest is made locally, other times at the head office, but most of the time it will be a combination of the two. Wherever the decision is made, the discussions will often happen behind closed doors, giving IPAs little opportunity to influence these conversations. However, sometimes foreign investors require help in preparing a detailed analysis of the exit cost. This may present a further opportunity to help the investor make a more exhaustive calculation, with the hope that a more detailed analysis will result in them reaching a different conclusion.

These decision dynamics in the corporate boardroom – and the sensitivity to divest – can be exacerbated by external economic shocks. For instance, the EY Global Corporate Divestment Study provides insight into what likely happened in boardrooms during Covid-19. They surveyed 1,010 global corporate executives and 25 global activist investors between November 2019 and January 2020, just before the Covid-19 pandemic started, and then surveyed another set of 300 corporate executives and 25 global activist investors following the onset of the crisis. They observed that "companies are pursuing divestments to rebalance portfolios as they face tough capital decisions and increased activism."[25] Indeed, 78% expect to divest within the next two years and 65% say they will reshape their portfolio to prepare for a post-crisis world. An important factor behind these decisions is the need to fund the technology investment required in a post-Covid world, with 54% saying that they will prepare or accelerate plans to divest as a result of the crisis.[26] While these figures reflect viewpoints made during the Covid-19 crisis, and so do not reflect a "normal" market, they do provide an insight into the rationale of investors, and how they take investment decisions.

6.3.1 Shareholder activism

Another factor worth understanding regarding boardroom decision making is shareholder activism. Most IPAs are not directly exposed to how shareholder activism impacts a foreign investor's decision making process, and consequently how it affects any divestment decisions. However, gaining an understanding of boardroom dynamics could help them better understand divestments in their host economies.

Activist investors are individuals or institutions who own stock in a public or private corporation. As owners, they elect a board of directors to oversee the corporation, and they wield their influence via their chosen board members.[27] Activism is not new. Indeed, "any publicly traded company that isn't number one in its peer group is going to have someone at least looking at them."[28] The Activist Investing Annual Review 2019 reported that 922 companies worldwide faced shareholder activist campaigns, compared to 520 in 2013. Moreover, activism is now a global phenomenon with almost half of the cases taking place outside the USA.[29]

Dan Romito, a senior analyst for Nasdaq writing in the *Harvard Business Review*, identifies 4 types of activist investors:

- **Activist investors who optimise yields**[30]: they will look at "how management is currently allocating capital, and how different strategies might better optimize shareholder yield (dividend yield plus buyback yield). This typically means they look to re-engineer the balance sheet to increase shareholder yield, over the shortest amount of time possible."[31] Activist investors will put pressure on boards to increase returns under the belief that "more aggressive rebalancing of portfolios will help companies free up capital and refocus on their core business."[32] Activist investors are looking for high total shareholder returns (TSR). Their rationale being that, since the global financial crisis in 2008, divestor companies have outperformed non-divestors by 24 TSR percentage points.[33]
- **Activist investors who combine close competitors**[34]: when competition is strong, particularly in volatile sectors such as industrials and materials, it might make more sense to join forces. "Activists look to see if opponents could be combined to form a more productive single entity, one that can capitalize on economies of scale and monopolize a given sector."[35] This type of activism will favour mergers.
- **Activist investors who separate different divisions**[36]: "When a company operates in non-complimentary divisions, it can be difficult to maintain a single balance sheet that optimizes overall shareholder return. Even if both divisions are profitable, the capital requirements of one may be completely different than the other."[37] Activists will propose capital structure reorganisations with the aim of optimising performance, resulting in splitting up divisions and divestments.
- **Activist investors who get rid of dead weight**[38]: this type of activist "pinpoints struggling business units that weaken the performance of the overall firm and pursue spin-offs to eliminate dead weight from the company." They are likely to suggest a sale or closure.

Whilst the first two types of activist are so called economic activist advocates as they seek changes to increase financial gains within the company, the latter two activist types are focused on governance work to change boards and decision making in order to achieve higher profits.[39] In addition, there is social and environmental activism that seeks to make a company's operations more ethically and ecologically aligned, with agendas such as sustainability, carbon-neutrality, climate change, anti-slavery or anti-child labour[40] featuring high in their priorities. These activists will put pressure on management to conduct business in a manner that is aligned with that agenda. They often favour pushing their companies to divest businesses, rather than to allow their financial assets to fuel business practices that are not aligned with their ethical principles.

The 2020 Global Corporate Divestment Study notes that "96% [of] activist investors will recommend carve-outs of underperforming or noncore businesses in the next 12 months."[41] This is something IPAs should take note of, as it may be a trend that continues for several years.

6.4 Project management during a corporate exit

Once a foreign investor has made the decision to exit, the next step is how to execute that decision. Shareholders consider three months to be a standard timeline[42] to execute a divestment, but PWC, a management consultancy, observes that "51% of companies report their divestment took five months or longer from sign[ing] to closing."[43]

At this point, both the head office and the subsidiary will generally want to know in more detail the answers to four questions:

- How much it will cost to exit?
- How long it will take to exit?
- How can we minimise disruption to our customers, suppliers and operations?
- How can we minimise any adverse impact on our brand and reputation, particularly with regards to media coverage, politicians and employees?

Most businesses have limited experience of closing a facility and hence are likely to require support from experts, such as lawyers, accountants, PR professionals and business continuity experts in order to close an operation in as efficient and cost-effective manner as possible. This offers another opportunity for IPAs to influence struggling investors.

In addition, there are a number of key areas a company needs to consider when planning to divest. These include the firm's employees,

Figure 6.3 Consideration of a corporate exit. © *Investment Aftercare Explained: A Guide for FDI Practitioners and Policymakers on How to Grow and Retain Investors.*

commercial relationships, financial and legal considerations, governance, communications strategy and risk and mitigation planning. What is at the very core is project management, as shown in Figure 6.3.

6.4.1 Employee considerations

The divestment of a subsidiary often entails closing some of its local facilities in the host country. The closure of a facility will lead to job losses, not just at the business to be closed, but also extending to companies in the local area, both formally and informally in their supply chain, such as suppliers and food outlets that will see their turnover diminished, potentially putting further jobs at risks – the reverse of the job multiplier effect of FDI.

A responsible investor will be keen to minimise the adverse impact on its reputation from closing a facility. This is a further area where the IPA should seek to work closely with the investor. Areas that require special attention include:

- **Unions and works councils**: in some countries unions and works councils play a significant role in how a business operates. Consulting and working closely and collaboratively with unions and work councils to effectively plan the wind down of operations is likely to result in a smoother exit. Early engagement is advised.

- **Key employees**: management will need to identify which staff are key to keeping operations running as the business is wound down, and may need to incentivise them to stay during the closure process.
- **Operations**: once the decision to close an operation is made, management needs to accept that, facing imminent closure, employees are likely to behave differently and so needs to plan accordingly. Possible changes in staff behaviour include demotivation, a decline in productivity, increased absenteeism, sudden resignations, sabotage and theft.

6.4.2 Commercial partnerships

The firm's customers and suppliers will be concerned when an organisation chooses to scale down its operations. Contracts may need to be renegotiated. Communicating early and openly with both customers and suppliers is key to retaining their support, co-operation and business, particularly if there is a desire to transfer a customer's business to another facility or to serve them remotely.[44]

6.4.3 Financial and legal considerations

Closing any facility is typically a costly exercise. It is good practice for a company to produce a wind-down profit and loss schedule and cash flow forecast for the weeks and months through to closure, and to monitor actual costs against forecast on a regular basis. Closure specific financial costs include:

- **Employee-related costs**: including severance costs, retention payments, unfunded pension schemes and retraining and job search costs for employees being laid off.
- **Contract termination and exit costs**: where contracts are terminated early for property, including dilapidations, and for plants, where leased or rented.
- **Grants that need to be repaid**: wholly or in part.
- **Taxes**: corporation tax, sales tax, payroll taxes, etc. This can include tax reductions granted at the time of expanding an operation on the basis of a specific job creation target.
- **Consultants' fees**: e.g. hiring PR experts, accountants and lawyers.
- **Asset realisation costs**.

- **Additional security costs**: during the closure period.
- **Actual and contingent liabilities**: such as outstanding legal cases. Legal costs are likely to include the legal process to solvently close a business in the relevant jurisdiction, data protection considerations, confidentiality clauses and novation or substitution of contracts.

6.4.4 *Governance*

Where an investor decides to close an operation, whether solvently or insolvently, the directors of the company should seek legal advice as to their responsibilities.

Regulatory filings will include final tax returns, accounts and paperwork to formally close a business. Where applicable, consideration should be taken of any industry specific regulatory issues. In addition, analysis should be made regarding whether or not any conditions attached to any incentives provided by the host government have been met and if not, whether any repayments need to be made.

6.4.5 *Communication strategy*

Employees, customers, suppliers, local government and the (local) media will all be disappointed or angry at the decision to close a facility, particularly if it comes as a surprise. Managing the message is crucial to minimise the reputational damage to the investor, and also disruption at the facility to be closed. Early, open and honest communication as to the reasons for closure and how the business plans to work with all stakeholders so as to minimise the impact on them is the best strategy to ensure a smooth exit.[45] Consideration should be given to employing a PR company specialising in crisis communications. Where appropriate they should also work closely with the government's PR team to minimise any communications crises, as these can evolve into a political crisis.

6.4.6 *Risk and mitigation planning*

Closing a business has risks, and so careful management and mitigation planning is required. As such, the closing down team needs to identify the key risks involved in the closure and a mitigation plan should be made for each risk. This includes logging each risk, rating it according to the likelihood of it happening and the severity of impact should it happen. Finally, each risk should be regularly monitored and reviewed.

6.4.7 Project management

Successfully closing down a business requires excellent project management. Given the wide range of actions that need to be taken, and that some of them need to be taken in a specific order, it is a critical role, and hence a very competent project manager is required when a significant operation is to be closed down. Sometimes this role is outsourced to a third party.

While this section explains what it takes to close an operation from an investor's point of view, IPAs also need to consider the effect that an investor exiting has on the local economy. Host governments often engage in crisis management and ensure strong coordination between public agencies and effective communication to prevent any escalation of the situation. Some of the common risks of disinvestment, in addition to the loss of jobs, are unfavourable perspectives shared in the business community, further exits of companies from the same industry and how these actions affect the public sector, politics and therefore the perception of funders and stakeholders regarding the effectiveness of the IPA. Well-run IPAs have crisis plans in place when it comes to managing the impact of exits by foreign investors.

6.5 Divestment considerations

This chapter illustrated that divestments are multi-factored – there are aspects of corporate management, boardroom dynamics, investor services and investment climate. Nonetheless, investor retention can and should start before an investment is made. It starts with the host government not overselling its economy when it seeks to attract investors. It follows with well-designed, executed and impactful Aftercare services. It continues with carefully monitoring investor enquiries, complaints and grievances, advocating for policy reforms that help investors thrive, as well as introducing research methods to effectively understand, monitor and evaluate divestment and disinvestments. All of this needs to be supported by effective policies in the host country that reduce the uncertainties faced by investors, and thereby lowers their costs of doing business.

Looked at another way, understanding how to retain investors in the long term is arguably the most important part of FDI services. Indeed, FDI longevity should be a key performance indicator when it comes to evaluating the performance of FDI attraction as a whole, as the inclusion of exit rates allows a holistic view of the possible outcomes of an investment. It also makes calculating the impact of investment facilitation more accurate and can highlight which IPA services have the greatest impact on (investor) growth. Monitoring failure rates can be complex, expensive and can carry some political risk. As a result, there is little evidence of the impact on FDI of the failure rate and/or voluntary exiting of foreign investors. There is also a dearth of official data comparing the promises made by investors, in terms of money to be invested and jobs to be created, with what actually happened (i.e. how much money was actually invested and how many jobs were actually created, both immediately after an investment was announced and also after several years of establishment, or for that matter how these jobs evolved in the long term, a topic that is explored in Chapter 9, The How of Investor Services). Most governments do not have the capability to accurately monitor FDI withdrawals, such as cancelled expansion projects, or the factors behind such investment pullback, and even fewer have the right tools to cope with such exiting.[46] In addition, performing this work could bring in to question the effectiveness of some FDI policies, making performing this type of research politically risky There is a role here for international organisations to undertake research and provide better insight into how to best monitor FDI divestment.

Notes

1 Borga, M., Ibarlucea-Flores, P. and Sztajerowska, M. 2020. *Disinvestments by Multinational Enterprises*. OECD, Paris [online]. Available at: https://www.oecd.org/investment/Divestments-by-multinational-enterprises-Investment-Policy-Insights.pdf.

2 World Bank, 2019. *Investment Policy and Promotion* [online]. Available at: https://www.worldbank.org/en/topic/investment-climate/brief/investment-policy-and-promotion.

3 Borga, M., Ibarlucea-Flores, P. and Sztajerowska, M. 2020. *Disinvestments by Multinational Enterprises*. OECD, Paris [online]. Available at: https://www.oecd.org/investment/Divestments-by-multinational-enterprises-Investment-Policy-Insights.pdf.

4 Ibid.

5 Ibid.

6 Ibid.

7 Ibid.

8 Borga, M., Ibarlucea-Flores, P. and Sztajerowska, M. 2020. "Drivers of divestment decisions of multinational enterprises – A cross-country firm-level perspective". *OECD Working Papers on International Investment*, Volume 2019/03.

9 Mohr, A., Konara, P. and Ganotakis, P. 2020. "Explaining the performance of divested overseas subsidiaries". *International Business Review*, 29(1), pp. 11–13.

10 Ragoussis, A. 2020. *How Beneficial Are Foreign Acquisitions of Firms in Developing Countries? Evidence from Six Countries*, Global Investment Competitiveness Report 2019/2020.: doi:10.1596/978-1-4648-1536-2.

11 OECD, 2020. *Foreign Direct Investment Statistics Explanatory Notes* [online]. Available at: https://www.oecd.org/daf/inv/FDI-statistics-explanatory-notes.pdf.

12 Konara, P. and Ganotakis, P. 2020. "Firm-specific resources and foreign divestments via selloffs: Value is in the eye of the beholder". *Journal of Business Research*, 110(1), pp. 423–434.

13 Ibid.

14 Berry, H. 2013. "When do firms divest foreign operations?" *Organization Science*, 24(1), pp. 246–261.

15 Soule, S.A. and Swaminathan, A. 2014. "The diffusion of foreign divestment from Burma". *Strategic Management Journal*, 35(7), pp. 1032–1052.

Guler, I. and Guillén, M.F. 2010. "Institutions and the internationalization of US venture capital firms". *Journal of International Business Studies*, 41(2), pp. 185–205.

García-Canal, E. and Guillén, M.F. 2008. "Risk and the strategy of foreign location choice in regulated industries". *Strategic Management Journal*, 29(10), pp. 1097–1115.

16 Donaubauer, J. and Dreger, C. 2018. "The end of cheap Labour: Are foreign investors leaving China?" *Asian Economic Papers*, 17(2), pp. 94–107.

17 Soule, S.A. and Swaminathan, A. 2014. "The diffusion of foreign divestment from Burma". *Strategic Management Journal*, 35(7), pp. 1032–1052.

18 Soule, S.A. and Swaminathan, A. 2014. "The diffusion of foreign divestment from Burma". *Strategic Management Journal*, 35(7), pp. 1032–1052.

Henisz, W.J. and Delios, A. 2001. "Uncertainty, imitation, and plant location: Japanese multinational corporations, 1990–1996". *Administrative Science Quarterly*, 46(3), pp. 443–475.

Henisz, W.J. and Macher, J.T. 2004. "Firm- and country-level trade-offs and contingencies in the evaluation of foreign investment: The semiconductor industry, 1994–2002". *Organization Science*, 15(5), pp. 537–554.

19 Tsang, E.W.K. and Yip, P.S.L. 2007. "Economic distance and the survival of foreign direct investments". *The Academy of Management Journal*, 50(5), pp. 1156-1168.

20 Borga, M., Ibarlucea-Flores, P. and Sztajerowska, M. 2020. *Disinvestments by Multinational Enterprises*. OECD, Paris [online]. Available at: https://www.oecd.org/investment/Divestments-by-multinational-enterprises-Investment-Policy-Insights.pdf.

21 Ibid.

22 Kahneman, D. and Tversky, A. 1979. "Prospect Theory: An analysis of decision under risk". *Econometrica*, 47(2), pp. 263–291.

Miller, K.D. and Reuer, J.J. 1996. "Measuring organizational downside risk". *Strategic Management Journal*, 17(9), pp. 671–691.

23 EY, 2020. *2020 Global Corporate Divestment Study* [online]. Available at: https://www.ey.com/en_gl/divestment-study.

24 PWC, 2020. *Deal Readiness to Build Value Immediately and Sustainably* [online]. Available at: https://www.pwc.com/us/en/services/deals/divestitures/operational-readiness.html.
25 EY, 2020. *2020 Global Corporate Divestment Study* [online]. Available at https://www.ey.com/en_gl/divestment-study.
26 Ibid.
27 Wolf, C. 2017. *Everything You Need to Know About Shareholder Activism* [online]. Available at: https://insidesources.com/everything-need-know-shareholder-activism/.
28 Ibid.
29 Ibid.
30 Yield is the income returned on an investment, such as the interest received from holding a security. The yield is usually expressed as an annual percentage rate based on the investment's cost, current market value or face value. Source: Investopedia.com.
31 Romito, D. 2015. "4 Types of activist investors and how to spot them". *Harvard Business Review,* 7 October. Available at: https://hbr.org/2015/10/4-types-of-activist-investors-and-how-to-spot-them.
32 EY, 2020. *2020 Global Corporate Divestment Study* [online]. Available at https://www.ey.com/en_gl/divestment-study.
33 Ibid.
34 Ibid.
35 Romito, D. 2015. "4 types of activist investors and how to spot them". *Harvard Business Review,* 7 October. Available at: "https://hbr.org/2015/10/4-types-of-activist-investors-and-how-to-spot-them.
36 Ibid.
37 Ibid.
38 Ibid.
39 Wolf, C. 2017. *Everything You Need to Know About Shareholder Activism* [online]. Available at: https://insidesources.com/everything-need-know-shareholder-activism/.
40 Ibid.
41 EY, 2020. *2020 Global Corporate Divestment Study* [online]. Available at: https://www.ey.com/en_gl/divestment-study.
42 PWC, 2020. *Deal Readiness to Build Value Immediately and Sustainably* [online]. Available at: https://www.pwc.com/us/en/services/deals/divestitures/operational-readiness.html.
43 Ibid.
44 Freeman, K.W. 2009. "The right way to close an operation". *Harvard Business Review,* 87(5), pp. 45–51.
45 Ibid.
46 World Bank, 2019. *Retention and Expansion of Foreign Direct Investment: Political Risk and Policy Responses,* Washington, DC: World Bank [online]. Available at: https://openknowledge.worldbank.org/handle/10986/33082.

7
PLACE AND ECOSYSTEM

Chapter highlights

- Outlines why Place matters and how place branding, place marketing and placemaking are gaining increasing importance when it comes to building communities where investors, talent and business can thrive.
- Explores the concept of Ecosystem and how value is created by fostering connectedness among stakeholders, whether they be global, local or personal.
- Introduces practical examples of how IPAs work with industry sectors and start-ups, how they support workforce development, collaborate with real estate, support local ambassadors, equip location storytellers and seek to improve their ranking, focusing on the criteria on which talent and investors base their decisions.

7.1 Introduction

"Place is supplanting the industrial corporation as the key economic and social organizing unit of capitalism. Density, the clustering of creative people – in cities, regions, and neighbourhoods – provides a key spur to innovation and competitiveness."[1] This quote from leading urbanist Richard Florida captures the importance of incorporating a physical aspect to FDI, both in

DOI: 10.4324/9781003174950-10

terms of a geographic characteristic, as well as a socio-economic system that has a unique character.

Historically *place* has been used to describe, as defined in *The Oxford English Dictionary*, "a particular position, point, or area in space; a location."[2] Places come in many different shapes and sizes, both large and small, and include nations, states, regions, cities and neighbourhoods. Moreover, each place has its own unique characteristics that make it more or less attractive to both people and businesses. The competitive advantage of a place was historically driven by its geography – its proximity and access to natural resources, and its transportation links to other (important) places. The great cities of the past were nearly all located alongside navigable rivers or close to natural harbours, and more recently in the vicinity of significant sources of natural resources. However, these natural advantages are much less important today as information technology has become one of the key drivers of growth. Hence, as people and capital are increasingly free to set up almost anywhere, there is a growing need for locations to differentiate themselves in new ways in order to attract and retain investors.

The link between Place, Ecosystems and established investment has been neatly summarised by the Project for Public Spaces (PPS), a New York based non-profit dedicated to helping people create and sustain public spaces that build strong communities, which states that "it takes a place to create a community and a community to create a place."[3] This principle also applies to FDI: foreign investors are attracted to a specific place that offers the best conditions to invest, and at the same time they become part of the local business community which actively advocates for improvements to the business climate.

Specific goals of Place-related activities are:

- To nurture activities that are conducive to strengthening local communities.
- To give a voice to local players and orchestrate these activities to develop a local identity.
- To support local efforts to help make a location a great place to live, play and work.
- To amplify storytelling efforts that convey the uniqueness and attractiveness of a place.

7.2 Place matters

The concept of *place* is an increasingly important factor when it comes to considering the set of variables that affect local economic growth. This is because a place has a value that goes beyond just its physical assets to include resources, ideas and capital. In any given place these factors, come together in different ways to create a unique identity. This is where the concept of a location brand comes in.

In 1991 David Aaker, Professor Emeritus at the University of California's Berkeley Haas School of Business, said that "a brand is the commercial value that derives from consumer perception of the brand name rather than from the product or service itself."[4] He went on to define brand equity as "a set of brand assets and liabilities linked to a brand name and symbol, which add to or subtract from the value provided by a product or service." Aaker proposed that brand equity has four dimensions – brand loyalty, brand awareness, brand associations and perceived quality. Brand experts consequently mapped the process of how to increase brand equity and provided a roadmap to manage the value creation of brands. Building on Aaker's work, brand experts have developed a process for increasing a brand's equity and a roadmap to manage the value creation of a brand.

From a brand perspective, places share many characteristics with products or services. Location names sometimes become the Place brand, for example Silicon Valley, and it is these Place brands that have a value and therefore Place equity. Paraphrasing Aaker's definition: *Place Equity is a set of assets and liabilities linked to a place's name and identity that adds or subtracts from the perceived attractiveness of a place.*

And as with consumer brands, places can follow a Place equity roadmap to manage that potential gain in value, as cities such as Hamburg, Edmonton, Mississauga, Lyon and London[5] are increasingly doing. The activity behind those efforts is called place branding.

7.2.1 Place branding

According to the International Place Branding Yearbook 2012, Place branding is "the process of discovering, creating, developing and realizing ideas and concepts for (re)constructing place identities, their defining traits and 'genius loci'"[6] and also by "subsequently building the sense of place, by efforts and investments in hardware (e.g. infrastructure, buildings), software (e.g. events, stories), orgware (e.g. co-operative organisational structuring) and virtual ware (e.g. symbols and symbolic actions, websites)."[7] Furthermore, there is an interesting dynamic between place and brand. Some locations will see placemaking as the ultimate goal, while others see it as an output of a strong Place brand. However, there is consensus among practitioners, "that – irrespective of the exact cause and effect – there is an opportunity for amplification of message when there is a concerted location-wide effort to deploy place branding values and assets across activities and organisations."[8] The perceived importance of Place branding means that it has been adopted by places across the world, whether large or small, from The Hague to Helsinki, from New Zealand to South Africa, with the aim of improving local or regional competitiveness in an increasingly competitive global market. Furthermore, according to the North American geography academics Evan Cleave et al, "Place-branding can be used to guide identification, enhancement and leveraging of the place-based advantages a city or region has to offer tailoring the image of the area to align with the needs of the business."[9] Cleave also goes on say that "this well-measured and substantive approach to coordination, organization and promotion of local resources that provides the best opportunity for effective policy development Place branding is being used as the compass to improve local capacity. Through this enhancement of place, a community become[s] 'sticky' enough to attract and retain business."[10] City Nation Place goes on to say that another strongly held view is that "country branding efforts appear to represent the views of the government or the funder, have a top-down approach and represent central government, but not necessary[necessarily] of the private sector or other local players."[11] To City Nation Place it then seems clear that, "[a]s a result, certain locations have moved away from centralised initiatives, to leave individual organisations [to] find their own voice."[12]

Samanth Subramanian, a journalist for *The Guardian* (a British newspaper), explores nation branding in his 2017 article, "How to sell a country: the booming business of nation branding". Subramanian states that, "in the 21st century nation branding has grown to be busy business with virtually every nation keen to hear how to best compose the face it presents to the world."[13] While Place branding consultants are busy travelling the world working with governments to create an identity for their nations, Subramanian presents a critical view of the Place branding consulting industry and suggests that the father of the term nation brand, the independent policy advisor Simon Anholt, "regrets coining 'nation brand' because he has watched it become 'nation branding': cynical acts of spin, void of any real reforms."[14] The argument goes that *the lie called nation-branding* "encourages so many countries, who really can't afford it, to blow wicked amounts of money on futile propaganda programmes, and the only people who benefit are these beastly PR agencies."[15] The journalists highlight that income from Place branding campaigns tend to flow to cities such as New York, Madrid, London and Paris, where specialists agencies "dispense advice to governments in Asia, Africa, Eastern Europe and Latin America on how best to present themselves – a configuration that can veer easily into cultural imperialism."[16]

However, Place brand expert Robert Govers, together with Erik van 't Klooster and Gerard Van Keken, is more positive, recognising that, "in a globalised world, places increasingly vie for attention. In such a highly competitive environment, place branding can help by building competitive identity."[17] They then bring this into more focus for action "in particular, sustainable competitive advantage can be created by building brand equity in relation to the identity of the nation, region, local area or city or town."[18] Govers et al go on to suggest 5 Place branding principles: distinctiveness, authenticity, memorable, co-creation and placemaking as different approaches to developing strong Place brands. Govers et al conclude that, "in the experience economy an integrative place branding strategy is needed to capture the hearts and attention of visitors. This means that the place brand should be supported by policies, innovations, events, structures, investments and symbolic actions."[19] This is where Place marketing comes into play.

7.2.2 Place marketing

According to the website Placebrandobserver.com, "place marketing is the development and implementation of a managerial process that assists places in order to achieve their objectives by adopting a market-oriented philosophy,"[20] and is also about ensuring that "the brand message and the story of an area are strategically and methodically delivered to the right audiences through the appropriate channels."[21] In particular, the focus should be on how to communicate the Place brand using conventional marketing tools and techniques.

However, there is no standard approach to Place marketing, and therefore different locations have taken different approaches. In Oslo, for example, the various organisations involved in marketing the city "have agreed to work with the same place brand strategy and criteria. No new organisation was required for this – it is handled as a shared responsibility that keeps each other on track and removes the activity from the political sphere."[22] In contrast, in The Hague there is an "officer in charge of brand management [who] has to sign off on bids for major projects etc. His role is not to decide whether or not an activity or project happens, however s/he does comment on whether or not the project is on brand."[23] Other locations have set up a "panel of senior stakeholders that [are the] custodians of the brand."[24] This approach has changed the output of Place branding from managing the Place brand to image brand orchestration. Furthermore, some locations also bring foreign investors onto these panels in order to get their perspective and input. Box 7.1 provides an overview of City Nation Place's key considerations for country and nation branding initiatives.

Box 7.1 The Nation Branding Playbook

The Nation Branding Playbook by City Nation Place (2017)

"Best practices:

1. Be Absolutely Clear on the Overall Objective. Before commencing work on the development of a nation brand strategy, countries need to be very clear on their objectives.
2. Be Realistic About the Expected Benefits. Countries need to be clear on the expected benefits, beyond increased general awareness, of spending time and money on refreshing/developing a national brand. Tangible benefits can include a combination of increased investment, growth in exports of goods and services, attraction and retention of talented people, increased tourism and more.
3. Be clear who will be responsible for creating or refreshing the national brand and how local and international stakeholders will be invited to participate.
4. Agree a Process for creating the brand strategy. Before embarking on the journey to create, deliver and manage a national brand strategy, the government and its partners need to understand and agree a process for doing so.

An effective national brand process would include:

a) Government having a very clear understanding of why it wants to create a national brand, its objectives and the benefits it wants to realise.
b) Government appointing a National Brand Champion to lead the process of brand development.
c) Government forming the initial National Brand Partnership and agreeing its terms of reference and scope of responsibilities (focussed and tight).
d) The Brand Partnership setting up its executive arm, the National Brand Team, agreeing its terms of reference and responsibilities, recruiting its membership and allocating funding for its activities.
e) Government pump-priming the process of brand development and using its connections to raise contributions from the private sector of cash or in-kind resources, e.g. undertaking research, seconding skilled and experienced staff to the Brand Team.
f) The National Brand Team drafting the brand development process and timetable for approval by the Brand Partnership and creating the process for managing this work (outputs, deadlines, meeting schedules, KPI's, etc). And compiling the work programmes for years 1 and 2, to be reviewed quarterly and annually."

This is a collaborative blog by experienced Place brand practitioners who have worked together – Malcolm Allan, Jose Torres and Gonzalo Vilar of Bloom Consulting, Jeannette Hanna of Trajectory, Roger Hobkinson of The Destination Developers, published by City Nation Place, the forum for place brand and place marketing.

Reproduced with kind permission from City Nation Place: www.citynationplace.com.

Link: http://www.citynationplace.com/the-nation-branding-playbook.

Both Place marketing and Place branding are particularly effective when it comes to addressing any post-purchase dissonance. The on-going nature of both these functions will expose an investor to messages that support their initial investment decision. They will also provide an investor with a reference point against which to compare their own experience. Additionally, positive Place content can help mitigate the impact of any negative experiences an investor may have had. A good messaging strategy can materially influence post-investment decisions.

7.2.3 Placemaking

The focus on Place, Place branding and Place marketing has resulted in a further concept in economic development, namely *placemaking*. According to the Project for Public Spaces, "placemaking inspires people to collectively reimagine and reinvent (public) spaces as the heart of every community." They create a specific goal, being "strengthening the connection between people and the places they share, placemaking refers to a collaborative process by which we can shape our public realm in order to maximise shared value for the stakeholders that use it."[25] And also provide a framework for action "more than just promoting better urban design, placemaking facilitates creative patterns of use, paying particular attention to the physical, cultural, and social identities that define a place and support its ongoing evolution."[26] Or as the digital placemaking advisory firm Calvium puts it, "placemaking can take many forms."[27] They note that it can be "small-scale or citywide, high-tech or lo-fi, but the one thing it always needs is a creative spark of inspiration. Whatever the project, it's the sense of connection, wonder and excitement which drives place-makers; bringing to life the potential of a place in a new and engaging way."[28] Meanwhile, Robert Govers, founding chairman of the International Place Branding Association (IPBA), has identified three types of global community: emerging communities, copied communities and imaginative communities. In particular, he describes imaginative communities "*as locations that reinforce or build local character and civic pride, while at the same time captivating outsiders.*"[29]

In the world of FDI, these "outsiders" are foreign investors, businesses and international talent. Moreover, these outsiders, once attracted to a location, can play a key role in shaping how the image, profile and self-confidence of a location develops. This is where post-investment services come in. By continuing to engage with investors throughout their investment journeys,

Aftercare can encourage investors to participate in developing a better Place, thereby improving the overall attractiveness of a location.

In addition, Place is important from the perspective of the relationships, connections and networks that are forged locally. These relationships, connections and networks play a key role in the development of Ecosystems.

7.3 Ecosystems make a difference

The term "ecosystem" was coined by the British botanist Sir Arthur Tansley in 1935 to describe a community of organisms interacting with each other and their environments – air, water, earth, etc. In order to thrive, these organisms compete and collaborate with each other for resources, co-evolve and jointly adapt to external disruptions. More than 50 years later, business strategist James Moore used the concept of Ecosystems to explain how businesses collaborate in a location to their mutual benefit, observing that "a business ecosystem, like its biological counterpart, gradually moves from a random collection of elements to a more structured community."[30]

From a business perspective, an Ecosystem can be seen as a network of organisations – including suppliers, distributors, customers, competitors and government agencies – involved in the simultaneous delivery of multiple products and services through both competition and cooperation. Each entity in the Ecosystem affects, and is affected by, the other entities, thereby creating a constantly evolving set of relationships in which each entity must be flexible and adaptable in order to survive, as in a biological ecosystem. Hence, over time, and as circumstances change, the entities in an Ecosystem co-evolve their capabilities and roles and tend to align themselves with one another.

Fast forward 20 years, and the concept of business Ecosystems has expanded beyond a single industry to include several sectors that co-evolve together. The automotive industry is a good example of this as, beyond core automotive engineering, car manufacturers work alongside data scientists to improve vehicle control, use industrial designers to improve the ergonomics of seats and work with the air-conditioning industry to regulate the temperature inside a car. Each industry is interdependent on how the other evolves, while at the same time influencing the behaviour of the other industries. Interestingly, there has been an increasing level of interaction between culture and business. Or as the British networker extraordinaire Rohan Silva, credited with being the brains behind Tech City, the fastest growing digital cluster in Europe, puts it, "we didn't just want to be about technology, we wanted to be where fashion meets design, meets art, meets finance, meets tech."[31] It is in this interplay between industries where Ecosystems can really thrive, where locations can become *imaginative communities* that build local character, while at the same time captivating outsiders, including foreign investors. Or put another way, paraphrasing the idea that it takes a village to raise a child, it takes a whole Ecosystem to grow a [foreign] company.

The growing interest in business Ecosystems has resulted in governments and academia wanting to understand how Ecosystems function in order to accelerate growth. The Finnish Ministry of Foreign Affairs and Employment, for example, recognises that competition in the global economy has moved away from individual organisations or industries and "increasingly become a battle between various networks or ecosystems." Companies can often no longer be competitive just by using their own know-how. Instead, and in addition to their own competitive advantages, they need the benefits offered by strong partners. They go on to say that "such partners may include other companies and public sector or civil society organisations. Various business incubators, business accelerators and organisations specialising in promoting the use of various technologies may have an important role as platforms for testing, developing."[32] Promoting ecosystem level business operations is a new challenge for the Finnish public sector.

However, this is not new. Business Ecosystems are closely linked to the concept of clusters, as defined in 1990 by the business guru Michael Porter describes clusters as, "geographic concentration of related companies, organisations, and institutions in a particular field that can be present in a region, state, or nation. Clusters arise because they raise a company's productivity, which is influenced by local assets and the presence of like firms, institutions, and infrastructure that surround it."[33] Porter goes on to say that "clusters are not unique, however, they are highly typical – and therein lies a paradox: the enduring competitive advantages in a global economy lie increasingly in local things – knowledge, relationships, motivation."[34] He notes that "clusters represent a kind of new spatial organisational form in between arm's-length markets on the one hand and hierarchies, or vertical integration, on the other. A cluster, then, is an alternative way of organising the value chain."[35] In the wake of Porter's comments, governments across the world have dedicated resources to studying, setting up and growing clusters.

In 2009, the European Union launched several cluster-related projects and initiatives aimed at improving the quality of cluster policy within Europe, and at enhancing the efficiency of existing efforts in cluster management. These initiatives brought together the most experienced people and organisations in Europe to identify and set up a meaningful set of training programmes, KPIs and peer-assessment procedures for cluster management. The outcome was The European Cluster Excellence Initiative and the European Foundation for Cluster Excellence with its related training programmes and thought leadership.

According to Victor Huang, vice president of Entrepreneurship at the Kauffman Foundation, "the terms 'cluster' or 'network' are rather static. They describe the mere presence of assets in a system, like blocks on a wall chart. An ecosystem, on the other hand, is about the dynamic interactions between things. It's about how people meet, talk, trust, share, collaborate, team, experiment and grow together."[36] Huang goes on to say that "when an ecosystem thrives, it means that the people have developed patterns of behaviour – or culture – that streamline the flow of ideas, talent, and capital throughout a system."[37] In other words, key features of Ecosystems are their adaptability and resilience as well as the competition between companies. Because of the key role that Ecosystems play in developing and growing businesses, there is a link between the competitiveness of a company and the competitiveness of a location. Astute investors are aware of this, and so monitor the "health" of a local Ecosystem before deciding where to grow next. In an era when many investors are location agnostic, locations cannot ignore the role their local Ecosystem plays when it comes to attracting (further) investment.

Specific goals of Ecosystem-related activities are:

- To nurture linkages between players across a wide range of networks conducive to business growth.
- To convene stakeholders from different business sectors to help raise the business game of the FDI industry by creating shared benefit.
- To orchestrate local activities that support foreign investment to further local growth.

Engagement with an Ecosystem can be horizontal (i.e. targeted at companies that provide similar services or compete for similar clients) or vertical (i.e. along the value chain of an industry). The very nature of an Ecosystem means that many different organisations have to contribute for an Ecosystem to grow and thrive. There is an organic element to this.

Ecosystem development is not something that can be centralised and controlled, and hence an IPA is just one of the players that can help nurture and grow a local ecosystem. It is worth noting that Ecosystems are not centralised, but multi-layered and therefore the function of engaging with it lies in different sectors and organisations of the host economy at any one time.

While there is much debate around whether Ecosystems are created or happen by chance, there are a series of concerted interventions and activities that are deployed today by countries, cities and regions to help build Ecosystems. Connectedness and linkages are the two principal ones. Linkages was covered in Chapter 4, Portfolio of Investor Services, and therefore the focus now is to explain connectedness, as it is the force behind linkages.

7.3.1 Connectedness

Ancient Roman merchants knew that being well connected was a key driver of business success. In the book, *The Organization of the Grain Trade in the Early Roman Empire*, David Kessler and Peter Temin noted that Roman merchants used a number of different tools to manage their grain imports in order to overcome the informational challenges of long-distance trade in an era when communication with remote locations took days, if not weeks. "The Roman wheat market was mostly private with a healthy mixture of government involvement. Wheat merchants and traders made use of agents, maritime loans, legal framework and financial provisions. Families, extended households of slaves and freedmen, and friends were used to reduce the extent of adverse selection."[38] It appeared to Kessler and Temin that "informal Roman institutions also proved useful in addressing problems of incomplete information. Agents and principals typically came from the same elite social groups, and their informal relations supported and aided their commercial transactions."[39] They noted that the connected place central to this was "primary physical institution for grain information exchange in Ostia was a large building with a colonnade surrounded by many small offices that housed numerous types of merchants, promoting casual communication between merchants."[40]

7.3.1.1 Global connectedness

Two millennia later, the "Global Start-up Ecosystem Report 2018", led by Start-up Genome, captured the voices of over 10,000 entrepreneurs from 170 countries, and confirmed the value of connectedness. They established "that globally-connected start-up ecosystems grow faster and perform better than less-connected places. These ecosystems tap into a worldwide circulation of ideas, knowledge, talent and capital."[41] They also noted that "global networks that are rooted in relationships between entrepreneurs, start-ups in these ecosystems can access global customers at a very early stage and develop globally-leading products and business models."[42] It is apparent through their work that "this is the foundation of the so-called unicorns, the trigger for ecosystem evolution and accelerated growth through attraction of international resources – and the multiplier of more connections. Conversely, ecosystems that are not well connected, do not experience fast growth."[43]

Connectedness not only matters for start-ups, as the DHL Global Connectedness Index (GCI) shows. Their research, which started in 2012, is led by globalisation expert Pankaj Ghemawat and measures flows of trade, capital, information and people across 140 countries. The 2016 GCI states that "deeper ties spur economic recovery and growth. Broader links bridge cultural differences. Shared information enables innovation. And more cooperation leads to less conflict. This is why connectedness matters."[44] Meanwhile, the 2018 GCI highlights "how emerging economies still lag behind on global connectedness. Even when emerging economies trade as intensively as advanced economies, advanced economies are about three times as deeply integrated into international capital flows, five times as much on people flows, and nine times with respect to information flows."[45]

The 2016 edition of the GCI also notes that "if emerging economies become more similar to advanced economies in terms of their connectedness levels, this would provide a powerful boost to overall connectedness," and therefore also to wealth creation.

The GCI 2016 edition goes on to suggest that there are two trends in globalisation (see note)[46]:

- **Semi-globalisation**: "international interactions, while non-negligible, are significantly less intense than domestic interactions. Flows often take place more intensively within large cities than between them."[47] It then goes on to provide an direct example pertaining to trade "the value of shipments within a given zip (postal) code in the US (with a median radius of just four miles) is three times larger than the value of shipments across zip code boundaries."[48] They also note that "in regard to capital flows, investment fund managers are more likely to buy or sell stocks when other managers in the same city are doing so."[49]

- **Distance**: "international interactions are dampened by distance along cultural, administrative, and geographic dimensions and are often affected by economic distance as well."[50] Distance in this case also includes a non-geographic dimension.

These trends are important for long-term foreign investment because connectedness influences the ability of a location to capture business growth. Furthermore, the 2018 GCI noted that "among the world's 100 largest corporations ranked by foreign assets, the average firm earns roughly 60% of its revenue in just four countries (home plus three international markets)."[51] Understanding where foreign investors generate revenue can open unexpected avenues of connectedness, particularly for smaller locations that can offer the ability to access markets that are important to an investor. Box 7.2 provides further insight into the Global Connectedness Index.

Box 7.2 Quotes from the Global Connectedness Index 2016 and 2018

"In prior editions of this report, we have highlighted discrepancies between popular perceptions of levels of globalization and the actual data, attaching the term 'globaloney' to the tendency of people to believe the world is more globalised than it really is. New evidence reveals that this phenomenon is even more widespread than previously known and can cause real damage in both business and public policy." (2016 edn, p. 13)

"Readers suspect that globaloney afflicts only Americans, on another survey of more than 3,000 students from 138 countries, respondents from every country for which a meaningful average could be calculated also overestimated levels of globalization – on average, again, by about 5 times. While globalization is far less advanced than is commonly perceived, globaloney does seem to be a global phenomenon." (2016 edn, p. 14)

"Consider Sassen's suggestion that as the connections among global cities grow, these cities become progressively less connected to their domestic hinterlands: a kind of world in which New York City might have more links with London, say, than with other US cities. While of obvious appeal to certain urban elites, this picture turns out to be factually wrong. While New York is usually rated as one of the world's top global cities, prior research using Sassen's preferred measure indicates that New York's greatest connectivity is with Washington, DC, ahead of Tokyo, and Chicago and Boston round out its top four connections. Other US cities are much less connected internationally: thus, the Los Angeles metro area, the fourth largest in the world in GDP terms after New York, Tokyo, and London, counts only one foreign city (Tokyo, at #8) among its top dozen connections." (2016 edn, p. 52)

"At the global level, this report shows that the world is actually far less globalised than most people believe, even after globalization's recent gains. The large majority of flows that could take place either within or between countries are still domestic rather than international. For example, just about 20% of economic output around the world is exported, foreign direct investment flows equal 7% of global gross fixed capital formation, roughly 7% of phone call minutes (including calls over the internet) are international, and only 3% of people live outside the countries where they were born. Furthermore, despite advances in transportation and telecommunications, distance and cross-country differences continue to serve as powerful constraints on international flows. If the world had really become "flat" and such constraints no longer mattered, international trade, capital, information, and people flows would be expected to travel 67% further than they do today. In fact, international flows are so far from global that about half take place between countries and just their top three origins and destinations." (2018 edn,– p. 8)

Sources: DHL, Global Connectedness Index, http://www.dhl.com/content/dam/downloads/g0/about_us/logistics_insights/gci_2016/DHL_GCI_2016_full_study.pdf. https://www.logistics.dhl/content/dam/dhl/global/core/documents/pdf/glo-core-gci-2018-full-study.pdf. Pankaj Ghemawat and Steven Altman, *The State of Globalization in an Age of Ambiguity*, 2016 edn. Steven Altman, Pankaj Ghemawat and Phillip Bastian, *The State of Globalization in a Fragile World*, 2018 edn.

Reproduced with kind permission from the authors.

Connectedness matters when it comes to FDI as it affects the state of development of the local cluster and therefore determines how fertile the host economy is to grow a foreign investment.

In the case of start-ups, research carried out for the "Global Start-up Ecosystem Report" revealed the weight host economies have when it comes to growth. "One in every three start-ups located outside the United States report having multiple connections to Silicon Valley."[52] "One in every four start-ups around the world have multiple connections to London."[53] "One in five start-ups around the world have multiple connections to New York."[54] Or put another way, these three hubs "cast the widest net of Global Connectedness: these are the places that start-ups everywhere want to connect to for access to advice, money, and ideas."[55] No other location comes close to these three in terms of what the report called "inbound" global connections.

Inbound global connectedness is calculated as "the percentage of startups around the world (excluding the United States) saying they have 2+ connections to other ecosystems."[56] This type of connectedness matters because even small companies benefit from inbound connectedness as it exposes them to world-class innovation. Companies of any size become "global customers, because they become knowledgeable of what the latest and greatest technologies are."[57] This is particularly the case in Silicon Valley where "founders, investors, and advisors can also become knowledgeable of the latest global customer needs and the latest innovations pretty much anywhere in the world."[58] Inbound connectedness makes innovation more accessible locally, therefore reducing the need to travel to another location in order to be exposed to it.

Outbound global connectedness "measures the ecosystems where start-ups report having the highest average number of significant connections to seven top ecosystems: Silicon Valley, New York City, London, Tel Aviv, Singapore, Berlin, and Shanghai. Outside of those six, Stockholm, Toronto-Waterloo, Sydney, and Mexico City are the most connected to the top-performing ecosystems."[59] Outbound connectedness is particularly important when looking for clients. Reaching out to foreign customers allows start-ups "to identify problems and solutions that are relevant to broad parts of the world,"[60] and therefore to develop a product with a wide customer base. Additionally, "productivity and innovation increase as start-ups go global – in any given economy, companies with more exposure to foreign markets are the 'frontier' firms that drive growth. A focus on foreign customers should therefore mean faster growth for start-ups and ecosystems."[61]

According to Swiss think tank the Gottlieb Duttweiler Institut (GDI), "cities are the new states. Around 50 cities worldwide have more inhabitants in their metropolitan area than the entire population of Switzerland (8.4 million); almost one billion people live in these 50 cities alone."[62] A striking point! They go on to note that "[i]n the age of globalisation, life and travel routes lead around the world – and almost always from city to city."[63] Joel Kotkin, writing on the business website Forbes.com, adds that "the greatest global cities were generally the largest and centres of the world's empires: London, Paris, New York and Tokyo. Today size is not so important."[64] The GDI examined the most important cities in the world to measure how well they fulfil their networking role in global terms. "Of the world's 10 most populous cities, only 3, namely Tokyo, New York and Beijing, rank among the top 10 world's most important cities. Instead, what matters today is influence."[65] And cities are also competitors, competing for companies, for investment and for people. GDI concludes by saying that "all metropolises connect people and cultures – but not all to the same extent."[66] Political scientist Parag Khanna adds that "cities will benefit from the fact that a multipolar, fragmented world is developing in international relations: as in the Middle Ages, cities will become the guarantors of security and progress."[67] He states that a "city's global connectivity is often at odds with its national significance. In a similar way to the Hanseatic League, city networks have developed into the economic and cultural centres of a world society."[68]

The GDI publishes a Global City Index, a ranking of the most important cities in the digital world based on the total number of connections on English-language Wikipedia, usage on Twitter and the number of Google searches. Overall, "the [digital] network analysis shows exciting similarities to the network created by global flight connections: many highly-placed cities [in the ranking] are hubs of global air traffic."[69] This analysis suggests that digital connectedness shows a similar pattern to physical infrastructure.

As the importance of cities continues to grow, so does the range of indices that measure them. In the 2016 edition of DHL's Global Connectedness Index, two new indices of particular interest were introduced:

- "The **Globalization Hotspots Index** ranks the cities with the most intense international flows of trade, capital, people, and information compared to their internal activity. The top Globalization Hotspots in 2015 were: Singapore, Manama (Bahrain), Hong Kong, Dubai, and Amsterdam."

And

- "The **Globalization Giants Index** looked beyond the cities themselves to assess their overall external projection by comparing directly the sizes of cities' international interactions [i.e. the four pillars of the index]. The leading Globalization Giants were Singapore, Hong Kong, London, New York, and Paris."[70]

One outcome of these new indices was that "London and New York, perennial leaders on rankings of global cities, place 3rd and 4th on the Globalization Giants index, but only 47th and 76th on the Globalization Hotspots index." Perhaps what makes New York and London so attractive to international business is not their international activity per se, but the platform they provide in the form of global connectedness, both inbound and outbound, and the value-add this creates.

7.3.1.2 Local connectedness

The "2018 Global Startup Ecosystem Report" (GSER) by Start-up Genome revealed that "start-up founders who are personally more connected [locally] see their start-ups grow faster."[71] This also applies to established businesses, including foreign investors, particularly as many foreign investors operate like start-ups when they first land in a country.

Businesses connectedness is crucial to the success of most companies, whether a start-up or a more mature company. Hence it is important that companies learn how to connect, how to interact with other businesses, how to collaborate with new partners and how to navigate the local Ecosystem.

The GSER goes on to say that "free-riding inside a connected community doesn't work."[72] This is something that some foreign investors get wrong. They assume that just by establishing a presence in a connected location that they will gain access to business opportunities and markets. Moreover, some investors see it as the role of the IPA to not only broker local connections, but also to instil the trust and to convey the reputation they enjoy at home (where their parent company is located) in the local business community. Unsurprisingly, it does not work like this. Connectedness is a hard-won asset that requires effort in the form of participation, face time and familiarity with people and new initiatives. Moreover, this is work that foreign investors must do for themselves. IPAs can only facilitate.

There are 4 key success factors when it comes to building local connectedness: a sense of community, the quality of local relationships, collisions and density.[73]

- **Sense of community**: in locations "where founders help each other, the ecosystem performs better at producing scaleups"[74] (fast-growth companies). Or put another way, there is a positive correlation between growing and helping others to grow. Hence the best entrepreneurs, investors and companies, as part of their strategy for growth and their search for competitive advantage, are all looking to become better connected to the right people, organisations, etc. By becoming well embedded in the local Ecosystem, companies develop the ability to relate to other businesses and other local constituencies in a way that converts potential for growth into actual growth. Although the Three Musketeers motto "all for one, one for all" is probably taking it a little too far, the concept of "my growth is our growth, our growth is my growth" is a mindset often found in thriving business Ecosystems.
- The **quantity of local relationships** also matters. Connectedness is partly a numbers game and partly a relationship game where

participants not only know each other, but also have a positive opinion of each other. The better the quality of the relationship, the stronger the Ecosystem will be. In essence, it is not just the more businesses based locally, the merrier, but the more active and friendly the business partners, the merrier.

- **Collisions**, or serendipitously bumping into people one already knows, are well known to have positive effects, both in the form of generating new ideas and different ways of looking at a problem or opportunity, and also through strengthening relationships within a company and between different stakeholders (indeed some companies, such as Apple, design their buildings to engineer more collisions).

There's a temptation in our networked age to think that ideas can be developed by email and iChat. That's crazy. Creativity comes from spontaneous meetings, from random discussions. You run into someone, you ask what they're doing, you say 'wow,' and soon you're cooking up all sorts of ideas.[75]

Steve Jobs

- And finally, **density**, which refers to how closely companies are based to each other and the geographical proximity between where founders or executives live and work. The closer companies are to each other, the more likely they are to collaborate, and also the more likely they are to bump into each other, thereby strengthening the Ecosystem.

In essence, connectedness is about both quantity and quality. It is not just event participation and community engagement that helps an Ecosystem. On one side, numbers facilitate participation and collisions. On the other side, the personal touch nurtures relationships which lead to the development of a sense of community, thereby creating a connected ecosystem that fosters growth.

Figure 7.1 illustrates a positively interactive loop of local connectedness for FDI growth. Numbers drivers density and collisions, while personal touch drive relationship and a sense of community. All four factors lead to a stronger Ecosystem in the local economy.

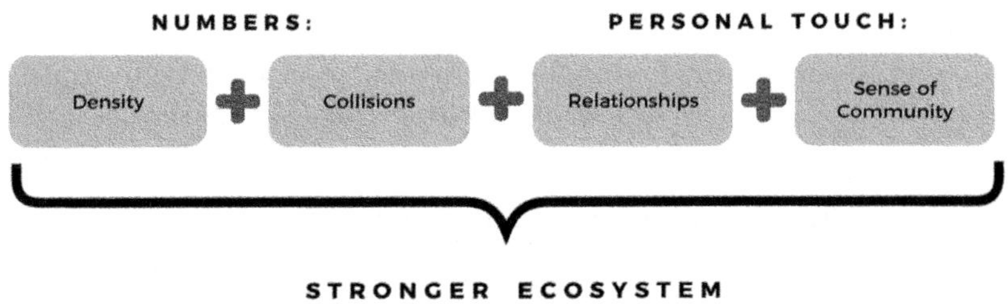

Figure 7.1 Local connectedness.

Source: Author's own design using data from Startup Genome, 2018. "Global Startup Ecosystem Report 2018".

7.3.1.3 Connectedness among people

According to the McKinsey Connectedness Index, "building global connections does not have to be left to national policy makers. Local businesses everywhere have the ability to forge their own global ties directly – and digital globalization gives them a multitude of new ways to pursue these opportunities."[76] And they do, facilitated by the ever-declining cost of travel and the advent of ever more sophisticated tools for connecting people, whether that be by phone, email, social media, on-line, industry forums, etc. "Whether it is deliberate or serendipitous, international cross-pollination is likely to continue and accelerate in a more digitally connected global world. But while digital platforms are enablers, they do not negate the need for local ties and personal connections based on trust."[77]

The 2017 Global Start-up Ecosystem Report states that, "when founders in a start-up ecosystem have meaningful relationships with their peers elsewhere (especially in the world's top ecosystems), it is associated with greater levels of global market reach, start-up growth, and overall ecosystem performance."[78] The report also noted that establishing more relationships between founders and executives in other parts of the world generates more ideas and more innovation, resulting in faster start-up growth and more vibrant Ecosystems. Businesses thrive on relationships and the exchange of ideas – with customers, investors, corporations and, especially, other businesses. These ideas fall into two types: "*hard* knowledge such as technical ideas about product improvement, new scientific ideas, and how to sell into different markets,"[79] and *soft* knowledge, "connectedness also brings the benefits, including giving introductions and being exposed to a pay-it-forward mentality. The exchange of this knowledge occurs through personal relationships, and more relationships leads to faster-growth."[80] The broader those connections are, the better the growth outcomes will be for the entire Ecosystem. According to the British "Tech Nation 2018 Report," they comment on both global and local connectedness as having the following attributes, it "drives innovation, and also extends the market reach of all players in an ecosystem. Since the success of firms in the knowledge-based economy is increasingly dependent on their ability to innovate, the importance of these global networks to the performance of [a] sector cannot be overstated."[81] It goes on to say that "physical proximity often aids collaboration, so we must not underestimate the value of domestic networks. But it is increasingly important that clusters are seen as local nodes within an international web."[82]

There is one more angle to connectedness and long-term foreign investment, resilience. According to the 100 Resilient Cities Initiative, "connections not only can provide critical support and lifelines in the event of a disaster, but also lead to **multi-stakeholder, multi-benefit problem solving** even under normal circumstances."[83] This is the reason why they include connectedness as a pillar of resilience programmes, all of which also support international trade and investment and, in particular, long-term expansions. This is because resilient locations recover faster from disruptions and provide an added layer of stability and predictability that foreign investors value. As a result, connectedness becomes an asset. It is exactly this asset-like nature of connectedness that makes it such a strong fit with post-investment. This is something that post-investment professionals can hone.

Figure 7.2 shows some of the institutions and organisations investors typically connect with. These organisations touch every aspect of a business and go beyond the core business to include, for example, affinity groups, including diaspora, faith groups and political groups in the community. A rich programme of activities, events, conferences, gatherings and opportunities to meet will enable connectedness to grow organically between different groups, which in turn will strengthen the connectedness and vibrancy of a local business Ecosystem. But connectedness is not only local, as it can move beyond physical borders when the local Ecosystem connects with another Ecosystem, both with incoming links and outgoing connections, thus broadening the network. It is this integrated connectedness that matters most and becomes an asset for a location.

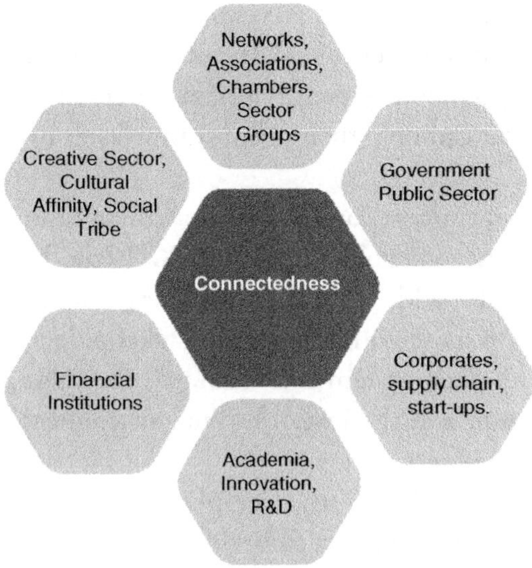

Figure 7.2 Organisations investors typically connect with. © *Investment Aftercare Explained: A Guide for FDI Practitioners and Policymakers on How to Grow and Retain Investors.*

Programmes that support connectedness exploit the factors mentioned above, including proximity, collisions, relationships and a sense of community, and create an environment that supports them.

One organisation that has embraced the value of connectedness as a business differentiator is Santander Bank, a leading Spanish bank, through their Santander Trade Portal. Santander uses the knowledge they have of local markets and of their own networks to enhance the international connectedness of the locations they work with. They do this systematically by giving access to this network to their clients, who therefore benefit from access to data and contacts, and provide preferential services designed to increase company connectedness in new markets. HSBC, a leading Hong Kong headquartered bank with strong presence in the UK, has a similar programme supporting companies wishing to enter Asian markets or the UK. Their slogan is, "At HSBC we know that good things happen when people connect." There are many other organisations who are maximising the value of connectedness in other ways. For example, there are many incubators, business accelerators and coworking businesses that seek to put entrepreneurs and (small) businesses together in the same real or virtual space, thus generating collisions and connections. Some tech companies have followed suit: Amazon Web services (AWS) organises Amazon Days to connect clients, using their cloud servers, to business support services. Stripe, the leading online payment business, enters into partnerships with local businesses that can help their clients grow faster in every new market they enter.

Programmes that support connectedness are many and varied. Figure 7.3 is an example of the stakeholders Uruguay XXI (the IPA from Uruguay) engages regularly, to add value to the foreign investor based locally. Examples of how to liaise with these other stakeholders are covered in the next section. The underlying aim is to maximise the value of connectedness for both the location and the investors, but not connectedness per se – it needs to be connectedness by design.

The IPA's role is to identify the key players, engage them, foster participation and create and support Ecosystem-wide initiatives that become springboards for both local and global collaboration. For example, many IPAs work with their peers in export promotion agencies to ensure

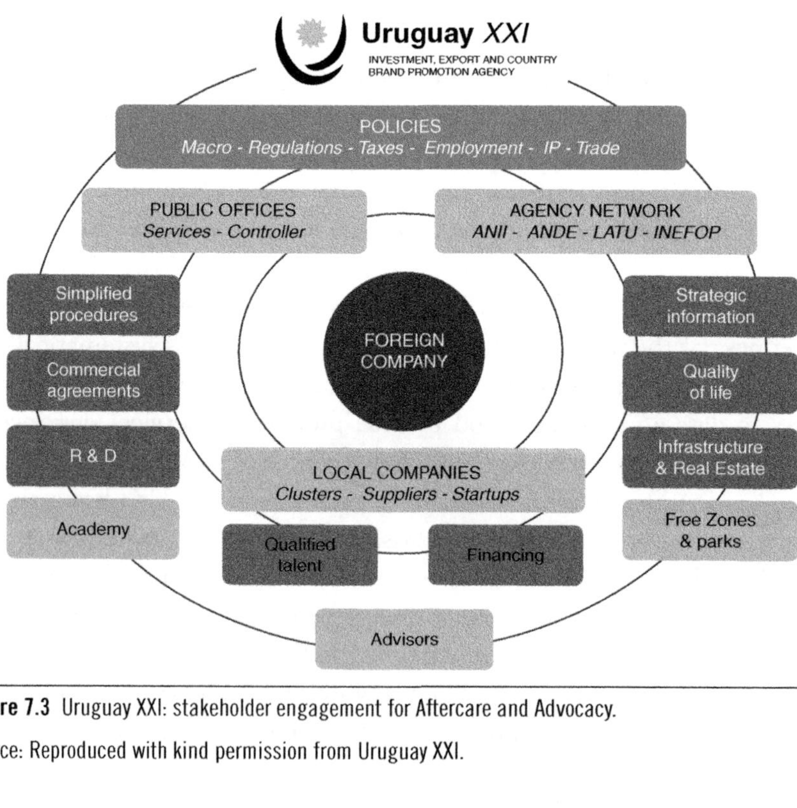

Figure 7.3 Uruguay XXI: stakeholder engagement for Aftercare and Advocacy.

Source: Reproduced with kind permission from Uruguay XXI.

established investors have access to clients in a third country, or they work closely with the start-up Ecosystem to drive innovation. However, it should be noted that Ecosystems respond to the interplay of cooperation and competition, simultaneous market forces that constantly change the landscape of the Ecosystem. As such, it is important that IPAs ask themselves what role they can play, and what type of programme provides the best support to investors seeking to navigate a constantly evolving Ecosystem. In many cases, the role is to orchestrate local programming, such as conferences, hackathons, seminars and meet the buyer weeks, and to set in motion initiatives that convene and amplify events led by third parties. In other situations, it is about identifying niches not served by other parties and to fill the gap.

7.4 Place and Ecosystem in action

The following pages explore a number of Place and Ecosystem-related programmes that have a distinctive role to play when it comes to strengthening a host Ecosystem in which investors can thrive, while also maximising the positive spill-over effects generated by their presence.

It is worth noting that while Investor Services are tailored for each company, Place and Ecosystem, interventions benefit the whole business community. The aim of these activities is to inject more dynamism into the area, to foster linkages or to make a location more welcoming to business. In contrast to programmes that focus directly on supporting an investor, this type of intervention will be open to both local and foreign companies and aims to create a positive, business-conducive climate a host economy can build on. While their impact on Investor Services might be less obvious, Place and Ecosystem programmes play a key role in generating economic growth and attracting long term investment, and hence are not an area that IPAs should ignore. The precise role IPAs play in these types of programmes is likely to vary significantly from host economy to host economy.

The following pages present examples of Place programmes.

7.4.1 Sectors as platforms for growth

"Foreign investment is more beneficial for a company when it takes root in a cluster, as spillovers of information and business practices diffuse quickly through tight-knit networks of firms and workers."[84] This quote from the "2016 Brookings Institute Report" provides insight into why companies are interested in becoming part of business communities in the locations they invest. In fact, "since the benefits of clusters are inseparable from place, companies that invest in locations with strong clusters are more likely to stay or expand."[85]

Sector specialisation is closely linked to business development. Indeed, in 2013 the European Union asked "national and regional authorities across Europe [to] design smart specialisation strategies in entrepreneurial discovery process."[86] The rationale behind this is that it will allow them to use European funds "more efficiently and [to identify] synergies between different EU, national and regional policies, as well as public and private investments."[87] Unsurprisingly, investors follow the same logic and seek sector insight in order to understand relevant local capabilities. However, this can be a time-consuming activity for an investor. "The most promising locations recognise the value of these specializations and double down on them, focusing on turning their strongest clusters and international relationships into *platforms* that companies can use to distinguish themselves and form valuable partnerships."[88]

A natural by-product of these relationships is *knowledge transfer* in both directions. A foreign investor is likely to bring industry knowledge from both their country of origin and from other markets where they have a presence, knowledge that they are likely to share with their (new) local partners. At the same time, an investor will also hope to access local knowledge that can help it become more competitive. IPAs can help facilitate this knowledge sharing process by introducing investors to innovation hubs, exposing them to local thinkers or introducing them to data sandbox projects where new technologies are tested, as is the case in Singapore.

In essence, the relationship between an investor and a sector is self-reinforcing. Investors are attracted by the business opportunities a particular sector offers, and so target these opportunities once they are established. Once the sector has reached a certain size, companies will have ambitions of their own and will organise their own forums, associations and chambers of commerce. These organisations will in turn seek to work with the local government to create the most favourable business conditions for their sector. This is where government institutions come into play with their plans (or lack of them) for a sector. It is in this dynamic coming together of stakeholders that sectors become platforms for locations to grow. The resulting dynamism is a valuable asset for a location and is usually referred to as cluster strength. Indeed, some political leaders assign the same level of importance to cluster development as they do to job creation and connectedness.

IPAs can act as the connector, co-creating new local sector initiatives and suggesting activities a company could participate in, and by doing so, help nurture the sector Ecosystem. This includes sector conferences, summits, forums, etc. A good example is London Tech Week, a week-long technology festival created by London & Partners (London's IPA) in 2014 to provide yet another reason to travel to London by leveraging the connections and industry knowledge of the Trade and Investment team. In organising this festival, London & Partners saw their role as simply to organise the opening event and to provide a platform for others to join and where they could organise their own events. Over 300 corporates and organisations responded to the call, and more than 50,000 people attended. In London & Partners words, they "co-founded London Tech Week to promote and build on the extraordinary success story"[89] of London's technology hub. By organising the festival, London & Partners helped give the local tech sector a voice, a reason to come together, to celebrate, to learn, to connect and to grow together.

7.4.2 Start-ups

A growing number of locations recognise the value of a dynamic start-up Ecosystem, as it attracts investors, upskills talent, unleashes funding and supports location branding. They also realise that a strong start-up Ecosystem is a location asset that can be leveraged to make a location more attractive to foreign investors. Consequently, many larger locations have concerted location-wide programmes to coordinate entrepreneurship activities. The most common types of support include the provision of flexible workspaces, training courses, event programmes, mentoring and coaching, introduction to potential customers, support in accessing finance and facilitation of partnerships. These types of programmes not only help start-up founders, they also pollinate other economic activities such as driving innovation on behalf of government and corporates. It is therefore not surprising that two thirds of IPAs interviewed for the OCO IPA Benchmark Study 2018 have included start-up support in their mandate.[90]

In his latest book, *Start-up Cities: Why Only a Few Cities Dominate the Global Start-up Scene and What the Rest Should Do About It*, the investor, and lecturer at Babson College, Peter Cohan, identified 6 core elements of a start-up Ecosystem. These pillars are companies, universities, human capital, investment capital, mentoring and values. These core elements "get strengthened in each generation of start-up success and failure. The benefits include lower unemployment rates, rising wages and housing values and higher tax revenues."[91] All these positive outputs are goals of FDI and Aftercare. Moreover, the link between start-up support and business growth is strong. Google, for example, was one of the first corporates to develop an international strategy to engage with start-ups. They understand the importance of supporting local entrepreneurs as a way to build digital Ecosystems and to access new technologies that may ultimately benefit Google's own expansion plans, as well as creating local digital capacity. Hence, Google established Google Campuses, collaborative spaces for entrepreneurs comprising work and event spaces, cafes and classrooms. The first Google Campus launched in London in 2012 under the banner of "Come start something. Strong community to show you the way. Strong coffee to start your journey." By 2017 there were more than 70,000 members across the globe. The start-ups have created around 3,000 new jobs every year, and since 2012 have raised in excess of £194 million (US$215 million) seed funding from partner investors, to help London based entrepreneurs grow.[92]

Encouraging foreign investors to play a role in fostering local entrepreneurs is gaining momentum everywhere. Multinationals are increasingly opening start-up accelerators and incubators on their premises across the world, and across many different sectors. For example, legal firm Mishcon De Reya has established MDR Labs focused on supporting disruption in the delivery of legal services, airline KLM is exploring how virtual reality and machine learning can innovate the passenger transport industry, while supermarket chain Metro, which operates in 31 countries, is looking for innovation ideas in the food and retail sector. These companies have also sought support from the public sector or have, due to their sheer size, become the natural partners for entrepreneurship programmes. Spanish telecommunications giant Telefonica, for example, has created Open Future, a programme designed to work with local governments to support the growth of local Ecosystems. Telefonica provides the growth methodology, the sector insight and access to experts, while the location provides the space and funding support.

Governments have played their part as well. For example, Qatar has partnered with Microsoft and invited them to join their mission to "develop the next QAR 100 million companies in Qatar."[93] The initiative is managed by The Qatar Business Incubation Center (QBIC), which is supported by the Qatar Development Bank, the Qatar Foundation and the Qatar Tourism Authority amongst others. Microsoft supports Qatari entrepreneurs with their BizSpark scheme, which provides free software and support for start-ups, as well as access to a global online community. Entrepreneurs also benefit from online and offline training guidance from Microsoft DirectX specialists, including the App Academy, Ask the Expert sessions and Microsoft's Virtual Academy.[94]

The Indian Government has chosen a different route, one that allows faster pace and reach. Their Start-up India Action Plan,[95] launched in 2016, comprises 278 government-run incubators across the country. In 2017, they invited the private sector to certify their in-house corporate accelerator programmes to deliver the Start-up India vision. As a result, 20 private sector companies were appointed to deliver incubator services on their behalf. German manufacturer Bosch, for example, offers access to labs and mentoring from its in-house engineers as part of the Start-up India Action Plan.

An alternative route for governments to play a role in encouraging entrepreneurship is via their e-government initiatives. Singapore, for example, observes that "with the rising popularity of social networking, Government can more easily tap [into] the collective intelligence of the crowd and data shared online. As such, the Government can go beyond its traditional role as a service provider, to also serve as a platform provider to encourage greater co-creation of new e-services."[96] Singapore also observes that "members of the public will be able to readily look for and download publicly available government data from data.gov.sg, which can be used for research purposes, as well as to encourage the development of innovative and impactful applications."[97] In this scenario the public sector does not perform the role of supporting entrepreneurship but seeks to enable it via the release of data. As such, it plays a role in growing the Ecosystem.

The importance of partnerships between start-ups, corporates and locations has resulted in the creation of new member organisations solely dedicated to facilitating such collaborations. This is something that Amsterdam has recognised and supports with their Start-up Amsterdam's Corporate Network (see Box 7.3). This private sector-led initiative developed a value proposition to enable corporates to contact local entrepreneurs, while at the same time welcoming the support and collaboration of the public sector. Many of the companies that have signed up for membership of the programme are foreign investors.

Box 7.3 Start-up Amsterdam's Corporate Network

"We are a community of over 80 corporates and multinationals, including Philips, Microsoft, KPMG, ABN Amro, TomTom, KLM and many more. We are a well-connected community of innovation managers, start-up liaisons and dedicated ambassadors of change from every industry you can think of. Together, we form a powerful player in Amsterdam's tech and start-up ecosystem.

- Bring your challenges to the right eyes, invest in initiatives and get assistance.
- Start-up ecosystem.
- Initiate your next corporate-start-up collaboration.
- Harness the talent and capabilities of Amsterdam's most ingenious start-ups and find tech solutions to your company's current innovation challenges.
- Connect to fellow innovation managers.

This is how Start-up Amsterdam supports corporates [including foreign investors].

- Request a corporate profile: Place your company on a platform where start-ups can easily find you and propose solutions to the challenges you define. Become Visible.
- Partner up with initiatives: Get involved! Become a mentor, speaker, launching customer, sponsor or event organiser. Browse project[s].
- Browse service providers: Should you have questions or need additional assistance, these service providers are on stand-by. Get Assistance.
- Launchpad Meetups: Apply for future meetups to have start-ups pitch their solutions to your innovation challenges."

Reproduced with kind permission from Startup Amsterdam: www.iamsterdam.com.

When it comes to helping companies grow, the only limiting factor is (your) creativity. For example, Austin, the state capital of Texas, has a particularly novel approach to helping their local start-ups access new markets. Austin has created the Midnight Live Pitch event that gives local businesses the opportunity to directly access Chinese entrepreneurs (see Box 7.4).

Box 7.4 Austin's Midnight Live Pitch Event

City of Austin Announces Alibaba Midnight Live Pitch Event

Businesses Live Pitch for Opportunity to Enter Chinese Global Market on March 12, 10PM – 2AM

"The City of Austin's International Program, within the Economic Development Department's Global Business Expansion Division, and Alibaba Group, the largest commerce company in the world, are pleased to bring the second Midnight Pitch Event to Austin, Texas. This LIVE stream Midnight Pitch Event will run from 10 PM to 2 AM on March 12 at Austin City Hall, 301 W 2nd St.

Nine entrepreneurs will take the stage to pitch their products to a captive audience of Chinese retailers on Taobao Global, Alibaba's solution that allows small-to-medium size businesses from outside of China to reach Chinese consumers via buying agents. This follows the first U.S. live pitch event in Austin, Texas last year, which garnered more than 13,000 views and 5 of 11 businesses received offers from Taobao Global to sell to China.

Alibaba Group serves as a gateway for businesses of all sizes to access China's large and growing middle class of more than 300 million consumers – expected to grow to 500 million in the next 5 years.

The Pitch Event aims to increase visibility of Austin brands and give businesses a chance to explore the Chinese consumer market, minus the expense of flying to tradeshows in China to meet buyers.

Participating businesses were coached by export experts, Blue Heron Holdings, LLC, Lee & Hays, PLLC, along with the Alibaba Group and the City of Austin Economic Development Department, prior to the pitch event to ensure fit and feasibility of importing their products into China and lay the groundwork for potential international expansion.

City of Austin Economic Development Department Global Business Expansion – International Program

The City of Austin Economic Development Department (EDD) develops and leads the innovative programs that increase the prosperity of Austin's citizens, our businesses, and our diverse neighbourhoods. The Global Business Expansion (GBE) Division merges International and Economic Development Programs within the Economic Development Department in order to 1) enhance global opportunities for locals in business, trade, education, and cultural activities, and 2) bring international attention to Austin-area investments, resources, and events. Ultimately, the GBE Division is dedicated to scaling Austin's position in the global marketplace to create a sustainable, vibrant economy that protects and enhances the environment, culture, and livability of the Austin area."

Reproduced with kind permission from the Economic Development Department of the City of Austin.

Link: http://www.austintexas.gov/news/city-austin-announces-alibaba-midnight-live-pitch-event.

While all IPAs have interactions with local entrepreneurs, they don't all have a mandate to support them. Those that do find it relatively straightforward to connect them with foreign investors. While IPAs that are not focused on entrepreneurs are more focused on coordinating their activities with existing programmes and partnering with incubators. Clearly their focus is on increasing the level of connectedness between the different local players, including foreign investors and start-ups, in such a way that it results in growth for all parties involved.

7.4.3 Workforce development

The war for talent is never-ending, and, as the *Financial Times* reported in 2016, "countries compete for [the] best workers. Policymakers are under pressure to help companies attract in-demand staff."[98] Moreover, many countries are reporting talent shortages, predominantly in highly-skilled or high-growth sectors. For example, the *South China Morning Post* points out that "China faces a severe talent shortage in its quest to become a global powerhouse in artificial intelligence by 2030,"[99] while the *Deutsche Welle* reports that "Germany faces [a] huge shortage of skilled workers. It's a gloomy prognosis, but a new study claims that by 2040 Germany could suffer from a major shortage of specialised skilled workers to fill important jobs,"[100] and the World Economic Forum reports that "Latin America has the biggest skills gap in the world."[101] Hence in this global fight for highly skilled talent, how much of this talent a location manages to attract is likely to have major implications for its economic prospects. If foreign employers can't find the talent they require, they can't create jobs, and so are much less likely to invest.

While the section on talent and recruitment in Chapter 4, Portfolio of Investor Services, focussed on providing services that help investors attract the right talent, the pages below explore how a location can attract talent which foreign investors can then hire locally.

7.4.3.1 Attracting talent

With talent becoming one of a location's strongest assets, attracting and retaining talent is key. In the United States, Development Counsellors International (DCI), a leading Place marketing consultancy with a specialist talent attraction team, produces "Talent War", a quarterly report aimed at helping economic developers understand how talent assesses new job opportunities and relocation decisions. DCI regularly interviews more than 1,000 working-age individuals across the USA in order to understand what it takes to attract and retain a quality workforce. DCI observes that "competition among locations trying to attract these workers is stiff. Once sleepy cities have transformed into 'millennial magnets,' and nearly every location claims they are the ideal live, work, play community."[102] Based on its work, DCI identified the following 4 factors that impact the ability of a location to attract and retain a high-quality workforce:

- **Employers are the biggest talent attraction asset**: talent looking for jobs typically focus on the job first, not the location. "How employers market themselves on top sources such as their company website, LinkedIn, a business and employment-oriented website, and Indeed, a recruitment portal, is more important than how the location markets itself."[103] Consequently, IPAs should collaborate with local employers in such a way that they also promote the location as part of the recruitment process.

- **Tourism is a door to accepting an offer**: candidates are likely to travel to a location before deciding about relocating. "While attractive job opportunities capture talent's attention, travel forms their perceptions." Hence IPAs should work with the tourism sector to "ensure that visitors can imagine themselves not just visiting but living in the community."[104]
- **Residents are location promoters**: "Despite the growing influence of digital sources such as websites and social media, family is both one of the top sources for finding new job opportunities and among the most important factors for relocation."[105] Hence IPAs should encourage residents to promote a location and its opportunities through their personal and professional networks. This is something that is often overlooked, yet can be very cost-effective.
- **Money talks**: "Money plays a major role in people's job search and relocation decisions."[106] While salaries and benefits are outside an IPA's remit, they can help position a location from a cost-benefit perspective, such as a lower cost of living, accessible housing and free public education. This can help differentiate a location when compared with higher-cost locations offering similar jobs but with higher salaries.

One example of how locations seek to attract new talent is the award-winning LookSee Campaign organised by Wellington in New Zealand (see Box 7.5).

Box 7.5 Wellington, New Zealand Attracts Global Tech Talent

"Wellington, New Zealand is a rising center for tech and creative industries, located at the very bottom of the country's North Island. With ocean views and a vibrant culture, this city would seem like an obvious choice for professionals looking to advance their careers. However, following an all too familiar narrative of places throughout the world, Wellington companies were struggling to attract talent, particularly in the tech industry.

The Wellington Regional Economic Development Agency (WREDA) recognised this problem and came up with a solution, the LookSee Wellington talent attraction campaign, launched in February 2017. This idea would eventually go on to earn them the 2017 Innovation award from Economic Development New Zealand. DCI recently had a conversation with David Jones, the General Manager of Growth and Innovation at WREDA, reflecting on the experience.

'What you'd find if you came to Wellington is that people are deeply passionate about this place. It's a compact city that seems to attract people who have an aspirational career and quality of life,' explains Jones.

Centered around global tech talent attraction, LookSee Wellington took the world by storm. Project partners WREDA, recruitment agency Work Here and Immigration NZ, created a well-designed website and video with a simple application, seeking qualified professionals interested in making the move to Wellington. In return? Selected candidates would be flown out free of charge and be given a week of networking with top New Zealand companies, as well as information sessions about immigration and daily life. Organisers of this campaign knew that to really attract talent to their location, candidates had to see the city for themselves, up close and personal.

After several top media outlets such as the New York Times, Forbes and Mashable got a hold of the story, qualified applicants from across the world flooded in, totalling well over 45,000. Jones explains, 'It's been an incredible campaign for the level of ROI, with millions of dollars in media coverage; for the level of investment we put in, it's fantastic.'

When it came time for the week of interviews, executives from top companies were thrilled with the candidates who were invited to Wellington. As of today, 40+ people have either begun living and working in Wellington, or are moving through the interview and immigration process.

'It's been great giving people the opportunity and platform to go and fulfil their ambitions. For us as a city, continuing to bring in more candidates will make an incredible difference to our economy,' says Jones.

The LookSee story doesn't stop there, either. Not only are candidates from the original applicant database connecting with new Wellington employers and job opportunities on an ongoing basis, other regions of New Zealand are lining up to present their employment opportunities to the talent pool. The LookSee model is also being expanded by Workhere for New Zealand's booming construction sector, with LookSee Build.

Allen Geer – one of the candidates selected from LookSee – puts it simply: 'There hasn't been a day that's gone by that I haven't been immensely thankful that somewhere on the other side of the world, on an isolated island in a little city, a group of folks put together a contest to bring me to Wellington."'

Reproduced with kind permission from Development Counsellors International (DCI).

Link: https://aboutdci.com/2017/12/wellington-attracts-global-tech-talent/.

In contrast to the Wellington example, which is publicly funded and aimed at people willing to relocate to New Zealand, the next example offers a different model. Tulsa Remote (see Box 7.6) is an initiative led by the City of Tulsa that partnered with a local organisation, the George Kaiser Family Foundation, which "believes in the power of privately-funded innovation and oversight, coupled with public support, for the scaling and replication of proven programs."[107] They developed in their programme an innovative approach to talent development. Tulsa Remote targets remote workers and digital nomads who are highly skilled in their fields. They define their ideal candidate as somebody who "is a fully-employed individual with the flexibility to work anywhere and is looking for a community to call home."[108] At the time of the book going to press, Tulsa had attracted 500 members to their Tulsa Remote community. It is precisely this community aspect that people look for, when determining where to work from. The pandemic has introduced a deep change in how companies related to their talent, with recent announcements of companies, such as SalesForce and Spotify with their work-from-anywhere programmes, reinforcing flexibility of where the job is actually done.

Box 7.6 Tulsa Remote

"Tulsa Remote, a program funded by the George Kaiser Family Foundation www.gkff.org, is offering 250 people the opportunity to make $10,000 by simply moving to Oklahoma, the organisers announced Tuesday. The money comes in the form of a grant and is distributed to the recipient over the course of a year.

The program was launched in 2018, and more than 10,000 applications came in from more than 150 countries, Tulsa Remote [founding] Executive Director Aaron Bolzle told CNN. More than 100 people were selected.

The initiative decided to expand their offer in 2020 by more than doubling the amount of people they would accept.

'We wanted to remove the barrier to come from other cities – and the money got people's attention,' Bolzle told CNN.

'Tulsa suffered from a lack of perception – we had an opportunity to expose the country and the world as to what was happening here.'

The rules are pretty simple. Applicants must be full-time remote workers or be self-employed outside of Oklahoma and eligible to work in the United States. They must be older than 18 and be able to move to Tulsa within six months. Once accepted, recipients agree to live in Tulsa for at least one year.

However, recipients get more than just a stack of cash. The program provides free workspace, housing specials on certain apartments and community hangouts and meetups.

'If we could get people to come for a year, we believed we could get them to stay longer,' Bolzle told CNN.

And it's proving to be true. Bolzle told CNN that 12 of this year's participants already bought houses in the city, and the people are buying into the community. Bolzle said some have started non-profits and the program has even inspired job creation.

'Taking the leap of faith to move to Tulsa was one of the best decisions I ever made,' said Taylor Allen, who was selected for the

2019 Tulsa Remote program. 'The community has been so welcoming and has quickly made Tulsa feel like home. I am thankful for the abundant opportunities to invest in Tulsa through what I'm already passionate about.'

So, if you are thinking about relocating, you might want to give Tulsa a shot.

Reproduced with kind permission from Tulsa Remote: www.tulsaremote.com.

Link: https://edition.cnn.com/2019/10/29/business/10k-for-tulsa-trnd/index.html.

A further example comes from Japan, where the IPA encourages local companies hiring foreign professionals as a means to strengthen diversity of skills. Their online portal "Open For Professionals" facilitates recruitment of highly-skilled foreign professionals in Japan. The site provides information of companies interested in hiring foreign professionals, lists related policies and events by government ministries and agencies, as well as career search, required paperwork and formalities and recruitment events, just to name a few.[109]

7.4.3.2 Expats

Expatriates can make an important contribution when it comes to Place and Ecosystem. One location that leverages its expat community well is Barcelona, which has two distinctive initiatives that involve both local organisations and expats already living in Barcelona to promote the city.

Barcelona Global is a private, independent and not-for-profit association made up of 200 of the city's leading companies, research centres, entrepreneurs, business schools, universities and cultural institutions who come together to "make Barcelona one of the world's best cities for talent and economic activity."[110] Barcelona Global develops strategic proposals for the future of Barcelona, promotes specific projects together with its partners, and mobilies them so they get to know the city and each other, to ultimately better support and promote Barcelona as a global talent hub. One of those projects is Hola Barcelona! described in Box 7.7.

Box 7.7 Hola Barcelona!

"Reaching out to internationals who have decided to live and work in Barcelona, drawing them in and getting them involved has been one of Barcelona Global's objectives from the outset. To do that, we support the following activities:

Hola Barcelona! Pack

Barcelona has a wide range of services, activities and facilities, which Barcelona Global wants to be known and available to the international talent living in our city. Hola Barcelona! Pack is a goody bag full of discounts and benefits designed for the association's international members, including culture, sport, leisure, institutions, transport and the media.

Hola Barcelona! Dinners

The task of integrating Barcelona's international community has been taken up by our members, who open up their homes and host dinner gatherings to connect internationals with locals and help them to build a social network. Since 2014 a total of 98 dinners have been held, with 959 participants, 60% of whom were from outside of Spain.

Hola Barcelona! Cocktail

Barcelona attracts millions of tourists but has not been so good at welcoming the foreign nationals who have decided to live and work in our city. Seven years ago, Barcelona Global decided to break the ice: each September, with the collaboration of the Ajuntament, we hold a welcome event, which is attended by more than 1500 people, including internationals of 80 nationalities.

Hola Barcelona! Activities

Barcelona is a city where things constantly happen. To the wide offer of local activities, there are more and more international events choosing Barcelona as the location for their celebration. From Barcelona Global, we want to bring all these big appointments to our members and we encourage their participation."

Reproduced with kind permission from Barcelona Global.

Link: www.barcelonaglobal.org.

7.4.3.3 Welcome centres

Some locations, such as London, New York, Silicon Valley and Bangalore, are natural talent magnets and therefore have to make little effort to attract highly skilled talent, while other locations need to work hard to attract skilled workers. However, irrespective of the amount of effort locations put into attracting talent, they should also ensure they make new arrivals feel (more) welcome. This includes helping them to quickly settle in and make the new location their home. First impressions and experiences when arriving in a new location can be decisive when it comes to talent retention. Amsterdam, for example, has made a concerted effort to simplify arrival processes for highly skilled workers and offers a range of services at their welcome centre (see Box 7.8).

Box 7.8 IN Amsterdam

"IN Amsterdam (formerly Expatcenter Amsterdam) provides a one-stop-shop service for international newcomers in the Amsterdam Area. We serve companies and their highly skilled migrant employees, scientific researchers, international entrepreneurs and international graduates. The IN Amsterdam procedure includes immigration elements such as residence and work permits (including the start-up visa), registration with the municipality, the 30% tax ruling and many other official matters.

IN Amsterdam services

With simplified processes and applications, IN Amsterdam aims to better meet the needs of international companies and their expatriate employees in the Amsterdam Metropolitan Area, as well as international graduates and international entrepreneurs/investors.

A streamlined process

Utilising the IN Amsterdam procedure begins with the completion of the appropriate application form from the IND website. On the form, the employer indicates that they would like to use IN Amsterdam's services and sends the completed form to the IND. Approximately four weeks later, the highly skilled migrant can visit the IN Amsterdam office to collect his or her residence permit and register with the municipality.

Advantages of using IN Amsterdam

By submitting one single form, the employer can initiate the necessary official procedures while the employee is still abroad, and schedule an appointment with IN Amsterdam for their arrival. Once the employee is in the Netherlands, all documents will be in place, allowing the employee to start work immediately after their visit to the IN Amsterdam office.

Service for EU citizens

EU citizens who have a work contract with a company that is an officially recognised sponsor by the IND can visit IN Amsterdam for their municipal registration.

Citizen Service Number

As a result of the municipal registration, IN Amsterdam clients will receive their citizen service number (burgerservicenummer, BSN) during their appointment. Those registering with the municipalities of Almere and Haarlemmermeer will receive their BSN in two days by email.

Early residence stamp

IN Amsterdam offers the possibility of an early approval for work. With this early approval, highly skilled migrants are able to start working within two weeks after the IND has received their application. Once the IND has made a decision on the application, an early residence stamp can be issued at the IN Amsterdam office (in the employee's passport). This service requires that the employee visit IN Amsterdam twice, however, the second visit is simply for the issuance of the residence card.

Residence permit extensions for highly skilled migrants and researchers

Highly skilled migrants and scientific researchers that have applied for an extension of their residence permit can collect their extended residence permit at one of the Expatcenter branches, including IN Amsterdam.

Residence permits for recent graduates

Recent graduates from Dutch colleges and universities and academics from abroad that have successfully applied for an Orientation Year permit, which allows graduates to search for employment in the Netherlands for up to a year, can collect their permit at an Expatcenter in the Netherlands and at IN Amsterdam.

Biometric data services

Highly skilled migrants, researchers and recent graduates applying for an Orientation Year permit can now deliver the required biometric photographs and fingerprints at an official Expatcenter, including IN Amsterdam. Check the list of official Expatcenters in the Netherlands.

Information for your expat employees

Expatriate employees can also visit IN Amsterdam for help with other government and expat-related issues, such as parking, taxes, healthcare, education and much more. The IN Amsterdam staff is ready and able to answer questions, provide information and offer advice on a wide range of topics. Furthermore, a wealth of information is also available throughout the Local section of this website, with detailed information on topics like finding a job, childcare or place to live.

Information for spouses and partners of expats

If an international has taken up employment in the Netherlands, it's vitally important for their spouse or partner to feel just as happy and settled in their new country. That's why IN Amsterdam offers a support service for accompanying partners of international workers, helping them to find employment, settle into Dutch life and access family support information. Find out more about the services offered for accompanying partners."

Reproduced with kind permission from IN Amsterdam: www.iamsterdam.com.

7.4.3.4 Skills academies

Most locations have skills development programmes. However, foreign investors can also play a major role in supporting and expanding these programmes. Reasons for investors to participate range from talent development and recruitment, to community engagement and corporate social responsibility. Many corporates include skills academies as part of their business models. Indeed, skills academies can also be part of the investment terms a foreign company has agreed with a local government. This is particularly common for infrastructure projects or large investments in heavily regulated industries such as mining, fishing or utilities. For example, the Chinese technology giant Huawei created its ICT Academy "to deal with a gap of 2 million ICT-related workers in the next 10 years,"[111] and so "Huawei plans to promote an education program portfolio to train a large number of professionals in IP and IT technologies."[112] The ICT Academy is a partnership project between Huawei and universities across the world. Through this project, participating universities deliver Huawei ICT technologies and courses, encourage students to get certified by Huawei and develop professionals with practical ICT skills. Thus far, Huawei has worked with more than 300 universities around the world and, according to the *Financial Times*, this programme is particularly strong in Africa, training over 12,000 students a year at centres in Angola, Congo, Egypt, Kenya, Morocco, Nigeria and South Africa.[113]

Participating in skills development not only helps investors secure the talent they need to grow, but can also benefit a location by upskilling local talent, driving an inclusion agenda and offering hope to communities at social risk. It also helps different players in the education, recruitment and skills development industries to collaborate, thereby strengthening local connectedness.

7.4.3.5 Talent positioning and mobility tools

While some people move to where the job they want is located, for others the attractiveness of a location plays a (key) role in where they choose to work. Indeed, some people first choose where they want to live, and then look for work there. And in the digital era there are now online tools to help them make these decisions. The Global Talent Competitive Index (GTCI) is one such tool. The GTCI recommends the best countries or cities to live in based on what personal and professional factors a person considers most important (see Box 7.9).

Box 7.9 Global Talent Competitiveness Index

"Developed by INSEAD, the Adecco Group and TATA Communications, the GTCI provides a benchmarking tool for governments, cities, businesses and not-for-profit organisations to help design their talent strategies, overcome talent mismatches and be competitive in the global marketplace."[114]

The GTCI monitors 155 cities and measures performance against 119 categories in the index, which broadly speaking can be grouped into 5 categories:

1. **Regulatory**: market, business and labour frameworks and how they attract (or put off) talent.
2. **Openness to people other than talent**: this measures inclusivity, attitudes to diversity and people from underprivileged backgrounds.
3. **Growth**: looks into how a location supports talent with education and lifelong learning.
4. **Play**: explores the joy of living in a location, which is a factor in talent retention and quality of life.
5. **Skills**: this includes vocational and technical skills, as well as global knowledge skills (workers in professional, managerial or leadership roles).

Source: https://gtcistudy.com/.

Another such tool is the annual Worldwide Quality of Living Ranking produced by Mercer, a consultancy and financial advisory group. Its 2018 report highlights that "an increasingly diverse workforce is both more mobile and digital with highly diverging requirements and aspirations in terms of career, lifestyle and ultimately where and how they want to work. Companies need to consider these factors in their value proposition to both their local and their expatriate employees."[115] This is true not only for companies, but also for host economies who also want to increase their attractiveness to both talent and companies. Consultancies such as Mercer offer valuable insight to host locations that helps them to understand the specific factors that affect their residents' quality of living, which in turn has an indirect effect on attracting and retaining both multinational companies and globally mobile talent. Moreover, Mercer's 2019 report expands on the overlap between talent attraction and FDI highlighting that, "the key is relevant, reliable data and standardised measurement, which are essential for employers to make critical decisions, from deciding where to establish offices to determining how to distribute, house and remunerate their global workforces."[116] It is therefore no surprise that many host locations work with consultants specialised in talent positioning tools to help them maximise their workforce development programmes. For further details about the ranking see Box 7.10.

Box 7.10 Mercer Worldwide Quality of Living Ranking methodology

Mercer's ranking evaluates local living conditions in more than 450 cities worldwide.

Living conditions are analysed according to 39 factors, grouped into the following categories:

1. Political and social environment (political stability, crime, law enforcement, etc.).
2. Economic environment (currency exchange regulations, banking services).
3. Socio-cultural environment (media availability and censorship, limitations on personal freedom).
4. Medical and health considerations (medical supplies and services, infectious diseases, sewage, waste disposal, air pollution, etc.).
5. Schools and education (standards and availability of international schools).
6. Public services and transportation (electricity, water, public transportation, traffic congestion, etc.).
7. Recreation (restaurants, theatres, cinemas, sports and leisure, etc.).

8. Consumer goods (availability of food/daily consumption items, cars, etc.).
9. Housing (rental housing, household appliances, furniture, maintenance services).
10. Natural environment (climate, record of natural disasters).

The scores attributed to each factor, which are weighted to reflect their relative importance to expatriates, permit objective city-to-city comparisons. The result is a Quality of Living index that compares relative differences between any two locations evaluated. For the indices to be used effectively, Mercer has created a grid that enables users to link the resulting index to a quality of living allowance amount by recommending a percentage value in relation to the index.

Reproduced with kind permission from Mercer: www.mercer.com.

Link: https://www.mercer.com/newsroom/2018-quality-of-living-survey.html.

Another set of tools comes from the recruitment sector. Job listing portals or résumé listing sites provide valuable insights into the talent pool available in a given location, including talent availability, shortages and mobility. In particular, LinkedIn's economic development data is a useful source of insight into the depth of the talent pool in a location as it shows what type of talent is actually working there, and what talent is relocating to it or moving away from it. Recruitment portals also provide data about vacancies that are difficult to fill, types of roles that are in high demand, etc. Such data provides further insight into how talent, skills and recruitment affect location attractiveness and job creation, insight that can help IPAs to strengthen their competitiveness storylines by crafting campaigns that highlight the location's capacity to develop, attract and retain talent.

7.4.3.6 Information and social capital

Most employers want to hire staff who are not only appropriately skilled, but also, where possible, well-informed about their industry and with strong networks in, and knowledge of, the local business community and/or industry-specific international community. There is also a social capital angle to this. According to the OECD, social capital refers to "networks together with shared norms, values and understandings that facilitate co-operation within or among groups."[117] Or put another way, companies are not only looking for informed candidates, they are also looking for connected industry professionals who can "hit the ground running."

IPAs with a mandate to develop talent can help talent (both local and expats) develop their professional networks and develop social capital for themselves by organising sector briefing events and networking opportunities, and by encouraging the local business community, innovation centres and think tanks to have an "open door" approach. The professional connectedness that results from these events, in additional to sector insight gathering exercises, creates value, improves recruitment processes, makes faster matches and increases the employment-readiness of a location. However, very few locations are currently taking this approach, and hence there is an opportunity to better support talent grooming and recruitment, which in turn supports location attractiveness.

7.4.3.7 Great place to live, work and play

As discussed, for skilled workers it's not just about the job. Talent is increasingly selective about where they chose to live, as work-life balance and quality of life become increasingly important factors when choosing a job. One location that has developed a holistic approach to talent attraction is Anchorage, the largest city in Alaska. Anchorage's "Live. Work. Play." campaign encourages the local community to come together to make the city "an amazing place to call home"[118] (see Box 7.11).

Box 7.11 Anchorage: a place to Live. Work. Play

"We have a vision for our future. By 2030, Anchorage is the best mid-size city in America in which to Live. Work. & Play.

Anchorage is a young and growing city for all ages where you can live close to work, make a competitive salary and have a plethora of options for entertainment and outdoor activities. There are many things that make this city an amazing place to call home; however, to be the best mid-sized city in the nation to live, work, and play we must continually improve and invest.

As Alaskans, we are proud of our state. We know that as the largest state in the nation we have more to offer. Our mountains are bigger, our trails are longer, and we share one common idea – we love where we live.

Live. Work. Play. is a grassroots effort focused on community improvement and engagement for the people who live here. The rationale for such a vision goes beyond the traditional economic development model and responds to a shift in paradigm – people are no longer forced to go where the jobs are, instead they are choosing places based on where they want to live and the jobs are following them. LWP works to foster the development of the city's economy by supporting community re-development efforts through a focused approach toward identifying and addressing issues, strategic partnerships and a rigorous data-driven evaluation of the movement's progress (set of over 30 quantitative metrics).

LWP has grown from 35 supporters in 2010, to over 200 in 2015, who are working on more than 40 projects with a shared objective. In 2015, AEDC announced the re-launch of our LWP initiative survey, in an effort to get a new pulse on Anchorage."

Reproduced with kind permission from Anchorage Economic Development Corporation: www.aedcweb.com.

Link: https://aedcweb.com/live-work-play/.

7.4.4 Real estate and developers

Another group that is particularly interested in making a location attractive to (foreign) investors is real estate. Many developers recognise that creating dynamic local communities will make a location a more attractive place to live and work, which in turn will contribute to the success of a development project, i.e. result in higher property prices, both commercial and residential. However, this requires a long-term strategy, one that starts at the planning stage with public consultations, community engagement and impact assessments. There are at least three areas where developers and IPAs can collaborate:

- Community engagement (which is often required to obtaining planning consent);
- International promotion of the investment opportunities of the development to attract anchor investors and an anchor tenant; and
- Placemaking (via events programmes and corporate social responsibility work).

These activities make developers natural allies for IPAs. To their mutual benefit they can work together on many activities including co-ordinating marketing budgets, selling a location, promoting new commercial developments and adding a new local destination that adds vibrancy to the host economy. MassDevelopment, Massachusetts economic development and finance agency, is one such example (see Box 7.12).

Box 7.12 MassDevelopment's Transformative Development Initiative

"MassDevelopment's Transformative Development Initiative (TDI) is a place-based development program for Gateway Cities designed to enhance local public-private engagement and community identity; stimulate an improved quality of life for local residents; and spur increased investment and economic activity.

TDI's goal is to concentrate efforts, resources and investments in a compact area to create a critical mass of activity that inspires investments by local residents, entrepreneurs, and businesses, and additional private development.

The initiative is rooted in three principles:

- Strategic district focus: TDI focuses efforts on a strategically located contiguous neighbourhood characterised by a primary land use (e.g. downtown main street, residential, light industrial) and a dense, mixed-use environment with a five-minute walking radius. The districts are locally selected and framed by recent public or private investments.
- Local collaborative partnerships: Successful development is rooted in strong partnerships that work together to create a vision, link resources to ideas, and move projects forward over

the long term. A 'TDI Partnership' is the public-private agent that identifies a TDI district and works with MassDevelopment to execute its vision for the district.

- Community engagement: TDI provides funding tools and supports local partners to reinforce local community engagement and further investment within a district.

The initiative is organised around these programmes:

- TDI Assistance, a technical assistance program through which MassDevelopment provides and manages tailored third-party professional services; community-building Placemaking projects; and TDI Fellows, a fellow program through which a MassDevelopment employee is embedded in and works with a TDI District's local partnership.
- TDI Investment, an equity investment program through which MassDevelopment makes equity investments in real estate within TDI Districts.
- TDI Cowork, a business growth tools program that will expand in 2016 and 2017 with new programs to support collaborative workspaces and innovative initiatives to catalyse business development.
- TDI Local, a small grants program initiated to pilot grants to help support local market development."

Reproduced with kind permission from the State of Massachusetts.

Link: https://www.massdevelopment.com/what-we-offer/key-initiatives/gateway-cities/.

7.4.4.1 Housing

According to the Centre for Cities, a British think tank dedicated to improving the economies of the UK's largest towns and cities, "housing matters to economic development. It can enhance economic performance and place competitiveness."[119] Their report, "Housing and Economic

Development: Moving Forward Together", identifies three ways the malfunctioning of housing supply impacts on economic growth:

- It affects the labour markets because "the lack of availability, inflexibility and unaffordability of housing prevents labour mobility."[120]
- It has a direct effect on infrastructure because the high demand for housing leads to a strain on infrastructure, which demands more infrastructure, while at the same time areas of low demand receive little attention, which again impacts upon labour mobility.
- It also affects business – areas of high demand are exposed to spiralling prices, which in turn put pressure on wages and increase rents for business.

In turn, poor housing options make it difficult for local businesses to attract people with the right skills. The report highlights that housing needs to be considered as part of an overall economic development story, which is the basis on which to build a competitive narrative for the host location.

Housing is a topic that is becoming an increasingly important part of an IPA's post-investment toolkit. It should be noted that there two clear trends. Smaller locations speak about the availability of housing in their marketing literature. However, highly dense locations include housing policy in their Policy Advocacy work. The rationale is that housing policy and investment shouldn't take place in isolation from the wider economic context. While housing might not seem to directly affect new investment, it is relevant to established investors when they seek to hire local talent, only to discover that the highly skilled talent they would like to hire lives two hours away from their office, and would either require a higher salary to move closer, or a flexible working arrangement to accommodate the need to travel outside peak times. This is the point where housing becomes part of the local value proposition investors buy in to.

Forbes recognises that "it's not only about numbers – x number of people needing housing, which equals y number of houses. It's about building them in the right way in the right place at the right price."[121] To summarise, talent is looking for affordable housing, good public transport, cultural amenities and skilled jobs. And while some IPAs might have little influence in these areas, other IPAs – particularly public ones working at a national or municipal level – have a major say when it comes to economic development decisions, to promoting particular local development projects and to providing investor services tailored to housing projects, as the following two examples show.

An example of housing work comes from Philippines (see Box 7.13), where the IPA takes an active role in driving the sector. Another one comes from Vladivostok in Russia where the local IPA facilitated a private-public partnership for housing development (see Box 7.14).

Box 7.13 Assistance to investors in hotel and housing in Philippines

BOI strengthens assistance to investors in hotel and housing sectors

"The Philippine Board of Investments (BOI) is further strengthening its assistance to investors in the hotel and housing sectors as the agency conducted an Investor Awareness Seminar at the Crowne Plaza Hotel in Ortigas Center, Pasig City recently (May 29, 2018). The seminar aims to enhance the awareness of potential investors on the requirements, rules and regulations, and policies and procedures, and processes in doing business in the Philippine hotel and housing sectors. Resource speakers from the Housing and Land Use Regulatory Board (HLURB), Department of Tourism (DOT), Bureau of Fire Protection (BFP) and the Bureau of Internal Revenue (BIR) also discussed their respective areas of concern related to doing business in the Philippine hotel and housing sectors. The seminar likewise aims to familiarise BOI-registered enterprises (RBEs) with the value chain of services that the agency readily provides including pre- and pos-t investment assistance, registration of investment projects, and availment of incentives. 'We are very much enthusiastic in providing assistance to these industries especially that we wanted more investors in the housing industry to come in and help address the current housing backlog. In the same manner, we also want to encourage more hotel investors in the country and address the need for 120,000 additional hotel rooms to boost local tourism,' said BOI Executive Director Raul Angeles."

Reproduced with kind permission from BOI Philippine – www.boi.ph.

Source: https://boi.gov.ph/boi-strengthens-assistance-to-investors-in-hotel-and-housing-sectors/.

Box 7.14 Invest Primorsky secures housing investment in Vladivostok

Investor from Hong Kong to build a housing complex in Vladivostok

"The resident of the Free Port of Vladivostok, LLC RKSK (subsidiary of AO TON corporation, Hong Kong) has started the construction of a housing complex in Zeleny Ugol city district. Amount of investments in this project will constitute up to 1,5 billion rubles.

'In order for this project to become real we have worked closely with the investors from Hong Kong. We have presented the advantages of our region and the special regimes that Primorye can offer to business. The key factor in investors' decision were the privileges that are provided to the residents of the Free Port,' said Denis Starodub, the deputy director of Primorye Investment Promotion Agency.

The tax relief that the developer has received as a resident of the Free Port of Vladivostok let them cut the costs and, as a result, to set an affordable price for a square meter.

The concept of the project implies the creation of a comfortable environment: forest view from every window, sports grounds and playgrounds for children, a stadium, areas to walk pets and no cars in the yard.

'Within the period of 25 years we have built dozens of modern residential areas in Asia, and we are currently ready to use this experience in Vladivostok. The zest of this project is the only kilometer long green pedestrian boulevard in the city, where the people will be able to walk and do outside sports. Pedestrian foot paths, jogging tracks, cycle lanes, as well as places for skateboarding and roller skating will be equipped here,' said Ren Shizhong, president of AO TON Corporation.

As a part of a full-service support from Primorye Investment Promotion Agency, the development company received the accreditation as mortgage loans partner from Rossiysky Capital bank – the subsidiary bank of DOM.RF.

'This will help us give out mortgage loans on an interest rate that is lower than the market average. The standard rate for the Green Boulevard currently equals 9,65% and for those participating in the

"Family mortgage loan" state programme equals to 6% per annum,' explained Anatoly Bondarenko – the head of the bank's regional branch.

The building in Green Boulevard housing complex is scheduled for commissioning in December 2019. Construction of two more blocks, as well as all related infrastructure will be completed by 2021.

Thanks to the state support measures that included the services of Primorye Investment Promotion Agency, special tax regime of the Free Port of Vladivostok and the preferential mortgage programs of DOM.RF, for the first time ever the region has managed to attract investments from China to the construction of affordable housing."

Reproduced with kind permission from Primorye Investment Agency; https://invest.primorsky.ru/en/.

Link: https://invest.primorsky.ru/en/news/91.

7.4.5 Local ambassadors

The notion of ambassadors as location promoters is one that different locations embrace to strengthen their placemaking capabilities. This can be a private sector-led initiative, where enthusiastic local players come together to raise the location's profile, for example, Team Lincolnshire in the UK (see Box 7.15). This can also be an initiative by the IPA that asks established business leaders and celebrities with a strong link to the host economy to endorse the location as a place to do business and invest. These engagements are often voluntary, unpaid and by invitation only – and hence risk losing momentum over time. Some IPAs go a step further and appoint honorary investment ambassadors with whom they have written terms of reference that outline the responsibilities of the role.

Box 7.15 Team Lincolnshire

"Team Lincolnshire is a powerful, independent partnership of ambitious, forward-thinking private and public sector organisations, united by the common goal of championing a stronger local economy. We're called Team Lincolnshire and we represent the whole of Greater Lincolnshire, Humber area and Rutland.

TEAM LINCOLNSHIRE IS FLOURISHING!

We love Greater Lincolnshire and are proud of our communities, our businesses and our quality of life. We're Team Lincolnshire, a fast-growing ambassador programme made up of ambitious organisations who are building on the region's successes to make it an even more desirable place to live, learn, work and invest.

Through strong leadership and governance, clear strategic objectives and a shared, common purpose, we break down barriers, foster selfless collaboration and create a more fertile environment for businesses of all sizes. It's all about working together to encourage investment, strengthen our economy and champion Greater Lincolnshire on the regional, national and international stage.

BENEFITS

By bringing the public and private sector together we really can influence the future of growth in our local economy and shape the environment and community we live in.

Team Lincolnshire offers a wide range of benefits:

- Promoting the region as an attractive place to live, work and invest
- An extensive event programme of webinars and digital seminars and also local, regional, national and international events, post Covid
- Facilitating investment into the region and creating jobs
- The opportunity to share knowledge and expertise with a network of like-minded businesses
- Access to key public sector departments
- Nurturing collaborative working

Join Team Lincolnshire and become part of a dynamic partnership of local organisations working together to grow their businesses, share their expertise, promote Greater Lincolnshire and improve the quality of life for our communities.

Whether you're looking to access new markets, increase your skills and knowledge or take your business to the next level, Team Lincolnshire will help you make the right connections and unlock a wealth of advice and support. We already have over 120 members from a wide range of sectors across Greater Lincolnshire and beyond. Join us and become part of making this region an even more desirable place to live, learn, work and invest."

Reproduced with kind permission from the Greater Lincolnshire Local Enterprise Partnership www.greaterlincolnshirelep.co.uk.

Link: https://www.greaterlincolnshirelep.co.uk/funding-and-projects/team-lincolnshire/.

7.4.6 Location storytellers

Prospective investors, both new and ones who are looking to further expand, generally perform due diligence on what it is like to invest in a location. This diligence is likely to include contacting local advisers, such as accountants and lawyers, and reaching out to existing foreign investors to learn first-hand what it takes to invest in the area. In a similar manner, more sophisticated investors considering a move to a new location will also perform their own diligence. They typically reach out to various individuals and organisations, via their personal networks or social media, to get an impression of the location, and they may also visit the location for a few days in order to make a more informed decision.

The people and organisations these prospective investors approach are therefore de-facto storytellers for that location. Hence, there is a case for "managing" the messages that foreign investors and talent are exposed to by providing key information to any parties that investors and talent are likely to contact. Having these parties "on message" can help attract further jobs and investment.

Estonia is a leading example of a country that has produced high quality materials to support professionals speaking on its behalf. Indeed, as part of its efforts to attract tech businesses, Estonia has rebranded itself as e-Estonia. In support of this, Estonia has created the e-Estonia Spokesperson's Toolkit (see Box 7.16).

Box 7.16 The e-Estonian Spokesperson's Toolkit

"The following materials are intended to serve the needs of anyone whose job it is to present and promote the e-services, IT-sector and companies of Estonia abroad. These materials are free to use and share for anyone promoting or interested in the success story that is the Estonian information society.

e-Estonia is an incredible success story that has grown out of a partnership between a forward-thinking government, a proactive IT sector and a switched-on, tech-savvy population. The associated brochure gives a quick overview of Estonia's information driven society and the developments of e-services there.

- e-stories about e-Estonia help unpack and explain our e-state solutions, beginning with the problems that we set out to solve and ultimately presenting the results we have achieved.
- e-Estonia factsheets help provide a brief overview of the background to most of the important fields in e-Estonia and present the different e-solutions created in these areas.
- Q&As: The most important questions about Estonia's information society are gathered together in our Q&A materials, which can be downloaded and presented or shared to anyone interested in the secrets of the success that is e-Estonia.
- e-Estonia presentation slideshow: The presentation provides an overview of the main indicators of the information society including electronic identification, e-services, interoperability and education, and provides relevant success stories complemented by the latest statistical data and speakers' comments.
- e-Estonia in numbers: The most important facts and figures about the impact of e-Estonia are gathered together in one tool

providing an insight into the astounding accomplishments of the e-State.

- Profiles of Estonian IT-companies: The Estonian IT cluster brochure provides an overview of our IT sector and presents one-pager company profiles of Estonian IT companies. The one-pagers cover core competences, achievements and the cooperation routes that best suit our main IT players. This material is a perfect tool for searching for business partners and planning matchmaking events and conferences.
- e-Estonia Briefing Centre services: The goal of e-Estonia Briefing Centre is to inspire global policy makers, political leaders, corporate executives, investors and international media to kick-off the digital transformation by sharing successful examples from e-Estonia and build links to the IT sector. Check out the services that the executive briefing centre offers to businesses and the public sector. – you can also add a link to our services: Services – e-Estonia (e-estonia.com)."

Reproduced with kind permission from Estonian Investment Agency: https://investinestonia.com/investment-agency/.

Link: https://e-estonia.com/e-estonia-toolkit/.

Meeting visiting business delegations offers another opportunity to sell a location to potential investors. These visits offer a unique opportunity for a location to showcase itself, the local growth opportunities and possible business partnerships. Many of these visiting delegations are coordinated by local chambers of commerce, innovation agencies or embassies. IPAs can help by opening doors, facilitating access to foreign investors and inviting other stakeholders to host the delegation. For example, Destination Detroit, a regional collaboration led by the Detroit Chamber of Commerce (DCC) and the principal economic development agencies in the area, plays an important role in selling the region to visiting delegations (see Box 7.17).

Box 7.17 Detroit welcomes delegations

The Detroit Regional Chamber regularly welcomes delegations and trade missions from around the globe. In 2017, the Chamber hosted more than 10 delegations including international groups from Africa, China, the Netherlands and Turkey, as well as the Chicago International Trade Commissioner's Association. Delegations are a vital component to attracting business to Southeast Michigan.

The Chamber's delegation services include:

- An overview of the Detroit region (30-min presentation) targeted to the delegation.
- Overview of services available to companies looking to explore and invest in our state and region.
- Marketing materials on the Detroit region.

Reproduced with kind permission from Detroit Chamber of Commerce: www.detroitchamber.com.

Link: www.detroitchamber.com/destinationdetroit/delegations/.

The DCC has also set up a Technology Showcase Programme to welcome visiting delegations or trade missions focussed on the automotive sector, a key sector for the city. The objective is twofold: to showcase local capabilities and to connect investors with relevant international players, as can be seen in Box 7.18. By organising these showcases, Detroit allows local tech stories to emerge, which reinforces location storytelling.

Box 7.18 Detroit Tech Showcase

In recent years, the Detroit Regional Chamber has built relationships with leading mobility Ecosystems across the globe. The mission is to identify these centres of mobility innovation and begin a dialogue around each respective areas of expertise, exchange ideas and build partnerships aimed at driving forward the future of mobility.

To formalise and enhance this exchange, the Chamber launched the Destination Detroit Tech Showcase series. A quarterly event, in which the Chamber will host the world's most advanced mobility countries and regions in Detroit, and aims to share, engage and explore possibilities for longer-term partnerships. The Chamber is seeking other global mobility communities to partner on future Tech Showcases.

Format: the visit to Detroit centres around the Tech Showcase, a half-day event hosted by the Chamber, which provides each visiting delegation (with) a platform to communicate how their community and stakeholders are leading in next-generation mobility.

The agenda for each Tech Showcase includes a keynote speaker who will introduce the delegation's mobility Ecosystem, best practices, and overview of the broader delegation. It will be followed by a panel discussion with 4 to 5 delegates – each delegate has the chance to briefly pitch their company to businesses and organisations from the Detroit region, followed by a Q&A. In addition to the Tech Showcase, the Chamber will help each mobility delegation with the development of a customised agenda based on each country's capabilities and interests. This includes meetings with appropriate partners from government, education and industry within the Detroit region.

Financial responsibilities: the Chamber will host each Tech Showcase and delegation expenses are the responsibility of each visiting group.

The delegation visit is one of several events the Chamber participates in throughout the auto show to promote Detroit and Michigan's story to a global audience.

Reproduced with kind permission from Detroit Chamber of Commerce: www.detroitchamber.com.

Link: http://www.detroitchamber.com/destinationdetroit/tech-showcase/.

7.4.7 Location rankings

If nobody is talking about a location, then people and businesses are unlikely to be aware of its strengths and attractions, and hence are unlikely to come, whether just to visit or permanently. On the other hand, when there is a "buzz" around a location, when people are talking about it, this can have a significant impact on "attractability". In this regard, location rankings play a key role when it comes to understanding where a location sits on the spectrum between buzz and silence.

The Gottlieb Duttweiler Institute (GDI) has researched how a city participates and remains relevant in the digital era. With a headline "hype is king – at least for metropolis(es),"[122] they note that "cities looking to attract the creative class or the most intelligent minds have to be able to offer something unique. This is influenced by 'hard' local factors (such as infrastructure, traffic, etc.) and 'soft' ones (culture, scene, image, etc)."[123] But even so, "these factors mean nothing without the attention to go with it: a city needs to be seen and heard, loved or hated, craved or controversial. Above all, it needs to be part of the general conversation."[124] They note that "idle chatter alone is not enough. The value of a particular city's brand is defined – much more so than the majority of consumer brands – by what its 'users' organise, host and stage there."[125] Because of this to "attract new customers [that is, new residents, talent, investors], cities have long relied on personal recommendation and direct contact over advertising messages. As with influencer marketing, it depends primarily on what people say about the brand, not what the brand says about itself."[126] The GDI ranks cities based on their coolness factor using Instagram as a proxy. A glance at the number of photos uploaded to Instagram with a city's hashtag reveals their Instagram ranking, with London, Paris, Dubai, New York and Istanbul at the top of the list, while the number of Wikipedia references ranks Paris, Moscow, Berlin, Rome and Santiago as the most internationally significant cities.

According to Chris Fair, CEO from Resonance Consultancy, a "destination's quality of place and perceived brand increasingly determines where talent and investment flows."[127] Based on these two characteristics, and the 6 pillars of Place discussed earlier, Resonance has ranked the top 100 cities in the world to produce their *Best City Index*.[128] Below are the top 5 cities, as published in the 2021[129] ranking:

- **#1 London**: as the "capital of capitals" negotiates the uncharted terrain of a post-Brexit world, for now it still reigns atop the planet's best cities for the fifth year running.
- **#2 New York**: America's urban heart was broken by the pandemic and has a long way back.

- **#3 Paris:** just as terrorism subsided, the Notre-Dame inferno struck Parisian resolve anew. But the City of Light builds on resiliently.
- **#4 Moscow:** Russia's beguiling capital is a cultural gold mine spanning the ages.
- **#5 Tokyo:** the futuristic metropolis is tapping its ancient feudal roots by investing in street-level liveability and residents' wellbeing – Olympics or no Olympics.

These rankings are important to Place and Ecosystem because they may influence consumer's decisions, whether they be local citizens, travellers, businessmen or investors. They also have an indirect impact on post-investment as they help to shape the view of decision makers about the attractability and business-friendliness of a location, and whether or not it is suitable for further investment and expansion. Consequently, a good messaging strategy can positively influence re-investment decisions. Locations are conscious of this effect. Those cities with a high-ranking mention this in their marketing material. Those cities with a low ranking often study the ones with a high ranking in order to improve their own performance. As ranking lists have increased in number and become more widely publicised, most locations now work hard to improve their ranking.

In summary, Place branding, Place marketing, placemaking, Ecosystem and connectedness together have the potential to accelerate economic growth. They are, by nature, inclusive and provide a platform from which companies can grow. This also applies to foreign investors. And because, as discussed earlier, it takes a whole business Ecosystem to grow a foreign company, these 5 disciplines are increasingly important to post-investment in general and to Aftercare professionals in particular. Together they help provide a more fertile landscape within which foreign companies can grow.

Notes

1 Cacioppe, J. 2014. *Casual Collisions, Spontaneous Meetings & Serendipity* [online]. Available at: https://medium.com/the-boundlss-blog/casual-collisions-spontaneous-meetings-serendipity-f632bc063b80.

2 Oxford, n.d. *Oxford English and Spanish Dictionary* [online]. Available at: https://www.lexico.com/definition/place.

3 Project for Public Spaces, n.d. *Great Public Spaces Strengthen Communities* [online]. Available at: https://www.pps.org/about.

4 Aaker, D.A. 1991. *Managing Brand Equity.* New York: Jossey-Bass.
5 The Place Brand Observer, 2017. *Top 5 City Branding Case Studies and Examples to Learn From: How They Do It* [online]. Available at: https://placebrandobserver.com/top-5-city-branding-case-studies-examples/.
6 Govers, R. and Go, F.M. 2012. *International Place Branding Yearbook 2012: Managing Smart Growth and Sustainability.* First edn. s.l: Palgrave Macmillan.
7 Ibid.
8 Ibid.
9 Cleave, E., Arku, G., Gilliland, J. and Sadler, R. 2016. "The role of place branding in local and regional economic development: bridging the gap between policy and practicality". *Regional Studies, Regional Science*, 6 April, 3(1), pp. 207–228.
10 Ibid.
11 City Nation Place, 2017. *City Nation Place Think Tank 2017 Round Up.* s.l. s.n.
12 Ibid.
13 Subramanian, S. 2017. *How to Sell a Country: The Booming Business of Ration Branding Published in the Guardian* [online]. Available at: https://www.theguardian.com/news/2017/nov/07/nation-branding-industry-how-to-sell-a-country.
14 Ibid.
15 Ibid.
16 Ibid.
17 Govers, R., van 't Klooster, E. and Van Keken, G. 2015. *5 Place Branding Principles for Successful Brand Development and Management* [online]. Available at: https://placebrandobserver.com/5-place-branding-principles-to-guide-brand-development-management/.
18 Ibid.
19 Ibid.
20 The Place Brand Observer, 2016. *Difference Between Place Branding and Place Marketing: Quick Guide* [online]. Available at: https://placebrandobserver.com/difference-place-branding-marketing-explained/.
21 Best Place Institute, 2015. *Place Marketing & Branding 2015+* [online]. Available at: http://bestplaceinstytut.org/en/raport-place-marketing-branding-2015/.
22 City Nation Place, 2017. *City Nation Place Think Tank 2017 Round Up.* s.l., s.n.
23 Ibid.
24 Ibid.
25 Project for Public Spaces, n.d. *Great Public Spaces Strengthen Communities* [online]. Available at: https://www.pps.org/about.
26 Ibid.
27 Harman, C. 2017. *9 of the World's Most Creative Placemaking Projects. Calvium* [online]. Available at: https://calvium.com/5-of-the-worlds-most-creative-Placemaking-projects.
28 Ibid.
29 Govers, R. 2018. *Imaginative Communities: Admired Cities, Regions and Countries.* s.l: Reputo Press.

30 Moore, J. 1999. "Predators and prey: A new ecology of competition". *Harvard Business Review*, 71(3), pp. 5–86.

31 Gapper, J. 2015. *Networker Extraordinaire Rohan Silva and His Second Home Start-up Hub* [online]. Available at: https://www.ft.com/content/61dc00e6-a1c1-11e4-bd03-00144feab7de.

32 Ministry of Economic Affairs and Employment of Finland. *Growth Ecosystems as a Tool in the New Industrial and Innovation Policy* [online]. Available at: http://tem.fi/en/ecosystems.

33 Porter, M. 1990. *The Competitive Advantage of Nations*. Illustrated edn. New York: Free Press.

34 Porter, M. 1998. "Clusters and the new economics of competition". *Harvard business review*, 76(6), pp. 77–90.

35 Ibid.

36 Hwang, V.W. 2014. *The Next Big Business Buzzword: Ecosystem?* [online]. Available at: https://www.forbes.com/sites/victorhwang/2014/04/16/the-next-big-business-buzzword-ecosystem/?sh=142c03885456#295624155456.

37 Ibid.

38 Kessler, D. and Temin, P. 2007. "The organization of the grain trade in the early Roman Empire". *The Economic History Review*, 60(2), pp. 313–332.

39 Ibid.

40 Ibid.

41 Startup Genome, 2018. *Global Startup Ecosystem Report 2018* [online]. Available at: https://startupgenome.com/report2018/.

42 Ibid.

43 Ibid.

44 Ghemawat, P. and Altman, S.A., 2016. *DHL Global Connectedness Index 2016 – The State of Globalization in an Age of Ambiguity*, s.l: DHL [online]. Available at; http://www.dhl.com/content/dam/downloads/g0/about_us/logistics_insights/gci_2016/DHL_GCI_2016_full_study.pdf.

45 Altman, S.A., Ghemawat, P. and Bastian, P. 2018. *DHL Global Connectedness Index 2018 – The State of Globalization in a Fragile World*, s.l: DHL [online]. Available at: https://www.dhl.com/content/dam/dhl/global/core/documents/pdf/glo-core-gci-2018-full-study.pdf.

46 These trends are referred to as "laws of globalization" in the book Ghemawat, P. 2017. *The Laws of Globalization and Business Applications*. Cambridge: Cambridge University Press. According to the author the laws of globalisation were informed by the same hard data as the DHL Global Connectedness Index. They represent generalizations – within the international domain – of the two laws of geography proposed decades ago by Waldo Tobler: the phenomenon external to (a geographic) area of interest affects what goes on in the inside; and that very thing is related to everything else, but near things are more related than distant things.

47 Ghemawat, P. and Altman, S.A. 2016. *DHL Global Connectedness Index 2016 – The State of Globalization in an Age of Ambiguity*, s.l: DHL [online]. Available at;

http://www.dhl.com/content/dam/downloads/g0/about_us/logistics_insights/gci_2016/DHL_GCI_2016_full_study.pdf.

48 Ibid.

49 Ibid.

50 Ibid.

51 Altman, S.A., Ghemawat, P. and Bastian, P. 2018. *DHL Global Connectedness Index 2018 – The State of Globalization in a Fragile World*, s.l: DHL [online]. Available at: https://www.dhl.com/content/dam/dhl/global/core/documents/pdf/glo-core-gci-2018-full-study.pdf.

52 Startup Genome, 2017. *Global Startup Ecosystem Report 2017* [online]. Available at: https://startupgenome.com/report2017/.

53 Ibid.

54 Ibid.

55 Ibid.

56 Ibid.

57 Ibid.

58 Ibid.

59 Ibid.

60 Ibid.

61 Ibid.

62 Gottlieb Duttweiler Institut (GDI), 2017. *Global City Index 2017: The Most Connected Cities* [online]. Available at: http://www.globalinfluence.world/en/global-city-index-2017-connected-cities/.

63 Ibid.

64 Kotkin, J. 2014. *The World's Most Influential Cities* [online]. Available at: https://www.forbes.com/sites/joelkotkin/2014/08/14/the-most-influential-cities-in-the-world/?sh=155ff56f7ad0.

65 Gottlieb Duttweiler Institut (GDI), 2017. *Global City Index 2017: The Most Connected Cities* [online]. Available at: http://www.globalinfluence.world/en/global-city-index-2017-connected-cities/.

66 Ibid.

67 Rittmeyer, F. 2012. *The Cities-State: Interview to Parag Khanna.* [Online] Available at: https://schweizermonat.ch/the-cities-state/.

68 Ibid

69 Gottlieb Duttweiler Institut (GDI), 2017. *Global City Index 2017: The Most Connected Cities* [online]. Available at: http://www.globalinfluence.world/en/global-city-index-2017-connected-cities/.

70 Ghemawat, P. and Altman, S.A. 2016. *DHL Global Connectedness Index 2016 - The State of Globalization in an Age of Ambiguity*, s.l: DHL [online]. Available at: http://www.dhl.com/content/dam/downloads/g0/about_us/logistics_insights/gci_2016/DHL_GCI_2016_full_study.pdf.

71 Startup Genome, 2018. *Global Startup Ecosystem Report 2018* [online]. Available at: https://startupgenome.com/report2018/.

72 Ibid.
73 Ibid.
74 Ibid.
75 Cacioppe,J.2014.*CasualCollisions, SpontaneousMeetings & Serendipity*[online].Available at: https://medium.com/the-boundlss-blog/casual-collisions-spontaneous-meetings-serendipity-f632bc063b80.
76 Mckinsey Global Institute, 2016. *Digital Globalization: The New Era of Global Flows*, s.l: Mckinsey & Company.
77 Ibid.
78 Startup Genome, 2017. *Global Startup Ecosystem Report 2017* [online]. Available at: https://startupgenome.com/report2017/.
79 Ibid.
80 Ibid.
81 Gregory, M. and O'Hanlon, D. 2018. *Technation Report 2018* [online]. Available at: https://technation.io/insights/report-2018/international-competitiveness/.
82 Ibid.
83 Berkeley, 2016. *Berkeley Resilience Strategy: A Strategic Preparedness Plan for Berkeley, a Community Known for Inclusiveness and Innovation* [online]. Available at: https://www.cityofberkeley.info/uploadedFiles/City_Manager/Resilient_Berkeley/Berkeley_Resilience_Strategy_LowRes.pdf.
84 McDearman, B. and Donahue, R. 2015. *The 10 Lessons from Global Trade and Investment Planning in U. S. Metro Areas* [online]. Available at: https://www.brookings.edu/research/the-10-lessons-from-global-trade-and-investment-planning-in-u-s-metro-areas/.
85 Ibid.
86 European Commission, 2014. *National/ Regional Innovation Strategies for Smart Specialisation (RIS3): Cohesion Policy 2014–2020*, s.l: s.n.
87 Ibid.
88 McDearman, B. and Donahue, R. 2015. *The 10 Lessons from Global Trade and Investment Planning in U.S. Metro Areas* [online]. Available at: https://www.brookings.edu/research/the-10-lessons-from-global-trade-and-investment-planning-in-u-s-metro-areas/.
89 https://www.londonandpartners.com/what-we-do/students/higher-education/news-and-events/events/london-tech-week-2018.
90 OCO Global, 2018. *Investment Promotion Agencies Benchmark Study*, s.l: s.n.
91 Cohan, P. 2013. "How can you attract start-ups to your region?" *MIT Entrepreneurship Review*, 26 October. Available at: http://miter.mit.edu/how-can-you-attract-start-ups-to-your-region/.
92 Source: https://www.campus.co/london/en/about/.
93 Source: http://www.qbic.qa/en/success-stories/.
94 Ibid.
95 Source: www.statupindiahub.org.in.

96 Source: Ministry of Finance of Singapore. https://www.mof.gov.sg/Policies/e-Government.

97 Ibid.

98 Murphy, H. 2016. *Global Mobility: Countries Compete for Best Workers* [online]. Available at: https://www.ft.com/content/606781b0-d0b2-11e5-92a1-c5e23ef99c77.

99 Dai, S. 2016. *World's Most Populous Country Lacks the One Thing It Needs to Become an AI Powerhouse: Enough Talented People* [online]. Available at: https://www.scmp.com/tech/china-tech/article/2123949/worlds-most-populous-country-lacks-one-thing-it-needs-become-ai.

100 DW, 2017. *Germany Faces Huge Shortage of Skilled Workers* [online]. Available at: https://www.dw.com/en/germany-faces-huge-shortage-of-skilled-workers/a-40294450.

101 Flores, M. and Melguizo, A. 2018. *Latin America Has the Biggest Skills Gap in the World. Here's How to Bridge It* [online]. Available at: https://www.weforum.org/agenda/2018/03/latin-america-has-the-biggest-skills-gap-in-the-world-here-s-how-to-bridge-it/.

102 Development Counsellors International, 2017. *Talent Wars: What People Look for in Jobs and Locations* [online]. Available at: http://aboutdci.com/wp-content/uploads/2017/03/TalentWars2017.pdf.

103 Ibid.

104 Ibid.

105 Ibid.

106 Ibid.

107 George Kaiser Family Foundation, n.d. *How We Work* [online]. Available at: https://www.gkff.org/who-we-are/how-we-work/.

108 Tulsa Remote, n.d. *Frequently Asked Questions* [online]. Available at: https://tulsaremote.com/faq/.

109 See https://www.jetro.go.jp/en/hrportal/.

110 Barcelonaglobal.org

111 Huawei ICT Academy Building Your Career Today Report 2017.

112 Ibid.

113 Pilling, D. 2017. *Chinese Investment in Africa: Beijing's Testing Ground* [online]. Available at: https://www.ft.com/content/0f534aa4-4549-11e7-8519-9f94ee97d996.

114 See: https://gtcistudy.com/.

115 Mercer, 2019. *Vienna Tops Mercer's 21st Quality of Living Ranking* [online. Available at: https://www.mercer.com/newsroom/2019-quality-of-living-survey.html.

116 Mercer, 2019. *Vienna Tops Mercer's 21st Quality of Living Ranking* [online]. Available at: https://www.mercer.com/newsroom/2019-quality-of-living-survey.html.

117 Keeley, B., 2007. Chapter 6: "A Bigger Picture". In *Human Capital: How What You Know Shapes Your Life*. s.l: OECD Publishing.

118 AEDC, n.d. *What is Live. Work. Play?* [online]. Available at: https://aedcweb.com/live-work-play/.

119 Glossop, C. 2008. *Housing and Economic Development: Moving Forward Together*, s.l.: Centre for Cities.

120 Ibid.

121 Talbot, D. 2018. *Housing Is Connected To Economic Growth – But Only The Right Housing In The Right Place* [online]. Available at: https://www.forbes.com/sites/deborahtalbot/2018/05/01/housing-connected-to-economic-growth/?sh=49b1ec041e30.

122 The Gottlieb Duttweiler Institute (2017) Global Cities in the Websphere: Tourism and Leisure: http://www.globalinfluence.world/en/global-cities-in-the-websphere-tourism-and-leisure/.

123 Ibid.

124 Ibid.

125 Ibid.

126 Ibid.

127 Source: www.bestcities.org.

128 Ibid.

129 Source: www.bestcities.org/reports/2021-worlds-best-cities/.

PART III

THE HOW

8
HOW TO SET UP AN AFTERCARE UNIT

Chapter highlights

- The three most common messages that post-investment practitioners and academics convey are: post-investment is learnt while doing; context is king when delivering services on the ground; and that they are on a mission to support economic growth.
- Post-investment services can be structured around 5 foundational building blocks that support both Investor Services and Policy Advocacy.
- These are to weight the relative importance of foreign investors in the host economy, to secure a mandate, to know what drives decision making, to define success and to secure resources.

8.1 Introduction

> The commitment from an IPA towards foreign investors needs to be strong. Without it, Aftercare efforts will not withstand the changes in politics, governments, budgets and leadership.
>
> (Marian Scheifler, director at FDI consultancy SIFDI)

While performing the research for this book, the authors spoke to dozens of stakeholders including foreign investors, Aftercare practitioners, policy

DOI: 10.4324/9781003174950-12

makers, IPAs and chambers of commerce. The three common messages came out of these conversations:

- **We learn post-investment while doing post-investment**: even academics and researchers place value on the practical, front-line reality of post-investment and observe that long-term FDI is less about economic development theories or studies and more about the practice that informs these theories. It is about daily interaction with investors, governments and the myriad FDI stakeholders who influence policy making, who drive economic development and who shape a host economy's competitiveness. It is about fostering dialogue that leads to collaboration, co-creation and ultimately the growth of the host economy. Key to successful post-investment support is the ability to listen carefully to what both investors and government are saying, and then to join the dots to come up with creative ideas to overcome any roadblock that IPAs might encounter.
- **Context is king when delivering services on the ground**: many IPAs don't really know or understand the theory of post-investment, and only a few have the luxury of an inhouse research team with the bandwidth to study best practice. However, IPAs are experts in their local reality, and it is this knowledge that guides them on how to perform Aftercare. They are resourceful, creative and agile in finding ways to deliver services, influence regulatory change and grow their host economy.
- **We are on a mission to support economic growth**: practitioners and policymakers alike are aware that FDI is affected by political cycles, business cycles and economic cycles. They also know that they have limited influence over exactly when their work will produce tangible results, and can't forecast how decisions made by government organisations or foreign investors will affect their work. Nonetheless they are inherently optimistic and know that eventually their work will result in new jobs, economic growth and opportunities for the host economy. The notion that post-investment is a moving target only applies to the short term; in the long term, practitioners and policymakers see themselves as impact-makers.

The following pages provide a roadmap for practitioners and policy makers on how to deliver post-investment and specifically Aftercare. It first looks at the basics that IPAs need to address when considering providing post-investment services, including Investor Services and Policy Advocacy. Place and Ecosystem delivery are not covered as this work is usually performed by specialist units that often are not under the control of the IPA. The chapter closes with considerations about the practicalities of delivering post-investment services.

8.2 The foundational blocks

Not supporting established investors is a risky strategy. The impact of the Covid-19 pandemic has exposed many IPAs in this regard, as they have found themselves ill-prepared to help established investors weather the crisis and also to help governments organise their recovery efforts. The best place to start is with the fundamentals of post-investment: to establish the relative importance of foreign investors, to secure a mandate, to know what drives decision making at the IPA, to define what success looks like and to secure resources. The steps are depicted in Figure 8.1.

8.2.1 Establish the relative importance of foreign investors

Understanding the relative importance of foreign investors to an economy is a key part of understanding how an IPA should approach its post-investment mandate. For example, when Invest Slovenia conducted an investment base review in 2016, they found that although foreign investors made up only

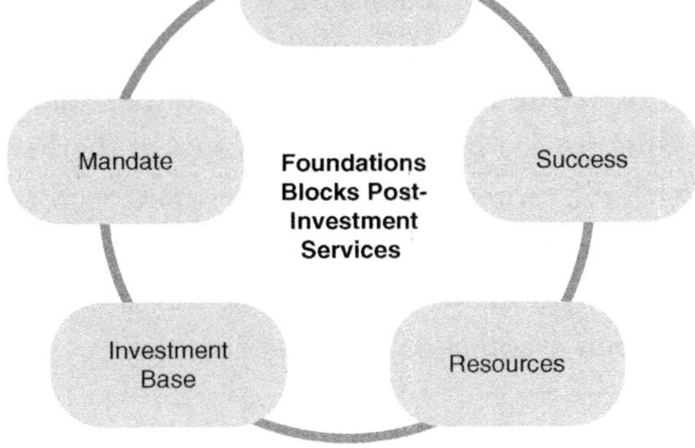

Figure 8.1 Foundations of post-investment services. © *Investment Aftercare Explained: A Guide for FDI Practitioners and Policymakers on How to Grow and Retain Investors.*

4.5% of local companies, they accounted for 22% of jobs, 19% of investment, owned 27% of all assets and were responsible for 39% of all exports and 45% of all imports.[1] Figures such as these show just how important foreign investors can be to a local economy, and hence how important it is that their thoughts, opinions and needs are heard by government and other stakeholders. This information can also help when an IPA is looking to secure support for its Aftercare activity, storytelling about the attractiveness of a location and when considering how best to deploy its resources.

According to UNCTAD, it is essential for an IPA wishing to deliver services to investors "to know which firms are established, what the nature of their activities is in the host region, and who the key corporate officials in the relevant decision-making units are."[2] Understanding the investor community starts with data obtained from desk and field research. It is likely that the IPA will draw information from different sources, including internal records and official data from the national statistics office, and then cross-checking this data with any studies undertaken by public organisations or academic institutions. "These databases can then be examined to see if there are any statistical characteristics of established firms, such as products, services provided, markets, export orientation, size and country of origin, that throw light on the nature of the established [investor]."[3]

While one might expect an IPA to understand its existing investor base, a surprisingly large number do not. Sometimes this is due to a lack of resources or no mandate to perform this work, and there is a significant amount of work involved. In other cases, it is because the IPA's focus has solely been on attracting new investors.

Understanding the investor community is no small task, particularly in those locations that are popular and have successfully attracted many foreign investors. IPAs should start small and, rather than researching all investors at the same time, a better approach is to study them one group at a time, starting with the more strategically important sectors, or in one specific region at a time, such as a special economic zone. One of the benefits of this work is that it will make clear who the key investors are, and what weight they have when it comes to the local economy.

8.2.2 Secure a mandate to deliver Aftercare

While the pillars of post-investment are well-established, there is no template as to how to deliver them in the field. The research for this book found that there are a variety of approaches currently being used, and that it is the local context that defines the approach taken.

The mandate for Aftercare will, most likely, be an extension of the mandate to provide services for investment attraction and facilitation. Servicing investor's enquiries can be seen as an extension of investment facilitation. IPAs in the public sector tend to have more explicit, and sometimes very specific, mandates, which define the support to be provided for investor expansion and retention. This level of detail is sometimes required to secure budget resources, as well as for transparency.

Although publications by the likes of the OECD and UNCTAD suggest that an IPA should have a simple, clear mandate for investment promotion, many agencies have several functions that go beyond FDI. Survey results indicate that "IPAs may be diluting their already scarce resources in too many mandates – on average an IPA has eight of them."[4] Hence the extent to which an IPA gets involved in post-investment depends to a large extent on the mandate it has from its board, the context in which it operates and the institutional structure of the IPA.

8.2.3 Know the IPA's why

In his book *Start with the Why*, the author and motivational speaker Simon Sinek researched communication patterns and identified that both successful people and successful organisations communicate in a very precise way, irrespective of the content. He identified that any communication answers three questions: the why, the how and the what. He then placed the questions in three concentric circles, The Golden Circle model, as shown in Figure 8.2.

He observed that, "people like Martin Luther King Jr., Steve Jobs, and the Wright Brothers had little in common, but they all started with why. They realised that people won't truly buy into a product, service, movement, or idea until they understand the why behind it."[5] He adds that "most leaders know what their organisation does, some know how, but very few know why."[6] He explained the difference with an example. The majority of computer manufacturers approach to selling is by saying "we make great computers. They are beautifully designed, easy to use and user-friendly. Do you want to buy one?"[7] Their communication focuses on the what, i.e. the computer. Their communication style is from the outside in. In contrast, Apple's approach is along the lines of, "we believe in challenging the status quo; we believe in thinking differently. The way we challenge the status quo

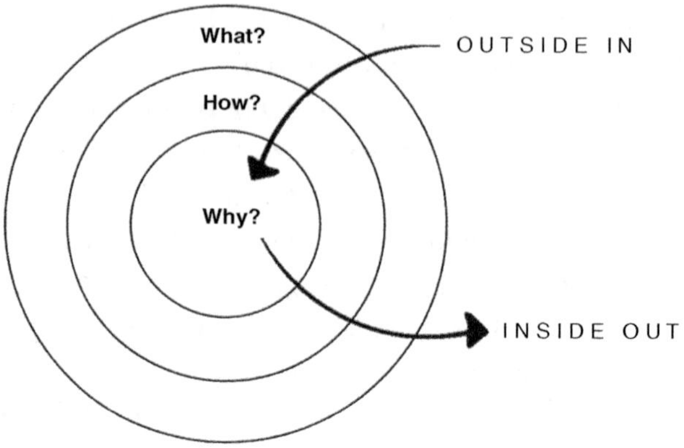

Figure 8.2 The Golden Circle – Simon Sinek.

Source: Adapted from Sinek, S. 2009. *Start With Why: How Great Leaders Inspire Everyone to Take Action*, p. 41. First edn. New York: Portfolio.

is by making our products beautifully designed, simple to use and user-friendly. We just happen to make great computers. Do you want to buy one?"[8] In this message they put their values centre-stage. After analysing hundreds of cases, Sinek concluded that leaders who communicate from the inside out are more effective, given that "people don't buy into what you do until they understand the *why* you do it."[9]

The Golden Circle model is also applicable to the design of post-investment services, as IPAs need to know what it is that their organisation places at the centre of their activities and to understand their *why*. When we asked IPAs about their why, some of them replied that their raison d'etre was the foreign investor. They exist to serve the investor; they design all their services around them. Other IPAs responded that their country's growth is the ultimate goal; they believe that economic development and the improvement in attractiveness, productivity and living standards for the country is what mobilises them. A third group stated that their organisations sought to serve both investors and local economic growth. Figure 8.3 shows the three different approaches IPAs take to post-investment and how this is reflected in their business. The investor-led IPA places the investor at the centre, the why, and economic development is an outcome of this focus. Meanwhile, the economic-development-led IPA, sees the why as economic growth and considers the investors as the beneficiary of their services to fulfil their mandate, which is to ultimately bring growth to their

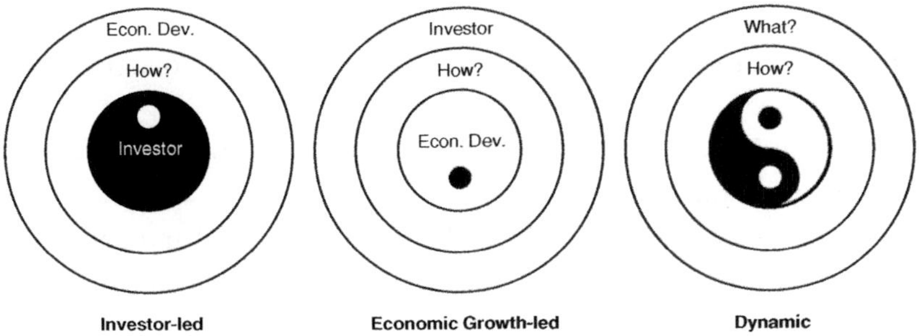

Figure 8.3 Different types of drivers IPAs respond to. © *Investment Aftercare Explained: A Guide for FDI Practitioners and Policymakers on How to Grow and Retain Investors.*

Source: Adapted from diagram from Sinek, S. 2009. *Start with Why: How Great Leaders Inspire Everyone to Take Action.* First edn. New York: Portfolio.

local economy. The dynamic approach, as shown on the right, is a balancing act between investor and growth. IPAs taking this approach answer the question of what they do in a fluid manner, based more on the contextual priorities of the why.

Post-investment services respond to the *what* question and the way these are conceptualised, designed, delivered and measured will be shaped differently depending on the answer to the question *why*. Clarity around the *why* is the first foundation stone when it comes to understanding post-investment.

8.2.4 Define success

Given that IPAs have different *whys*, they will also have different definitions of success, and success in post-investment is much more than the number of jobs created and the amount of financial investment secured. The different audiences for, and stakeholders in, FDI (discussed in Chapter 2, Understanding Aftercare) and the distinct objectives FDI seeks to achieve mean that success has several different dimensions, and, by extension, each stakeholder will have a different view of what success looks like. For example:

- Foreign investors evaluate Aftercare through a commercial lens and assess a location on its ability to help meet their strategic, operational and financial objectives.
- Public bodies are most concerned about economic growth and job creation, an attractive investment climate and increased competitiveness.

- Tax authorities seek higher tax receipts.
- The local workforce will assess the quality and quantity of jobs delivered.
- The business sector will be looking for a healthy pipeline of commercial opportunities.
- Other objectives may include alignment with local and national economic priorities, a stronger business Ecosystem, sustainability, inclusion, etc.

Figure 8.4 provides a simplified overview of the various KPIs that make regular appearances when it comes to defining success. Typically, IPAs use a basket of KPIs to monitor performance against the goals of their different stakeholders. For example, Invest in Madrid has defined success as "to facilitate the growth of our Aftercare clients and the attraction of new business lines to the region, as well as to learn about international investment practices and identify business barriers and policy suggestions that need to be overcome/implemented to improve the business climate at a regional and national level."[10]

Some specific short and long-term outputs of post-investment work include:

- More jobs and capital investment: these are the most commonly used KPIs by IPAs.
- Satisfied foreign investors who are committed to the location become advocates for the location, thereby helping to attract new investors.

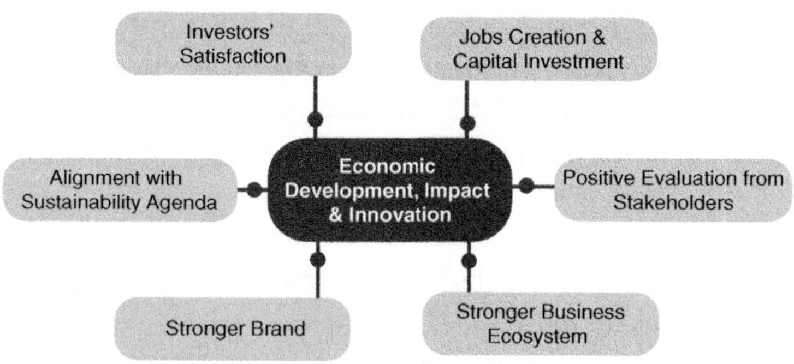

Figure 8.4 Success is a local definition. © *Investment Aftercare Explained: A Guide for FDI Practitioners and Policymakers on How to Grow and Retain Investors.*

- Positive evaluation by stakeholders of how Aftercare services are delivered. IPAs are closely scrutinised by their boards in terms of how the Aftercare function supports the prevailing political and economic agenda. Some locations measure this in terms of positive press coverage and media opportunities, others by how the IPA supports specific government programmes.
- Stronger business Ecosystem, which may be assessed in terms of contracts won by local SMEs with foreign businesses and new partnerships between academia and foreign investors' R&D teams.
- Stronger brand for both the location and the IPA. Many Aftercare practitioners report that there is some sort of tension when it comes to brand. Some believe that the only brand that needs developing is the location brand. Others see the need to push the brand of their IPA. The reality is that they are targeting different audiences and that a balance needs to be found between the two.
- Alignment with a wider sustainability agenda. Sustainability KPIs are likely to be location-specific and may include, for example, greener business practices or diversity targets. Aftercare will be evaluated in terms of the contribution it makes to achieving these targets.

The best IPAs realise that post-investment success combines a range of tangible deliverables relevant to the local economy. To deliver against them, IPAs need to remain alert to changes in the local business environment, be flexible and have the ability to adapt to changing external priorities. Addressing these many demands can be difficult for IPAs. It requires the ability to tell a coherent story of the value they add, while at the same time addressing the particular demands of individual stakeholders and clients.

Defining success also determines how the performance of the IPA is evaluated, how its impact is measured and monitored, and how the return on investment of the work undertaken is calculated. This will be discussed in detail in Chapter 10, Impact Evaluation.

8.2.5 Secure resources

Managing budgets is an important part of post-investment. Unfortunately, budgets tend to be small and so many post-investment units are under-resourced. The World Bank observed that "in 2005, more than 50 percent of agencies had budgets up to US$500,000, whereas in 2018, most of them had budgets up to US$1 million."[11] The OECD added that "investment promotion budgets vary widely across IPAs – ranging from USD 0.26 million to USD 351 million in 2016 – reflecting the disparities in size and income levels among OECD countries but also potentially the priority given to investment promotion."[12] And OECD members receive most of their budgets, about 90%, from the government.

OECD members on average dedicate 30% of the IPA's budget and 34% of the IPA's personnel to investment facilitation and retention.[13] They do not provide a breakdown of how much of their facilitation work corresponds to new investment versus established investment. Of the total facilitation activities, 36%[14] relate to Aftercare. Applying the same proportions as above (30% and 34%) to the total facilitation budget figure of 36% would mean that about 10% of budgets and approximately 12% of personnel are dedicated specifically to Aftercare.

Delivery of post-investment services, and specifically of Aftercare, must be built on a solid foundation. Only when the 5 foundation blocks of investment base, mandate, why, success and resources are fully understood by all parties involved, will the IPA be well placed to deliver effective and efficient post-investment services.

Notes

1 Invest Slovenia (2016). Tools and best practices: Aftercare services and Roles of IPAs. Presentation given in Torino to ITCLO (International Training Center for the International Labour Organisation) by Matej Skocir.

2 UNCTAD, 2007. *Aftercare: A Core Function in Investment Promotion* [online]. Available at: https://unctad.org/system/files/official-document/iteipc20071_en.pdf.

3 Ibid.

4 Sanchiz, A. and Omic, A. 2020. *State of Investment Promotion Agencies: Evidence from WAIPA-WBG's Joint Global Survey.* World Bank, Washington, DC. WAIPA (World Association of Investment Promotion Agencies), Geneva [online]. Available at: http://documents1.worldbank.org/curated/en/499971594008431029/pdf/State-of-Investment-Promotion-Agencies-Evidence-from-WAIPA-WBG-s-Joint-Global-Survey.pdf.

5 Sinek, S. 2009. *Start with Why: How Great Leaders Inspire Everyone to Take Action.* New York: Portfolio.

6 Ibid.

7 Ibid.

8 Ibid.

9 Ibid.

10 Insight gathered by this book's research team – Interview Invest in Madrid 2017.

11 World Bank Group, 2020. *Global Investment Competitiveness Report 2019/2020: Rebuilding Investor Confidence in Times of Uncertainty.* Washington, DC: World Bank.

12 OECD, 2018. *Mapping of investment promotion agencies in OECD countries* [online]. Available at: http://www.oecd.org/investment/Mapping-of-Investment-Promotion-Agencies-in-OECD-Countries.htm.

13 Ibid.

14 Ibid.

9
THE "HOW" OF INVESTOR SERVICES

Chapters highlights

- Investor Services need to be aligned with key stakeholders' business, political and economic agendas, while delivering the highest ROI given time spent, resources utilised, and relationships made.
- There are 7 building blocks to deliver Investor Services. These are: to know the local economy; to know and understand the investor; to segment the investor base; to define relevant value propositions; to choose delivery models that best fit the context; to orchestrate the local Ecosystem to jointly create FDI value; and to build a comprehensive Aftercare toolkit.
- There is also a discussion of points to consider when delivering Aftercare services to ensure they incorporate good governance practices and also on how best to set up Aftercare teams.

9.1 Introduction

Investor services is to Aftercare what the taste of the food is to online food delivery. All the beautiful pictures of the website mean nothing if the food is not delivered on time, doesn't look yummy and isn't tasty. The same is valid in FDI; all the promises of services given in attraction and facilitation phase mean nothing if Investors Services do not meet needs and expectations.

DOI: 10.4324/9781003174950-13

Regardless of whether an Investor Services programme has large or small ambitions, careful planning is needed during the design stage to ensure that not only is it aligned with key stakeholders' business, political and economic agenda, but also that it delivers the highest ROI given time spent, resources utilised and relationships made. As UNCTAD said in 2007, "In essence, these correspond to what is to be expected from any professional program: know the market, know the customer; identify and target the most desirable segments; design and deliver services that meet customer needs; and monitor, evaluate and adjust the service as required."[1] The key elements of a robust Aftercare programme are shown in Figure 9.1. They are: know your market; know your customers; and know your competition, so that you can generate relevant insight and therefore bring to market an Aftercare offer that creates impact, while also delivering excellent service. This is then supported by Place and Ecosystem, Policy Advocacy and evaluation and monitoring, in order to continuously improve the services offered, the investment climate and local connectedness. While in the diagram each element is shown as a standalone process, in practice these steps overlap and therefore should not be considered in isolation.

9.2 The 7 Building Blocks of Investor Services

In the authors' experiences of advising IPAs, they have observed that knowing the different characteristics and models of Investor Services

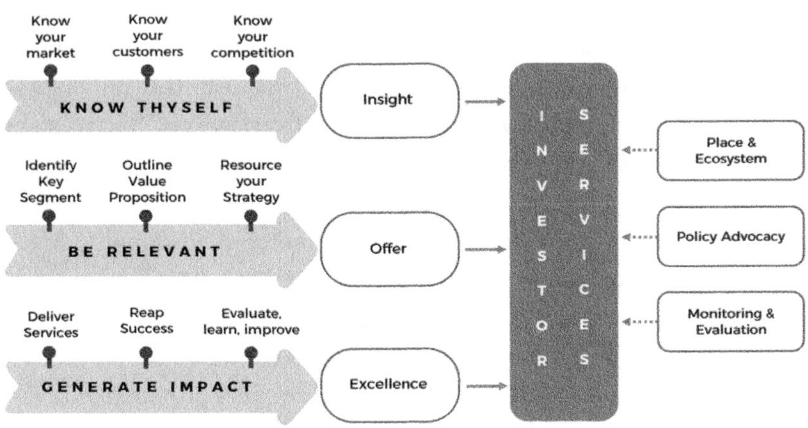

Figure 9.1 Design and delivery of Investor Services. © *Investment Aftercare Explained: A Guide for FDI Practitioners and Policymakers on How to Grow and Retain Investors.*

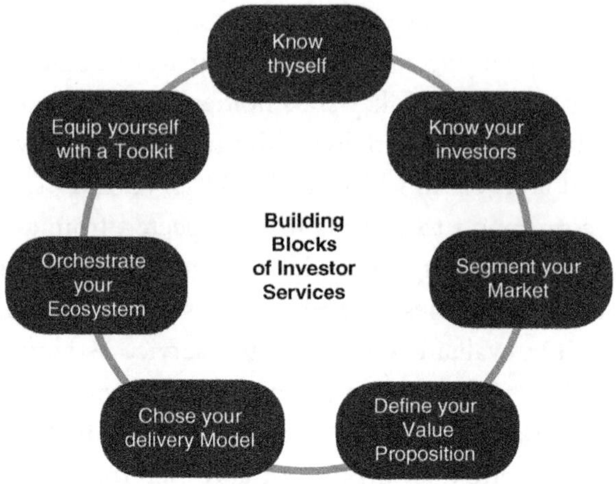

Figure 9.2 Building blocks of Investor Services. © *Investment Aftercare Explained: A Guide for FDI Practitioners and Policymakers on How to Grow and Retain Investors.*

is not sufficient to optimise their design, and that many IPAs needed an additional framework to put their knowledge into action. This led us to develop the concept of the "7 Building Blocks of Investor Services". This is a step-by-step model for designing Investor Services, and while some of this content has been discussed earlier in the book, it is referenced again here to help understanding of the whole model. The 7 blocks are presented in Figure 9.2.

9.2.1 Building block 1: know thyself

Designing Investor Services starts with knowing the location, the market, the client and the competition, as the insights gained from this understanding form the foundation of any investor service offer. Investor Services should be built on superior knowledge, data and insight into the host economy. There is little sense in putting together an Aftercare programme that is not deeply embedded in the fabric of the local market. Additionally, Aftercare professionals are expected to know the local market better than the foreign investor, and hence be able to present growth opportunities to an investor that they are likely to be unaware of.

The previous chapters included examples of services provided to investors. All of them were based on knowing in detail what it is the host economy can offer to the investor. IPAs curate the best offers from the host economy and bring them to investors. To do this, they constantly scan their local economy and take note of the characteristics of each particular sector: opportunities they can bring to investors; weaknesses when compared to other locations; and threats that could eliminate a well-established strength of the location, such as garment manufacturing, which is constantly under threat from the search for lower cost locations and also from nearshoring.[2]

There are many tools to better understand what a host economy offers; the most commonly used tool is a SWOT analysis: Strengths, Weaknesses, Opportunities and Threats. A SWOT diagram analyses a project or business venture by focusing on each of these factors. Strengths and weaknesses are internal factors and relate to the location itself, while opportunities and threats are external factors, whether current or future. By clearly outlining all the positive and negative factors of a location, a SWOT analysis helps clarify how to present and (further) sell a location to an investor. It is important to remember that this "sell" is different to the one made at the attraction phase. Aftercare requires identifying different rationales and narratives that will convince clients to expand locally. It is not enough to quote attractiveness rankings issued by international institutions; established investors already know them and expect IPAs to add real value. This is why Aftercare Investor Services is based on deep knowledge of the local market. IPAs need to know the local market better than investors do, otherwise investors may see them as irrelevant.

There are a few IPAs that consider their locations to be the best in their niche, and hence believe that they have no real competitors. This complacency can open the door to new threats. When it comes to Aftercare, a location is often competing with other locations that can offer a similar business climate, may be located nearby, or have developed a competitive advantage. As such, competition can come in a number of forms:

- When an investor is considering several locations, it may be open to offers. For example, when Amazon announced that its second headquarters in North America would be built in the location "where the biggest growth opportunity is."[3] For Amazon it was less about the characteristics of a location – which are often difficult to differentiate – and more about the business case, after taking account of any value proposition offered by a location. Hence, the best-placed locations are normally those that can deliver the growth an investor is looking for, in terms of market opportunity, resources or efficiency.

- Sometimes investors considering an expansion are open to offers, but they do not make a public announcement (as Amazon did with its HQ2 project). This is a challenge for an IPA, particularly when either the local affiliate is unaware of the growth plans of its parent company, or the affiliate fails to submit a case for expansion to its parent company. This may represent a missed opportunity. Hence IPAs should always be on the lookout for potential opportunities, monitor the press, develop relationships at head office level and keep an open dialogue with the local management team about the strategy of its parent company.
- Some foreign investors considering expanding one of their locations conduct an internal competition. The local IPA, through a targeted Aftercare programme, may be able to help increase the attractiveness of the affiliate based in its location and therefore increase its chances of winning the expansion project. IPAs can do this, for example, by making the affiliate aware of all the available incentives. This applies whether an investor is considering investing in one of several facilities to expand an existing function, or is choosing which opportunity represents the best use of its investment dollars, for example, a choice between expanding a factory in Detroit or an R&D facility in Tokyo.

Indeed, as the Brookings Institute's 2015 report, "The 10 lessons from global trade and investment planning in US metro areas," noted, when one local affiliate was asked what competition was for them, they responded by saying, "our biggest competitor is not another company or low-cost production in the Far East. For us, the competition comes from other locations where our company is already based and has similar manufacturing capabilities to us."[4] In this case, the competition takes place within the company's functions. For them, the question is "who is going to get the largest portion of production assigned, this plant or another plant somewhere else. We have to fight for our share of our own company's production and bring this capacity production home. IPAs can provide us with arguments and facts that we can take to HQ."[5]

In summary, Investor Services are deeply rooted in the knowledge that the IPA and the whole FDI Ecosystem develops about its own economy together with the IPA's ability to connect the dots and articulate the value that is relevant to foreign investors. Part of that knowledge includes understanding that there is more than one type of competitor for a location, and how to make the local offer as compelling as possible.

9.2.2 Building block 2: know your investors

Knowing investors is quintessential to providing good services. But first, a caveat. Defining who the recipients of Aftercare services are requires careful thinking. The first potential challenge is the increasing complexity of ownership structures of multinational companies. In response to ever-changing market conditions, organisations have adapted by becoming more sophisticated – multinational companies are adopting increasingly complex business ownership structures that make it difficult to classify companies as either local or foreign. The 2016 World Investment Report noted that more than 40% of foreign affiliates worldwide have multiple "passports", meaning that these companies can claim to belong to different jurisdictions. These "affiliates are often part of complex ownership structures with multiple cross-border links involving, on average, three jurisdictions. Moreover, the nationality of investors in, and owners of, foreign affiliates is becoming increasingly blurred."[6]

To understand why companies increasingly have "multiple passports", the report points to the rise of indirect foreign ownership, transit investment through third countries, and round-tripping. The top 100 MNEs in UNCTAD's Transnationality Index have, on average, more than 500 affiliates spread across more than 50 countries. They have 7 hierarchical levels in their ownership structure (ownership links to affiliates could potentially cross 6 borders), around 20 holding companies owning affiliates across multiple jurisdictions, and almost 70 entities in offshore investment hubs. Research undertaken by Pankaj Ghemawat and Niccolò Pisani[7] in 2012 on the Fortune Global 500 identified an average of 2,500 entities per multinational. UNCTAD adds that linked to an increased specialisation of corporates, foreign subsidiaries have a tendency to integrate into corporate ecosystems run as company networks or holdings. This applies to companies run hierarchically as groups, and also those that operate independently in each country.

Another potential challenge for effectively delivering Aftercare is the rise in cross-border mergers and acquisitions activities and private equity deals, as these transactions often complicate a company's ownership. Almost overnight, local companies can become foreign-owned. These new companies are then subject to corporate decision making in another jurisdiction. Private equity can have a similar impact; active international investors typically only invest in a business on the condition that they can influence its strategy and how it is managed. Either way, a local business will become an affiliate of a foreign-owned organisation, and hence a candidate for Aftercare support.

The final complexity is how local companies in some countries can obtain "foreign" treatment by investing "out of state", but within the same country. In this context, national companies that are not actually "foreign," but are from another part of the same country become Aftercare clients. As competition to attract companies gets increasingly fierce, not only internationally, but also within a country, region or state, locations are increasingly unconcerned about where an investor is actually from. Illustrating this all too clearly is the example of the 2017–2018 competition to become Amazon's second US headquarters (HQ2), with the promise of the creation of up to 50,000 high paying jobs to a host location within North America.

There is, therefore, a wide range of definitions of what a foreign investor is, and consequently determining who should qualify for Aftercare services is, in practice, quite complex. Whilst some locations rely on the OECD guideline of a simple 10% of ownership to determine how they deploy resources and to whom they grant access to different sources of funding, others take a more practical approach. They are less concerned about where precisely an investor is from and are more focused on identifying and working with those companies they believe will contribute the most to the local economy.

The combined effect of unpredictable timelines, over-optimistic forecasts, how and when to claim credit, scrutiny and the subjective nature of additionality means an IPA requires a deep understanding of Aftercare in order to effectively deliver services that are both relevant and impactful. Some IPAs find themselves alone in this quest, questioned by policy makers with little patience or interest in understanding the multidimensional nature of Investor Services. This is unfortunate and can weaken post-investment efforts to the detriment of the host economy. Faced with these challenges, managing the expectations of all stakeholders, not just an investor's, is key.

Spending time explaining what is feasible and what may prove more difficult to deliver is a key part of protecting and maintaining an IPA's reputation.

Once the baseline of who qualifies for Investor Services has been determined, there are 5 attributes foreign investors have that can help IPAs understand their clients: what drove them to invest in the first instance; their size; their attitude towards FDI; their preferred engagement style, irrespective of geography; and their needs for specific services.

9.2.2.1 Investors' drivers for FDI

In his book *Global Capitalism, FDI and Competitiveness,*[8] economist John Harry Dunning explained why companies choose to invest in foreign markets. According to Dunning, in most cases investors choose to expand their overseas operations for broadly similar reasons:

- **Natural resource seeking**: foreign investors looking for access to raw materials or geography-specific resources, for example, a mining company seeking to open a new gold mine in Australia in order to increase its market share. Definition of growth for this type of investors will be efficient local extraction and exports of natural resources or resource-based products
- **Market seeking**: firms grow to serve new buyers for their goods and services as they believe their products are unique or superior to the competition. They may also be able to generate higher returns than in other markets. What attracts the company is the client base they can secure locally, for example, an Italian wine company entering China to serve and exploit the growing demand for wine there that results from changing consumer patterns. These types of investors define growth by attractive volumes of domestic sales of final products to consumers or intermediaries.
- **Efficiency seeking**: multinational companies sometimes reorganise their overseas operations in response to broader economic opportunities. For example, the creation of a new free trade agreement among a group of countries may overnight increase the competitiveness of a facility located in one of these countries due to its access to lower tariffs and attractive tax regimes. Fluctuations in exchange rates may also change the profit calculation of a firm, and consequently a company may change the allocation of its resources in order to exploit

these opportunities. This type of investors will define growth by the local capacity to add value to their own products that they then export.

- **Strategic asset seeking**: here growth is driven by an investor's desire to gain access to strategic assets, such as distribution networks and new technology, tap into cheaper or higher-skilled talent pools or to leverage the brand and reputation of a premium location (e.g. Silicon Valley) or cluster. This type of investor defines growth by the level of increase in their in their overall competitive advantage. They will usually ship final goods to their home country or to third countries.

Companies looking to grow internationally are normally looking to benefit from one or more of these drivers. Articulating offers that respond to these ambitions can play an important role in convincing existing foreign investors to further invest in a location. Figure 9.3 outlines how the different investment drivers result in different outputs, as well as expectations of what constitutes local growth. In addition, growth will not only depend on the different drivers, but also on the different investment stages of the investment cycle (see Chapter 3 Investor Services, Figure 3.3). For example, the expectation of growth when a company invests in a country is different

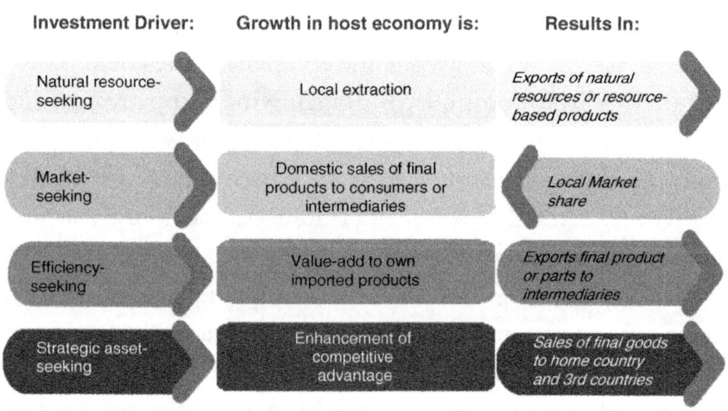

Figure 9.3 Investment drivers.

Source: Author's own design adapted from Global Investment Competitiveness Report 2017 / 2018, World Bank, who adapted material from *Global Capitalism, FDI and Competitiveness* by John Harry Dunning, J. H., 2002. 2nd ed. Northampton, MA: Edward Elgar Publishing.

to when the company is established in the country, to when it is growing locally or adapting to market changes. Growth is also linked to the role the subsidiary plays in the global company and what headquarters define as growth. Some will understand growth as number of local clients, others will define it as tons produced, profit generated or market share achieved. In essence, growth is a moving target.

9.2.2.2 Investors' size

Good IPAs realise that one-size doesn't fit all and that different businesses, different industries and different investors require different services, and hence a tailored approach, based on the unique demands of each investor, is more appropriate. Among the major groups of foreign investors are multinational corporations, small and medium sized businesses, and mega deals such as infrastructure development. According to the World Bank, "nearly all IPAs provide services to both groups; 97 % of IPAs provide services to small and medium size enterprises and 96% to multinationals and large foreign firms."[9] When it comes to resources, 34% are consumed by larger foreign firms, while smaller foreign firms receive 27% and megadeals take 10%. The balance of resources is deployed as follows: 17% to small and medium sized domestic firms; 13% to joint ventures between foreign and domestic firms; and 12% to large domestic firms.[10] Due to how the research was conducted, the IPAs were asked to allocate their resources to the 6 categories above. The figures reflect a simple average of the percentage in each category, not the total; same resources were allocated to more than one category, hence the sum total is greater than 100%. Unfortunately, the report does not split these figures between new investment, and retention and expansions. Nonetheless, these figures do provide an indication of priorities.

Multinational companies (MNCs): foreign investors make their FDI decisions in a host country based on many factors. Large MNCs are usually attracted to new markets for their products, lower production costs, talent acquisition and risk diversification. As a result, among the key priorities for MNCs operating in a host country, especially a developing one, is working with reliable local suppliers that are cost competitive in their operations as well as reputable in their business practices.

Small and medium sized businesses (SMBs): SMBs investing abroad are also likely to be pursuing growth as they seek to enter new markets, to diversify their risks and acquire new resources.[11] For these organisations, which also include start-ups, learning from and working with their local partners are often a high priority. MNC's typically have all the knowledge and resources needed in-house, such as technological capabilities, managerial expertise, proprietary assets and knowledge of the host country.[12] In contrast, SMBs are often taking greater risks, and are therefore the type of firm most in need of post-investment support. Compared to MNCs, these SMBs face a greater "liability of foreignness" in terms of having much fewer resources available to effectively navigate a new foreign environment – such "liability of foreignness" includes greater communication, coordination and information search costs when operating in a new country. Foreign SMBs often feel that host governments are focussed on meeting MNC's needs, which risks creating the perception among these SMBs that they are not really wanted by their host country.[13] Consequently, according to many economists, smaller firms are less likely to invest abroad in the first place – particularly in highly competitive industries – due the high costs and deep local knowledge required to compete effectively with local firms and foreign MNCs. The data largely supports this view – FDI investments from the US to Canada and to the UK tend to be made by the largest firms in their respective industries.[14]

However, overlooking foreign SMBs is not in the interest of host economies. Host countries, especially developing ones, that do not give foreign SMBs the same priority as MNCs are missing out on opportunities to create value. There are also many cases where SMBs collectively contribute to the majority of FDI in other countries. For example, SMBs, particularly from ethnically Chinese economies such as Taiwan, Singapore, Hong Kong, and Malaysia, collectively represented the majority of FDI inflows into China in the 1990s and early 2000s.[15] In addition, foreign SMBs from the four East Asian Tiger economies (South Korea, Taiwan, Singapore and Hong Kong) have invested heavily in neighbouring Southeast Asia, which collectively serves as a significant driver of economic growth in those host countries.

In particular, technology start-ups and SMBs can serve as a catalyst for growth in a host economy because they are often among the most innovative firms in their respective industries. These ventures typically produce high-value technology products, and they may even establish R&D research centres in the host countries as they seek to hire local talent and better understand local markets. These new ventures are also likely to be nimbler, and better at exploiting niche opportunities within sectors – niches that are often neglected by larger firms, whether locally or foreign owned.[16] In addition, these new ventures often play a key role in developing the skills and knowledge of their local workforce, and of local companies and their employees.

While some SMBs may be "pushed" away from a potential host country by its harsh regulatory environment, they are likely to "pulled" by other host countries that have more business-friendly policies.[17] For example, when it comes to financial securities listings, countries with strong institutions and policies find it easier to get foreign companies to list on their markets – this explains the success of London and New York in attracting overseas companies to list on their exchanges. Indeed, countries with underdeveloped institutions and policies can even "force" homegrown companies to move overseas.

Finally, effective post-investment policies to support SMBs need to consider their preferred mode of entry into a host country – particularly if they are from developing countries, as is increasingly the case. For example, among the top 100 fastest growing firms (both large and small) based in Asia that are investing abroad, 15 of them are new ventures based in developing countries. SMBs from developing countries are often more resource constrained and thus their preferred modes of entry may often be mergers or alliances with local players – which often involve greater knowledge flow between these foreign SMBs and their local partners, as well as driving secondary effects such as accelerated technology adoption to other local stakeholders such as their suppliers.[18]

Megadeals: these are large-scale construction, infrastructure or regeneration projects, most of the time tendered by the government. Of IPAs surveyed in the joint study by the World Bank and WAIPA,[19] 62% are active in mega-deals and dedicate up to 10% of their client service resources to them. Many of these mega-deals are large infrastructure projects, such as airports, highways or large-scale regeneration projects, are managed in collaboration with other government departments and are the subject of open tenders.

9.2.2.3 Investors' attitude to FDI

Research undertaken for this book has identified 7 different investor profiles when it comes to how they engage locally and how they approach IPAs or the local Ecosystem:

> **Expansion novices** are new to international expansion, have a presence in only a handful of locations, and tend to be more loyal to locations they have already invested in. For them, expanding to another location is high risk and resource-intensive and hence they tend to be location-loyal.
>
> **Experienced multi-nationals** typically have a presence in many markets and the capability in-house to expand into almost any geography. They therefore are neither inclined to stay in, nor are fearful of leaving, a location. For them, the business opportunity is paramount and they are therefore often location-agnostic; they stay or go depending on the local growth opportunities.
>
> **Embedded companies** typically have a significant stake in a location; hence moving would either be expensive or would take significant effort, and their preferred option is to grow locally. If successful, they often become investment anchors attracting their peers and competitors to the area, thereby improving the overall attractiveness of a location. These companies can be difficult to engage with because they consider themselves to be sufficiently well-established that they no longer need assistance from an IPA. It should be noted that while embedded companies are *satisfied enough* with a location to stay, this does not mean they "love" the location.
>
> **Loyal companies** have decided to stay in a location for the long term. The market meets their needs, and hence the investors are content and consider that the location delivers the returns they are seeking. There is every likelihood that, should the opportunity arise, they will further invest in the location.
>
> **Brand/Cluster seekers** are looking to benefit from associating their business with either the reputation of a location, such as London, Singapore and New York as open international cities, or the need to be located close to their industry cluster, for example Silicon Valley (tech), or Milan (fashion), and the Ecosystem that

supports that industry. As long as these location benefits persist, investors are likely to grow locally. They are also relatively immune to messages from competing locations that do not offer the same brand or cluster value.

Supply chain followers are part of larger value chains and initially chose a location in order to take advantage of the local supply chain. The existence of the supply chain is the key determinant of whether they stay or go. These types of companies are client-led rather than tied to a location. An example would be a construction company engaged on a large regeneration project. Their initial plan might be to stay in a country for 5 years with the intention of closing the operation once the project is complete. The key to retaining these jobs is helping the investor to win new contracts. These companies are good potential Aftercare clients.

Disruptors are typically location-agnostic companies who are leveraging the power and reach of the internet to disrupt certain industries. Such companies include Amazon, Spotify, Uber, Facebook and Airbnb. These companies are less "sticky" to a location, and often have the backing of investors with deep pockets seeking rapid growth (and ultimately big returns). Expansion projects are often likely, but if business does not prosper, they are likely to leave fast.

These 7 types of investor behave, see growth and relate to a location in different ways. Hence there is a need to understand the nature and strategy of each investor, and what their future development plans are likely to be for a location, in order to develop services that meet the investor's (and the location's) needs.

9.2.2.4 Investors' preferred style of engagement

Irrespective of their nature, investors typically take one of 4 approaches when it comes to interacting with an IPA: low-profile and self-reliant, transactional, profile-seeking or collaborative:

- **Low-profile** investors keep themselves to themselves, use independent consultants and keep their interactions with their local

IPA to a minimum. This can be for a number of reasons, including guidance from their head office, management style of the local affiliate or simply a question of priorities. This doesn't necessarily reflect a lack of enthusiasm on the part of the investor, and IPAs should continue to monitor these companies.

- **Transactional** focused investors only contact an IPA when they need something or have a problem. Often the reason they minimise interaction with their local IPA is because they are concerned that, while the IPA might say that certain services are free, in reality the IPA wants something in return. Hence, they don't buy into the idea of free services and so prefer to reduce their transactions with the IPA to a minimum, as they believe that by accepting free services, at some point in the future the IPA will seek "payback", typically in the form of time, endorsement, requests to complete surveys or the association of the investor's brand with the local IPA.
- **Profile-seekers** want to cultivate a public profile. This may be driven by a real desire to collaborate with the local business community, including the IPA, the personality of a charismatic leader, an interest in maximising marketing opportunities or alignment with their public relations strategy. This type of company has the potential to become an ambassador for a location, to give testimonials about the benefits of locating there and will likely attend events and be actively engaged in Policy Advocacy in order to ensure the location continues to thrive. IPAs can work with profile-seekers to the mutual benefit of both parties.
- **Collaborative investors** are the ideal type of client, as the investor sees the IPA as a partner organisation that can help it grow faster. These investors understand that they cannot do it all alone and that, at the same time, they can make a contribution to their host location. There are two scenarios where investors tend to display this behaviour. First, when they land in a new country and are relatively unsure how to "play the system." Second, when an investor is more established and they understand the benefits that the local IPA can bring to their business. As investors transition from newcomers to well-established firms there is often a period of self-reliance. It is at this point that they may evolve into one of the other three profiles. This can be attributed to a lack of knowledge about new services, staff

churn or simply focusing on their own business. A well-designed and relevant value proposition based on real investor needs is the best tool to reduce this self-reliance period.

Understanding what type of investor a company is will help an IPA develop the most constructive possible relationship, even if any interactions are, in reality, relatively small, as may be the case with a low key, but highly experienced multi-national or an established and self-reliant investor. Understanding the value each investor brings to an economy, and how each of them can help deliver the objectives of Aftercare, will increase the efficiency and reputation of the IPA.

9.2.2.5 Investors' needs

As discussed in Chapter 4, Portfolio of Investor Services, investors have different investment drivers, which result in different definitions of growth and therefore they will respond to different services. These fall into 5 categories, as shown in Figure 9.4. The first three are administration, operations and strategy, categories outlined by UNCTAD in 2007.[20] In addition, there are needs around value chains, which the economic disruption caused by the Covid-19 pandemic made evident. Likewise, sustainability, governance and international treaties bring an additional set of demands, both from investors and from the host economy. Meeting these 5 different needs helps meet an investor's primary objective, to grow the company in the host location.

When designing Investor Services, taking into account their mandate and resources, IPAs need to have clarity about which of these different needs they should focus on. This is also relevant when it comes to collaborating

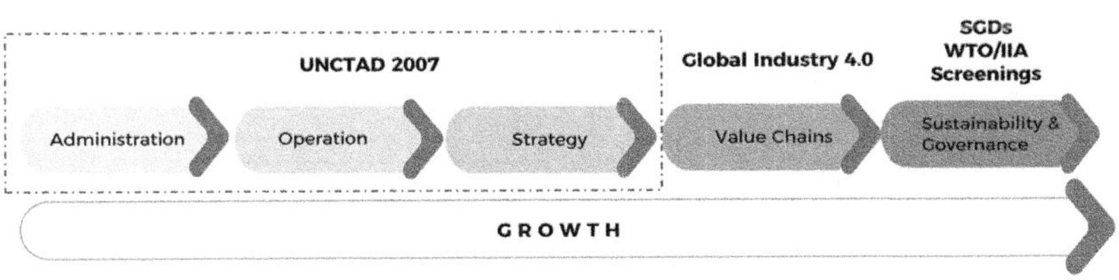

Figure 9.4 Five needs of an investor. © *Investment Aftercare Explained: A Guide for FDI Practitioners and Policymakers on How to Grow and Retain Investors.*

Source: Adapted from UNCTAD, 2007. *Aftercare: A Core Function in Investment Promotion.*

with other public agencies and stakeholders in order to avoid duplication of effort and unnecessary bureaucracy, and also to manage expectations about what services the IPA can effectively provide.

9.2.2.6 Investor's attitude to service

Susanne Lambregts-Winters, from Brabant Development Agency BOM in the Netherlands, was surprised when an investor indicated that "we might be stubborn, but we do not have any need for your type of services." To find out why an investor might have such an opinion, she studied investors' engagement preferences and segmentation for her master's thesis, *See and be seen: Added value for foreign investors in Brabant.*[21] In particular, she looked at the model of added value outlined by Professor Kent B. Monroe in 1990 in his book *Pricing: Making Profitable Decisions*,[22] which can be summarised in a formula, as shown in Figure 9.5.

Lambregts-Winters found that investors compare the benefits to be gained with the sacrifices they will need to make when deciding whether or not to engage with an IPA. Benefits can, for example, be saving money or time, accessing new suppliers or developing a relationship with the public sector. However, while a service may be free of charge, some investors prefer to keep matters in-house, and hence using an IPA's services can be seen as a *sacrifice*[23] of their time, of their privacy policies or their preference to make decisions behind closed doors. The more strategic the services offered and the higher the value delivered by the IPA, the greater the probability that the investor perceives the services offered as a benefit and will therefore be more willing to "sacrifice" something they value in exchange.

The level of added value that IPAs can bring relates to the different types of services they provide to investors. Figure 9.6 contrasts the 5 types of service provided to investors with the level of trust involved. While some

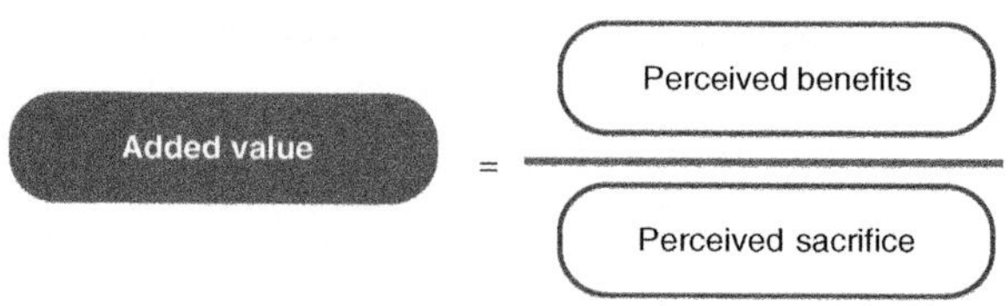

Figure 9.5 Formula of added value.

Source: Authors' own design, adapted from Monroe, K. B. (1990). *Pricing: making profitable decisions* (2nd ed.). Boston: McGraw-Hill.

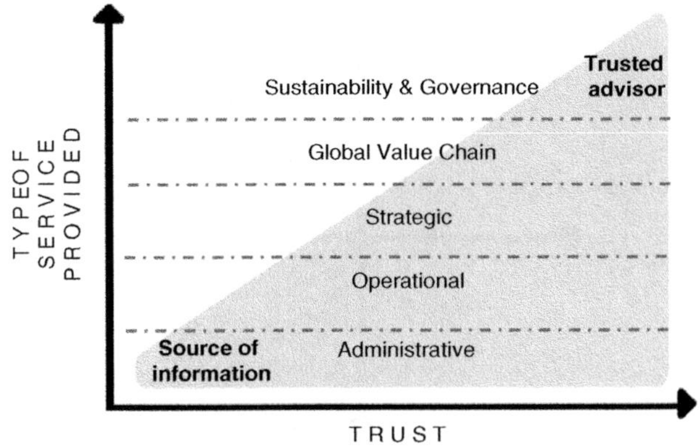

Figure 9.6 Type of service and trust diagram.

Source: Lambregts-Winters, S. 2016. "See and be seen: Added value for foreign investors in Brabant." Thesis for MSc in Marketing, Tilburg University and Eindhoven University of Technology, TIAS.

administrative services might seem basic in nature, they can nevertheless be of great value to an investor. As the level of trust increases, and the investor starts to use higher value services, the IPA becomes a trusted advisor.[24]

Irrespective of the type of services offered and the level of trust involved, foreign investors have different attitudes when it comes to engaging with the IPA. Swedish academics Dan Hjalmarsson and Anders W. Johansson, who specialise in competitiveness and entrepreneurship, studied advisory services in their paper, "Public advisory services-theory and practice. Entrepreneurship & regional development." They identified that there are different attitudes when company managers relate to consultants: there are the ones who are simply anti-consultant and are not interested in any advice, as they perceive it as detrimental to their own knowledge or judgment. There are those who consider that consultants have a role as a sounding board or that they can provide solutions to specific problems. And finally, there are the ones who not only accept, but also seek guidance from an advisor whom they see as a knowledge authority or role model.[25]

Lambregts-Winters contrasted this model with local foreign investors and established that different types of investors have different degrees of need for, and willingness to use advice from, an IPA. The profiles she identified are influenced by the investor's attitude towards services, whereby investors differentiate themselves by their approach to using external advisers, a preference that can be influenced by their corporate culture, the

Figure 9.7 Investor profile based on type of support and service take-up.

Source: Lambregts-Winters, S. 2016. "See and be seen: Added value for foreign investors in Brabant." Thesis for MSc in Marketing, Tilburg University and Eindhoven University of Technology, TIAS.

cultural background of their country of origin, the size of the company, the "age" of the company, the degree of experience it has in operating internationally, the sector, the nature of the operations it performs in the area (e.g. sales, manufacturing or R&D) and the perceived opportunity available locally.

Figure 9.7 shows the 4 profiles Lambregts-Winters identified:

- **I don't need you**: these clients are of the view that they can better address their needs themselves, rarely take up services, and in the rare case they do, they only take up low value support such as administrative services.
- **Inspire me**: these clients are not really interested in engaging with the IPA; but they are open to high value services that would otherwise be out of their reach, or that align with their strategy. Possible starting points for engagement are contacts at the head office and connections at the strategic level.
- **Take care of me**: these investors have a high degree of service take-up; however, they mainly take advantage of lower value-added services.
- **Develop with me**: this group is open to working with the IPA, is willing to disclose information, will take up high value services and

> is a regular user of the IPA's services. The IPA becomes a "partner to further develop the company and jointly influence the head office."[26]

Engaging with the profiles on the left-hand side of the diagram requires careful consideration. Dealing with "I don't need you" investors can be frustrating as no amount of effort is likely to overcome the investor's view of external advisors, whether from the IPA or anybody else. "Inspire me" investors can be resource-intensive to serve, and whether or not they are worth the effort is often not clear. "The return of efforts to establish a relationship with companies in this segment might results in a low yield for Brabant; it is only justified in a small proportion of companies which have a strategic value for us."[27] The "develop with me" and "take care of me" type of investor is willing to develop a strong relationship with the IPA, will share the information needed for the IPA to better understand their needs and will be willing to co-create services and drive innovation with the IPA. As such, these investors should be the focus of a proactive communication and engagement plan.

Once clients have been profiled, the next step is to assess their strategic importance to the IPA, and then to allocate resources appropriately. Segmentation is key to doing this.

9.2.3 Building block 3: segment your market

Locations that have proved successful at attracting new FDI and follow-on investment face a further challenge – how to manage and support the ever-increasing volume of established investors present in their host economy, sometimes referred to as the stock of investors. A commonly used approach is to segment investors into different groups.

According to marketing guru Philip Kotler, market segmentation is the sub-dividing of customers into homogenous sub-set of customers who share similar characteristics. By making this division there is a high chance that each group responds in favour to a specific market strategy.[28] Kotler argues that "all customers are important, but some are more important than others."[29]

A 2007 UNCTAD survey found that while 60% of business support programmes work with their entire client base, the other 40% choose to focus on sub-sectors aligned to political priorities and local economic development policies.[30] The joint study by the World Bank and WAIPA in 2020 noted that, "sector targeting is one part of a successful investment promotion strategy. Existing research shows that sector targeting results in higher FDI inflows."[31] They add that IPAs tend to have a "large number of priority sectors: according to the survey findings, an IPA has 11 priority sectors on average."[32]

Some IPAs spend a significant amount of time and effort segmenting their investors by analysing data from different sources, working closely with the office of national statistics or their central bank. They then combine their findings with datasets and insight from other sources such as chambers of commerce, research institutes and academia. Other IPAs take a more pragmatic approach, choosing to focus on the businesses they believe are most likely to invest again. Most important in this work is to remember Kotler's words: "if markets are to be segmented and cultivated, they must meet certain requirements. Segments must be measurable, substantial, accessible, differentiable, and actionable."[33] Harvard University professors Benson Shapiro and Thomas V. Bonoma were the first ones to study industrial and business-to-business segmentation and suggested a "nested hierarchy – like a set of boxes that fit one into the other. Moving from the outer nest toward the inner, these criteria are: demographics, operating variables [such as the use technology or production methodologies], customer purchasing approaches, situational factors, and personal characteristics of the buyers."[34] This model is widely used around the globe and has influence IPA segmentation to certain degree.

The following pages explore alternative types of segmentations commonly used by IPAs such as industry, growth stage, how much they can influence an investors alignment with the IPA's strategies, public programmes, affiliation to strategic groups and negative segmentation.

9.2.3.1 Industry segmentation

The FDI industry model developed by Andrew Charlton et al[35] is a commonly used segmentation framework that focuses on the desirability and "attractability" of different industry sectors (see Figure 9.8).

- **Desirability**: the benefits obtained from attracting another company from a specific industry to a location, and the externalities that subsequently flow into the local economy. In the case of Amazon, the desirability was the 50,000 new technology jobs, the associated

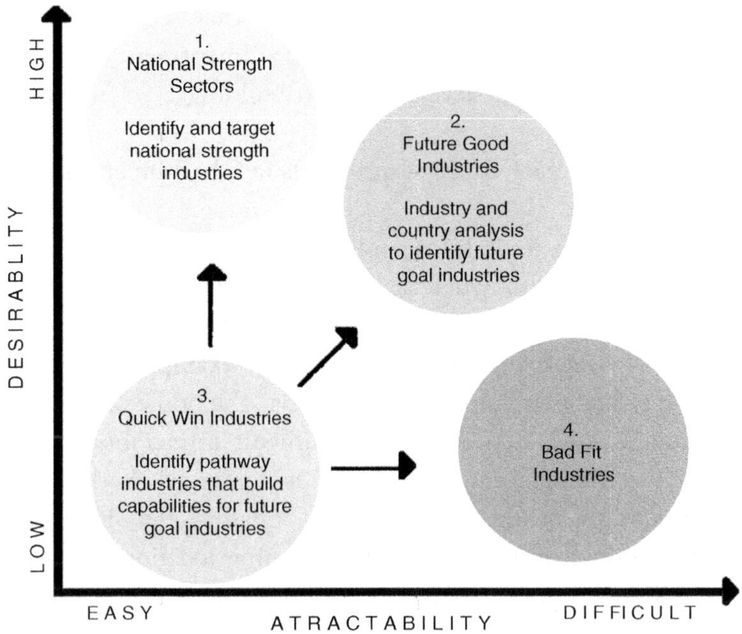

Figure 9.8 Segmentation of FDI industries. © *Investment Aftercare Explained: A Guide for FDI Practitioners and Policymakers on How to Grow and Retain Investors.*

financial investment by Amazon and the expected spillover effect of around US$1.40 for every dollar invested by Amazon.[36]

- **Attractability**: the cost of attracting firms from a particular sector to the location. Cost is expressed in terms of how easy or how difficult it is to secure investment. Put another way, locations that are perceived to be less attractive are likely to have to offer greater incentives to an investor than a more "attractive" location. Costs can include the hours involved in preparing a bid, including teams from different organisations, fees paid to consultancies, engagement with civic organisations to discuss the projects, public relations and the alternative use of the assets that a location is willing to deploy to the prospective project.

According to FDI consultant Dr Ashraf Mahate, the "targeting of sectors is seen as a choice between **costs** of attracting a sector against the benefit that is derived from it. In most cases the final choice of selecting sectors is a balance of those two factors."[37] He adds that segmentation allows meeting "short-term goals of attracting inward investment with the long-term national objectives of developing and building a strong sustainable economy."[38]

Looking in turn at each of the 4 quadrants in Charlton et al's model:

Quadrant 1: high desirability and easy attractability. This is typically an industry sector where a location is already strong, and hence attracting new businesses and encouraging expansion projects should be relatively straightforward, for example, attracting more film production companies to Mumbai, the home of Bollywood.

Quadrant 2: high desirability and difficult attractability. Amazon's HQ2 is the perfect example of a company in this quadrant. Attracting a business of Amazon's "quality" and size will have a lot of follow-on benefits for the winning location in the form of jobs and attracting businesses keen to support Amazon. However, Amazon's initial selection of New York and Washington, two already highly attractive cities that are at the centre of financial and political power in the US, showed how difficult, and perhaps unrealistic, it was for many of the other bidders to try and attract a business of the size of Amazon, even when offering highly attractive incentive packages.

Quadrant 3: low desirability and easy attractability: Attracting companies in this quadrant represent quick wins and offers the possibility of becoming a hub for that industry in the future. For example, Stockholm has emerged as a new gastro-destination with a strong Ecosystem of food-related companies and a focus on prioritising food-tech investors. Attracting a new restaurant is now relatively easy. Local organisations, such as SwedenFoodTech and The FoodTechVillage, focus their efforts on attracting companies who can help them accelerate transformative entrepreneurship for the next-generation food system, driven by tech, data and innovation. As such, they do not focus on restaurants, but on attracting companies that have a strong tech component that disrupt the food value chain.[39]

Quadrant 4: low desirability and difficult attractability. Companies in these industry sectors are either a bad fit for a location or in declining industries, and hence are unlikely to attract other businesses at a later date. These sectors should therefore not be a priority and services should only be provided on the basis of demand. For example, if a company from such a sector chooses to expand, the IPA should of course "make them feel welcome," while at the same time being careful in its use of resources.

Dr. Mahate explains that "the model helps identify the national strength followed by translating the strategy for the geography (or even the different strategies, e.g. economic strategy, innovation strategy, employment strategy, etc.) into a list of sectors that are considered 'good for the economy.'"[40] This is followed by the "design [of] a roadmap that allows the IPA to move from a quadrant of quick win industries to the quadrant of future good industries."[41]

9.2.3.2 Growth stage segmentation

Another approach to segmenting companies is by using the growth model developed by UNESCAP.[42] This model, based around a transnational corporation (TNC), breaks down the development of an investor's business into 8 stages:

1. Establish the start-up.
2. Carry out the basic mandate satisfactorily.
3. Perform the basic mandate in a "superior" way (efficiency gains).
4. Extend the basic mandate – low-risk moves.
5. Extend the basic mandate – strategic activities.
6. Become a strategic centre for the TNC[43] – centre of excellence.
7. Become a strategic centre for key activities.
8. Become a stand-alone strategy-making unit of the TNC (i.e. regional head office).

The growth stage model helps an IPA identify the type of companies a location needs to attract in order to realise its ambition and vision. For example, if a government's strategy is to become a centre of excellence in circuit board manufacturing, it should target local affiliates that are seeking to become a strategic centre for their group (stage 6). This type of segmentation seeks to align the growth objectives of a location with the current stage of development of the investor company, thereby making the location more attractive to similar businesses.

9.2.3.3 Influence and growth phase segmentation

The nature of Investor Services means there are a couple of further factors to consider when segmenting companies: influence and investment.

- **Influence** refers to the capacity of an IPA to persuade foreign investors to make further investments, or to minimise the risk of disinvestment. According to UNESCAP, "two-thirds [of established foreign companies] say that Aftercare positively influences their expansion plans."[44] Hence an IPA needs to understand how much it is able to influence any individual decision. As ever, a good relationship with investors is key.
- **Investment** refers to the nature of the investment, whether it is directed at growth or preventing contraction.

Combining both factors results in 4 distinct quadrants, as can be seen in Figure 9.9.

The upper two quadrants are where an IPA can have the most influence, and hence the potential to generate significant results, whether in the form

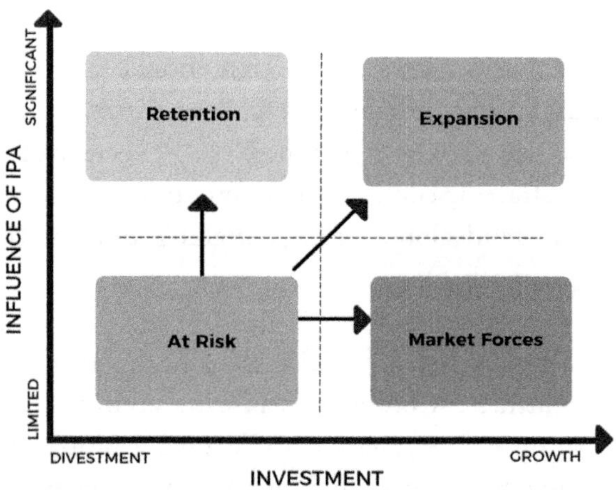

Figure 9.9 Influence and investment segmentation. © *Investment Aftercare Explained: A Guide for FDI Practitioners and Policymakers on How to Grow and Retain Investors.*

of retentions or expansion. Therefore, this is where most of the Investor Service offer should be focused.

The *At Risk* quadrant is where a foreign investor is considering disinvestment and it is likely that the IPA will have little or no influence over the outcome. Nevertheless, companies in this quadrant should not be neglected, and efforts should be made to move an *At Risk* company into one of the other quadrants if at all possible, particularly when there is the possibility that a company in this quadrant may decide to exit the location, with the consequence media coverage and political interest in the case.

Companies in the *Market Forces* quadrant do not seek or need assistance from their local IPA to expand, as their growth is market driven or they are self-reliant.

The influence-investment segmentation offers a practical approach to increasing the effectiveness of Aftercare teams by providing guidance on where they should focus their efforts. It is of particular relevance to company-friendly service models and IPAs who are new to Aftercare.

9.2.3.4 Strategic segmentation

Another frequently used segmentation model involves focusing services on those segments that are aligned with the overall IPA's strategy, which will usually be aligned with the government's strategy. Strategic segments include:

- **Sector**: the focus is on priority sectors aligned with a location's economic development strategy and those subsectors that provide niche business opportunities in higher value-added segments. An example of this is the automotive sector in Spain, which represents approximately 10% of national GDP, a figure that increases to 25% of GDP in Navarra in the north of Spain. The local IPA, Invest In Navarra, focuses primarily on the automotive industry working with a wide range of local stakeholders such as CEMITEC, a multidisciplinary R&D centre, ACAN, the automotive cluster association, and SODENA, the local economic development organisation. SODENA is tasked with managing incentives and expansion grants and developing tailored growth programmes for the more than 120 automotive companies based in the area.
- **Countries**: here the focus is on investor companies from specific countries and may be aligned to international ambitions, or the

historical or cultural affinity of an investor. IPAs sometimes group investors from certain geographies together where there is a high concentration of companies operating in a priority segment. For example, Hamburg, in northern Germany, has links with China that go back many decades thanks to a consistent effort from the local government to position Hamburg as the natural port of entry for Chinese products. Despite the shipping market changing, which resulted in more cargo flowing through Rotterdam, Hamburg has developed and maintained an Aftercare programme tailored to the particular needs of the Chinese community. Hamburg was not only one of the first cities in Europe to support the celebration of Chinese New Year and other Chinese cultural activities, it also supported Chinese expatriates and their families, for example by providing Chinese schools many years before other cities followed suit. Hamburg also maintains a close dialogue with locally based Chinese business leaders and invites executives from their parent companies to visit the city so they better understand the local opportunities. In addition, Hamburg has connected local companies doing business in China with Chinese companies with operations in Hamburg as a means of strengthening not only business links, but also to create a sense of community for those involved in trade and investment between China and Hamburg. Having sustained these efforts for over 20 years, Hamburg remains one of the leading cities in the EU when it comes to attracting Chinese investment.

- **Geography**: here the focus is on a specific location in the host economy. There are many reasons for this type of segmentation. These include ease of access, the availability of talent, the concentration of players in a particular sector and the political ambition to support and develop a region that either offers attractive opportunities or is relatively deprived, and hence a focus for economic growth. One such example is the Special Economic Zones (SEZs) in China – defined areas or regions that are permitted to carry out certain activities under a different regulatory or taxation regime to other parts of the country. SEZs were initially created along the Chinese border with Hong Kong in order to take advantage of the low utility and labour costs in mainland China. In particular, the SEZ's local authorities have specific programmes targeting international companies based in these zones.

- **Regional presence**: this type of segmentation is common for countries that seek to attract regional HQs or innovation centres. For example, Denmark has a strong offer when it comes to attracting investors looking to establish a regional office to serve the Scandinavian countries. They target companies that have a presence in neighbouring countries who might benefit from managing regional operations from a single location.
- **Function**: the objective is to target foreign investors with the potential to expand a specific function or department within the company's structure. For example, Taiwan, has a strategy to attract research and development (R&D) functions and has become a magnet for R&D departments, as can be seen in Box 9.1.

Box 9.1 Multinational innovative R&D centre in Taiwan

"The Program of Multinational Innovative R&D centre in Taiwan" is an important element in the International Innovation and R&D Base Plan, which forms part of the National Development Plan. The aim is to get multinational corporations collaborating with local Taiwanese firms so that Taiwan can establish itself as a regional R&D centre within the Asia Pacific region. This in turn will help to support multinational production activities, thereby enhancing the role that Taiwan plays in global R&D, giving the R&D activity of Taiwanese industry greater depth and encouraging Taiwanese companies to focus on cutting-edge research. Implementation of the plan began in 2002. Until October 2011, several leading international corporations including Intel, HP, Dell, Sony, Microsoft, IBM and Ericsson have established 51 R&D centres in Taiwan. Among these companies, many found that the industry environment and infrastructure here are much better than what they had expected, and some even expanded the scale of their R&D centres. This proves Taiwan to be an ideal location for multinational corporations to establish their R&D bases for innovative R&D activities. The introduction of key technology by these R&D centres will help Taiwan to become a valued partner to the world's multinational corporations in the area of technology and will contribute to the further development of Taiwanese industry.

Reproduced with kind permission from Invest Taiwan: www.investtaiwan.nat.gov.tw.

Link: https://investtaiwan.nat.gov.tw/showPage?lang=eng&search=433.

- **Size and value of potential investment**: a further layer of segmentation is to prioritise companies according to their investment potential. Size usually relates to the scale of investment, either the number of new jobs promised, the capital investment to be made or the size of the property to be acquired or built. Value takes account of the spillover effect an investment is expected to have on a location. For example, the presence of larger businesses is likely to attract other businesses to a location in a similar way to how shopping centres are often built around an anchor tenant. Cities bidding for Amazon's HQ2 clearly expected there to be a spillover effect. Key factors to consider include a company's brand strength and reputation, the likelihood that it will further invest, particularly if an initial investment is relatively small, the level of integration into the local economy and the potential added value to the business ecosystem.

9.2.3.5 Programme-based segmentation

Research for this book has found that some Aftercare practitioners take a more pragmatic approach to segmentation. As a delivery arm of government with a mission to support the activities of other government departments that are of interest to international investors, they segment by programme. That is to say, they identify programmes that provide value to their clients and bring them to market. They do this by matching their clients' strategic priorities with specific government programmes. For example, IDA Ireland works in partnership with Enterprise Ireland and supports the enrolment of companies in their various programmes. One of these programmes is the Lean Business Offer, which "is designed to encourage clients to adopt

Lean business principles in their organisation to increase performance and competitiveness."[45] IDA Ireland selects companies in their client base who have the ambition to be leaner and works together with Enterprise Ireland to deliver the programme.

Policy-led segmentation works in a similar way, as IPAs follow political mandates and select companies based on their potential to meet them. Some of these policies include supporting knowledge transfer from foreign companies to organisations in the local Ecosystem, working with companies that foster local supply chains and supporting foreign investors with the potential to export.

9.2.3.6 Diasporas

According to Inter American Bank's 2012 Policy Briefing, The Diaspora Direct Investment Policy Options for Development, "about 215 million people live away from their home country and many members of such diasporas are prospering abroad and are eager to extend such success by investing in their homeland."[46] These "transnational populations, living in one place – often permanently, while still maintaining relations with their homelands, and being both 'here' and 'there',"[47] represent a significant opportunity for a location as they can "leverage their networks and" help decision makers "to contextualise local information faster than their competitors."[48]

Diasporas influence FDI in different ways: first they invest directly in their homelands, usually called diaspora direct investment (DDI); second, they drive receiving investment from their homeland to their host country; and third, they influence FDI decision making.

9.2.3.6.1 DIASPORA DIRECT INVESTMENT (DDI)

The Indian diaspora is estimated to have invested US$2.6 billion, out of a total of US$10 billion of FDI, in India between 1991 and 2001.[49] In 2020 there are approximately 35 million Indians either living abroad or of Indian origin. In 2018 they collectively sent US$80 billion of remittances back to India.[50] Remittances "aid in socio-economic development as it is used for the recipient family's personal use (accounting for 50 percent of household expenditure in rural areas), in temple building, and for donations to schools."[51] Alongside remittances, diasporas also invest in their home country, which in the case of India has largely been concentrated in land, property and securities.[52]

According to Wei Yingqi and V.N. Balasumbramanyam, academics at Lancaster University in the UK, diasporas are not only a source of funds, they are also a rich source of skills and knowhow. Diasporas act as important intermediaries linking traditional development actors and local communities. Thanks to this early access to information, diasporas are likely to be early movers, while at the same time their motives to invest "are not entirely profit-driven as many of them wish to establish a long-term base."[53] In addition, they "are also better informed of market conditions, the domestic labour and economic policies and consequently have more realistic expectations of time frames for project completions and investment returns."[54] As such, diaspora investment tends to be more stable and more resilient in times of economic uncertainty when compared to investment with no links to diasporas. Wei and Balasubramanyam argue that this edge makes a difference and "that the social rate of return to a unit of diaspora investments may be higher than that for a unit of foreign direct investment from non-diaspora sources."[55]

Diasporas are an important group of foreign investors to nurture and so it is important to understand their unique characteristics and preferences. "A boost in investments through DDI becomes an alternative for countries that are lacking sufficient investments through 'traditional' FDI. This is the case in Africa, where FDI has been steadily declining due to a combination of cultural barriers and inappropriate (government) policies."[56]

A country that has aggressively sought to increase diaspora investment is India, which has a dedicated investor help desk for Indian diaspora (see Box 9.2). In addition, India has a programme that targets young people of Indian origin. This programme seeks to make them more aware of both the history and current nature of India with the long-term goal of driving future investment (see Box 9.3)

Box 9.2 People of Indian Origin Investor Helpdesk

Invest India set up a dedicated team to handhold People of Indian Origin (PIO), easing their investment journey and ensuring a smooth process at every step. This helpdesk will allow potential PIO investors to seek assistance and raise issues at any point before, during or post the investment.

Source: https://www.investindia.gov.in/pio-investor-helpdesk.

Box 9.3 Know India Programme

Know India Programme (KIP) is a flagship initiative for diaspora engagement that familiarises Indian-origin youth with their Indian roots and contemporary India, through an orientation programme. This programme aims at providing young PIOs with an exposure to India's progress in areas including infrastructure, technology and innovation.

Source: https://kip.gov.in/

9.2.3.6.2 DRIVING INVESTMENT INTO LOCATIONS THAT WELCOME DIASPORA

The 2016 study by Konrad B. Burchardi, Thomas Chaney and Tarek A. Hassan of the North American National Bureau of Economic Research looked at the opposite effect – how countries who have welcomed diasporas perform as investors into the home countries of those diasporas. Using 130 years of US immigration data, the study identified that migration and FDI creates two parallel global networks, one of ethnic connections and one of parent-subsidiary linkages, and looked at how these two networks connect. The study showed "that immigration and FDI are intimately related: The ethnic diversity created by migrations reaching back more than a century has a large positive causal effect on the propensity of US firms to engage in FDI with the historical migrants' countries of origin; and this effect appears to transmit itself primarily through a reduction of information frictions. For an average US county, doubling the number of individuals with ancestry from a given origin country increases by 4 percentage points the probability that at least one firm from this US county engages in FDI with that origin country, and increases by 7% the number of local jobs at subsidiaries of firms headquartered in that origin country. These effects persist over generations."[57]

Locations that have welcomed diaspora investors and have successfully nurtured them undertake an informal, but systematic, effort to educate themselves about potential opportunities in the migrant's home country. As a result, there is an increased probability that they will invest and reinvest in the country of origin of the local diaspora. According to Burchardi et al (2016), ancestral connections result in higher FDI success rates, particularly in the long term, as a result of improved information flow. "Residents of areas that received relatively more migration from a given origin country in the past systematically acquire more information about the politics, culture, and language of that country."[58] This additional information flow, let's call it ancestry spillover, results in more FDI and relates to the longevity aspects highlighted by the 2016 Burchardi study. The impact works both ways – more migrants into the US also increases the likelihood that US companies will expand by establishing subsidiaries in these migrants' home countries. The effect, according to the authors, unfolds over many generations and gets stronger as the diversity of the local population increases, the farther the country is from the US and the higher the quality of the judicial institutions in the diaspora's home country.

While the engagement of diaspora in FDI is well developed in some countries or regions, for example from Ireland, Palestine and Africa, ancestry-related investment and former migration-related FDI still tends to be overlooked. This may represent an opportunity. Box 9.4 shows how the US city of Detroit leverages its German diaspora to attract and retain investment.

Box 9.4 German Americans in Detroit

"Maybe it's because of Michigan's two million German-Americans – the largest population of any ethnic group in the state. It could be our universities, great lakes, natural resources and international reputation for the Motown sound.

Whatever it is, Germans love doing business here! Our 350 German companies in Michigan employ some 78,000 people here – more than those from any other nation. Michigan leads in German capital stock investment among all states and import-export data places Germany as the state's top European trading partner.

The shared values and deep roots make Michigan a second home to Germans and the most logical place for Germans to invest and reinvest."

Reproduced with kind permission from Detroit Chamber: www.detroitchamber.com.

Locations that have welcomed diasporas enjoy economic benefits such as new talent and increased global connectedness. Moreover, these places are more likely to receive a subsidiary from a company headquartered in the homeland of the migrants, even if the migrants are not involved. Furthermore, this investment tends to be more stable than an investment in another region. And there is also strong evidence that the investment effects of migration, diaspora and ancestry are long-term in nature. As such, while efforts to generate economic benefit from these networks and connections is long-term in nature, the opportunities should not be overlooked.

9.2.3.6.3 INFLUENCE OVER FDI DECISION MAKING

Diaspora can also influence FDI decision making. For example, a Japanese executive working in Frankfurt for a German headquartered company is well placed to persuade their German bosses to further invest in its Japanese subsidiary due to their direct links and networks in Japan and their greater ability to contextualise information. This type of connection increases the likelihood that the company will expand its Japanese subsidiary.

Diaspora influence over FDI decision making is a strategy that Ireland has excelled at. They set up a dedicated organisation, Connect Ireland, to engage with the Irish diaspora as a means to secure investment and expansions. So far, they have participated in projects with 94 international companies that resulted in the creation of 2,822 new jobs in Ireland, and also the building of a network of 90,000 Irish connectors in 147 countries.[59]

9.2.3.7 Negative segmentation

In addition to the 6 types of segmentation mentioned above, there are some segments, reflecting local government policy or guidance, that IPAs do not serve. These are:

- **Blacklisted sectors**: the growing importance of governance has led a number of IPAs to negatively segment, or blacklist, certain industries. Typical industries to be blacklisted include gaming, pornography and tobacco. Deciding to blacklist certain industries has pros, such as introducing transparency to all government agencies to stay away from an industry, and cons, such as overlooking geographic-specific contexts, which, when analysed in detail, might result in a different outcome. The pros and cons of blacklisting a sector should be carefully considered prior to making a decision.

- **Discarded sectors**: segmentation is all about selecting what services to offer and to whom, and hence implicitly what services are not offered. With increased scrutiny on providing the highest return on investment, and also on good governance, some IPAs are now clearly stating on their websites the industry segments they don't support. For example, the Australian Trade and Investment Commission, Austrade, states, "Please note we do not assist with real estate and portfolio investments, sales or representation offices, straight acquisitions, hostile takeovers or investments by individuals."[60] The 2020 World Bank/WAIPA joint study listed a number of sectors that a proportion of their members don't serve. These include the real estate sector, which 15% of surveyed IPAs don't serve, media and entertainment (9%), construction (8%), wholesale and retail trade (8%) and financial services (8%). In the authors' experience, the reasons IPAs choose not to serve certain sectors include: public sector guidelines that restrict IPAs from getting involved, for example mergers and acquisitions that are simply seen as a flow of capital; sectors such as online services that are unlikely to pay significant tax locally; companies where it is difficult to identify the exact nature of their business, such as online services listed as entertainment but are actually focussed on gambling; or construction jobs that are temporary in nature and hence do not meet FDI reporting criteria and so do not count towards targets.

As discussed, IPAs have many different options when it comes to segmentation. Indeed, they often take a blended approach to segmentation that takes account of a number of different objectives including political, strategic, geographical and sector. As we enter the era of big data, and also of open data, a number of IPAs are using advanced modelling techniques to identify and then select companies who might benefit from their services by looking for trends in investor behaviour, company movements, etc. Some of the factors IPAs are tracking include the size of both the HQ and the local affiliate measured by turnover, jobs, capitalisation, funds raised and financial backers, other locations where the company is present, rate of recruitment including vacancies advertised, awards and accolades won, public appearances of the leadership team, etc. For example, Invest in Spain dedicates additional resources to the highest scoring projects (i.e. most attractive projects) and assigns specific levels of additional service to particularly important target companies. Some IPAs go even further and only work on projects with a potential investment above a certain threshold, for example Invest in Holland sets this figure at a minimum of US$5 million.

The OECD notes that all their member agencies prioritise certain sectors and countries, two thirds prioritise specific investment projects and over one third specific investors. They offer a categorisation:

- Basic prioritisers: that only prioritise certain sectors or countries.
- Project-centred prioritisers: prioritise specific investment projects.
- Investor-centred prioritisers: who specialise in specific companies.
- Super-prioritisers: prioritise sectors and countries, projects and investors.

The OECD adds that "over three quarters of OECD IPAs take a project-centric view on prioritisation, on top of the priority sectors and countries, focusing on specific investment projects identified as 'priority' projects; often also referred to as 'high-quality' or 'strategic' investment projects."[61] The reasons listed for choosing one project over another include a "[s]trong domestic capacity (64%), a strong competitive position vis-à-vis other countries (58%) and the potential to diversify the economy (58%) are the most frequently cited reasons for prioritising certain sectors."[62] Other reasons include access to high-technology and strong economic or political ties. In addition, almost 70% of IPAs "have preestablished criteria that a project needs to satisfy to qualify, particularly the impact on innovation (83%), priority sector (83%), job creation (79%) and the size of the investment (75%). IPAs that prioritise projects or investors have on average higher budgets than those that do not."[63]

9.2.4 Building block 4: define your value proposition

On Aftercare courses delivered by the lead author, one of the most frequently asked questions by client-facing FDI professionals is: "How to be relevant to established foreign investors who don't really need us?" The answer is by offering a compelling value proposition. Foreign investors do not really respond to the *selling* of post-investment services, they are

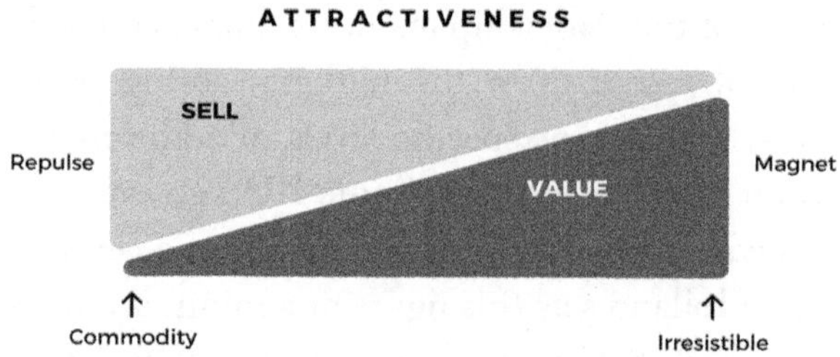

Figure 9.10 From commodity to irresistible.

Source: The Trusted Advisory Project https://thetrustedadvisorproject.com/programs/. Reproduced with kind permission from Roger Jones.

attracted by the *value* these services will bring to them. Roger E. Jones, CEO of the Trusted Advisor Project, describes the journey organisations need to make to better attract clients as one of "from commodity to irresistible", as shown in Figure 9.10.[64] The model proposes that people don't want to be sold commodity products, which repel many people; people want to see value that is irresistible, that they are attracted to and that pulls them in as if by a magnet.

9.2.4.1 What is a value proposition in Investor Services?

According to Michael Skok, Entrepreneur in Residence at Harvard Business School, a value proposition is a "*positioning statement that explains what benefit you provide for who and how you do it uniquely well.*"[65] The statement will usually include "the target client, the problem you solve, and why you're distinctly better than the alternatives. [It] is easy to dive headlong into the solution before really understanding the problem they're looking to solve."[66] Skok goes on to stress the importance of identifying a problem that requires an intervention. As discussed earlier, the provision of Aftercare services is also subject to a "is-there-a-need-for-intervention" debate, which makes Skok's model particularly relevant for Aftercare Investor Services. The model suggests asking 4 questions:

- Is the problem **Unworkable**? Does the Investor Services programme fix a specific problem where there are real and measurable consequences to inaction?
- Is fixing the problem **Unavoidable**? Is it driven by a mandate with implications associated with governance or regulatory control?

- Is the problem **Urgent?** Is it one of the top priorities for a company?
- Is the problem **Underserved**? Is there a conspicuous absence of valid solutions to the problem the IPA is looking to solve?

When the answer to all 4 of these questions is *yes*, there is a greater likelihood that an offer can be developed that will appeal to clients and so become, in Roger E. Jones's words, *irresistible*. There is no magic formula. Every location needs to identify its own value proposition. It should not only consider what the private sector is looking for, it should also encapsulate the vision and ambitions of the public sector, as well taking an honest look at the strengths and assets of the host economy.

The first step in developing a value proposition is to understand foreign investors' requirements. The FDI Market's 2018 FDI Reinvestment Ranking[67] provides key insights into the reasons foreign investors return to the same location and invest additional resources in markets in which they are already well-established. It found that 25% of investors cited a location's growth potential as the key driver behind their decision making, closely followed by the availability of a skilled local talent pool and proximity to new clients.

The Brookings Institute's 2015 report on lessons from global trade and investment noted that foreign investors expect a high level of service and responsiveness from potential host locations, commenting that "practitioners must be prepared to respond to needs more like businesspeople and not bureaucrats."[68] In other words, when a foreign investor is considering a follow-on investment they are always asking "what can the location do for me?" If an IPA is not ready, willing or able to answer this question in a manner that addresses the investor's needs, there is an increased risk of the IPA being ignored by the investor.

A value proposition should also take account of two other factors: the needs of the public sector and the characteristics of the host economy (i.e. the local opportunity), as shown in Figure 9.11.

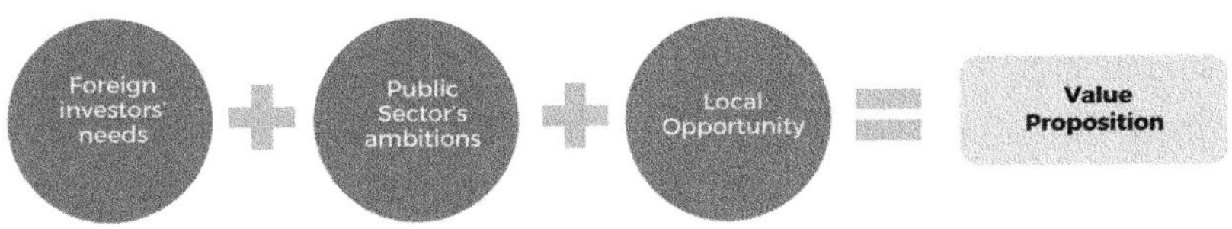

Figure 9.11 Elements of an Aftercare value proposition. © *Investment Aftercare Explained: A Guide for FDI Practitioners and Policymakers on How to Grow and Retain Investors.*

Regarding the needs of the public sector, value propositions tend to be aligned with the future vision and priorities of the government, and so will include proposals to address those areas of focus. For example, public sector priorities often include a focus on the development of infrastructure, the regeneration of deprived neighbourhoods and the development of brownfield sites. These priorities will result in a portfolio of investment propositions IPAs can take to market.

The third element of the value proposition is to understand the local market. In 2015, the Brookings Institute reported that to deliver a successful Aftercare programme, practitioners "must know their local economies, industry clusters, and available services better than anyone else, and add value by translating it for their investors."[69] That is to say, the key to developing good Investor Services is identifying local opportunities and understanding the sector opportunities an investor can access and benefit from. One way of doing this is to develop (and maintain) knowledge of key clusters in a location as a means of piquing an investor's interest. Foreign investors value and expect the IPA to have detailed knowledge of the local landscape and access to influential connections. Meanwhile, local governments value in-depth knowledge of the private sector's views and opinions as it helps guide policymaking.

In summary, an Investor Service value proposition is the unique offer that blends private sector need with public sector ambition and local opportunity. It is a platform through which to better embed the investor in the local economy.

9.2.4.2 Frameworks for developing a value proposition

Developing a solid value proposition is both a science and an art. It entails assessing what a host economy has to offer, and then bringing a few highly curated products and services to the investor. There are at least two frameworks that can help IPAs structure their value proposition: the SEE formula and the CREED formula.

9.2.4.2.1 THE SEE FORMULA

If growth potential is the key to reinvestment, then helping to facilitate that growth is the most effective way to encourage reinvestment. One methodology, developed by the lead author in her consultancy work, is to focus on Supporting, Equipping and Empowering (SEE) foreign investors to tap into the growth opportunities a location can offer. It usually centres on one specific project, for example an expansion. From that perspective, the SEE approach is particularly suitable for IPAs with few resources or who have only just started providing Aftercare services. The SEE approach helps a host location structure its services in a way that is attractive to the investor, therefore increasing the chances that the investor will take advantage of any local opportunity, and also that they will make use of the IPA's services.

Copenhagen Capacity's Aftercare catalogue uses the SEE methodology to support investors.

Support: the objective is to provide incremental support to the foreign investor in order to develop a relationship with them, and thereby earn their trust. This support will typically be for specific business needs that are common among investors or that support a particular sector the IPA wants to help grow. For example, Copenhagen Capacity asks its clients, "Are you seeking improvements in your logistics processes and sustainable supply chain activities so as to create growth, become more competitive and build a profitable supply chain?"[70] The support step starts from the assumption that the foreign investor already knows what it wants to achieve, and that the role of Copenhagen Capacity and Invest in Denmark is to help them realise their goals.

Equip: in this step, the IPA supports the investor's decision making process by providing information and services that complement the investor's inhouse team so that when the time comes, they can execute faster, bigger and better. This step will usually consider strategic needs, look into value chains and also at sustainability. Copenhagen Capacity provides services to equip a company when it is developing the case for investing in Denmark, pointing out that "[w]e can provide data for you to objectively compare Denmark/ Copenhagen with up to 300 global locations in parameters including salary and office rents, as well as qualitative factors. We can identify technological know-how, research and scientific output in Denmark to support your R&D project."[71] This may be supported with a report that highlights Denmark's relative cost competitiveness and, if appropriate, may also suggest regional consolidation as an option. Copenhagen Capacity describes a picture of their ideal target: "Your Scandinavian operations have grown to a size at which consolidation of your management team or business functions i.e. finance, HR, IT or customer support can benefit from centralising your activities to support your overall Scandinavian or international business strategy."[72] They go on to say that "establishing a shared services centre in Denmark will bring you highly skilled employees, the largest pool of Scandinavian language speakers, the most flexible working hours and an unsurpassed labour market flexibility which allows your company to scale up and down to meet the actual needs."[73] Copenhagen Capacity goes on to describe how they can help the investor take each of these steps.

Empower: finally, Copenhagen Capacity empowers a company to perform the due diligence it needs to do prior to taking the decision as to whether or not to reinvest. They want to make their client feel ambitious and confident about their expansion in Copenhagen. Indeed, they go one step further: "Take the initiative – a smart move. Regionalisation strategies typically originate from company headquarters. If the issue of regionalisation has not yet arisen, you can be reasonably sure that it will at some point. Seizing the initiative and bringing the idea of regionalisation to the table – before your HQ does – is a smart management move."[74] They continue by outlining how they can help the manager of the local subsidiary make a case: "We can help you with the initiation of a business meeting at your company headquarters to discuss key investment issues concerning your Danish operation and the advantages of Denmark, with the participation of government officials and other political stakeholders."[75]

The SEE approach can also be used as a template for the day-to-day engagements of an IPA. For example, a client-facing executive can prepare for a client meeting by listing ways in which the IPA can support, equip or empower the investor. This is of particular importance when it comes to establishing common ground from which to co-create new ways of jointly developing new value and when creating programmes that champion the location.

9.2.4.2.2 THE CREED FORMULA

UNESCAP[76] cites a different approach to structuring a value proposition: Consolidate, Retain, Embed, Expand and Diversify (CREED[77]). In contrast to the SEE formula, which focuses on what an IPA can do for an investor, CREED proposes 5 actions an IPA can take to increase its own effectiveness:

Consolidate: as discussed earlier, investors tend to be over-optimistic when it comes to estimating the number of jobs they are going to create with an investment. Quite often, a proportion of planned jobs do not materialise, sometimes referred to as projects with a low implementation rate. The implementation rate is the pace at which a foreign investor realises its initial vision for a location or a project. When an IPA focuses on consolidating projects, it works with a foreign investor to reduce over-optimism and improve the job implementation rate. Focussing on the job implementation rate is particularly important when incentives and grants are linked to the number of jobs created, and vice-versa.

Retain: a focus on retention usually occurs during periods of uncertainty or change. In the run up to the Catalan election in autumn 2017, several multinationals and Spanish companies headquartered in Catalonia assessed the risk of the region declaring independence from the rest of Spain and the consequences this would have for their businesses. According to the *Financial Times*, "the rush of companies either moving or threatening to move their legal headquarters out of Catalonia started with the region's two largest banks, Sabadell and CaixaBank. Following the banks, six out of seven companies of Spain's Ibex 35 stock market index companies based in the region said they are transferring their headquarters due to the secessionist challenge, including construction company Abertis."[78] Roughly 20 other large and medium-sized companies made the same decision. Such an exodus is a serious threat to an economy and requires the local IPA to rapidly focus on reassuring and retaining businesses to minimise the risk that investors downsize or close their local operations.

Embed: embedding actions, by integrating a company more deeply into the local (business) Ecosystem, have the objective of making it more difficult for an investor to leave a location, while also delivering benefits to both the company and the location. This has been the case in Vietnam where, according to data from the Vietnamese Foreign Investment Agency (FIA), foreign investment in the processing and manufacturing industries accounts for 45%of total investment flows into Vietnam. However, "the role of local Vietnamese enterprises remains limited to the low-added-value segment of the [international] global supply chain"[79] of that industry. As a result, FIA developed services to strengthen links with multinationals such as Samsung to help them find local partners for their supply chain. The agency goes on to say that "FDI businesses need to strengthen co-operation and connect with Vietnamese ones, support them to improve corporate governance and transfer technology."[80] In 2016, Samsung invited 200 Vietnamese businesses to a Global Supply

Chain Expo and held talks with roughly 70 local companies wishing to join Samsung's supply chain. They also facilitated a partnership between Samsung and Ho Chi Minh City's Department of Industry and Trade to find ways to enhance competitiveness in the field of parts production for Vietnam's hi-tech industry.

Expand: here the focus is to work with an investor to identify opportunities to grow a company's operations in a location. Sometimes this work also includes helping the investor find the funds to deliver such an expansion. This can include applying for incentives or encouraging the investor to apply to relevant business support programmes.

Diversify: identify and support opportunities for existing investors to diversify their businesses locally by moving into other business sectors. IPAs offering diversification support are likely to already have sophisticated account programmes in place. They are also well-positioned to broker opportunities for diversification due to the skills, networks and sector knowledge they already have. An example of diversification comes from Nigeria where the Singapore headquartered Tolaram Group first established operations in 1977. Over the years their operations expanded into manufacturing, power generation, road transportation and distribution. Tolaram's latest business expansion is a public-private partnership with the local government to promote the Lagos Free Trade Zone. During all this time, Tolaram Nigeria has stayed close to the Nigeria Investment Promotion Commission (NIPC), while the local government has brought local investment opportunities to the attention of Tolaram's parent company in Singapore.[81]

The CREED methodology can also help an IPA design Aftercare services from scratch. Its step-by-step approach helps IPAs to target companies that are likely to respond to actions in these 5 areas. It can also help Aftercare teams focus their attention on areas where they can be more effective.

9.2.4.3 Examples of value propositions

The following boxes provide some insight into the value propositions being offered by host economies. The first one comes from comes from San Diego (see Box 9.5), which places emphasis on dealing with local government and navigating local players, regulations and institutions, together with a mini case study to illustrate each service.

Box 9.5 Value proposition from San Diego Regional Economic Development Corporation

Here's how San Diego Regional EDC supports business:

Regulatory/permitting support: EDC serves as an interface between employers and municipalities or public agencies to address regulatory and permitting issues. EDC helps overcome permitting process delays and raises regulatory matters to the appropriate authority to seek quick relief. Example: TuSimple navigates autonomous vehicles regulation

Economic incentive consulting: EDC provides education, recommendations and application support for various local, state and federal programmes that incentivise business growth or retention, often creating a customised package of applicable programs. Example: General Dynamics NASSCO wins Cal Competes Tax Credit.

Expansion services/site selection: San Diego has a wide selection of building and land inventory to accommodate a diversity of businesses. EDC works with businesses, consultants and brokers to aggregate a list of applicable sites, provide introductions to vetted service providers and/or respond to detailed requests for proposals (RFPS) for campuses or locations. Example: EDC submitted regional proposal to Amazon HQ2 Project.

Marketing/visibility: EDC supports expanding innovation economy and client companies by promoting company growth stories to elected officials, media and key business contacts, both locally and nationally. Example: Makers Quarter Development in two *New York Times* articles.

Intelligence/research*: companies and public agencies rely on economic research to drive decision making. EDC's research bureau produces independent, economic analyses for municipalities, real estate projects and companies. Examples: profiles for the City of Vista and San Marcos.

International Support: in addition to EDC's business assistance services, World Trade Centre San Diego (WTC), an affiliate of San Diego Regional EDC, works directly with San Diego businesses to support internationalisation efforts, and advises foreign-owned business entering the San Diego market.

Export logistics consulting: before a product leaves US soil, companies must consider numerous regulatory and logistical factors. WTC works with vetted logistics providers to get San Diego products overseas and aligns closely with the US Department of Commerce to advise companies on market compliance and regulations. Example: VAVi logistical support to Australia.

Inbound investment support: WTC supports foreign businesses looking to invest in vetted San Diego businesses and projects. WTC also provides Aftercare support to international companies that acquire San Diego businesses. Example: Chinese investment in Gafcon project.

Market strategy: companies must be strategic about global expansion. WTC works one-on-one with San Diego businesses looking to enter foreign markets by advising on market selection and providing vetted introductions to drive international sales. Examples: Deering Banjo goes to India (via MetroConnect program).

Reproduced with kind permission form San Diego Regional Economic Development Corporation: www.sandiegobusiness.org.

PRONicaragua explains why they offer services to existing investors, as well as the responsibilities of the Aftercare department. Interestingly they split their offer between services and benefits (see Box 9.6).

Box 9.6 Value proposition from PRONicaragua

With the belief that a satisfied investor is the best country promoter, the department's main objective is to facilitate the development of companies already established locally by guaranteeing that their operations run smoothly, supporting the full implementation of their investment plans and promoting reinvestment. Additionally, it encourages the establishment of strategic alliances between companies to boost Nicaragua's economic growth.

The Aftercare department is responsible for channelling investors' concerns to the appropriate institutions of the central and municipal government through a close relationship, and by providing support to these institutions.

Services:

- Support in carrying out and speeding up government procedures.
- Identification of the ideal real estate option for the investment project.
- Identification of potential local partners to create productive chains and joint ventures.
- Assistance in solving inconveniences related to the operation of the company.
- Assistance to investors and their families in the process of establishing in the country.
- Support in the planning, development and start-up stages of reinvestment projects.
- Facilitate communication between the Government of Nicaragua and the investor, through the Government – Investor Network (GIN).

Benefits:

- Facilitation in the formulation and evaluation processes of investment projects.
- Facilitation in the process of cultural adaptation of foreign investors and their families in Nicaragua.
- Be part of a network of contacts of public and private institutions.
- Improvement of the country's investment climate.

Reproduced with kind permission from PRONicaragua: www.pronicaragua.gob.ni.

The next example comes from Tshwane Metropolitan Municipality in the province of Gauteng in South Africa, which also outlines Covid-19 specific services (see Box 9.7).

Box 9.7 Aftercare service offer from Tshwane, South Africa

The key objective of the investor Aftercare programme is to retain and expand existing businesses in order to generate and revitalise the city's economy, proliferate employment opportunities, stimulate re-investment and ensure the highest levels of investor satisfaction.

The following services are provided:

- Executive company visitation programme aimed at maintaining and enhancing relationships with existing investors.
- Providing information on issues such as the investment environment, business establishment, the taxation regime, investment regulations, skills availability and immigration.
- Providing introductions to key stakeholders and role-players.
- Facilitating and hosting inbound and outbound investment missions.
- Providing information on financing options and investment incentives.
- Assisting investors to access local supply chains.
- Providing assistance in obtaining and facilitating access to suitable land, factory space, etc.
- Assisting existing firms to expand and re-invest.
- Providing advice and facilitate all aspects of export development and promotion.

Socio-economic stimulus package towards economic recovery in the aftermath of the Covid-19 pandemic

- **Facilitate access to existing Covid-19 support**: facilitate access for qualifying businesses to National Covid-19 Relief Funding Programme.
- **Financial relief**: payment holiday for small business on property rates and taxes. Establishment of Township Enterprise Development Fund (TEDF).

- **Enterprise development and support for small business**: offer preferential procurement opportunities to vulnerable businesses. Bias towards procuring locally made goods.
- **Job creation**: facilitate creation of jobs through implementation of capital projects. Partner with companies and institutions to quickly identify and fill employment opportunities.
- **Investment Aftercare**: honour infrastructure and service delivery pacts with investors in key industrial nodes. Fast-track approval processes for strategic investment projects. Automation of all permitting processes. Implement an "Ease of Doing Business" programme.

Reproduced with kind permission from the City of Tshwane, South Africa: www.tshwane.gov.za.

The final example of value proposition comes from the region of Lombardy in Italy (see Box 9.8). Promos Italia brings a wide-ranging offer "from analysis to strategic stakeholder's connections, from company awareness on the field to business networking, from management training to new partnership development."

Box 9.8 Value proposition Invest in Lombardy

"Invest in Lombardy takes care of your existing operations and business expansion on the territory. Our team of experts is at your complete disposal to support and enhance your presence in Lombardy/Italy: from analysis to strategic stakeholder's connections, from company awareness on the field to business networking, from management training to new partnership development.

1. Follow-up analysis: sector/market, competitors: We provide useful information on your sector/market and help you evaluating the opportunities for your business to grow. Ambitious companies need to continuously improve the knowledge of the local business environment by a stable network of contacts

and collaborations on the field. We can help you dealing with information and data research for sector/market analysis, competitors/partners, new business opportunities for your company.

2. Relationship with the territory: Feel like at home: we facilitate and foster the connections with private and public stakeholders on the field. Invest in Lombardy can share with you the valuable extensive knowledge of the territory by providing you with direct links and facilitations to national, regional and municipal governments, international foreign offices representatives, chambers of commerce, associations, universities and local authorities in general.
3. Moving and relocating: Thinking of moving from your old offices, looking for more suitable space and new opportunities for your daily operations: we can support you exploring new and existing locations. Invest in Lombardy, thanks to its private network of professionals and its close interactions with the municipalities, we can help you with:
   - Definition and presentation of the features of the 'territorial offer' of the Region
   - Research and selection of suitable locations for your business (offices, temporary offices/shops, industrial properties and more)
   - Managing of the contacts with municipalities, real estate agencies, business centers, incubators, science and technological parks and other players on the field
   - Support in the overall building maintenance and renovation processes
4. Business Networking & Dedicated activities: Are you looking for a dedicated prestigious location for your company's promotional events and presentations? Want to be involved in useful business networking activities? Invest in Lombardy offers a various remarkable choice of historical venues in the heart of Milan business and cultural district for both existing events

and customised opportunities of promotion and networking for your company.

5. Marketing and communication solutions: How do you promote your business in Lombardy and Italy? How do you reach the right business targets? Invest in Lombardy can help you to assess your existing approach to the market and stakeholders together with PR-marketing specialists. Make your marketing mix suitable for the challenges of the competition in a very dynamic business environment.
6. Education, training and living in Lombardy: Improve your company's skills, knowledge of the market and your employee's toolbox for working and living in Lombardy/Italy. Invest in Lombardy can provide a customised offer of courses for foreign companies and managers with a high-level education package, covering all the subjects of doing business and investments in Italy. In particular, through NIBI (the New International Business Institute) we offer a wide range of subjects and the support of a network of outstanding experts selected among University professors, consultants and professionals within the business community. For more information: www.nibi-milano.it.
7. Partner research and customers scouting: Strengthen the business network in Lombardy and Italy through our support in the selection of suitable partners and customers in your sector. Invest in Lombardy can accompany you in your partners research, helping you foster your relationships with the Italian business counterparts. In particular, through the dedicated promotional departments of Promos Italia, we are able to evaluate and propose a customised service of partners and customers scouting."

Reproduced with kind permission from Promos Italia: www.promositalia.camcom.it.

Links: www.investinlombardy.it, and www.yesmilano.it.

9.2.5 Building block 5: choose your delivery model

Once the IPA has defined its segment and value proposition, the next step is to take that offer to market. In 1994, academics from Strathclyde University, Stephen Young and Neil Hood, identified 4 different service models for doing this: company-friendly, project-based, team-based and integrated.[82]

The **company-friendly model** is used most frequently during the initial investment period, with existing investors receiving informational and some limited operational support. For example, an investor may ask for an introduction to a law firm specialising in employment law. This level of assistance is normally sufficient for a new investor but is likely to have little impact when working with established investors. It is also referred to as the "minimalist investor service model."

The **project-based model** takes a more targeted approach, assigning resources to critical or predetermined components of an Investor Services program. Activities could include office relocation support, help developing a supplier base and assistance in attracting talent. This type of activity is usually reactive, providing a solution to a specific problem.

The **team-based model** approach establishes a dedicated team to support a company post-investment. In essence, once established, an investor migrates from the new investment team to a specialised Aftercare team. This model has pros and cons. By separating the new investment team from the Aftercare team there is a risk that some of the relationships developed with a client by the new investment team are lost when the client is "handed over" to the Aftercare team. However, separating the teams will result in the Aftercare team becoming more specialised in helping investors grow, better at convening stakeholders to provide post-investment support and, as a result, delivering a higher quality service to investors.

The **integrated model** is by far the most ambitious and expensive approach as it views Investor Services as a critical component of a well-developed economic development strategy. This model is most effective in more complex business and economic landscapes that require well-defined and well-resourced service provision, and it is also closely aligned with local and/or national government priorities. Young and Hood also point out that "[t]his model also recognises the need to include indigenous companies"[83] as they also add value to the foreign investors. Box 9.9 briefly summarises the UK's approach.

Box 9.9 The UK's integrated model: Global Accounts

The UK Department for International Trade operates an advanced, integrated model, "Global Accounts", which targets significant foreign businesses with operations across the UK who have invested heavily and created thousands of jobs. A cross-ministerial team works closely with senior company executives to support their interactions with all relevant government departments, offering a full-service support package. Each minister/Secretary of State manages a small portfolio of major foreign companies, oversees Investor Services and has regular engagements with the investor's businesses, both in the UK and in the investor's home market.

Source: Insight gathered by this book's research team: Interviews 2017.

Link: https://www.gov.uk/government/organisations/department-for-international-trade.

9.2.5.1 Partners on the journey

In parallel to the work of FDI, there is a significant amount of work done at a local level to drive economic development. In the United States it is called Business Retention and Expansion (BRE) and in Europe it falls under the economic development banner. A formal BRE-style program is a structured effort involving a broad cross-section of community interests engaged in an ongoing dialogue with the business community with the goal of helping existing businesses remain profitable, competitive and efficient.[84] The focus here is on coordinating local efforts in their engagement with companies. BRE programs are not concerned about the nationality of the business but with the fact that there is a company active locally, and, as a result, they also serve foreign investors, so there can be a significant overlap with Aftercare teams.

Academics highlight that BRE is an asset-based approach,[85] that is to say, focussed on building on what the location already has. While some Aftercare professionals find themselves constrained by a lack of resources, BRE practitioners work with what is locally available. This small but profound difference empowers BRE professionals. They take a practical approach and look to systematically strengthen the connection between businesses and the community while also encouraging each business to continue operations and expand in the community.[86] Moreover, BRE professionals state that BRE helps them to focus "on the community's existing businesses instead of those it doesn't have."[87] In an interview, Michael Darger, an academic from the University of Minnesota and author of *Business Retention and Expansion (BRE), A Practical Approach to Economic Development*, highlighted that BRE has developed a range of methodologies that broadly correspond to the following principles:

- **Intentional**: BRE favours a proactive approach to growth.
- **Client-first**: BRE seeks to respond to client needs and has developed a series of protocols to achieve them, including visit programmes in collaboration with other stakeholders or volunteers.
- **Data driven**: BRE is based on data gathered locally with a particular emphasis on surveys incorporating recent public data. They have developed best practices on how to get data, process data and act on data. Data becomes the guide to deciding where to focus effort.
- **Solution based**: BRE services offer practical help to access public resources, navigate the local business community, write applications and connect with suppliers.
- **Community oriented**: BRE professionals focus on developing relationships within the community, which allows them to help businesses to grow.

BRE puts an emphasis on engaging with companies; they utilise diverse ways of reaching out and responding to existing businesses. These include many of the approaches that traditional Aftercare uses, such as tapping into business clusters, supporting entrepreneurship, linkages and sustainability. Talent and workforce development are also a high priority, to which BRE adds practical aspects such as housing. One specific area of BRE that is growing in importance is business succession, referred to as the strategic transferring of ownership that ensures business continuity after a company's most important people move on to new opportunities, retire or pass away.[88] Services around business succession are linked to opportunities for mergers and acquisitions and therefore the arrival of foreign investors.

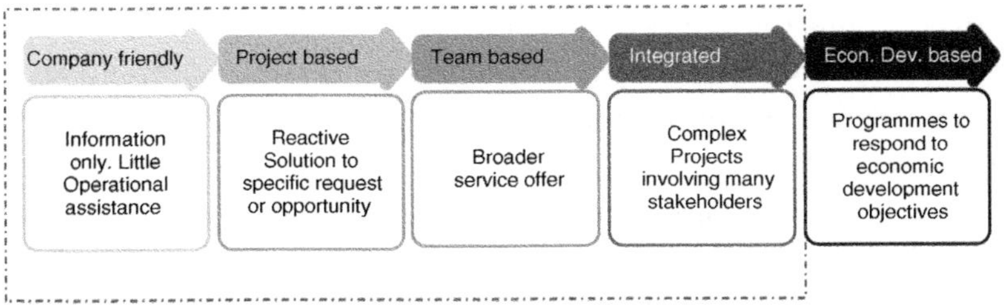

Figure 9.12 Type of service models.

Source: Author's own design adapted from: Young, S. and Hood, N. 1994. "Designing developmental aftercare programmes for foreign direct investors in the European Union". *Transnational Corporations*, 3(2), pp. 45–72.

BRE and Aftercare share the same objectives and have many similarities in the way value is created. Unsurprisingly, Aftercare and BRE teams have a lot of common skills. Nevertheless, they could also learn from each other, and it is good to see that in many locations collaboration between these two groups is increasing.

Figure 9.12 summarises the 5 different types of service models for engaging with companies. They all have their pros and cons and IPAs need to decide which model best fits their specific context.

9.2.5.2 How clients buy

Irrespective of the type of service model that an IPA chooses to use, delivering the service is what matters, what salespeople call "the moment of truth." Every Aftercare situation is different, and the range of support services that investors may require is broad. Nonetheless, there are three key steps that are common to the delivery of the majority of services:

- Winning the investor's trust (or building on any existing relationship);
- Maintaining a consistent dialogue with the investor; and
- Identifying opportunities to help the investor.

Winning an investor's trust: trust is growing in importance in business management books. Indeed, in a competitive marketplace, it is not enough to focus on "technical mastery of a discipline, but rather, the key to professional success in the service industry is the ability to earn the trust and confidence of clients."[89] IPAs know this all too well and that in their work with the investor and the Ecosystem, collaboration is the foundation for services and value-creation. Because "work gets done with and through people. There's nothing more impactful on people, their work, and their performance, than trust. Trust is the glue."[90]

Foreign investors typically come in two forms: those who prefer to work with an IPA from the outset, and who consequently reach out to IPAs at the start of their growth journey, and those investors who seek to establish themselves independently, perhaps with the help of an expansion consultant. The first group generally presents few challenges for an Aftercare team. The second group can be more challenging to engage with. There may be many reasons for this. Investors might want to keep their growth plans confidential; they might be unaware of how an IPA can add value, and therefore choose to work alone; or they work with consultants who prefer not to collaborate with IPAs (often in order to demonstrate their impartiality). Navigating these dynamics can sometimes be challenging, and so IPAs should seek creative and diplomatic ways to engage with both investors and advisers. For example, Invest Buenos Aires tries to engage potential clients through an invitation to a "Request for an Investor Workshop." They encourage investors to "be part of a tailored-made session with our team of experts and local partners to learn everything you need to know to [grow] your business in BA."[91] Other IPAs prepare introduction letters from the local authority, a state minister or even the CEO of the parent company should they visit the local affiliate, or by leveraging their diplomatic offices in the country of the parent.

Maintaining a dialogue: delivering Investor Services should not be a one-off exercise. It should form part of an ongoing "conversation" with an investor and its local affiliate. An IPA's focus should always be on the medium to long term, seeking opportunities for open and honest discussions with an investor in order to better understand their plans and concerns. There are many ways this can be achieved, including informal conversations around a coffee, or more formal situations, such as inviting the investor to participate in a business climate study or to participate at a ministerial roundtable. However, at any interaction the IPA should always look to bring something of interest to the investor in order to ensure on-going engagement, as regularly contacting an investor simply with the aim of staying in touch is time consuming for both sides, may frustrate both parties and also damage the IPA's reputation.

Identify opportunities to help an investor: this can take time. Both parties first need to get to know each other. Trust needs to build (on both sides, but particularly from the investor) such that all parties can identify and recognise the value each can bring to the table. Some IPAs talk about a "six-interventions rule," in that it typically requires 6 carefully designed encounters between an IPA and a foreign investor before real value can be added, and hence any strategy to engage an investor should take this into account. In early meetings it can sometimes be difficult to identify what services an investor requires. Aftercare professionals who have previously worked in the private sector are well-equipped to relate to business priorities and mentality.

Business authors Tom McMakin and Doug Fletcher, in their book *How Clients Buy*, mapped out how clients buy in the services industry and identified 7 steps when engaging with clients. Their model also applies to how foreign investors "buy" services from an IPA, irrespective of whether these services are paid for or are free of charge. The 7 steps are the prospective client:

1. Is aware of your existence;
2. Understands who you are and what you do;
3. Develops an interest in you;
4. Trusts you have their best interests at heart;
5. Respects your work;
6. Has the ability to secure resources and organisational support; and
7. Is ready for action.

IPAs can use this model to map their interactions with foreign investors and to design activities that help them progress from one step to the next. This approach also helps manage expectations when it comes to engaging the client. Some client-facing professionals mistakenly believe that offering free services should be enough to engage a foreign investor, only to see their offer of help politely turned down. Others blame the value proposition for not being strong enough, or that some investors simply don't want outside support, when in fact their lack of enthusiasm might be due to one of the 5 needs (outlined in Figure 9.13) not being met. Other reasons could be a lack of authority to engage, insufficient resources being available or that the timing is not right.

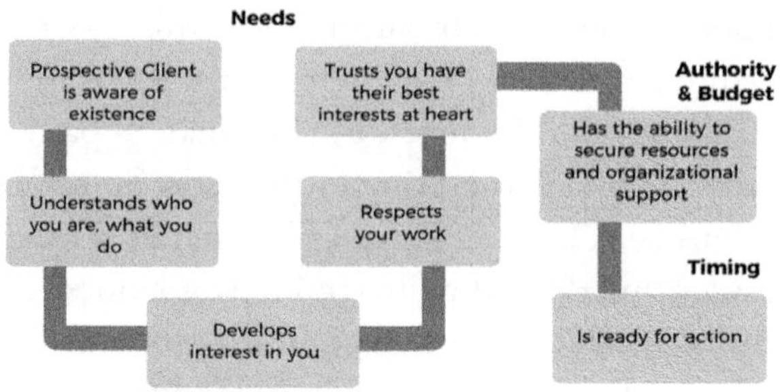

Figure 9.13 How clients buy.

Source: Author's own design adapted from McMakin, T. and Fletcher, D. 2018. *How Clients Buy: A Practical Guide to Business Development for Consulting and Professional Services.* 1st edn. s.l: Wiley.

The combination of an adequate service model, plus a carefully designed engagement plan that addresses the 7 stages of service acquisition provides a solid platform from which to deliver services.

9.2.5.3 Stage your services

When deploying Investor Services, it is important to understand the nature of company growth, the company's decision making process and their level of confidence in the host economy. Figure 9.14, taken from the 2017 UNESCAP report, "Promotion and Facilitation of Foreign Direct Investment for Sustainable Development in Asia Pacific,"[92] charts the growth journey British Airways (BA) has taken in India. The chart shows that BA took a relatively cautious and low risk approach to expansion in India, steadily increasing the number of operations it performed, commencing with relatively simple operations, such as reservations and customer relations, and then later, as it became more established, adding increasingly more complex services, such as engineering and finance.

The incremental approach to setting up operations in a new country is often used by investors – starting small and gradually increasing their commitment as they build up more knowledge, more experience and more relationships in that country. Consequently, the approach to delivering Investor Services to these companies should also be incremental and focused on the investor's specific needs at each stage of their investment journey.

Another example of an incremental approach to entering a new country would be starting with alliances with local players, then increasing equity investments in these partnerships, potentially acquiring some of these

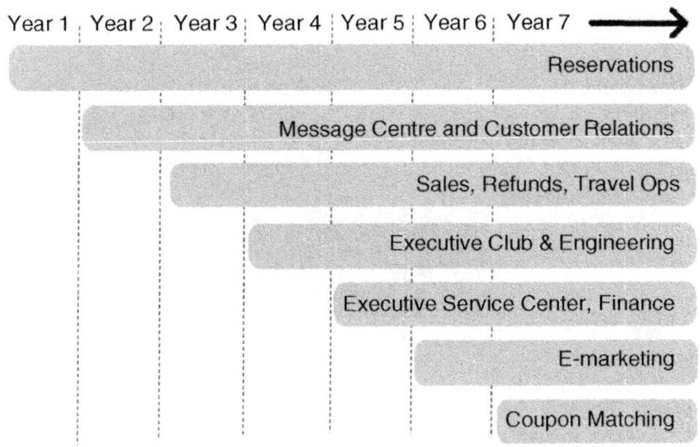

Figure 9.14 Expansion of British Airways in India.

Source: Authors' own design adapted from *Handbook on Policies, Promotion & Facilitation of Foreign Direct Investment for Sustainable Development in Asia Pacific*, United Nation ESCAP (2017).

players and ultimately, perhaps, making a greenfield investment such as building a factory.[93] Of course, a major reason that companies often take an incremental approach is in order to minimise financial risk.[94]

9.2.6 Building block 6: orchestrate your Ecosystem

It takes a village to grow a child.

(African proverb)

Chapter 7, Place and Ecosystem, provided an overview of how the local community adds value to FDI, while Chapter 4, Portfolio of Investor Services, presented several examples of services that are provided to foreign investors in collaboration with a wide network of stakeholders, partners and supporters. Indeed, the essence of Aftercare is the ability to jointly create value that helps the investor grow, as well as to generate spill-over benefits for the whole Ecosystem. In a nutshell, it takes a whole (local) business community to grow a foreign investor. There is a caveat: communities have many different agendas, respond to different logics and have a diverse range of values they offer and values they want, as can be seen in Figure 9.15. While the investor offers jobs, taxes and innovation, it wants a business-friendly environment, adequate support services and to secure growth for the local subsidiary and profit for the parent company. The FDI support Ecosystem offers its expertise in niche sectors, networks, linkages, events

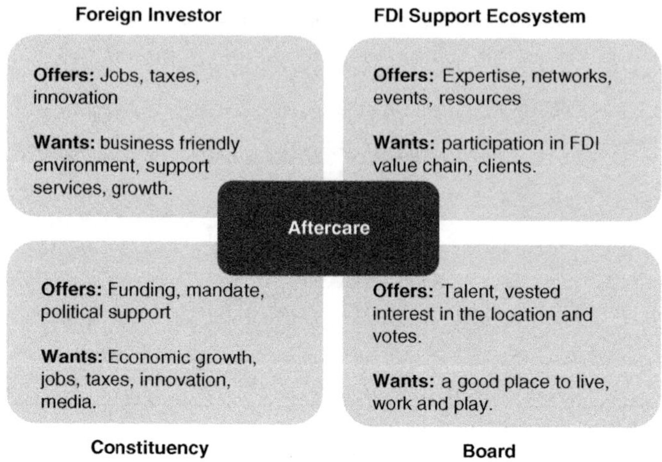

Figure 9.15 Offers and wants in Aftercare. © *Investment Aftercare Explained: A Guide for FDI Practitioners and Policymakers on How to Grow and Retain Investors.*

and resources, and in exchange wants to be included in the FDI value chain in the belief they can find clients, members and support for their activities. The IPA board, whether public or private, offers a mandate, funding and sometimes political support and leadership, and in return expects economic growth, which can be in the form of jobs, taxes, innovation and sometimes also favourable media coverage. Finally, the local population wants their community to be an attractive place to live, work and play and in return they offer their skills, a vested interest in the location and votes.

Understanding these different offers and wants is critical to the ability of an IPA to connect organisations and jointly create value that is relevant to the different players. It helps IPAs and policy makers to see the bigger picture, as well as identifying opportunities to match complementary interests with services and policies.

A key difference between Aftercare for foreign investors and customer service in other industries is the dependence on third parties for delivery. IPAs generally rely on the support, engagement and the goodwill of partners and stakeholders for delivery. Often this is done without any formal agreement, relying solely on the strong relationships the IPA has with these third parties, and the trust in them to deliver the high levels of service foreign investors expect. Aftercare professionals therefore work closely with their partners to keep abreast of market developments, share information and build strong networks. This enables them to better determine what resources are available and which organisations are best placed to deliver the support an investor requires.

However, while co-operation is crucial to efficient and effective delivery, care should also be taken to ensure that the investor does not have to manage too many relationships. From an investor perspective, what counts is the delivery of the service, not the names of the organisations that provide the services. It is not unusual to hear of investors who are surprised by the number of organisations they are expected to engage with, the amount of time this consumes and the amount of paperwork involved. It is therefore important to think about the foreign investor's experience when delivering through partners, and to minimise their bureaucratic workload as far as possible.

The 2020 World Bank/WAIPA Joint Survey on the State of Investment Promotion Agencies identified that the three most common institutional coordination mechanisms between agencies and other entities, used by over 90% of surveyed members, are regular interagency meetings, specific interagency working groups and memoranda of understanding/association. Shared online portals and service level agreements are used by almost 75% of the agencies surveyed. Some of the challenges in inter-organisational collaboration include: unresponsiveness of partners; complaints about the lack of capacity or knowledge within partners; the lack of a mandate or the power to ensure effective cooperation; the lack of designated focal points; and finally, not having established cooperation channels with relevant agencies.[95] In 2018 the OECD noted that their member IPAs interact on average with 25 different organisations and commented that "the most strategic relationships for IPAs involve their sponsor minister, the ministry of foreign affairs and diplomatic missions abroad, sub-national agencies (affiliated or not to the IPA), and local authorities."[96]

Orchestrating the local ecosystem is an ongoing process that requires planning, and therefore some IPAs hold regular meetings with key stakeholders in the local community, which ensures that there is a consistent two-way dialogue on any key issues and propositions.

9.2.7 Building block 7: equip yourself with an Aftercare toolkit

The final building block of Investor Services is the development of an Aftercare toolkit that helps practitioners bring relevant Investor Services to clients, while at the same time engaging with the ecosystem to create and/or broker value propositions that match the different offers and wants of the FDI ecosystem.

An IPA's toolkit should reflect the level of complexity of its service model and therefore be highly tailored to the local situation. Nevertheless, there are some basic components no Aftercare team should be without. Some obvious ones include:

9.2.7.1 Website and other marketing collateral

These days clients and prospective partners expect information about post-investment services and other relevant information to be online. Even more so in 2020 as the Covid-19 pandemic has accelerated the move towards the digitalisation of so many businesses. Hence, a well-designed and informative website should be a key focus as it can help an IPA capture additional economic value by enabling the reader to understand why Investor Services are relevant and how the different stakeholders can be part of value creation.

While an online presence should be the first priority of Aftercare, somewhat surprisingly, a majority of IPAs surveyed do not have an explicit Aftercare offer outlined on their websites. Some IPAs mention the word Aftercare, but do not provide details about the services offered, nor what an investor can expect. Other IPAs offer a small set of Aftercare services but do not mention them on their websites. Unsurprisingly, foreign investors like to see a clearly defined offer. Good examples include the websites for Invest in Holland, CzechInvest and Invest in Croatia. All three outline what they can do for the investor and how the investor can benefit from engaging with the IPA.

Websites can, and should, provide a wealth of information to the foreign investor. In this day and age, investors expect it. IPAs should be using their websites to showcase what they can do for investors in a way that makes investors want to engage with them. Content should include information about how the IPA adds value, incentive programmes, tax rates, recent location-relevant news, industry specific information, a map highlighting investor-relevant information, information on the particular sector capabilities of any academic or R&D focussed institutions, etc. Clearly, the information should be kept up to date – something that is not always the case. The IPA should also consider including some basic guidelines on their website or develop a specific brochure explaining how external partners can join efforts to grow and retain local investors.

Aftercare is also partly sales, and hence there is a requirement for materials to promote a location and its advantages, as well as the benefit of being part of a thriving local community and Ecosystem. These materials should be tailored to the needs and aspirations of a foreign investor, and hence should not be about *why* to grow in the location, but about *how* to grow in the location. Focussing on the *why*, rather than the *how* is a common mistake. Re-purposing collateral produced for new investors can help tell the story only if it responds to the question of *how*. Using recent case studies is a good way of doing this.

9.2.7.2 What to ask a foreign investor

As every investment is different, and some or all of the needs of the foreign investor may be unknown, identifying opportunities to help is often more art than science. Many client-facing Aftercare professionals find this part challenging. While developing a relationship with a client and winning their trust is the first step when engaging with clients, equipping teams with some general questions can help them gain an insight into an investor's thinking.

The questions below are intended to help these professionals better understand the investor's business, and also to identify areas where the IPA is able to help the company. For clarity, they have been written in direct language, but they should be rephrased according to the strength and nature of the relationship with an investor.

- How is business going? How did last year go (compared to plan)?
- Where do you see the business in 5 years' time? How does this fit into your parent company's strategy?
- What factors, if any, are inhibiting your growth here? Legal, regulatory, supply chain, other?
- How are your staff settling into the area? Are there any issues/concerns?
- How well are your local suppliers performing?
- Is your R&D programme achieving its objectives?
- Do you see your market growing or shrinking? What would explain this? How would this affect current headcount?

- How satisfied are you with this location? What would you like to see done to further improve the location from your perspective? Do you have any concerns?
- Do you know of any consolidation plans for your business?
- Is your organisation considering centralising any local activities? What are you seeking to achieve (it could be cost cutting, efficiency, etc.)?
- Have you thought about expanding your local offer to incorporate areas such as shared services and R&D?

Where appropriate, every question can be followed up by asking something along the lines of, "Is there anything we (the IPA) can do to help you achieve this goal/unblock this challenge/create more value?"

A note should be made on the use of language. No foreign investor calls their activities FDI, or considers themselves to be foreign investors – they use language such as "expanding into new markets," "chasing resources" or "local talent." Words that are meaningful to them. The advice is not using FDI jargon with foreign investors, as it risks undermining the perceived value of the IPA by making it appear more government-centric rather than focussed on the needs and wants of the foreign investor.

9.2.7.3 CRM systems and client meetings

Customer relationship management (CRM) systems help monitor, centralise and track the many interactions with clients, stakeholders and intermediaries. Almost half of IPAs use custom-made software, while 43% percent use off-the-shelf software.[97] There are many commercial software suppliers that provide FDI-specific solutions such as Geovadis, Wavteq, Enovado and ExecutivePulse, in addition to the wide range of commercial sales software that can be used to manage opportunity pipelines such as Salesforce and Zoho CRM.

The World Bank/WAIPA study also noted that IPAs need "at least the following three internal systems to provide [a] good service to investors and to manage relationships with them: (a) standard operating procedures (SOPs); (b) an investor information system (IIS), and (c) an investor relationship management system (IRMS) built on customer relationship management (CRM) software."[98] In the experience of the authors, there is also a fourth system that is needed – a digital project management tool. While IIS and IRMS provide tools to support client-facing activities, there is a need for back-office support other than Microsoft Excel when it comes to creating value with partners and stakeholders. This is of relevance to both Investor Services and Policy Advocacy. Dashboards to visualise progress against targets, as well as systems that enable inter-agency collaboration will help manage the many mini projects usually needed to delivery Investor Services.

CRM systems are also useful tools when it comes to planning and managing client visits. Covid-19 has restricted the volume of face-to-face visits, giving space to online and digital meetings. Many IPAs developed new digital content, introduced a "virtual first" policy with itineraries delivered remotely via videos, site cameras, drones or satellite imagery. Box 9.10 provides insight into how Kenya approaches client visits during the pandemic.

Box 9.10 Client visits in Kenya

Aftercare approach and methodology by KenInvest.

"In line with the Kenyan Government's directive aimed at combating the spread of COVID-19 Virus, KenInvest will continue to extend services to investors but without physical meetings unless these are very essential. We will continue to provide to our investor's quality services through digital tools.

We take the health, safety, and well-being of our employees, investors and other members of our community very seriously and are committed to play our role in the fight against the virus.

During the crisis, you will be able to reach us via text, mobile, email and through our Case and Inquiry Management System (CMS) available online.

Thus, if you have any question or concerns, or you would like to start the process of implementing your investment project please do not hesitate to contact us through the CMS, usual email addresses, and the listed telephone numbers:

We believe the virus will be crushed and our normal services will resume the soonest possible. In the meantime, we thank you for making Kenya your investment home and wish you and your families good health and safety during this crisis period and beyond.

We shall be posting regular updates on COVID-19 here. You can also visit https://www.health.go.ke/ for more information."

In regular times, KenInvest Aftercare services/activities are planned and carried out quarterly.

First, a project visit schedule is drawn and planned for the quarter based on the target of each given quarter (number of companies to be visited)

At each visit issues are picked out to be discussed, mainly with the aim to get feedback on the status of the company and whether they require any services or facilitation from KenInvest sharing with them current government policies and priority areas for them to take advantage.

These services offered can be categorized/grouped under three headings:

ADMINISTRATIVE SERVICES

These services facilitate operations and include obtaining permits and permissions to operate or expand, obtaining work permits for foreign nationals or spouses, introductions to providers of services such as banking, legal and accounting services, or property agents/brokers, and help in finding homes for transferred staff or schools for their children.

OPERATIONAL SERVICES

These are services that promote efficiency and effectiveness of investors. They include support for training, help with export promotion, obtaining larger premises for expansions, identifying local suppliers and developing cluster organisations or other networks to improve productivity and competitiveness.

STRATEGIC SERVICES

These services impact on the future direction of the business, enabling development of new capabilities and overall corporate development of the firm. They include encouraging and supporting the development of new, upgraded, higher value-added products and services of strategic value to the firm's network, nurturing local suppliers to international standards, linking the top management of FDIs and DDIs to high level national policy and influential networks, and Policy Advocacy activities.

The aim of all these activities is to ensure the investors are happy in the existing investment climate to re-invest and expand. Most of these services are undertaken through the one stop centre.

Reproduced with kind permission from KenInvest: http://www.invest.go.ke/.

9.2.7.4 Forms and templates

Love them or loathe them, forms are a useful way of gathering the information an IPA requires to deliver services to investors. Some of the most common forms and templates used by Investor Services include:

- **Initial assessment form**: some IPAs ask potential clients to complete a form at the beginning of an engagement as a way of gathering information about the company and the proposed project. This information helps the IPA understand the potential of a project, timelines and resources required – hence whether the proposed project meets the IPA's services criteria, and if so, how it can best assist the investor. Another benefit of a written initial assessment is that it should state the number of existing jobs in the company at the beginning of the engagement with the client. A key piece of information when reporting is the number of jobs created or retained at the end of an Aftercare project.
- **Terms of engagement form**: while engagement policy is typically broad in nature, terms of engagement are much more specific. Some investors want clarity about free versus paid services, as well as what expectations the IPA has of the investor. Other investors, particularly larger ones, often request engagement documents up front as a standard condition of engaging with an IPA. Some IPAs have a tick box on their websites asking users to agree to their terms and conditions to simplify this process, although a few investors want to have terms formally signed by both sides.

- **Completion/confirmation of investment form**: investors are normally asked to confirm that they have successfully completed a new project. This document is gaining importance from a governance perspective as it captures evidence of growth and is confirmed by the client. To provide more transparency, many IPAs outsource the verification of confirmation to an independent third party (typically a large accounting firm or consultancy). This topic is discussed further in the Chapter 10, Impact Evaluation.
- **Evaluation (feedback) form**: IPAs often ask clients to evaluate the quality of the services they have received. This form can also be used to gather broader information such as a client's perception of the investment climate in a location, etc. This intelligence is of particular value for service improvement and also for Policy Advocacy.
- **Non-disclosure agreement (NDA) template**: based on research for this book, less than 10% of clients request an NDA or confidentiality agreement. Nonetheless, a standard NDA should be available in the toolkit for those clients that require it. Depending on the specific circumstances and local regulations, NDAs can be signed by an Aftercare professional or by the legal representative of the IPA.
- **Letter of introduction (LOI) template**: LOIs are a good way of first reaching out to a company and can be sent by a state minister, the local authority, a CEO of a chamber of commerce, a local influencer or the Aftercare team. The objective of a LOI is to engage a foreign business by introducing the IPA's services and the support it, and other parts of the local business ecosystem, can offer. LOIs can also be sent to the local affiliate's parent company if appropriate. Sometimes delivering a LOI via diplomatic channels can be effective, leveraging a country's network of embassies and consulates.
- **Letter of visa sponsorship**: most FDI projects result in the relocation of staff who may require visas and/or work permits for themselves and their families. Some IPAs provide this type of letter. Clearly any template should be validated by legal advisers to ensure it complies with the latest migration regulations.

- **Letter of endorsement**: some foreign investors need to raise funds locally in order to complete an expansion project. To strengthen their funding application, they may request an endorsement letter showing they have local support. IPAs should have a policy clearly detailing who has the authority to issue such a letter and under what circumstances.

While all these forms and templates have their uses, care should be taken not to over-engineer services or to become too bureaucratic, while at the same time complying with best practice and minimising risk.

9.2.7.5 Social media

The 2020 World Bank/WAIPA joint study on the State of Investment Promotion Agencies identified that the most effective social media for their particular investment promotion task is LinkedIn, "especially for identifying and recruiting staff, identifying investors, and gathering investor intelligence."[99] Facebook was identified "as the most effective social media (platform) to inform the general public about the value of the IPA's activities."[100] The study also found that a quarter of the surveyed IPAs spend up to US$10,000 annually on social media, while another quarter spent more than US$100,000 annually. From a staffing perspective, most participants dedicated up to two full-time equivalent employees to social media.[101]

9.2.7.6 Testimonials

Investor testimonials are valuable indicators of success, because ultimately it is the customer's view that matters most. Success described by an investor is more likely to resonate with potential future investors as to the attractiveness of a location and the value and support the local IPA has delivered. It is therefore important that IPAs make every effort to get feedback from clients.

The following example (see Box 9.11) not only describes a success story, it also provides insight into the many players that can be involved in securing an investment, the various political agendas at play and how an investor can help shape a location, its skills and capabilities, as well as its future economic growth.

Box 9.11 Lockheed Martin to expand and create 500 jobs in Orlando, USA

"ORLANDO, Fla. (February 14, 2018) – Today, Governor Scott announced Lockheed Martin, a global security and aerospace company, will be expanding in Orlando and creating 500 new jobs. The average wage of the 500 new jobs will be $87,064. The company will also invest more than $50 million in their Orlando facility. Lockheed Martin currently employs over 14,000 Floridians at 73 locations.

Governor Scott said, 'I am proud to announce Lockheed Martin is continuing to invest in Florida by creating 500 new jobs as part of their expansion in Orlando. Lockheed Martin is already a major job creator for our state, and our commitment to cutting taxes and making Florida business-friendly is making it easier for this global business to continue to create thousands of opportunities for Florida families.'

Lockheed Martin employs approximately 100,000 people worldwide and is principally engaged in the research, design, development, manufacture, integration and sustainment of advanced, technology systems, products and services.

Frank St. John, Lockheed Martin Missiles and Fire Control executive vice president, said, 'With this expansion, Lockheed Martin is further solidifying its already robust presence in Florida and supporting our business growth. The Research & Development II building underscores our customer commitments to provide the most modern facilities for our talented workforce to produce critical capabilities for the U.S. and allies for years to come.'

Peter Antonacci, CEO of EFI, said, 'Lockheed Martin's continued investment in Florida sends a strong message to aerospace and aviation business leaders that Florida is the most business-friendly state in the United States for aerospace and aviation companies.'

Cissy Proctor, Executive Director of the Florida Department of Economic Opportunity, said, 'Lockheed Martin is globally recognised and attracts a diverse group of talent to our state. This expansion is an outstanding contribution to our state's thriving economy and is a significant win for the families in the Orlando area.'

Orlando Mayor Buddy Dyer said, 'More than 60 years ago, Lockheed Martin opened its first location in Central Florida, planting the roots that have transformed Orlando into the innovative city it is today and solidifying Central Florida as the world's epicenter for modelling, simulation and training. We welcome the company's continued investment in Orlando which is an example of our success in creating long-term partnerships that bring high quality jobs to residents, and is a testament to our dynamic business environment and our high quality of life.'

Orange County Mayor Teresa Jacobs said, 'I'm delighted to join in today's ground-breaking ceremony. Already we're a global leader in the modelling, simulation and training industries, and as the world's number one defense contractor, Lockheed Martin is a huge part of that success. Today's announcement tells the world that we have a skilled workforce and an economic climate in which high-tech manufacturing and development can succeed. And it tells our local community that we're building an economy with depth, diversification, and opportunity.'

Tim Giuliani, president and CEO of the Orlando Economic Partnership, said, 'Lockheed Martin has been an important part of Orlando's economic growth for more than 50 years not only because of the company's innovations in technology but because of its commitment to supporting our community's STEM education initiatives. The Partnership is honoured that Lockheed has chosen to expand in Orlando. Our region's high-tech industry, strong engineering programs and talent pipeline highlight why this remains the ideal location for Lockheed's continued success.'"

Reproduced with kind permission from Enterprise Florida: www.enterpriseflorida.com.

Link: https://www.enterpriseflorida.com/news/lockheed-martin-expand-create-500-jobs-orlando/.

The 7 Building Blocks of Investor Services provide a practical approach to designing investors services and cover the most common themes that come up when delivering services to foreign investors.

9.3 Aftercare teams

There are many ways to deliver Aftercare services. Different governments and IPAs are structured in different ways, and inevitably this impacts how Aftercare services are delivered. Some governments and IPAs keep Aftercare in-house, others delegate the service to subnational or specialised agencies, while others outsource Aftercare services to private sector consultancies, or support chambers of commerce or business networks when they are performing these roles. In some IPAs Aftercare has its own dedicated department, in others it is part of a larger department and occasionally Aftercare services are spread across a number of departments in a "bits-and-pieces" fashion. Reporting lines are not standardised either, as some place the function in the Facilitation team, whilst others find a better fit when working within the Operations teams that usually includes a one-stop-shop. Some combine the client facing role with the Ecosystem engagement role, while others have them sitting in different teams. Consequently, reporting lines can be confusing, and KPIs are likely to vary according to both the IPA's mandate as well as to how the department in general operates. For example, job creation targets, monitoring the quality of services delivered, the quantity of enquires served, etc., may not be able to be meaningfully compared between IPAs.

The variety of organisational structures speaks to both the localised nature of government and to the local economic environment the IPA is working in. Therefore, context is everything when working out how best to service established foreign investors and how to get different stakeholders to collaborate, while all the time supporting local value creation.

An area where our interviewees broadly agreed was around the skills required for the Aftercare team. To ensure the effectiveness of an agency and to successfully build and deliver Investor Services, Aftercare needs to be delivered not by a group of individuals, but by a team, who "are on a mission to equip, support and empower foreign investors to tap into the growth opportunities the location can offer."[102] As well as having an Aftercare mindset, Aftercare teams need to be motivated, resourceful and empowered. To build such a team requires strategic recruitment, structured learning and development and career planning, as with setting up and managing any high-performing team.

Based on dozens of conversations with recruiters and HR teams, Aftercare roles can be broken down into 7 distinctive skillsets. These are:

- **Client engagement**: Aftercare professionals need to be skilled at identifying both (future) opportunities for reinvestment and also areas where the Aftercare team can add value in the short term.
- **Ecosystem navigation**: this relates to the active role Aftercare professionals play in the local community where they are constantly looking for market insights, opportunities, resources and connections that might be of current or future use.
- **Business development**: understanding business is key when designing growth services that are based on market insights, which appeal to the business instincts of the foreign investor, and which the IPA has the resources to effectively deliver. This requires consultative selling skills that place importance on listening, require a deep understanding of how the industry works, as well as the capacity and ability to create tailor-made solutions.
- **Analytical mindset**: the capacity to understand, contextualise and interpretate data, reports and a wide range of fragmented messages from many different sources is key to making sense of the many moving pieces that influence Aftercare.
- **Political acumen**: Aftercare professionals need the ability to navigate fluid political environments while also translating the governing party's agenda into action. At the same time, they need to remain technical experts and provide advice to government while refraining from giving political opinions.
- **Situational leadership**: Aftercare professionals are exposed to many different environments; one day they will be sitting with a state minister in front of the press, the following day sitting in a port helping an investor solve delays with custom clearances, only to be sitting the next day in a board meeting presenting the case for an expansion. The variety of settings in which Aftercare takes place needs to be reflected in the skills of practitioners, who are constantly honing their situational leadership skills.
- **Storytelling**: as the point people for a location, Aftercare professionals need to be able to articulate to investors and other stakeholders all aspects of Aftercare, from selling to delivery to announcing success. Storytelling turns data, insight and activities into a (compelling) narrative. According to Ann Badillo, a futurist author specialising in accelerating start-ups and Ecosystems around the world, it is these

narratives that help make sense of a situation, and provide a framework for understanding, organising and contextualising information in a way that brings both order and clarity.[103]

These 7 skills, summarised in Figure 9.16, together provide the professionalism, resilience and creativity needed to help foreign investors grow in the local economy, ensure partners join and support the IPA's work, and foster long-term economic development.

Aftercare teams perform 5 distinctive roles. There is the *strategy role*, that determines where to go and how to get there; the *ecosystem broker*, which creates value by integrating with the ecosystem; the *sector expert*, who brings the specific knowledge needed to create value in a certain type of situation; the *project manager*, who brings these different elements together and works closely with the *client-facing professional* to respond to specific needs. Job descriptions for an Aftercare professional will vary depending on the specific role or whether a person performs various roles simultaneously. Irrespective of this, the role description usually states that the successful

Figure 9.16 Skills for Aftercare roles. © *Investment Aftercare Explained: A Guide for FDI Practitioners and Policymakers on How to Grow and Retain Investors.*

candidate will be required to manage a mixed portfolio of projects, and to deliver on some, or all, of the following tasks:

- Design, resource and deliver bespoke services to Aftercare clients.
- Articulate location-wide opportunities for the whole FDI Ecosystem.
- Build relationships at a senior level with investors to identify growth opportunities and associated service needs.
- Influence investors to choose the location over other destinations.
- Organise visits and familiarisation programmes and escort visiting delegations.
- Join, convene and manage complex projects requiring location-wide collaboration.
- Develop and maintain successful relationships with a wide range of stakeholders.
- Actively research, review and share market intelligence and trends that lead to business growth.
- Evaluate investor sentiment and channel feedback appropriately.
- Advocate for the best possible business climate.
- Embrace placemaking as a way to create local value and increase location loyalty.
- Collaborate with internal and external teams on location-wide initiatives.
- Maximise press and marketing opportunities to publicise the location.
- Broadcast local success stories to relevant audiences.
- Help build the profile of the IPA among key stakeholders.

The interviews conducted for this book allowed insights into why people enjoy working in Aftercare. Participants commented that the Aftercare industry offered them unique, exciting and challenging career opportunities and experiences. In particular, they mentioned:

- Exposure to c-suite level executives.
- Significant interaction and engagement with senior politicians and the media.
- Exposure to highly confidential strategic, business and political information.

- The development of wide and influential personal networks.
- The satisfaction they gain when they see they made a difference (such as creating jobs for "my neighbours" and seeing a location grow and develop into an attractive destination).

Interviewees also reported that Aftercare presents some unique challenges. For example:

- Such a diverse group of clients and stakeholders can make demands that are sometimes contradictory.
- Trying to generate value with relatively limited resources while navigating an ever-changing business and political landscape.
- Being "distracted" from core Aftercare work by other parts of government/agency who want to tap into the deep local knowledge and understanding Aftercare professionals have acquired in the course of their work.
- Operating in a role (Aftercare) that is often not understood by the "people at the top." As one Aftercare professional mentioned, "[i]t doesn't help that neither the director nor the board really understand Aftercare."
- Operating in a field where success is often not easy to define or measure, and hence forever having to justify one's existence.

A 2020 WBG/WAIPA study looked into salaries as they recognise it is an important factor in attracting a qualified workforce. While their study reflects the whole IPA and not only post-investment teams, the data serves as a reference point to readers interested in benchmarking salaries. "Survey responses indicate that 42% (of) the agencies offer public sector level wages. A significant proportion of agencies offer either wages that are above public sector wages but below private sector wages or offer wages that are comparable with the private sector."[104] They add that performance-based bonuses are also common practice.

9.4 Considerations when delivering Investor Services

Some basic considerations when delivering Investor Services include an understanding of when success can be declared, i.e. completing an Aftercare project, and the mechanics of job creation that underpin it.

9.4.1 Mechanics of completing Aftercare projects

When it comes to completing an Aftercare project, practitioners need to manage many variables, such as unpredictable times, over-optimistic forecasting, whether or not to claim credit, public scrutiny and the subjective nature of additionality – concepts that are briefly explained below.

9.4.1.1 Unpredictable timelines

Timelines can be unpredictable when it comes to Aftercare projects. This can affect when an IPA can claim credit for the support it provided. For example, some Aftercare services produce results relatively quickly, e.g. administrative support, while more strategic projects may take months or even years to complete. There are also projects with no specific completion date, but for which there is an ongoing commitment to support the investor. As a result, the timing of when credit can be claimed may be left to the discretion of the IPA. This can lead to questions being asked by external stakeholders who are not necessarily familiar with the nature and dynamics of the Aftercare industry.

9.4.1.2 Over-optimistic forecasting

Although there is little oversight about the effective rate of job creation when compared to investor forecasting, anecdotal evidence gained from the interviews for this book suggests that investors are over-optimistic about how successful their investments will be. IPAs may also be complicit in this when the investor knows that a higher estimated job creation level may lead to more IPA services being brought to bear, i.e. there is no penalty on the Foreign Investor for getting their forecast wrong; there is no incentive for the IPA to verify whether declared jobs are accurate. Notable takeaways include:

- The degree of over-optimism depends to some extent on the industry, the country of origin and the size of the company. For example,
  - Retail, hospitality and leisure firms are typically fast to expand, but also quick to exit a market.
  - New technology firms, who are often highly dependent on incentives, are also quick to exit. For example, several solar energy companies follow grants and exit when they are no longer available.
  - Physical proximity helps drive stable growth. Experience suggests that the further an investor's HQ is from a subsidiary, the less

likely it is that the subsidiary will deliver the number of jobs initially forecast.

- Experience also indicates that mid-sized companies (50–250 employers) are more likely to deliver the forecast new jobs than smaller companies or (large) multinationals.

- The authors' experience also indicates that underperformance is often hidden by summary figures. An estimated 80% of investors fail to generate the growth initially forecast. However, 20% of investors significantly outperform their initial growth forecasts, partially offsetting the shortfall in jobs created by the underperformers. However, despite the strong performance of a few investors, overall, the total number of new jobs created is usually significantly lower than the number promised.

9.4.1.3 Claiming credit

In the day-to-day work of an IPA, declaring success is not a clear-cut process. For example, OECD guidelines[105] state that organic growth should be excluded when calculating the incremental growth generated by an expansion project. Organic growth can be difficult to calculate, hence it is important to gather relevant data at the start of a project, notably the number of employees by function at the existing location at the beginning of the engagement, in order to make it easier to calculate growth once a project is completed. The onus for this is on the IPA, as this information is of no particular interest to an investor.

Another example is when exactly to publicly declare that a project is concluded. OECD guidelines state that FDI job gains or losses should be recorded by an IPA once, and stipulate explicitly that it must be in the financial year in which the investor makes a public announcement. However, the timing of when an investor makes an announcement can vary significantly. For example, the announcement could be made at any time during an expansion project, the beginning, the middle or on completion; the investor might make an announcement on expanding a factory at the moment it has secured financing, even though the new factory won't open for several years. Another foreign company may only announce the opening of a new division at the inauguration of a new facility, or once all new jobs have been filled. From an IPA's perspective, multiple timelines they cannot influence can be problematic, particularly when it comes to internal administration, claiming credit and reporting to external stakeholders, as it can affect how performance is evaluated.

Per OECD guidelines, jobs that have been announced by the investor can only be claimed during the same financial year. Hence, if an IPA has failed to engage with the client, or to provide any impactful support during the financial year when the announcement was made, then it is unable to count these jobs towards any OECD-aligned targets, even when these jobs are actually created in future years. This can be frustrating for IPAs when they have job creation targets to meet. Clearly, from meeting an IPA's job-creation targets perspective, the most attractive projects to support are those that have not yet been publicly announced. In reality, IPAs typically have a mixed portfolio of projects, some of which will count towards their job creation targets, while others will not. Nevertheless, teams should make their bosses aware of (and keep records on) the work they perform in helping investors create new jobs that do not count towards the IPA's job creation targets. Likewise, not being able to claim credit on OECD targets should not stop them engaging with the company and providing the support the investor requires in order to ensure that these new jobs are actually created. Ultimately, supporting the investor is the most important goal.

Irrespective of the timing of when an investor makes an announcement, and whether jobs can or cannot be counted towards targets, projects that come to a successful conclusion should be celebrated, as this is a clear opportunity to raise the profile of the investor, the IPA and the host economy. Local media love a local good news story, so this is the time to get them on board to share the good work done. Care should be given to coordinate any publicity with the investor, as some have strict PR policies that prevent them from engaging with local media.

9.4.1.4 Big projects attract scrutiny

Occasionally a single project can have a major impact on a location, whether it be in terms of job creation, impact on the local economy or the profile of the location. As investors often tread carefully when first entering a new market, subsequent expansion projects are often much larger and therefore have a much greater economic impact on a location. And unsurprisingly, it is the bigger projects, and the (large) number of new jobs associated with them, that gain the attention of stakeholders, funders, politicians and the media.

Auditing teams within the IPA or from external audit bodies tend to look at large projects more closely to check whether the foreign investor has really created all the jobs claimed. They may also insist that some due diligence is performed before allowing any success to be publicly announced. Local communities are also likely to closely scrutinise any plans, particularly when it comes to proposed job losses, but also with regards to the sustainability of any new jobs. IPAs, and in particular those funded with public money, should therefore take care and, as appropriate, qualify the numbers reported by a client and only claim credit for those jobs they were directly involved in creating.

9.4.1.5 Subjective nature of additionality

There is an old joke in the Aftercare industry that says that if an alien spaceship were to land in the main square of a town, the local IPA would declare it a success and claim credit for their role in securing the expansion. However, there is a serious point here in that it is often difficult to calculate the additional value generated by an IPA. Sometimes the impact an IPA makes is clear, such as when an IPA brings an opportunity to the attention of an investor that the investor was unaware of. Should the investor take the opportunity, the jobs created would be attributable to the IPA. However, much of the time identifying the difference made by an IPA is difficult. While most Aftercare interventions help a company grow, or grow faster, and this is generally appreciated by stakeholders, the precise impact of an IPA's work is often less tangible and hence difficult to calculate due to the lack of a straightforward benchmark against which to measure the IPA's work. Nonetheless, IPAs with strong project completion processes and evaluation methodologies, including clear guidance as to how and when to claim additionality, should be in a good position to answer any questions. This topic is covered in depth in Chapter 10, Impact Evaluation.

One commonly discussed challenge is how to convince an investor that it is worth investing their time and energy working with the IPA. Institutional credibility with the private sector can facilitate engagement, but in other cases it is the lack of it that hinders engagement. If an investor has not heard from the IPA before, it is unlikely they will understand the value the IPA can bring and will therefore be reluctant to engage.

There are also times when investors feel either neglected or taken for granted, for example, having engaged with an IPA, delivered expansion projects, created jobs and also opportunities for local firms, they nonetheless can't secure the attendance of a political figure to a launch event or get press coverage for the opening of a new facility. This can confuse investors, particularly when they don't fully understand the local political landscape.

Another challenge commonly cited by investors in emerging economies, economies in transition or developing countries relates to immature or poorly developed institutions with unnecessarily long-winded administrative procedures and/or a lack of basic infrastructure to support growth (such as wifi, electricity, transport, etc.). UNESCAP recognises the difficulties of operating in such an environment, and in 2017 commented that "excellent Aftercare can be an important competitive factor but cannot replace a conducive business climate."[106]

9.4.1.6 Changing workforce of the foreign investor

A final challenge of the IPA is dealing with staff turnover at the foreign investor. In the author's experience, all too often a brilliant support project is made difficult to claim downstream as the "old manager" has left and the "new manager" is not aware of the IPA, let alone who they have assisted in the past.

9.4.2 The mechanics of job creation

At the very core of completing an Aftercare project is claiming credit for the work done. At that moment, IPAs will declare the number of jobs the investors created. Job creation is perhaps the most commonly quoted performance indicator of Aftercare practitioners. Publicly funded IPAs typically have job-creation targets, while private-sector IPAs closely monitor the number of new jobs they help create. International organisations who support FDI activities in developing countries also look at jobs. They expect governments that receive their funding to put mechanisms in place that maximise the likelihood of long-term and successful foreign investment. This is a key role of Aftercare.

Figure 9.17 shows a hypothetical example of the complexity involved in monitoring job creation when a foreign investor enters a new market with a plan to create 100 jobs in its first year. It represents a phase of growth and expansion and charts different possible outcomes:

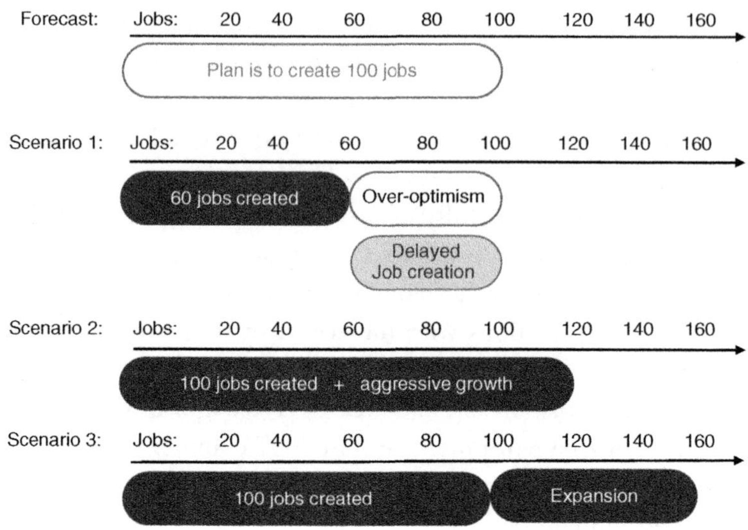

Figure 9.17 Job creation in expansion phase © *Investment Aftercare Explained: A Guide for FDI Practitioners and Policymakers on How to Grow and Retain Investors.*

a) The forecast is that by the end of the first year it has created the 100 jobs.
b) However, that case is unlikely; 80% of investors[107] tend to be over-optimistic in their job creation plans. A more realistic approach is that only 60 new jobs are created, a shortfall of 40 jobs against plan. This is referred to as over-optimism. In some cases, the investor might catch up in years later (shown in the diagram as delayed job creation).
c) The remaining 20% of investors will create more jobs than initially planned. In the figure, it is show as aggressive growth, adding 20 jobs, which total 120 jobs. This is good news.
d) The next scenario represents a company growing; the investor expands its operation, opens a new division creating an additional 60 jobs.

Different is the case when the company goes through a contraction phase, as depicted in Figure 9.18:

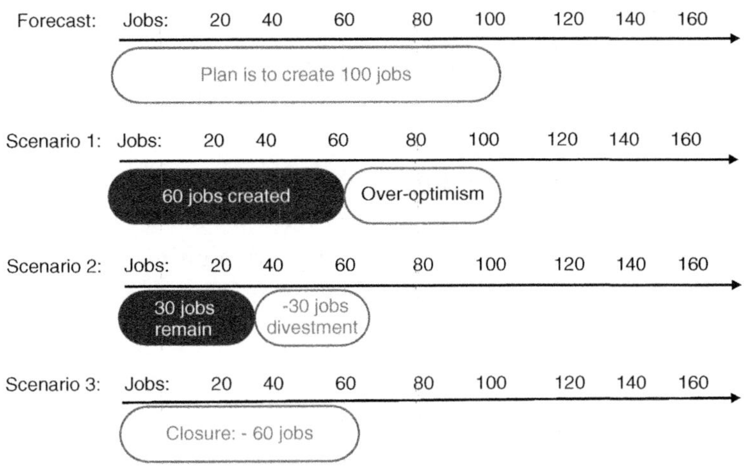

Figure 9.18 Job creation in contraction phase. © *Investment Aftercare Explained: A Guide for FDI Practitioners and Policymakers on How to Grow and Retain Investors.*

e) The investor created 60 of the 100 forecasted. However, business does not go as planned and the investor remains in the location but reduces its presence to 30 jobs.
f) Market conditions change and the investor decides to close their facility resulting in all 60 jobs being lost.

Job creation is at the very core of an IPA's work. However, as the industry changes and becomes more mature, the role of the IPA also evolves. While IPAs "used to manage aftercare programs, they now also have a role as ecosystem brokers. While they used to manage budgets, they now need to create partnerships to add value in a rapidly changing environment. While they used to count jobs, they are now asked to deliver social impact."[108]

Ultimately, Investor Services support economic development in the host country by maximising job creation or job safeguarding. The counting of new jobs created, retained or lost is an important part of how an IPA's performance is evaluated, and also of the overall impact of FDI. However, different parts of government count the creation, retention or loss of jobs in different ways in terms of both the timing and the quantum. This inconsistency first makes tracking these numbers complicated for an IPA, and second makes reporting them to different stakeholders often a political issue. This topic will be explored in more detail in Chapter 10, Impact Evaluation.

In summary, this chapter covered the practical aspects of delivering Investor Services with the aim of guiding practitioners, as well as informing policy makers of the challenges practitioners face when working with foreign investors.

The good news is that when Investor Services are well designed and professionally delivered, they become a much-needed external arm of a foreign investor's business. This close-knitted collaboration ultimately becomes co-creation of new value that benefits both the company and the host economy.

Notes

1 UNCTAD, 2007. *Aftercare: A Core Function in Investment Promotion* [online]. Available at: https://unctad.org/system/files/official-document/iteipc20071_en.pdf.

2 Andersson, J. et al. 2018. *Is Apparel Manufacturing Coming Home? Nearshoring, Automation, and Sustainability – Establishing a Demand- focused Apparel Value Chain* [online]. Available at: https://www.mckinsey.com/industries/retail/our-insights/is-apparel-manufacturing-coming-home.

3 Amazon, 2017. *Amazon HQ2 Request for Proposal* [online]. Available at: https://images-na.ssl-images-amazon.com/images/G/01/Anything/test/images/usa/RFP_3._V516043504_.pdf.

4 McDearman, B. and Donahue, R. 2015. *The 10 Lessons from Global Trade and Investment Planning in U.S. Metro Areas* [online]. Available at: https://www.brookings.edu/research/the-10-lessons-from-global-trade-and-investment-planning-in-u-s-metro-areas/.

5 Ibid.

6 UNCTAD, 2016. *World Investment Report 2016. Investor Nationality: Policy Challenges.* New York: United Nations Publication.

7 Ghemawat, P. and Pisani, N. 2014. *The Fortune Global 500 Isn't All That Global* [online]. Available at: https://hbr.org/2014/11/the-fortune-global-500-isnt-all-that-global.

8 Dunning, J.H. 2002. *Global Capitalism, FDI and Competitiveness.* 2nd ed.. Northampton, MA: Edward Elgar Publishing.

9 Sanchiz, A. and Omic, A. 2020. *State of Investment Promotion Agencies: Evidence from WAIPA-WBG's Joint Global Survey.* World Bank, Washington, DC. WAIPA (World Association of Investment Promotion Agencies), Geneva [online]. Available at: http://documents1.worldbank.org/curated/en/499971594008431029/pdf/State-of-Investment-Promotion-Agencies-Evidence-from-WAIPA-WBG-s-Joint-Global-Survey.pdf.

10 Ibid.

11 Rugman, A.M. and Wright, R.W. 1999. *International Entrepreneurship: Globalization of Emerging Businesses. Series: Research in Global Strategic Management.* vol 7 edn. Stamford, CT: Emerald Group Publishing Limited.

12 Zaheer, S. 1995. "Overcoming the liability of foreignness". *The Academy of Management Journal*, 38(2), pp. 341–363.

13 UNCTAD, 2002. *World Investment Report 2002: Transnational Corporations and Export Competitiveness.* New York and Geneva: United Nations Publication.

14 Caves, R.E. 1974. "Causes of direct investment: Foreign firms' shares in Canadian and United Kingdom manufacturing industries". *The Review of Economics and Statistic,* 56(3), pp. 279–293.

Taylor, C. and Henisz, W. 1994. *U.S. Manufacturers in the Global Marketplace.* New York, The Conference Board.

15 Wang, Z. 1998. *Japanese Corporations' Investment in China.* 1st edn. Beijing, China: China Economic Press.

Wang, Z. 1996. *Korean Corporations' Investment in China.* 1st edn. Beijing, China: China Economic Press.

16 Caves, R.E. 2007. *Multinational Enterprise and Economic Analysis.* 3rd edn. Cambridgee: Cambridge University Press.

Pitelis, C. and Teece, D. 2010. "Cross-border market co-creation, dynamic capabilities and the entrepreneurial theory of the multinational enterprise". *Industrial and Corporate Change,* 19(4), pp. 1247–1270.

17 Lee, S.-H., Peng, M.W. and Barney, J.B. 2007. "Bankruptcy law and entrepreneurship development: A real options perspective". *The Academy of Management Review,* 32(1), pp. 257–272.

Peng, M.W. 2003. "Institutional transitions and strategic choices". *The Academy of Management Review,* 28(2), pp. 275–296.

Puffer, S.M. and McCarthy, D.J. 2001. "Navigating the hostile maze: A framework for Russian entrepreneurship". *The Academy of Management Executive,* 15(4), pp. 24-36.

18 Barkley, D. & Mcnamara, K., 1994. "Manufacturers' location decisions: Do surveys provide helpful insights?". *International Regional Science Review,* 17(1), pp. 23–47.

UNCTAD, 2000. *World Investment Report 2000: Cross-Border Mergers and Acquisitions and Development.* New York and Geneva: United Nations Publication.

19 Sanchiz, A. and Omic, A. 2020. *State of Investment Promotion Agencies: Evidence from WAIPA-WBG's Joint Global Survey.* World Bank, Washington, DC. WAIPA (World Association of Investment Promotion Agencies), Geneva [online]. Available at: http://documents1.worldbank.org/curated/en/499971594008431029/pdf/State-of-Investment-Promotion-Agencies-Evidence-from-WAIPA-WBG-s-Joint-Global-Survey.pdf.

20 UNCTAD, 2007. *Aftercare: A Core Function in Investment Promotion* [online]. Available at: https://unctad.org/system/files/official-document/iteipc20071_en.pdf.

21 Lambregts-Winters, S. 2016. "See and Be Seen: Added Value for Foreign Investors in Brabant". Thesis for MSc in Marketing, TIAS School for Business & Society.

22 Monroe, K.B. 1990. *Pricing: Making Profitable Decisions.* 2nd edn. Boston: McGraw-Hill.

23 Lambregts-Winters, S. 2016. *Added Value for Your Customer* [online]. Available at: https://www.linkedin.com/pulse/added-value-your-customer-susanne-lambregts-winters/.

24 Lambregts-Winters, S. 2016. "See and Be Seen: Added Value for Foreign Investors in Brabant". Thesis for MSc in Marketing, TIAS School for Business & Society.

25 Hjalmarsson, D. and Johansson, A.W. 2003. "Public advisory services – theory and practice". *Entrepreneurship & Regional Development International Journal*, 15:1, 83–98 [online]. Available at: https://www.tandfonline.com/doi/abs/10.1080/0898562021000011205.

26 Lambregts-Winters, S. 2016. "See and Be Seen: Added Value for Foreign Investors in Brabant". Thesis for MSc in Marketing, TIAS School for Business & Society.

27 Ibid.

28 See www.pkotler.org.

29 Ibid.

30 UNCTAD, 2007. *Aftercare: A Core Function in Investment Promotion* [online]. Available at: https://unctad.org/system/files/official-document/iteipc20071_en.pdf.

31 Sanchiz, A. and Omic, A. 2020. *State of Investment Promotion Agencies: Evidence from WAIPA-WBG's Joint Global Survey*. World Bank, Washington, DC. WAIPA (World Association of Investment Promotion Agencies), Geneva [online]. Available at: http://documents1.worldbank.org/curated/en/499971594008431029/pdf/State-of-Investment-Promotion-Agencies-Evidence-from-WAIPA-WBG-s-Joint-Global-Survey.pdf.

32 Ibid.

33 See www.pkotler.org.

34 Shapiro, B.P. and Bonoma, T.V. 1984. *How to Segment Industrial Markets*. Harvard Business Review, 64 [online]. Available at: https://hbr.org/1984/05/how-to-segment-industrial-markets.

35 Charlton, A. et al. 2004. *Industry Targeting for Investment Promotion: A Survey of 126 IPAs*, Oxford Investment Research Working Papers.

36 Amazon, 2017. *Amazon HQ2 Request for Proposal* [online]. Available at: https://images-na.ssl-images-amazon.com/images/G/01/Anything/test/images/usa/RFP_3._V516043504_.pdf.

37 Mahate, A. 2017. *Module 3 IPA's Service Catalogue*, s.l: Course: Towards the next generation of IPAs by Inter-American Development Bank – Inter-American Development Bank (IDB).

38 Ibid.

39 Seeds&Chips, 2019. *Exploring Nordic Foodtech Innovation: Setting a Course for Stockholm* [online]. Available at: https://www.foodtechaccelerator.io/exploring-nordic-foodtech-innovation-setting-a-course-for-stockholm/.

40 Ibid.

41 Ibid.

42 UNESCAP, 2017. *Handbook on Policies, Promotion & Facilitation of Foreign Direct Investment for Sustainable Development in Asia Pacific*, Bangkok: United Nations publication.

43 TNC, Trans-National Corporation.

44 UNESCAP, 2017. *Handbook on Policies, Promotion & Facilitation of Foreign Direct Investment for Sustainable Development in Asia Pacific*. Bangkok: United Nations publication.

45 Enterprise Ireland, 2019. *First Steps to Green Competitiveness Guidebook for Services/ Office based companies* [online]. Available at: https://www.leanbusinessireland.ie/wp-content/uploads/2017/05/First-Steps-to-Green-Competitiveness-Guidebook-for-Services-or-Office-based-companies.pdf.

46 Rodríguez-Montemayor, E. 2012. "Diaspora direct investment policy: Options for development". *IADB Integration and Trade Sector. Policy Brief*, Volume IDB-PB-183.

47 Ibid.

48 Ibid.

49 Wei, Y. and Balasubramanyam, V.N. 2006. "Diaspora and development". *World Economy*, 29(11), pp. 1599–1609.

50 Sanghvi, D. 2019. *Where the Indian Diaspora's Money Is Going* [online]. Available at: https://www.livemint.com/money/personal-finance/where-the-indian-diaspora-s-money-is-going-1568892998596.html.

51 Challagalla, S. 2018. "The diaspora and India's growth story". *Observer Research Foundation*, Issue 232.

52 Ministry of Overseas Indian Affairs, 2015. *Annual Report 2014–2015*, s.l: Government of India.

53 Challagalla, S. 2018. "The diaspora and India's growth story". *Observer Research Foundation*, Issue 232.

54 Ibid

55 Wei, Y. and Balasubramanyam, V.N. 2006. "Diaspora and development". *World Economy*, 29(11), pp. 15991609.

56 Rodríguez-Montemayor, E. 2012. Diaspora Direct Investment Policy: Options for Development. *IADB Integration and Trade Sector. Policy Brief*, Volume IDB-PB-183.

57 Burchardi, K.B., Chaney, T. and Hassan, T.A. 2016. "Migrants, ancestors, and investment". *Working Paper 21847, National Bureau of Economic Research.*

58 Ibid.

59 See Connect Ireland www.connectireland.com.

60 Australian Trade and Investment Commision, n.d. *How Austrade can help* [online]. Available at: https://www.austrade.gov.au/International/Invest/Investment-Specialists/How-Austrade-can-help.

61 OECD, 2018. *Mapping of Investment Promotion Agencies in OECD Countrie*, s.l: OECD.

62 Ibid.

63 Ibid.

64 The Trusted Advisory Project https://thetrustedadvisorproject.com/programs/.

65 Skok, M. 2013. *4 Steps To Building A Compelling Value Proposition* [online]. Available at: https://www.forbes.com/sites/michaelskok/2013/06/14/4-steps-to-building-a-compelling-value-proposition/?sh=3fb83aa64695.

66 Ibid.

67 FDI Markets, 2018. *FDI Reinvestment Ranking 2018* [online]. Available at: https://www.fdiintelligence.com/content/download/71002/2026169/file/fDi%20Reinvestment%20Ranking%202018.pdf.

68 McDearman, B. and Donahue, R. 2015. *The 10 Lessons from Global Trade and Investment Planning in U.S. Metro Areas* [online]. Available at: https://www.brookings.edu/research/the-10-lessons-from-global-trade-and-investment-planning-in-u-s-metro-areas/.

69 Ibid.

70 Copenhagen Capacity Aftercare Service Catalogue. See www.copcap.com.

71 Ibid.

72 Ibid.

73 Ibid.

74 Ibid.

75 Ibid.

76 UNESCAP, 2017. *Handbook on Policies, Promotion & Facilitation of Foreign Direct Investment for Sustainable Development in Asia Pacific*, Bangkok: United Nations publication.

77 See https://prezi.com/mpixn0dfthis/how-to-develop-after-care.

78 Stothard, M. 2017. "Catalan business exodus signals deep corporate concerns". *Financial Times*, 15 October. [online] Available at: https://www.ft.com/content/e91df296-b00d-11e7-beba-5521c713abf4

79 Huong, N. 2017. *Strengthening Llinkages Between FDI and Domestic Enterprises to Support Industry Development* [online] Available at: https://www.vir.com.vn/strengthening-linkages-between-fdi-and-domestic-enterprises-to-support-industry-development-54753.html.

80 Anh, H. 2016. *Samsung Looks to Strengthen Lineup of Vietnamese Suppliers* [online]. Available at: https://www.vir.com.vn/samsung-looks-to-strengthen-lineup-of-vietnamese-suppliers-44511.html.

81 Speech by Mr Zainul Abidin Rasheed, Senior Minister of State for Foreign Affairs and Mayor of North East Community Development Council, at the Nigeria-Singapore Business and Investment Forum (2009) https://www.nas.gov.sg/archivesonline/data/pdfdoc/20090824003.htm.

82 Young, S. and Hood, N. 1994. "Designing developmental after-care programmes for foreign direct investors in the European Union". *Transnational Corporations*, 3(2), pp. 45–72.

83 Ibid.

84 Morse, G.W. 1990. *The Retention and Expansion of Existing Businesses: Theory and Practice in Business Visitation Programs.* 1st edn. s.l: Iowa State University Press.

85 Darger, M., Barefield, A. and Hales, B.D. 2019. *Business Retention and Expansion (BRE), A Practical Approach to Economic Development.* 1st edn. s.l: Routledge.

86 Ibid.

87 Ibid.

88 Kenton, W. 2020. *Succession Planning* [online]. Available at: https://www.investopedia.com/terms/s/succession-planning.asp.

89 Maister, D.H., Green, C.H. Galford, R.M. (2000). *The Trusted Advisor*. New York: Free Press.

90 Covery, S.R. 2008. *Speed of Trust: The One Thing That Changes Everything*. FranklinCovey, New York.

91 InvestBA, *Assistance to Investors* [online]. Available at: https://investba.buenosaires.gob.ar/en/static/inverti-ba-servicios.

92 UNESCAP, 2017. *Handbook on Policies, Promotion & Facilitation of Foreign Direct Investment for Sustainable Development in Asia Pacific*, Bangkok: United Nations publication.

93 Barkema, H.G. and Rian, D. 2007. "Internationalising in Small, incremental or larger steps?" *Journal of International Business*, 38(7), pp. 1132–1148.
Jones, M.V. and Coviello, N.E. 2005. "Internationalisation: Conceptualising an entrepreneurial process of behaviour in time". *Journal of International Business Studies*, 36(3), pp. 284–303.

94 Johanson, J. and Vahlne, J.-E. 1990. "The mechanism of internationalism". *International Marketing Review*, 7(4). www.emerald.com/insight/content/doi/10.1108/02651339010137414/full/html.

95 Sanchiz, A. and Omic, A. 2020. *State of Investment Promotion Agencies: Evidence from WAIPA-WBG's Joint Global Survey*. World Bank, Washington, DC. WAIPA (World Association of Investment Promotion Agencies), Geneva [online]. Available at: http://documents1.worldbank.org/curated/en/499971594008431029/pdf/State-of-Investment-Promotion-Agencies-Evidence-from-WAIPA-WBG-s-Joint-Global-Survey.pdf.

96 OECD, 2018. *Mapping of Investment Promotion Agencies in OECD Countrie*, s.l: OECD. [online]. Available at: http://www.oecd.org/investment/Mapping-of-Investment-Promotion-Agencies-in-OECD-Countries.htm.

97 Ibid.

98 Ibid.

99 Sanchiz, A. and Omic, A. 2020. *State of Investment Promotion Agencies: Evidence from WAIPA-WBG's Joint Global Survey*. World Bank, Washington, DC. WAIPA (World Association of Investment Promotion Agencies), Geneva [online]. Available at: http://documents1.worldbank.org/curated/en/499971594008431029/pdf/State-of-Investment-Promotion-Agencies-Evidence-from-WAIPA-WBG-s-Joint-Global-Survey.pdf.

100 Ibid.

101 Ibid.

102 Arriagada Peters, C. 2017. *Module 5 Aftercare and Policy Advocacy*, s.l: Course: Towards the next generation of IPAs by Inter-American Development Bank – Inter-American Development Bank (IDB).

103 Badillo, A., Donovan, T. and Trevarthen, T. 2016. *Narrative Generation: Why Narrative Will Become Your Most Valuable Asset in the Next 5 Years*. 1st edn. s.l: 21st Century Narrative.

104 Sanchiz, A. and Omic, A. 2020. State of Investment Promotion Agencies: Evidence from WAIPA-WBG's Joint Global Survey. World Bank, Washington, DC. WAIPA (World Association of Investment Promotion Agencies), Geneva [online]. Available at:http://documents1.worldbank.org/curated/en/499971594008431029/pdf/State-of-Investment-Promotion-Agencies-Evidence-from-WAIPA-WBG-s-Joint-Global-Survey.pdf.

105 OECD, 2004. *Benchmark Definition of Foreign Direct Investment.* 4th edn. s.l.: OECD.

106 UNESCAP, 2017. *Handbook on Policies, Promotion & Facilitation of Foreign Direct Investment for Sustainable Development in Asia Pacific*, Bangkok: United Nations publication.

107 Insight gathered by this book's research team.

108 Arriagada Peters, C. 2020. "Investment aftercare matters". *Columbia FDI Perspectives*, Issue 276.

10
IMPACT EVALUATION

Author: David Coble

Chapter highlights

- Impact evaluation and monitoring play a crucial role in understanding how an IPA's actions affect (re)investment and policy outcomes.
- Few IPAs currently perform effective impact evaluation and monitoring.
- IPAs' main challenges in this field are to expand and deepen their tools for effective impact evaluation and measurement of their actions.
- This chapter provides general ideas on how IPAs could approach impact evaluation and monitoring, and includes some examples of how this could be done.

10.1 The importance of monitoring and impact evaluation for IPAs

As post-investment matures as an industry, impact measurement is increasingly important for IPAs. In 2016, the OECD held a workshop with IPAs, policymakers, researchers, the private sector and several multilateral organisations including the World Bank, to exclusively share experiences and the tools IPAs were using to measure the impact of their activities on projects and host economies. In their summary, the OECD noted that "all IPAs [attending the workshop] were interested in measuring the impact of

DOI: 10.4324/9781003174950-14

their activities on investment projects and the local economy. This does not only help them tailor and adjust their own activities, but also communicate with the government and the general public at large on the impact of their efforts and the role of investment in the economy more generally."[1]

Earlier chapters of this book described the activities IPAs perform in order to achieve their objectives. To monitor performance and to manage progress against targets, policymakers and managers define appropriate key performance indicators (KPIs). This improves strategic decision making by identifying those activities that bring the highest return on investment (ROI). Monitoring and impact evaluation also help an IPA's leaders to reassess their objectives and to re-allocate resources more efficiently. It also increases an IPA's transparency and accountability, especially if it is publicly funded.[2]

Unfortunately, not all IPAs put sufficient effort into monitoring and evaluation. The vast majority have some form of customer relationship management system (CRM), which is useful for tracking an IPA's relationships with investors and the Ecosystem and measuring basic KPIs, such as the number of jobs created, total value of FDI attracted/retained, number of projects, etc. However, these KPIs are not sufficient to assess the effectiveness of an IPA's actions.

10.1.1 What types of impact can an IPA measure?

The very nature of the different types of audiences IPAs serve, and the distinct objectives of these stakeholders, results in a multifaceted definition of success. Consequently, many questions can be asked in relation to the IPA's performance. For example:

- Did the IPA succeed in attracting investment from foreign companies, securing expansion projects, maximising job retention and minimising disinvestment?
- Did post-investment services make a difference in retaining investment and creating more jobs?
- Have these efforts resulted in increased tax revenues for the local economy?
- Is the quality and quantity of jobs delivered by the foreign companies the IPA serves better than, say, other foreign companies?

Other questions and objectives may be around alignment with local and national economic priorities, a stronger Ecosystem, sustainability, inclusion and so forth, irrespective of the internal questions the IPA asks, or the KPIs it uses to evaluate its own activities. Measurement and evaluation will always depend on the availability of data to assess the impact.

10.2 Main challenges in monitoring and evaluation faced by IPAs

Many IPAs use CRM technologies to trace their actions and activities, and as a way to manage information that helps them comply with their objectives. They also track data from third party sources as appropriate. Oftentimes, however, tracking actions are confused with the evaluation of an IPA's programs. Although monitoring and evaluation are related, they are not the same. Monitoring data is focused on observing actions and keeping track of the achievements of the IPA. Monitoring can also help gather data, which can be used in an impact evaluation. Evaluation, on the other hand, uses monitored and other data to define whether certain actions made a difference over a pre-defined outcome, such as the number of jobs created or post investment activities.

Meaningful impact evaluation requires econometric skills and certain types of data, some of which can be difficult to obtain. However, most IPAs can obtain this data, either through a third party or with a collaborator. In 2019, the OECD and IDB launched a document that, among other topics, studied how IPAs currently perform monitoring and data collection.[3] They propose a simple measure – the IPA Evaluation Index (EI) – as a way to summarise their current state of advance in this matter. It takes into account whether or not the agency: (i) has a dedicated evaluation unit; (ii) uses accepted econometric methods to evaluate the impact,;(iii) uses other (non-econometric) methods to evaluate impact; and (iv) the number of investment promotion activities being tracked by a CRM. All these factors increase the Evaluation Index, which signals the state of monitoring and evaluation of an IPA.

The evaluation index combines these factors as follows:

$$EI = \frac{1}{4}\left[EU + ECONOMETRIC + \frac{EM}{EM^{max}} + \frac{NA}{NA^{Total}} \right],$$

where EU is equal to one if the IPA has a research or evaluation unit, and zero otherwise; $ECONOMETRIC$ is also a binary variable that takes the value of one if the IPA uses econometrics methods to measure the impact of the IPA's actions, and zero otherwise; EM is the number of other evaluation methods used by the IPA; EM^{max} is the maximum number of other evaluation methods that could be used by the IPA; NA is the number of investment promotion activities covered by the IPA's CRM; and NA^{Total} is the number of investment promotion activities carried out by the IPA.

EI then fluctuates between zero and one. The larger the value of EI, the more engaged the IPA is with monitoring and evaluation activities. Volpe and Sztajerowska (2019) show the evaluation index for OECD IPAs. These vary wildly between 0.05 (Poland) and 0.95 (Germany). Only a few countries have an index above 0.6, while more than a third of countries IPAs' evaluation index is lower than 0.4.

This finding suggests that many IPAs have significant scope to improve how they monitor and evaluate their activities.

Other interesting findings of this study include:

i. **Small evaluation units**: although many IPAs have research or evaluation units, these are generally small. In addition, only about half of their staff hold Masters or PhD degrees in a relevant discipline that would better equip them to undertake an impact assessment.
ii. **Very few IPAs perform econometric impact evaluation analyses**: even though IPAs use a variety of methods to assess the effectiveness of their activities, econometric-based analyses are the least common approach. Many IPAs use satisfaction or perception surveys, focus groups, consultations with stakeholders, benchmarking exercises against other IPAs and case studies to assess their performance. However, these are not proper evaluation methods, as they do not compare against a counterfactual, a statistically comparable scenario that necessarily must be estimated by econometric techniques. This topic will be discussed further in the following sections.
iii. **CRM systems are the most common source of information**: more than 90% of IPAs use CRM systems to record their activities and interactions with foreign companies. The most

common activities IPAs track are investment facilitation and investment generation. In contrast, Policy Advocacy and image building activities are the least tracked. Aftercare activities are not specifically mentioned in the article, and it is highly likely that they are also poorly tracked.

iv. **Lack of data is very common among IPAs**: much of the data IPAs require to perform monitoring and evaluations is held by National Statistical Offices, Central Banks or other relevant offices. However, obtaining access to this data is not a given; sometimes IPAs have to make formal requests for partnerships and arrangements in order to gain access. In other cases, there are legal limitations, or little interest from political authorities in sharing data. Hence, there are IPAs that require political support in order to be able to measure the impact of their activities.

According to the findings of Volpe and Sztajerowska's study, IPAs are used to dealing with data. Many IPAs look for new and innovative ways to evaluate their performance. But even though some IPAs may have large amounts of data, they may also be less familiar with formal impact evaluations. Proper training and access to data appear to be the main challenges. The following section seeks to address these difficulties by equipping practitioners with the key concepts and methodologies of evaluation, and the data required to do this.

10.3 Impact evaluation

10.3.1 The problem

Impact evaluation calculates the change in an outcome – such as the number of jobs created – attributable to a particular activity, project, program or policy, for example, for post-investment, promotion or Policy Advocacy actions. As discussed earlier, this is different to outcome monitoring, which evaluates whether some goals have been achieved. Impact evaluation aims to answer a particular, yet very important question: how would the outcomes have been different *if the intervention or new policy had not been implemented*? The answer to this question is not trivial, as it would need to compare what happened with a "parallel universe," which, by definition, is not observable. This assessment is called *counterfactual analysis*, that is to say, "a comparison between what actually happened and what would have happened in the absence of the intervention."[4] It is similar in concept to the trials that assess the effectiveness of a new drug, where half the patients receive the drug under test, while the other half receive a placebo.

To illustrate this point, let's look at an example. Well-run IPAs know how many foreign firms their actions attracted, how many jobs these companies created, how much money was invested by these firms, and many other relevant outcomes. Is this enough? No, as in reality, there are many other factors that influence a foreign company's decisions, and not all these factors will have been influenced by the IPA's actions. For example, the foreign investor may have already decided to invest in the location, regardless of the IPA's assistance. Alternatively, the IPA may have made a real difference. But what would have happened if the IPA had done nothing at all? Would these companies have invested anyway? How many jobs would have been created if the IPA had not assisted them? The answers to these questions are crucial to properly assessing the performance of an IPA. In order to do this, IPAs need to compare the outcome they observe against the *counterfactual reality* these questions raise. In this situation, the only way to do this is by calculating these counterfactuals – this is done using standard econometric methods.

10.3.2 What type of data is needed to perform impact evaluations?

Ideally, there would be an experiment: a group of identical, or very similar, foreign firms would consider investing in similar locations at about the same time, and the local IPAs would randomly decide whether or not to assist them – ultimately assisting a significant portion of them. The comparison in outcomes between the two groups would show the impact of assisting foreign firms. As this does not happen in reality, other means need to be used, and so we use statistical techniques to infer the performance of the "counterfactual" group. The companies that receive IPA support are called the "treatment group," the companies that don't receive IPA assistance are called "the control group." Over time, IPAs track certain KPIs of the treatment group, but still need the inference of the control group. Data on both groups must be obtained to evaluate the impact of the IPA's actions. This subsection will briefly show what data needs to be collected.

Suppose that the outcome to be assessed is whether foreign companies decided to invest in the local economy. To assess whether the actions of the

IPA made a difference, data is required about 4 groups of companies, split between the treatment group and the control group, and whether or not the company is already established in the local economy:

a. Treatment group firms that are established in the local economy (A).
b. Treatment group firms that are not established in the local economy (B).
c. Control group firms that are established in the local economy (C).
d. Control group firms that are not established in the local economy (D).

These and other data points, such as the local unemployment rate, government spending, etc., control for the influence of other factors that are beyond the control of the IPA, such as the state of the economy, the rule of law, etc. Most of this information should already be collated by an IPA, and, if not, should be readily available as they are standard metrics from private data providers (e.g. ORBIS, Thomson Reuters, Bloomberg, etc.), public bodies (Internal Revenue Services, National Statistical Offices, Central Bank, etc.), and other countries' IPAs, for companies not present in the local economy.

The longer the span of time for which the data is available, the more accurate and reliable any evaluation will be. The following section shows a general setup of impact evaluation procedures that may be undertaken. There are also some examples that may be useful to the reader.

10.3.3 Impact evaluation model

The main idea of this section is to show a simple and effective method to measure the impact of an IPA's activities. The objective is to estimate the effects of assisting foreign companies in the decision to settle (investment for the first time in the country) or to expand (reinvestment of a firm already installed). To do this, it is necessary to gather all variables that may affect the decision, both observable and unobservable factors. Examples of these variables are the size of the multinational firm, its age, changes in national investment attraction policies (for example, implement/stop implementing a priority sector policy), sector-specific policies that could affect foreign investment decisions (such as incentive policies for technological investment), among many others. In addition, the model includes specific assistance variables that the IPA may have provided, that could affect both the specific firm and its environment – affecting productive sectors – or decisions of other firms that are unobserved by nature.

As a starting point, the following theoretical model is used as a basis for comparison to measure the decision to invest by a foreign company[5]:

$$\mathbb{I}\left(FDI\right)_{fhst} = \mathbb{W}\delta + \mathbb{X}\beta + \mathbb{F} + \varepsilon_{fhst}$$

$\mathbb{I}\left(FDI\right)_{fhst}$ is a binary indicator variable that takes the value one if the foreign firm f with capital from country h of the economic sector s invests in home country during year t. In this sense, the dependent variable shows a decision of the firm whether to invest/reinvest. Another somewhat different definition of this variable begins by differentiating the sample between those companies that have not yet settled in the host country and those that potentially can invest. In this case, the dependent variable would be equal to one when the foreign company establishes, and would remain at that value for all the years in which it is present in the host country. The second group includes only the companies that, being already established in the host country, decided to reinvest, in which case this variable would take the value one when that happens. As mentioned in the previous section, the sample considers all those firms that, given their previously defined characteristics, are liable to be treated and attracted by the IPA.[6] A possible alternative on the left-hand side is the number of subsidiaries of the multinational in the country. Other possible dependent variables include the number of highly skilled jobs created, exports, R&D spending, etc.

On the other hand, matrix $\mathbb{W}$ represents the services the IPA offers to the foreign company. In other words, $\mathbb{W}$ are the "treatments" the evaluator would like to evaluate, and δ is the vector of effects to be estimated. $\mathbb{W}$ may be represented as a set of indicators, which can be binary or non-binary, that define the type (or amount) of assistance that the IPA provided in the years prior to the decision to invest. This variable can also be defined as the different categories of assistance variables. The grouping of these variables depends on the nature of the service offered by the agency, the time of assistance and the degree of granularity that the evaluator would like to add to the model. For now, $\mathbb{W}$ is defined as a matrix of actions carried out by the agency that could influence the post-investment decisions of foreign companies. Consequently, the impact of the agency's actions is captured by the vector of parameters of interest δ, which is defined according to the dimension taken by $\mathbb{W}$.[7] It is expected that δ will take a positive and significant value to justify an impact of the IPA's work.

The rest are control variables. On the one hand, $\mathbb{X}$ is a matrix of controls that may or may not vary by firm (f), country of origin (h), economic sector (s) and year (t), or by a combination of variations between them. Additionally, and given the characteristics of the database, $\mathbb{F}$ represents a set of fixed effects for f, h, s, and year t, and/or a combination of them. Variables contained in $\mathbb{F}$ control for all the uncontrolled factors in matrix $\mathbb{X}$ that can generate a scale effect on the probability of investing.

Finally, an error term ε_{fsht} is assumed to have a zero mean and to vary with f, h, s, and t. It is expected that in the estimation stage, it will be controlled for variation within the firm and/or sector using clusters.

10.3.4 Comments on the estimation procedure

The primary objective of impact evaluation is to estimate the effects of the agency's actions on the decision to establish or to reinvest. Impact evaluation methodologies require that the application of the treatment be *exogenous*, which means that this treatment must not affect or be affected by variables that cannot be included in the model. As mentioned before, this would require that the companies to which they provide services be chosen at random, regardless of strategic considerations (neither of the agency nor of the firms), such as the prioritisation of sectors, or that more time and effort was invested in certain projects. This is practically impossible to observe in reality so we have to recognise that the average treatment effect to be measured is difficult to measure accurately and without bias unless we have at least one acceptable instrumental variable.

One way to circumvent this issue is not to focus so much on the average treatment effect, but rather on the sign and statistical significance of the parameters of interest. In this sense, an estimation by the ordinary least squares method (OLS) is sufficient to estimate a linear probability model. In this case, the effect would be whether the treatment made a difference or not, and not how much of a difference it made. It keeps being good information to have, though to learn about the average effect OLS would be biased and inconsistent.

These and other estimation challenges are not new in the theoretical econometrics literature. However, the empirical literature, and in particular the impact evaluation literature of IPAs, is very much in the early stages of development.[8]

10.3.5 Other alternatives to impact evaluation in IPAs

As discussed earlier, most IPAs do not perform the type of impact evaluation analyses described in this chapter. There are alternative approaches that, even though they do not measure the impact of an IPA's activities as a causal factor for success, they do monitor and attempt to evaluate using other informative and intuitive methods. A non-comprehensive list of these methodologies includes the following:

1. **The gross value added (GVA) method**: GVA is the value of the goods and services produced in an area, industry or sector of an economy. It can also be defined as a measure of the productivity of a specific service or good produced by a firm or a set of firms in the economy. GVA is calculated by subtracting the total value of the inputs used from the total value of the outputs. For a firm, it is simply the profit created by their operations. For FDI attraction and retention, it is one of the most commonly used methods to evaluate the activities of IPAs. An example from London can be found in the Box 10.1. For these purposes, the GVA method is useful in the sense that it provides information to the authorities about which sector is most profitable, and therefore where there may be productivity gaps to close. The disadvantage of the GVA method is that any change in a company's profits is likely to be the result of more than just an IPA's actions, and hence does not solve the issue of identification discussed previously.
2. **Satisfaction or perception surveys**: surveys are useful investor service and policy tools that are sufficiently flexible to assess a variety of questions, solve problems, establish baselines, analyse trends, select goals and learn about the needs of an organisation, its stakeholders or the public. This type of survey can be performed relatively quickly and cheaply by an IPA. However, as it is by nature

qualitative and subjective, it is a relatively crude way of assessing the impact of specific actions. Moreover, as with many other types of surveys, if the sampling is poorly designed the results can be flawed. A helpful source to consult about perception surveys is the OECD's guide, *Practitioner's Guide to Perception Surveys*.[9]

3. **Focus groups**: focus groups are used to gain insights from, and to identify issues concerning, selected groups of people. Focus groups are performed as a group interview that establishes general areas of interest or concern of the interviewees through a series of structured questions. Regarding monitoring and evaluation, focus groups help obtain data when little or no information is available. While they are a very commonly used technique, conclusions drawn from focus groups can be misleading if the group being interviewed is not sufficiently large or sufficiently representative of the population of interest.
4. **Benchmarking**: "Benchmarking is the practice of comparing business processes and performance metrics to industry bests and best practices from other companies."[10] For IPAs, benchmarking exercises are a useful way to compare KPIs across different agencies. In order for benchmarking to be effective, it is crucial to access information that is comparable. However, this is often not the case, particularly when comparing new or very specific practices – where comparable data is unlikely to exist.

Box 10.1 London & Partners' methodology to evaluate economic impact

"The additional economic impact of London & Partners is defined as the extra benefits generated as a direct result of our intervention, compared to what would have happened without our work.

Measurement of this additional economic value, 'gross value added' (GVA), is calculated mainly by surveying a representative sample of our audiences.

How is London & Partners' impact measured?

Gross value added (GVA)

- GVA is the economic added value created when producing goods or providing services.
- It is the difference between the price paid for a good or service and the cost of inputs used in its production.
- GVA measures profits and wages of London-based businesses and London's employees. By measuring our impact on increasing GVA, we are reporting our economic contribution to London.

Performance indicators

- Our key performance indicators for measuring the economic benefits to the city are gross value added (GVA) and jobs retained.
- Economic impact figures are expressed in terms of GVA (economic wealth), unless otherwise stated.
- We also estimate additional leisure tourists, business delegates, major event-goers and additional sales made by London['s] small and medium-sized enterprises (SMEs) that have been part of our programmes.

Jobs created and supported

- By attracting foreign direct investment in key sectors for London, we generate new, high-value jobs for the London economy.
- We also create new and safeguard existing jobs in London by attracting the spend of tourists, business delegates, major event spectators and students.
- We cannot track these jobs directly but we use a robust model to estimate the number of jobs that our promotional activities support.

Evaluation methodology

The Evaluation Methodology 2018 report outlines the work undertaken by London & Partners and GLA Economics to evaluate impact across our five major business areas: leisure tourism, business tourism, major events, foreign direct investment and higher education. Read the Evaluation Methodology 2018 report for full information about how we measure our impact."

Reproduced with kind permission from London & Partners: www.londonandpartners.com.

Link: https://www.londonandpartners.com/about-us/how-we-measure-our-impact.

10.4 Examples of impact evaluation: Investor Services

The following pages present three variations of evaluation examples. In particular, it will be focused on the evaluation of Investor Services, as this practice tends to be longer in nature and therefore provides a good framework to explain how evaluation and monitoring works in practice.

Impact evaluation is difficult, especially for Investor Services. Oftentimes, it involves a long-term project that includes many people and counterparties, is collaborative and complex in nature, and happens in a dynamic and flexible environment. For this reason, thinking about impact evaluation requires defining the strategies necessary to monitor activities, outcomes, changes in policies, etc.

10.4.1 Example 1: homogeneous effects[11]

Suppose that the left-hand side of the equation represents a binary variable that is equal to one if the investor's decision is to reinvest in the country, and zero otherwise. Additionally, variable $\mathbb{I}(IPA)_{fhst-k}$ takes the value one if the IPA provided any Investor Services to the firm in year $t-k$. Furthermore, $X^{j}_{fhst-1} = \left\{X^{1}_{fhst-1}, \ldots, X^{J}_{fhst-1}\right\}$ is a set of control variables that could affect firm f from the country h, belonging to sector s, carried out in year $t-1$. The fixed effects λ_{fhs}, ρ_{st} and θ_{ht} are added to this specification.[12] In addition, $\mathbb{I}(Other)_{fhst-k}$ is a binary variable that takes the value of one if the firm was affected by any other policy effort – different than Investor Services – made by the IPA.

In this situation, which is a particular example of all the possible cases that the empirical model could take, we have the following equation to estimate:

$$\mathbb{I}(FDI)_{fhst} = \sum_{k=0}^{K} \delta_k \mathbb{I}(IPA)_{fhst-k} + \sum_{k=0}^{K} \omega_k \mathbb{I}(Other)_{fhst-k} + \sum_{j=0}^{J} \beta_j X^j_{fhst-1} + \lambda_{fhs} + \rho_{st} + \theta_{ht} + \varepsilon_{fhst}$$

In this case, a homogeneous effect of any IPA service on the probability of investing is being estimated, and this effect varies with the number of years during which the services have been provided to the foreign firm. In addition, the effect of the particular treatment being measured continues to be included, and J controls are added that may vary by firm, country of origin, sector and year. Finally, three fixed effects are included. The first is specific to the combination of firm, country of origin and sector, the second is specific to the combination of sector and year. Finally, a fixed effect by country of origin and year.

The advantage of this method is that it is relatively simple to include all the different services provided into a binary category. Investor services effects on the probability of reinvesting are captured by parameters δ_k, and are "homogeneous" in the sense that they do not distinguish between the distinct services that may vary widely in nature or extent. In some cases, the simplicity of the homogeneous approach brings costs, as it cannot identify which effort is more profitable. This is the reason for the following example.

10.4.2 Example 2: heterogeneous effects

Using the same nomenclature as in the previous example, more heterogeneity in the impact of the IPA's services is included. Suppose the IPA would like to understand which of its services has the greatest impact on foreign investment. Thus, an information provision service, which requires relatively few resources, could generate a much greater relative impact than, for example, a costly but highly specialised service. While both services must be delivered by the IPA, it is also important to know how much of this impact is due to each particular service. For example, in the following specification, three types of services are categorised: installation assistance ($\mathbb{I}(Instal)_{fhst-k}$), assistance in completing administrative procedures $\left(\mathbb{I}\left(Adm\right)_{fhst-k}\right)$, and Aftercare support ($\mathbb{I}\left(AC\right)_{fhst-k}$). Given that these services – set up, administrative procedures and Aftercare support – have different natures and purposes, the effects are also expected to be different. In the case of reinvestment, Aftercare services are expected to have greater effects, while for the installation, the first two services will have greater effects. In this case, the heterogeneous effects could be captured by including these three categories in the base equation in example 1:

$$\mathbb{I}\left(FDI\right)_{fhst} = \sum_{k=0}^{K} \delta_k^I \mathbb{I}\left(Instal\right)_{fhst-k} + \sum_{k=0}^{K} \delta_k^{Adm} \mathbb{I}\left(Adm\right)_{fhst-k} + \sum_{k=0}^{K} \delta_k^{AC} \mathbb{I}\left(AC\right)_{fhst-k}$$
$$+ \sum_{j=0}^{J} \beta_j X^j_{fhst-1} + \lambda_{fhs} + \rho_{st} + \theta_{ht} + \varepsilon_{fhst}$$

In this case, the set of effects $\{\delta_k^I, \delta_k^{Adm}, \delta_k^{AC}\}$ are differentiated, and are probably very different for projects at different stages. This approach is superior to the homogeneous approach shown above. However, it requires a richer dataset and a great deal of historical data in order to estimate it robustly.

10.4.3 Example 3: proactive policy

In this example, a different way of thinking about the impact evaluation is provided. Let example 1 be the starting point. Assume the IPA wants to evaluate whether a proactive policy – i.e. the IPA contacted the foreign firm first, instead of the foreign company contacting the IPA first (reactive policy) – made a difference to the company's decision to invest (or reinvest) in the local country. Variable d captures whether the *first contact* was made by the IPA (in which case $d = 1$), or by the foreign company ($d = 0$). If this variable is relevant – i.e. proactive policy has an effect – parameter α is expected to be positive and statistically significant. The empirical model would take the following form:

$$\mathbb{I}\left(FDI\right)_{fhst} = \sum_{k=0}^{K} \delta_k \mathbb{I}\left(IPA\right)_{fhst-k} + \alpha d + \sum_{j=0}^{J} \beta_j X^j_{fhst-1}$$
$$+ \lambda_{fhs} + \rho_{st} + \theta_{ht} + \varepsilon_{fhst}$$

Here, the evaluator looks to answer a somewhat different and interesting question that requires a different type of data to be collected. On the other hand, one can also think of different ways of evaluating the impact of any other IPA activity by embracing the availability and the nature of the data available. This methodology can be as flexible as it needs to be. As mentioned before, the empirical specification may take several different forms, as the above model can also account for, say, heterogeneous effects as with the previous example.

In closing, ongoing impact measuring and evaluation is essential, as it allows identifying those IPAs programmes and activities that are most effective and beneficial from an economic point of view. They also promote public accountability and a continuous improvement of public policies. This chapter discussed the importance of impact evaluation and monitoring the activities of IPAs, with special relevance to Investor Services. It showed the relevance of appropriately facing the challenge of measuring causal impact by using econometric techniques that are currently not widely used by IPAs, but are relatively standard in the literature. Some examples were shown, which may be useful when considering the most appropriate monitoring system.

As seen in this chapter, for many IPAs there is still a long way to go. The cost and difficulty in obtaining the right type of data and a highly skilled team of evaluators leaves this area less attended than other areas of the IPA. Fortunately, interest in filling this gap is increasing, as many international organisations, such as UNCTAD, the OECD, IADB and the World Bank, actively recognise the importance of evaluating the activities of investment promotion agencies.

Notes

1 OECD, 2016. *Workshop on Good Practices in Investment Promotion & Facilitation. How to improve Investment Promotion Agencies' impact and relevance* [online]. Available at: http://www.oecd.org/daf/inv/investment-policy/Summary-OECD-workshop-on-good-practices-in-investment-promotion-and-facilitation.pdf.

2 Sztajerowska, M. 2019. *Monitoring and Evaluation: A Brief Guide for Investment Promotion Agencies*. Paris: OECD Investment Insight.

3 Volpe, C. and Sztajerowska, M. 2019. *How to Solve the Investment Promotion Puzzle: A Mapping of Investment Promotion Agencies in Latin America and the Caribbean and OECD Countries* [online]. Available at: http://dx.doi.org/10.18235/0001767.

4 White, H. 2006. "Impact evaluation: The experience of the Independent Evaluation Group of the World Bank". *MPRA Paper*. Issue 1111.

5 Model inspired by Volpe, C., Carballo, J., Marra de Artiñano, I. and Blyde, J. 2020. *How Effective is Investment Promotion? Firm-Level Evidence*. IDB Discussion Paper, IDB-DP(00741)

6 This definition is relatively vague. However, it allows extending the range of possible companies to the entire universe of multinational companies of which there is a record. This is the case presented by Volpe et al (2020). Despite this, another interesting but limited definition of the universe is the set of firms that are defined as "lead" firms. The advantage of the latter is that the definition is conditional on a predetermined set of observable characteristics, which is necessarily a more manageable and self-contained subset. The registration of lead companies will be contained in customer relationship management (CRM), even though the IPA and the multinational have not yet generated the first contact.

7 The evaluator must decide which variables, and the definition of the categories that enter $\mathbb{W}$. This section shows a structure that could serve as an initial proposal.

8 A great source to learn more about Impact Evaluation, especially how to implement it in practice is Gertler, P.J. et al. 2016. *Impact Evaluation in Practice.* 2nd edn. Washington, DC: World Bank.

9 OECD, 2012. *Measuring Regulatory Performance: A Practitioner's Guide to Perception Surveys*, s.l: OECD Publishing.

10 Wikipedia. *Benchmarking* [online]. Available at: https://en.wikipedia.org/wiki/Benchmarking.

11 This example is inspired from Volpe et al (2020).

12 Fixed effects are binary variables that take the value one if the subscripts are activated for the particular observations, and zero in other cases. For example, the fixed effect λ_{fhs}=1 for each *f* from country *h* that potentially invests in the host country in sectors.

11
EPILOGUE

At the time of going to print, the IMF reported that "foreign investors have withdrawn or disinvested over 80 billion US dollars from developing countries since the start of the pandemic – and this amounts to the largest outflow of capital ever recorded."[1] This backdrop offers an unprecedented opportunity to rethink current FDI practices and to embrace the long-term FDI perspective this book is advocating for.

For FDI to mitigate some of the effects of the pandemic and be effective as a driver for recovery, more robust post-investment work is needed in almost all IPAs. It's in this sometimes neglected phase of the investment cycle where the majority of FDI value surfaces, the absorptive capacity of the host economy is tested and positive externalities materialise. This value is a critical part of building inclusive societies. This book invites – or perhaps demands that – policy makers and FDI practitioners to give post-investment more attention. This will result in IPAs moving away from focusing on just being an attractive Place to invest to being a welcoming destination and fertile ground where foreign investors can effortlessly grow. These post-investment drivers ought to be reflected in every national FDI strategy, as well as in every IPA's business plan.

FDI perspectives that focus on an investor's one-time *acquisition* of a country's value proposition are outdated; a post-Covid approach demands a wider perspective that considers repetitive *sales*. The FDI industry would

DOI: 10.4324/9781003174950-15

also benefit from considering the concept of customer life-time value (CLV), which is well-established in business development and private equity circles. CLV estimates how valuable a customer is, not just on the first purchase, but across the whole relationship. Commercially, it's also well known that it's easier and cheaper to sell to existing customers than to attract new ones. As the *Harvard Business Review* states, "depending on which study you believe, and what industry you are in, acquiring a new customer is anywhere from 5 to 25 times more expensive than retaining an existing one."[2]

A CLV approach, or perhaps we can coin the phrase "an investor life-time value" (ILV) approach, can contribute to FDI value creation in 4 different ways:

First: it would include the jobs created and the capex invested by the new investment.
Second: it would take into account the value in the variation in permanent jobs due to expansion or contractions, taxes paid and profit re-invested.
Third: it would incorporate any externalities generated, such as knowledge transfer, upskilling of talent and local spend, which is reflected in contracts with local suppliers, and the charitable activities of the foreign entity.
Fourth, it would consider the impact of co-creation; a stronger Ecosystem, an improved business climate and any sustainable development.

The life-time value of an investment is the sum of all the above, as can be seen in Figure 11.1.

A life-time value approach would lead to new decision making throughout the whole FDI value chain, and would also bring the notion of transformative FDI closer to home. In private enterprise, sales teams are normally split between developing new business and the account management of existing customers. These teams require different goals, skills, team structures, personality types and tools. Each is considered as important as the other and both are supported by marketing in different ways. Customer life-time value is a function of both team's work.

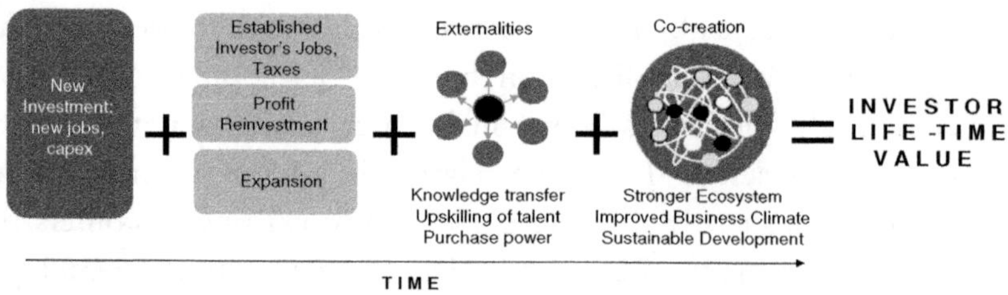

Figure 11.1 Investor life-time value. © *Investment Aftercare Explained: A Guide for FDI Practitioners and Policymakers on How to Grow and Retain Investors.*

Translated to an FDI setting, Aftercare would finally become mainstream, with dedicated account managers focussed on generating the repeat business of further investment while also preventing the loss of existing investment. Policy makers would need to come up with policies targeting those sectors that represent the maximum life-time value for the host economy; Ecosystem brokers would scan their local communities to identify services they could upsell and cross-sell to established foreign investors. In addition, life-time value calculations would provide a strong framework that budget-holders could use to offset the cost of delivering Aftercare services and with which they could identify stakeholders willing to share the costs of joint-programme delivery.

Investor life-time value ought to be a priority for the FDI industry. For this to take place, three things need to happen first: research is needed to guide the formulation of a decision making model; new tools to help FDI practitioners in their daily work need to be developed; and there needs to be strong leadership to encourage creativity, collaboration and some risk taking to explore new ways in which long-term FDI can further contribute to an investment-led local and global recovery founded on resilience and sustainable development.

The challenge and the rewards are there to be claimed. We can do this.

Notes

1 WAIPA. 2020. *Annual Report 2019–2020* [online]. Available at: https://waipa.org/waipa-content/uploads/Annual-Report-2019-2020.pdf.

2 Gallo, A. 2014. "The value of keeping the right customers", *Harvard Business Review*, Oct. 29, 2014. Available at: https://hbr.org/2014/10/the-value-of-keeping-the-right-customers.

INDEX